AI, Analytics, and Assessment in Higher Education

Hany Zaky
Eastern International College, USA

IGI Global
Scientific Publishing
Publishing Tomorrow's Research Today

Vice President of Editorial Melissa Wagner
Director of Acquisitions Mikaela Felty
Director of Book Development Jocelynn Hessler
Production Manager Mike Brehm
Cover Design Jose Rosado

Published in the United States of America by
IGI Global Scientific Publishing
701 East Chocolate Avenue
Hershey, PA, 17033, USA
Tel: 717-533-8845 | Fax: 717-533-7115
Website: https://www.igi-global.com E-mail: cust@igi-global.com

Library of Congress Cataloging-in-Publication Data

LCCN: 2025041618 (CIP Data Pending)
ISBN13: 9798337370576
Isbn13Softcover: 9798337370583
EISBN13: 9798337370590

British Cataloguing in Publication Data
A Cataloguing in Publication record for this book is available from the British Library.

Table of Contents

Detailed Table of Contents

This chapter examines the theoretical and practical underpinnings of assessment in higher education, outlining its progression from positivist traditions to constructivist and critical paradigms. It offers a thorough framework that unifies curriculum, pedagogy, and evaluation, highlighting inclusive, genuine, and technology-enhanced assessment methodologies. Essential principles encompass Assessment for Learning (AfL), Universal Design for Learning (UDL), and authentic assessment corresponding to graduate qualities. The discourse encompasses ethical issues in technology-based assessments and the significance of institutional preparedness and policy reform. The chapter anticipates learner-centered, data-informed, and competency-based assessment frameworks that facilitate personalized learning and promote social justice. This integrative approach guarantees that evaluation not only evaluates learning results but also promotes deeper engagement, lifelong learning, and comprehensive student growth in a progressively intricate educational environment.

The integration of Artificial Intelligence (AI) into education is transforming traditional approaches to teaching, learning, and assessment. This chapter explores the evolving landscape of AI-driven assessment, with a particular focus on ChatGPT, a generative AI language model developed by OpenAI, and its growing role in educational settings. Unlike conventional tools, ChatGPT enables dynamic, interactive engagement, supporting both students and educators in tasks ranging from essay writing to instructional design. The chapter critically examines how such

(LLM). Conceptualizing the G-Maritime LMS, a retrieval-augmented generation (RAG) system supported with a maritime-specific LLM is provided. Moreover, the system is guided by well-established instructional design techniques (SJT, ADDIE, Bloom) that maximize the benefits of AI integration into learning and assessment environment. Therefore, G-Maritime is fundamentally capable of delivering personalized learning and assessments. In addition to conceptual proposal, the study addresses probable challenges such as compliance, certification, and accessibility. A pilot implementation roadmap is also proposed to test the system. The study offers a valuable insight for trainers, policymakers, industry professionals, and investors seeking to understand and support maritime skill transition with generative LMS solutions. By integrating domain-specific AI capabilities with personalized content delivery, G-Maritime LMS represents a scalable model for future maritime learning ecosystems. G-Maritime has potential to become an accelerator for human-centred digital transformation in global shipping.

Chapter 5

Matthew Abiola Oladipupo, University of Salford, UK
Amaonwu Onyebuchi, Hussaini Adamu Federal Polytechnic, Nigeria
Ugochukwu Okwudili Matthew, Federal University of Lavras, Brazil
Morgan Nwaiku, Teesside University, UK
David Taiwo Oyekunle, University of Salford, UK
Ogechukwu Nkiruka Onyedibe, Federal University of Technology, Nigeria
Mgbike Francisca Chinenye, Federal College of Education (Technical), Umunze, Nigeria
Godwin Nse Ebong, University of Salford, UK

The Industry 5.0 concept for emerging sustainable education involves transforming every lesson into an interactive Virtual Reality (VR), Augmented Reality (AR), and Mixed Reality (MR) experimental gamification. By producing immersive and engaging experiences that were previously unthinkable, Extended Reality (XR) technology is transforming a number of sectors, including education. The present study investigated the domain of simulation-based learning, shedding light on its significance, challenges, and boundless possibilities in the context of health technology education. The paper advanced hi-tech educational technology adoption in the development of interactive educational pedagogy in Society 5.0 and Education 5.0 by describing the technological underpinnings, guiding principles, essential values, and key components of Industry 5.0 in education. The study adopted Actor-Network Theory (ANT) model to explore the implication of technological pedagogy content knowledge (TPCK) model instruction design for immersive education technology.

Constructing a valid and reliable measurement instrument is essential in education and research to ensure that all respondents are evaluated on the same scale. Validity and reliability ensure that inferences made from the instrument are trustworthy. This chapter discusses the Rasch analysis as a practical method for improving assessments to promote fair and inclusive practices. Consequently, this chapter aims to demonstrate the viability of Rasch analysis as a valuable tool for establishing validity, while also highlighting aspects that prospective Rasch analysis users should carefully consider when applying Rasch analysis to improve assessments. Rasch analysis appears to be a vital method for validating instruments because the model provides outputs that enable the designer to evaluate the dimensionality of the instrument, test hypotheses, and verify the instrument's internal consistency. The model offers statistics that can be used to assess the goodness-of-fit of the instrument items and to identify items that may function differently for respondents. However, Rasch analysis users are advised to carefully select the sample size, pay attention to misfitting items, and address issues related to missing data. Rasch analysis can be recommended as a practical approach for enhancing assessments.

This chapter explores portfolio assessment in undergraduate education, offering practical guidance for students and instructors. It examines three common portfolio formats: websites, USB flash drives, and compact discs. The chapter provides strategies for effective implementation. These strategies include but are not limited to the planning and the selection phase of your portfolio contents and the design considerations needed for enhancing your portfolio's aesthetics to improve self-branding and viewer engagement. Other strategies in the chapter include some sample ideas and adaptable rubrics drawn from several generalizable fields of study, with the goal of providing applicable and adaptable resources for readers. Since the chapter is written for a broad and transferable understanding of the topic of portfolio evaluations, the chapter's material is relevant to students, instructors, and instructional support professionals across a wide range of disciplines in higher education.

We are entering a new dawn where we are making considerable strides in realising value from People Analytics interventions. For over twenty years, researchers and professionals have been scrutinising the role of people analytics in accelerating the efficiency and effectiveness of human resource functions within an organisation. As a result, they advocate for people analytics as a driving force behind HR's strategic partnership. Despite the increasing recognition of People Analytics in driving data-driven decision-making within human resources, current academic literature largely overlooks a structured framework for understanding the role of people analytics and its linkage with the competitive advantage of higher education institutions (HEIs). Previous studies focus broadly on the generic benefits of analytics in HEIs without systematically examining its key functions. The role of the seven crucial pillars of people analytics still needs deeper insights in the context of HEIs. On digging deeper into the field of People Analytics in HEIs, we encounter a significant research gap that persists in our understanding of the key pillars of PA (Workforce Planning, Talent Sourcing, Talent Acquisition and Hiring, Onboarding & Engagement, Performance Management, Talent Retention and Employee Wellness) and their linkage with the competitive advantage of HEIs.

This chapter explores data-driven strategies that can enhance decision-making, resource allocation, instruction effectiveness, and promote institutional openness to change. The study integrates new learning analytics trends, artificial intelligence in educational evaluation, data visualization techniques, and forecasting modeling to develop a multi-faceted approach to organizational resilience. The authors present a new Resilience Analytics Framework (RAF) that integrates diverse data sources and analytic techniques for strategic growth initiatives in higher education. The chapter also discusses the ethical implications and pragmatic challenges of analytics use and provides actionable recommendations for institutions at different analytics maturity levels. The chapter concludes with potential research directions, citing future technologies like machine learning, natural language processing, and

Preface

The higher education landscape is at an unprecedented crossroads, with artificial intelligence, learning analytics, and innovative assessment methods fundamentally transforming our understanding of teaching, learning, and educational results. Navigating the complexities of the 21st-century educational environment requires integrating these three vital areas—AI, analytics, and assessment—not just as an option but as a necessity for institutions seeking to enhance student success, foster educational equity, and remain relevant in a rapidly digitalizing world.

This edited volume stems from the ongoing debate within the higher education community about how to best incorporate AI into learning and work (EDUCAUSE, 2024). The rapid pace of technological advances, combined with this uncertainty, creates both unique opportunities and major challenges for educational leaders, faculty, and students. As editors, we have curated a diverse selection of scholarly works from top researchers, practitioners, and thought leaders who are pushing the boundaries of AI, analytics, and assessment in higher education. Recent surveys indicate that only 9 percent believe higher education is adequately prepared for AI's growing impact (Inside Higher Ed, 2024), emphasizing the urgent need for clear guidance to align technological developments with effective teaching practices.

The impact of artificial intelligence on education extends far beyond basic automation and efficiency gains. It can address major educational issues, enable innovative teaching approaches, and accelerate the achievement of SDG 4 (UNESCO, 2025). Nonetheless, UNESCO highlights that fast technological progress brings risks and challenges that must be managed carefully. AI's strength lies not only in its computational ability but also in its capacity to personalize learning, provide immediate feedback, and facilitate large-scale data-driven decisions.

Learning analytics, the second pillar of our exploration, signifies a major shift from intuition-based to evidence-based education. It involves examining educational data to enhance learning experiences and environments. Recently, the field has advanced from simple data collection to sophisticated analysis that can forecast student performance, identify those who are struggling, and recommend personalized interventions. By leveraging various educational data, LA shifts the focus from general feedback to tailored support, thereby improving learning outcomes and promoting equity (Sharif & Atif, 2024; Inside Higher Ed., 2024; Samuel et al, 2025). Its strength lies in uncovering hidden patterns in student learning, enabling educators to better address individual needs and institutional challenges.

Assessment, the third pillar of our framework, has undergone significant changes in the age of AI and analytics. Traditional, mostly static and summative methods are giving way to dynamic, formative approaches that leverage real-time data to support continual learning. Although formative assessment is widely regarded as crucial for enhancing teaching and learning, implementing it effectively remains challenging due to systemic misalignments (Seyyed et al., 2025). AI and analytics present significant opportunities to address these challenges by developing assessment systems that are more responsive to students' needs and better aligned with institutional learning objectives.

This collection showcases our commitment to providing both theoretical insights and practical applications from multiple perspectives and institutional contexts. Each chapter builds on the previous ones, creating a comprehensive framework for understanding how AI, analytics, and assessment work together to enhance educational outcomes. Our authors come from diverse backgrounds, including research universities, liberal arts colleges, community colleges, and educational technology organizations, providing readers with a broad range of viewpoints and experiences.

As we begin this exploration, it is important to recognize that the fields of AI, analytics, and assessment in higher education are marked by both great potential and significant uncertainty. The technologies develop quickly, and their long-term impact on higher education remains unpredictable. However, one thing is certain: these technologies will keep shaping the educational landscape. Institutions that approach these changes thoughtfully and proactively will be better equipped to support their students and meet their educational goals.

This edited collection is guided by the principle that technology should support pedagogy rather than dictate it. We contend that the most effective application of AI, analytics, and assessment begins with well-defined educational objectives and uses technology as a means to achieve these objectives more effectively. This human-centered perspective, consistently evident across all chapters, ensures that as we examine the potential of these advanced technologies, our focus remains on the fundamental mission of higher education: fostering learning, encouraging critical thinking, and equipping students for meaningful lives and careers. All contributors share this commitment to prioritizing educational outcomes in technological advancements.

We invite readers to engage with this material enthusiastically, exploring the opportunities while maintaining a critical perspective on the potential challenges.

The future of higher education will depend not on the technologies themselves but on how deliberately and thoughtfully we incorporate them into our teaching methods. We aim for this book to serve as both a helpful guide and a catalyst for that essential effort.

The chapters presented offer valuable insights for academics, administrators, instructional designers, and policymakers. By integrating empirical analysis, conceptual frameworks, and innovative case studies, this book aims to foster the evolution of higher education into a more data-driven, learner-centered, and resilient system.

CHAPTER OVERVIEW

Chapter 1: Foundations of Assessment Theories: A Framework for Higher Education

This chapter provides a comprehensive foundation for understanding assessment through historical and theoretical lenses. It presents a unified framework that connects curriculum, pedagogy, and evaluation, emphasizing inclusive and ethical assessment practices aligned with student growth and lifelong learning.

Chapter 2: Navigating Challenges and Seizing Opportunities in AI-Driven Assessment: Insights from ChatGPT

This chapter examines the transformative impact of AI tools, such as ChatGPT, on educational assessment. It critically evaluates both the opportunities and risks of utilizing generative AI in higher education, including its implications for academic integrity and pedagogical practices.

Chapter 3: Transforming Assessment: The Role of Technology in Higher Education

Building on the prior discussion of AI, this chapter explores a broader range of digital technologies that are reshaping assessment strategies. It focuses on learner-centered and inclusive practices that utilize e-portfolios, simulations, and learning analytics to foster authentic and adaptive assessment.

Chapter 4: Conceptualizing a Novel Generative Maritime Learning Management System: G-Maritime

Introducing an innovative application of AI in specialized professional education, this chapter outlines the development of G-Maritime, a domain-specific learning and assessment platform for the maritime industry. It highlights how instructional design and large language models can support personalized learning in a high-stakes environment.

Chapter 5: Immersive Reality Technology-Based Gamification on Sustainable Education

This chapter explores the application of immersive technologies such as Virtual Reality and Mixed Reality in education. By integrating Actor-Network Theory and TPCK, it showcases how gamified and simulation-based learning experiences can advance sustainability and innovation in higher education.

Chapter 6: The Use of Rasch Analysis to Enhance Measurement Instruments in Education

Focused on measurement precision, this chapter introduces Rasch analysis as a powerful tool for validating assessment instruments. It explains how Rasch modeling ensures reliability, dimensionality, and fairness in assessment, while also highlighting the methodological considerations involved in its implementation.

Chapter 7: Portfolio Assessment in Higher Education: General Uses and Various Applications

Offering practical guidance, this chapter explores diverse portfolio formats and strategies to enhance student self-presentation and reflective learning. It provides adaptable rubrics and design recommendations that make portfolio assessment accessible across various disciplines.

Chapter 8: Scrutinizing the Seven Key Pillars of People Analytics and Their Linkage with the Competitive Advantage of Higher Education Institutions

This chapter identifies and analyzes seven foundational pillars of people analytics in Higher education. It explores how data-driven human resource strategies can foster institutional competitiveness and outlines a structured framework to guide their application.

Chapter 9: Advancing Organizational Resilience through Learning and Development Analytics: A Data-Driven Approach to Strategic Growth

Addressing institutional strategy, this chapter introduces a Resilience Analytics Framework that integrates AI, data visualization, and predictive modeling to strengthen organizational responsiveness and sustainability in higher education.

Chapter 10: Artificial Intelligence and Critical Thinking Endorsement: Investigating Higher Education Institutional Tools and Strategies

Concluding the volume, this chapter examines the interplay between AI technologies and critical thinking skills. It proposes institutional strategies and frameworks to effectively integrate AI into teaching and learning, emphasizing the importance of fostering analytical, ethical, and independent thought in a digital age.

Together, the contributions in this volume offer a comprehensive overview of current and emerging practices in assessment, analytics, and AI integration in higher education. While grounded in diverse educational contexts and disciplines, the unifying thread is a commitment to transforming assessment into a tool that not only measures learning but actively drives it forward.

In conclusion, this edited volume provides a snapshot of a rapidly evolving field, viewed through the diverse perspectives of our authors. By the time readers engage with this material, new developments, challenges, and opportunities will likely have emerged. This is not a shortcoming but a reminder of the continuous nature of educational innovation. As editors, our goal is not to present definitive answers but to offer a compilation of perspectives, frameworks, tools, and experiences that can guide readers through the ongoing transformation of higher education in the AI era. The collective insights of our contributors offer multiple pathways forward, recognizing that different institutions may require tailored strategies to integrate AI, analytics, and assessment effectively.

-Hana Zaky

REFERENCES

EDUCAUSE. (2024). *The future of AI in higher education*. EDUCAUSE AI Landscape Study. Retrieved from https://www.educause.edu/ecar/research-publications/2024/2024-educause-ai-landscape-study/the-future-of-ai-in-higher-education

Inside Higher Ed. (2024). *How will AI influence higher ed in 2025?* Retrieved from https://www.insidehighered.com/news/tech-innovation/artificial-intelligence/2024/12/19/how-will-ai-influence-higher-ed-2025

Samuel, O., Joseph, E., Sylvia, M., & Charles, O. (2025). Artificial intelligence in higher education institutions: Review of innovations, opportunities, and challenges. *Frontiers in Education*, *10*, 1530247.

Seyyed, K., Banihashem, Dragon, G. & Omid, N. (2025). A critical review of using learning analytics for formative assessment: Progress, pitfalls, and the way forward. *Journal of Computer Assisted Learning*.

Sharif, H., & Atif, A. (2024). The Evolving Classroom: How Learning Analytics Is Shaping the Future of Education and Feedback Mechanisms. *Education Sciences*, *14*(2), 176. DOI: 10.3390/educsci14020176

UNESCO. (2025). *Artificial intelligence in education*. Retrieved from https://www.unesco.org/en/digital-education/artificial-intelligence

Chapter 1
Foundations of Assessment Theories:
A Framework for Higher Education

Andi Asrifan
http://orcid.org/0000-0002-9934-6129
Universitas Negeri Makassar, Indonesia

Rismawati Sudirman
http://orcid.org/0000-0001-8046-6764
Universitas Muhammadiyah Palopo, Indonesia

Maemuna Muhayyang
Universitas Negeri Makassar, Indonesia

Nurfaida Tasni
http://orcid.org/0000-0003-4256-6849
Universitas Negeri Makassar, Indonesia

Isumarni Isumarni
Universitas Muhammadiyah Sidenreng Rappang, Indonesia

ABSTRACT

This chapter examines the theoretical and practical underpinnings of assessment in higher education, outlining its progression from positivist traditions to constructivist and critical paradigms. It offers a thorough framework that unifies curriculum, pedagogy, and evaluation, highlighting inclusive, genuine, and technology-enhanced assessment methodologies. Essential principles encompass Assessment for Learning (AfL), Universal Design for Learning (UDL), and authentic assessment corresponding to graduate qualities. The discourse encompasses ethical issues in technology-based

DOI: 10.4018/979-8-3373-7057-6.ch001

assessments and the significance of institutional preparedness and policy reform. The chapter anticipates learner-centered, data-informed, and competency-based assessment frameworks that facilitate personalized learning and promote social justice. This integrative approach guarantees that evaluation not only evaluates learning results but also promotes deeper engagement, lifelong learning, and comprehensive student growth in a progressively intricate educational environment.

HISTORICAL AND PHILOSOPHICAL UNDERPINNINGS OF ASSESSMENT IN HIGHER EDUCATION

1.1. The Evolution of Educational Assessment

The history of educational evaluation demonstrates a dynamic interaction among pedagogical ideas, regulatory mandates, and public expectations. Initially, assessment in higher education was informal and qualitative, influenced by oral disputations and master-apprentice evaluations throughout the medieval university era (Herzog-Punzenberger et al., 2020). a. As industrialization progressed and mass education expanded in the 19th and early 20th centuries, evaluation transformed into more standardized and quantitative formats, motivated by the necessity to categorize learners, validate competency, and guarantee comparability across growing institutions.

The positivist tradition that prevailed in early assessment procedures prioritized objectivity, measurement, and reliability. Multiple-choice assessments, norm-referenced evaluation, and psychometric precision emerged as defining features of the system, especially within Western educational frameworks. This period was characterized by the prevalence of Assessment of Learning (AoL), wherein examinations primarily functioned as final measures to evaluate performance and confer qualifications. Nevertheless, these methodologies frequently overlooked contextual, cultural, and developmental subtleties, inadvertently perpetuating injustices and promoting test-centric education (Chiziwa & Kunkwenzu, 2021; Swiecki et al., 2022).

Since the late 20th century, a notable paradigmatic change has transpired, shaped by constructivist epistemologies and learner-centered pedagogies. The notion of Assessment for Learning (AfL) has gained prominence, highlighting feedback, learner agency, and the formative function of assessment in facilitating improvement. This transition was not solely educational but also philosophical—questioning the belief that learning can be entirely quantified through objective assessment. Rubrics, self-evaluations, peer assessments, and performance-oriented tasks started to augment and, in certain instances, supplant conventional examinations.

The digital revolution significantly expedited this transformation. Digital platforms, electronic portfolios, and AI-driven evaluations have facilitated immediate feedback, customized learning pathways, and data-informed pedagogy. However, they also elicit apprehensions around surveillance, data ethics, and equitable access. Consequently, although evaluation tools have diversified, their development is still constrained by fundamental epistemological discussions regarding the nature of knowledge, its definition, and the methods of its demonstration (Giray et al., 2024; Gouseti et al., 2024).

The growth of educational evaluation is a complex process influenced by values, ideologies, and technology advancements. A fundamental comprehension of this history is crucial for higher education stakeholders aiming to develop equitable, inclusive, and future-oriented evaluation systems.

1.2. Philosophical Foundations

The philosophical underpinnings of assessment in higher education offer essential insights into the conceptualization, valuation, and measurement of learning. Assessment fundamentally embodies profound epistemological and ontological assumptions regarding the essence of knowledge, its acquisition, and its demonstration. Throughout history, three predominant paradigms—positivism, constructivism, and critical theory—have influenced assessment theories and practices in unique manners (Plummer et al., 2022; Swiecki et al., 2022).

The positivist paradigm, originating from the Enlightenment and empiricism, defines knowledge as objective, quantifiable, and generalizable. In this context, assessment is intended to be uniform, measurable, and reproducible. Conventional instruments like multiple-choice assessments, true/false propositions, and performance indicators correspond with this ideology. The focus is on summative results, reliability, and statistical validity, frequently downplaying the significance of learner context, reflection, or individual differences. This method, although efficient for extensive testing, has been criticized for oversimplifying intricate learning into basic results (Blundell, 2021; Swiecki et al., 2022).

Conversely, constructivist philosophy perceives knowledge as actively generated by learners through experience, reflection, and social interaction. Consequently, assessment transforms into a dialogic and formative process, intricately integrated inside teaching and learning. Instruments like as reflective journals, portfolios, problem-based exams, and peer evaluations arise from this perspective. Constructivist-informed evaluation prioritizes authenticity, learner autonomy, and developmental feedback, valuing the learning process equally with the outcome. It redefines educators as facilitators and learners as engaged participants in the construction of meaning (Do et al., 2023; Smith & Wyness, 2024).

The critical theory tradition, inspired by intellectuals like Paulo Freire and Jürgen Habermas, interrogates prevailing power relations in education. It emphasizes matters of equity, representation, and liberation in evaluation. Viewed through this perspective, traditional evaluation is frequently regarded as a tool of control, reinforcing hegemonic norms and suppressing minority learners. Critical assessment techniques promote participatory methodologies, culturally responsive evaluation, and reflexive research that empower students as co-creators of knowledge. It examines the designers of assessments, the knowledge being evaluated, and the underlying intent.

These philosophical paradigms are not incompatible. In modern higher education, hybrid models frequently arise, combining positivist rigor with constructivist participation and critical awareness. Comprehending these philosophical foundations allows educators, curriculum developers, and legislators to make educated decisions that connect assessment with overarching educational principles and societal obligations.

1.3. Changing Purposes of Assessment

The function of evaluation in higher education has transformed alongside changes in educational philosophy, societal expectations, and institutional accountability structures. Historically, assessment functioned mostly as a tool for certification and selection, designed to rate pupils, verify learning results, and guarantee that only the "qualified" advanced along academic or professional trajectories. This pragmatic perspective strongly corresponds with the Assessment of Learning (AoL) framework, emphasizing outcomes, summative evaluations, and the finality of assessment (Chiziwa & Kunkwenzu, 2021; Spowart & Turner, 2021).

As the massification of higher education increased access to a wider demographic, evaluation evolved to serve goals beyond simple credentialing. A notable transition has occurred towards Assessment for Learning (AfL)—a formative methodology that integrates assessment into the learning process. The objective is not solely to assess knowledge but to augment it through feedback, debate, and reflection. Assessment serves as a mechanism for facilitating student development, enhancing metacognition, and aiding individualized learning paths (Stoll, 2020).

A third, growing purpose of assessment in the 21st century is Assessment as Learning (AaL). This learner-focused approach fosters the cultivation of critical thinking, self-regulation, and lifelong learning competencies. In this context, evaluation enables students to establish personal objectives, track their advancement, and contemplate their learning methodologies. This objective aligns closely with the constructivist and transformative learning paradigms, which prioritize agency, autonomy, and identity development.

Furthermore, in a time of heightened institutional accountability and globalization, assessment fulfills administrative and policy-related functions. Accreditation organizations, governmental entities, and ranking institutions utilize assessment data to appraise institutional quality, guarantee compliance, and compare performance across areas and systems. Although these techniques enhance transparency and quality assurance, they also elicit concerns over curriculum constriction, test-oriented instruction, and the commercialization of education (Spowart & Turner, 2021).

n the era of digital transformation and artificial intelligence, assessment is now anticipated to facilitate real-time analytics, predictive feedback, and adaptive learning systems. This enhances its objective—promoting educational innovation while ensuring ethical and equitable data utilization.

Comprehending the evolving objectives of assessment is crucial for synchronizing assessment techniques with overarching educational aims. Regardless of being formative or summative, diagnostic or evaluative, assessment must consistently function as a tool to enhance learning and address the changing requirements of varied learners and communities.

CORE THEORIES OF LEARNING AND THEIR ASSESSMENT IMPLICATIONS

2.1. Behaviorist, Cognitivist, and Constructivist Theories

Theoretical frameworks about individual learning are fundamental for creating effective assessment processes in higher education. Prominent paradigms include behaviorism, cognitivism, and constructivism, each presenting unique assumptions on learning processes and their respective implications for assessment design (Baker et al., 2021; Hickey & Harris, 2021).

Behaviorism, advocated by B.F. Skinner and based on the contributions of early psychologists like as Pavlov and Thorndike, perceives learning as a modification in observable behavior induced by external stimuli. Learning is deemed successful when the intended response is produced and reinforced. In this framework, assessment is generally summative, standardized, and concentrated on quantifiable results. Multiple-choice questions, true/false items, and performance checklists effectively correspond with behaviorist concepts, as they facilitate the explicit showing of mastery through accurate responses and repetition. This technique prioritizes objectivity, reliability, and efficiency, rendering it appropriate for extensive evaluations.

Cognitivism, conversely, focuses on internal mechanisms, highlighting mental functions like memory, problem-solving, and information processing. Learning is defined as the active arrangement of knowledge inside the learner's cognitive frameworks. This theoretical perspective led to evaluations that extend beyond mere memorization, prioritizing tasks that test understanding, analysis, and application. Examples encompass systematic problem-solving assignments, essay composition, and concept mapping. Assessment under the cognitivist framework seeks to elucidate the learner's comprehension and cognitive representation of knowledge, promoting instructional coherence with Bloom's Taxonomy and metacognitive methods (Evans & Jeong, 2023; Swiecki et al., 2022).

Constructivism, promoted by thinkers such as Piaget and Vygotsky, asserts that learners derive meaning via engagement with their environment and social context. Knowledge is not conveyed but collaboratively generated. From this viewpoint, assessment is formative, authentic, and focussed on the learner. It frequently encompasses reflective journals, project-based evaluations, peer assessments, and collaborative assignments. The emphasis is on process rather than result, contextual comprehension, and the learner's capacity to apply knowledge in intricate, real-world situations (Lippmann, 2021).

These three paradigms persist in shaping assessment practices in higher education currently. Behaviorist techniques provide structure and scalability, but cognitivist and constructivist models prioritize depth, relevance, and learner empowerment. Effective assessment design frequently incorporates components from several theories to address distinct learning requirements and educational objectives.

2.2. Socio-Cultural and Situated Learning Perspectives

Socio-cultural and situated learning theories provide an insightful framework for comprehending the dynamics of learning within social, cultural, and contextual settings. Unlike individualistic paradigms, these approaches highlight the relational, interactive, and contextual aspects of learning, necessitating evaluation practices that acknowledge knowledge as socially generated and culturally mediated.

Socio-cultural theory, based on Lev Vygotsky's work, asserts that learning is inherently a social process influenced by tools, language, and encounters with more informed others. The core of this theory is the notion of the Zone of Proximal Development (ZPD)—the interval between a learner's autonomous capabilities and what they can accomplish with assistance. Evaluation, from this perspective, must recognize and assist learners within their Zone of Proximal Development, highlighting formative strategies that incorporate scaffolding, dialogic feedback, and peer cooperation. Observations, learning dialogues, and dynamic assessment techniques are more congruent with this theoretical framework than standardized testing (Anumanthan & Hashim, 2022; Hickey & Harris, 2021; Nicholas et al., 2021).

Situated learning theory, proposed by Jean Lave and Etienne Wenger, expands upon socio-cultural ideas while emphasizing the contextual context of learning environments. This idea posits that knowledge is inextricably linked to the activity, context, and culture in which it is cultivated. Knowledge is acquired by legitimate peripheral participation in communities of practice, where novices progressively develop expertise by engaging meaningfully with authentic tasks. Assessment must encompass learners' engagement, identity formation, and proficiency in practical applications. This necessitates performance-based, contextualized, and portfolio evaluations that accurately represent the learner's developing competency in genuine situations (Karunanayaka & Naidu, 2021; Wahyuni et al., 2021).

Both theories contest traditional evaluation techniques that detach learners from their social and cultural contexts. They promote assessments that are adaptive, culturally pertinent, and woven into the learning process. They emphasize the significance of discourse, reflection, and collaboration as essential components of both learning and assessment.

In higher education, implementing socio-cultural and situated perspectives necessitates a transition towards more inclusive, participatory, and practice-oriented evaluations, especially in fields where knowledge is utilized in dynamic, real-world situations. These frameworks are particularly beneficial in tackling fairness, access, and diversity, guaranteeing that evaluations not only evaluate performance but also promote significant learning within intricate social contexts.

2.3. Assessment for Learning (AfL) vs. Assessment of Learning (AoL)

The differentiation between Assessment for Learning (AfL) and Assessment of Learning (AoL) is crucial in modern higher education, influencing educational approaches and student experiences. Although both play essential roles in the educational ecosystem, their conceptual foundations, goals, and implementation methods vary considerably.

Assessment of Learning (AoL) is conventionally associated with summative assessment methodologies. It emphasizes the assessment of student performance at the conclusion of an educational cycle, typically via standardized assessments, culminating projects, or examinations. Assessment of Learning (AoL) is outcome-oriented, predominantly employed for evaluation, certification, or advancement determinations. It underscores objectivity, comparability, and accountability—attributes esteemed in regulatory and institutional frameworks. Nonetheless, its constraints stem from its retroactive character; it frequently does not offer prompt feedback that may enhance learning throughout the process (Dakkaki et al., 2021; Lodhia et al., 2020). AoL sometimes diminishes learning to mere numerical scores, potentially overlooking critical thinking, creativity, and personal development.

Conversely, Assessment for Learning (AfL) is inherently formative and essential to the teaching process. The primary objective is to enhance learning by delivering ongoing, actionable feedback to both students and educators. Assessment for Learning promotes learners to contemplate their comprehension, recognize areas needing enhancement, and assume responsibility for their educational progression.

Methods including inquiry, formative quizzes, peer assessment, and rubric-based self-evaluation show Assessment for Learning (AfL) in practice. This method promotes metacognition, enhances motivation, and facilitates deeper engagement with material. From an educational perspective, Assessment for Learning (AfL) closely correlates with constructivist and socio-cultural theories that perceive learning as iterative, contextual, and collaboratively built (Hosseini & Nimehchisalem, 2021; Ndawo, 2022).

Significantly, AfL does not supplant AoL but rather enhances it. An equitable evaluation method in higher education amalgamates two paradigms—employing Assessment for Learning (AfL) to enhance instructional practices and Assessment of Learning (AoL) to record and convey success. In recent years, hybrid methods like blended formative-summative assessments and assessment as learning (AaL) have arisen, emphasizing the significance of learner agency and reflective activities.

Comprehending the differentiation and interaction between AfL and AoL is crucial for developing inclusive, adaptive, and significant assessment frameworks. As higher education progresses to emphasize student-centered learning and comprehensive development, Assessment for Learning (AfL) emerges as a pivotal influence in fostering self-regulated, lifelong learners.

PRINCIPLES OF EFFECTIVE AND INCLUSIVE ASSESSMENT DESIGN

3.1. Validity, Reliability, and Fairness

The principles of validity, reliability, and fairness constitute the foundation of successful and inclusive assessment design in higher education. These fundamental principles guarantee that exams accurately evaluate their intended objectives while maintaining consistency and fairness across varied learner demographics.

Validity denotes the degree to which an assessment accurately reflects the particular construct or ability it aims to evaluate. Various forms of validity exist: content validity guarantees alignment of the assessment with learning objectives; construct validity verifies that the instrument accurately represents the theoretical construct being measured; and criterion-related validity associates assessment results with external standards or future performance. In the absence of validity, even the most dependable evaluation loses its significance. In higher education, the validation of an instrument include matching it with curriculum objectives, consulting expert reviewers, and piloting assessment tools with representative learners (Elangovan & Sundaravel, 2021; Varoquaux & Colliot, 2023).

Reliability pertains to the consistency and stability of assessment results. An accurate evaluation produces comparable outcomes under uniform conditions, regardless of variations in time, evaluators, or student cohorts. Methods include test-retest reliability, inter-rater reliability, and internal consistency (e.g., Cronbach's alpha) are employed to measure and enhance reliability. Nonetheless, it is crucial to recognize that great dependability does not ensure validity. An evaluation may be persistently inaccurate if it fails to measure the target construct (Masuwai et al., 2024).

Fairness underscores equity, accessibility, and the elimination of prejudice in the design and execution of assessments. Equitable evaluations provide all learners, irrespective of background, aptitude, or identity, an equal opportunity to exhibit their competencies. This encompasses providing accommodations for pupils with disabilities, employing culturally responsive language, and refraining from tasks that favor some groups over others. Fairness encompasses transparency—explicitly conveying expectations, assessment criteria, and feedback mechanisms (Voulgarides et al., 2023).

The interaction among these principles is essential. An evaluation can be dependable yet not valid, or valid yet inequitable. Consequently, effective assessment design necessitates methodical preparation, inclusive methodologies, and ongoing evaluation. In varied and globalized classrooms, prioritizing equity is crucial to maintain academic integrity and social justice (Tai et al., 2022).

By anchoring assessment in validity, reliability, and fairness, educators may cultivate accurate and credible evaluations, as well as a more inclusive and empowered educational atmosphere.

3.2. Universal Design for Learning (UDL) in Assessment

Universal Design for Learning (UDL) is an innovative educational paradigm that fosters inclusive pedagogy and evaluation by addressing the varied requirements of all students. Grounded in cognitive neuroscience and educational psychology, Universal Design for Learning (UDL) aims to eradicate obstacles to education by intentionally creating learning environments—including assessments—that are accessible, adaptable, and equitable from the beginning (Almumen, 2020; Novak, 2023).

The fundamental concepts of UDL consist of three key elements: diverse methods of engagement, varied forms of representation, and different avenues for action and expression. These principles, when applied to assessment, assist educators in designing activities that facilitate numerous modes of engagement, exhibit comprehension in many forms, and sustain motivation and relevance across a spectrum of learner profiles.

Multiple Means of Engagement guarantees that tests align with students' interests, present suitable challenges, and maintain motivation. Providing options in themes or assessment formats—such as written reports, oral presentations, or multimedia projects—can enhance motivation and ownership while evaluating the same learning outcomes.

Multiple Means of Representation underscores the necessity of delivering instructions, rubrics, and evaluation materials in many modalities—such as text, graphics, or audio—to cater to diverse learning preferences and mitigate cognitive overload. This principle emphasizes the significance of language precision and cultural inclusion in the design of assessments.

Multiple Means of Action and Expression enables learners to exhibit their knowledge through diverse outputs that correspond to their strengths and requirements. A student may opt to submit a podcast in lieu of a written essay, as long as both media evaluate the same competencies. This flexibility does not compromise rigor; instead, it enhances accessibility.

Assessments influenced by Universal Design for Learning (UDL) are especially pertinent in higher education, as classrooms exhibit growing variety in language, aptitude, socioeconomic status, and neurodiversity. Instead of modifying accommodations for individual students, UDL advocates for anticipatory design, guaranteeing accessibility for all from the outset (Sheppard-Jones et al., 2020; Ünal et al., 2020).

Implementing Universal Design for Learning in assessments further advances institutional objectives of equity, inclusiveness, and student achievement. It compels educators to reconsider conventional uniform methodologies and embrace more adaptive and principled assessment strategies. By adopting UDL principles, higher education institutions can cultivate learning environments that enable all students to realize their full potential.

3.3. Authentic Assessment: Aligning Tasks with Real-World Competence and Graduate Attributes

Authentic assessment is an educational method that prioritizes the congruence of assessment tasks with real-world issues, professional practices, and critical graduate competencies. In contrast to conventional assessments that frequently emphasize rote memorization and discrete abilities, genuine assessments emulate significant applications of information within intricate, contextualized environments, hence promoting profound learning and transferable competence (Lippmann, 2021; Ndawo, 2022).

Authentic assessment is grounded in constructivist and experiential learning theories, which assert that knowledge is most effectively gained and exhibited through active participation in tasks that reflect real-world complexity. This is particularly pertinent in higher education, where the objective is not solely to evaluate discipline knowledge but also to equip graduates with the ability to think critically, solve issues, collaborate efficiently, and act ethically in varied professional contexts (Lewis & Sarkadi, 2024; Mudhol, 2024).

Essential characteristics of authentic assessment encompass:

Authentic and intricate tasks: Learners are required to utilize their knowledge in scenarios that mirror those faced in professional or civic contexts—such as doing a policy analysis, formulating a business proposal, or designing a digital campaign. Integrated skills and knowledge:

1. Tasks need that students utilize many competencies—cognitive, interpersonal, and intrapersonal—demonstrating the interdisciplinary character of real-world issues.
2. Opportunities for contemplation and modification: Genuine evaluations frequently incorporate iterative procedures, feedback loops, and chances for learners to enhance their work, so strengthening metacognitive abilities and fostering ongoing growth.
3. Authentic assessment enhances the significance of academic learning by connecting evaluation with graduate attributes, including communication, creativity, critical thinking, and ethical reasoning. It enables students to exhibit not only their knowledge but also their ability to apply that knowledge meaningfully within context.

Furthermore, genuine assessment enhances student motivation, engagement, and identity formation by embedding learning in purposeful and personally significant activities. It is intrinsically inclusive, valuing multiple epistemologies and practices, while promoting culturally responsive pedagogies (Bourke, 2020).

To effectively adopt authentic assessment, institutions must engage in assessment literacy, adapt curriculum to focus on competency-based outcomes, and foster supportive environments that encourage innovation and risk-taking in teaching and learning. When well structured, authentic assessment functions not merely as an evaluative instrument but as a transforming educational experience that prepares students for life beyond the classroom.

EMERGING PARADIGMS AND DIGITAL SHIFTS IN ASSESSMENT

4.1. Technological Advancements in Assessment: AI, Learning Analytics, and E-Assessment Tools

The digital transformation of higher education has profoundly altered assessment procedures, creating a new era of technology-enhanced evaluation techniques. Artificial intelligence (AI), learning analytics, and e-assessment platforms signify a paradigm change from old methodologies, advancing toward more personalized, scalable, and data-driven approaches to measuring student learning (Binhammad et al., 2024).

Artificial Intelligence (AI) in evaluation has facilitated the automation of feedback, adaptive testing, and predictive analytics. Intelligent tutoring systems, automated essay evaluation, and chatbot-driven formative evaluations illustrate how AI may deliver immediate, personalized assistance, hence improving learner engagement and advancement. AI aids educators by examining extensive amounts of student work to identify misconceptions, patterns, and learning deficiencies, therefore guiding focused instructional strategies. Nonetheless, ethical issues regarding algorithmic bias, transparency, and data privacy require careful and responsible implementation (Roshanaei et al., 2023; Swist et al., 2024).

Learning Analytics (LA) encompasses the collecting, analysis, and interpretation of data regarding learners and their environments to enhance educational results. In evaluation, learning analytics allows educators to monitor student performance over time, identify at-risk students, and evaluate the efficacy of teaching methods. Dashboards, heat maps, and early warning systems render learning progress observable, facilitating evidence-based decision-making at both individual and institutional tiers. Learning analytics enables students to assume responsibility for their education by providing graphical performance statistics and goal-setting instruments.

E-assessment instruments, such as online quizzes, simulations, digital portfolios, and peer-assessment platforms, provide flexibility, scalability, and interactivity. These tools facilitate formative and summative assessments that are accessible across time and geography, promoting continuity in learning even in hybrid or remote environments. Additionally, attributes like automatic grading, multimedia integration, and collaboration capabilities enhance the assessment experience. When adhering to universal design principles, e-assessment can enhance inclusivity and accessibility for a varied range of learners (Qu & Cross, 2023; Tai et al., 2022).

Although technology improvements present significant potential, its application must be firmly rooted in pedagogy and focused on equity. Technology should not govern assessment practices but should be utilized to augment authenticity, inclusivity, and student autonomy.

In summary, AI, learning analytics, and e-assessment tools signify a revolutionary advancement in the evaluation of higher education. When judiciously incorporated, they may establish dynamic, responsive, and learner-centered environments that equip students for the digital knowledge economy.

4.2. Open Book, Peer, and Portfolio-Based Assessments

In reaction to changing educational philosophies and the growing diversity of students in higher education, assessment models have transitioned from conventional high-stakes examinations to alternative assessment methods that prioritize profound comprehension, collaboration, and genuine demonstration of learning. Notable emerging methods include open book assessments, peer evaluations, and portfolio-based assessments (Swiecki et al., 2022).

Open book assessments contest the traditional concept of closed-memory evaluations by permitting pupils to reference learning materials throughout examinations. Open book tests are intended to assess higher-order thinking skills, including application, analysis, synthesis, and evaluation, rather than merely evaluating rote memory. These evaluations foster academic integrity, alleviate anxiety, and more accurately reflect real-world problem-solving scenarios where information access is standard. Designing effective open book assignments necessitates meticulous alignment with learning outcomes and an emphasis on intricate, contextualized problems that cannot be resolved through mere search (Kurniawan & Sofyan, 2020).

Peer assessment entails students appraising the work of their colleagues based on explicitly established criteria and rubrics. This approach is based on constructivist and socio-cultural learning theories, highlighting active participation, critical reflection, and collaborative interpretation. Peer evaluation augments students' metacognitive awareness, develops feedback literacy, and cultivates a sense of collective responsibility in the learning process. It also fosters soft skills such communication, empathy, and evaluative judgment—crucial for employability (Joh, 2021). Effective and equitable peer assessment necessitates meticulous scaffolding through training, moderation, and the cultivation of a culture of trust and respect.

Portfolio-based evaluation allows students to create a comprehensive and continuous record of their learning progress across time. Portfolios may encompass written comments, project work, multimedia artifacts, and self-assessments, offering a comprehensive account of development and accomplishment. They facilitate individualized learning, promote autonomous investigation, and enable students to exhibit proficiency through many forms of expression. Portfolios are especially advantageous for fields that prioritize creativity, critical analysis, and professional preparedness. Digital portfolios (e-portfolios) improve accessibility and can function as documentation for academic and career advancement.

Collectively, these alternative assessment methodologies signify a comprehensive transition towards student-centered, process-oriented, and authentic evaluative procedures in higher education. When judiciously executed, open book, peer, and portfolio-based evaluations promote enhanced engagement, inclusivity, and dispositions for lifelong learning.

4.3. Ethical Concerns and Data Privacy in Tech-Driven Evaluation

The use of digital technologies into assessment systems has transformed educational evaluation, facilitating individualized learning, scalable feedback, and real-time analytics. Nonetheless, these improvements provide intricate ethical dilemmas and data privacy issues that require thorough scrutiny to guarantee that evaluation processes maintain the principles of justice, transparency, and human dignity.

A key ethical concern in technology-driven evaluation is the possibility of algorithmic prejudice. Artificial intelligence and machine learning techniques that automate grading or forecast student achievement frequently depend on historical data that may embody prevailing disparities. If unregulated, these systems can sustain or intensify gaps associated with race, gender, socioeconomic status, or learning requirements. Guaranteeing algorithmic fairness necessitates transparent design, consistent auditing, and inclusive datasets that reflect the diversity of learners (Chinta et al., 2024; Cossette-Lefebvre & Maclure, 2022; Dieterle et al., 2022; "The Potential Impact of Artificial Intelligence on Equity and Inclusion in Education," 2024).

A significant concern is informed consent and data ownership. Students frequently engage with many digital platforms that gather detailed data on their actions, reactions, and emotional involvement. However, students may lack a comprehensive understanding of the utilization of their data, the others who have access to it, or the duration of its retention. Ethical assessment systems must emphasize student agency by including explicit privacy notifications, opt-out alternatives, and the capacity to access or manage one's own data (Palada et al., 2024; Swist et al., 2024).

Concerns over surveillance arise when educational institutions employ proctoring software, biometric verification, or location tracking under the guise of academic integrity. Although these technologies intend to prevent cheating, they may foster an atmosphere of mistrust, fear, and intrusion into personal boundaries, especially among underprivileged students. Achieving equilibrium between preserving assessment integrity and honoring student liberty is essential (Nguyen & Goto, 2024).

Furthermore, the security of digital infrastructures must be guaranteed to avert unwanted access, data breaches, or manipulation of evaluation outcomes. Institutions must develop stringent cybersecurity protocols, adhere to data protection regulations (e.g., GDPR), and establish governance frameworks that delineate ethical obligations among stakeholders.

Ultimately, as evaluation in higher education becomes progressively data-driven, it must retain a human-centric focus. Ethical frameworks must direct the design and execution of technology-enhanced evaluations, guaranteeing they are effective, equitable, respectful, and reliable. Incorporating ethical literacy into institutional policy and educator practice is essential for developing assessment systems that really benefit the public good.

TOWARD A HOLISTIC ASSESSMENT FRAMEWORK FOR THE FUTURE OF HIGHER EDUCATION

5.1. Designing Integrated Assessment Ecosystems: Interlinking Curriculum, Pedagogy, and Evaluation

A comprehensive evaluation framework for higher education necessitates more than isolated instruments or intermittent assessments. It advocates for the establishment of an integrated assessment ecosystem—a unified framework whereby curriculum, pedagogy, and evaluation are interconnected to facilitate meaningful learning, equitable practices, and institutional efficacy.

Curriculum alignment is fundamental to an integrated ecosystem. Assessment must be conceived as a fundamental component of curriculum creation rather than an ancillary consideration. Learning outcomes must explicitly define the knowledge and skills students are expected to acquire, while assessments should accurately evaluate these goals across cognitive, affective, and practical domains. When curriculum design, instructional delivery, and assessment are synchronized, students encounter coherence, clarity, and purpose in their learning journey (Hickey & Harris, 2021; Wahyuni et al., 2021).

Pedagogical integration further solidifies this alignment. Assessment must align with and reinforce the pedagogical methods utilized—be they inquiry-based, experiential, project-oriented, or competency-focused. Active learning methodologies, such as collaborative problem-solving and case-based training, necessitate evaluations that evaluate complex thinking, creativity, and teamwork. Integrating assessment into pedagogical practice converts it from a distinct evaluating activity into an ongoing learning-focused process.

An effectively structured assessment ecosystem guarantees systemic feedback loops that link learners, educators, and institutional leaders. Students receive prompt, formative feedback that enhances self-regulation and metacognition; educators utilize assessment data to evaluate instructional efficacy and modify techniques; and institutions employ aggregated data to guide quality assurance, program evaluation, and accreditation procedures. Feedback-rich environments facilitate ongoing enhancement at all levels (Choudhary, 2024; Mowling & Sims, 2021).

Furthermore, integrated ecosystems acknowledge variety, inclusion, and adaptability, understanding that assessment must be adaptable to many disciplines, modalities (online, mixed, in-person), and learner situations. Digital technologies, learning analytics, and AI-enhanced platforms can enable seamless integration, contingent upon the establishment of ethical and pedagogical protections (Feuerriegel et al., 2023).

Establishing such ecosystems necessitates cooperative planning, evaluative proficiency, and conducive policies. Faculty, instructional designers, assessment specialists, and students must collaboratively develop frameworks that are contextually pertinent and forward-looking.

Ultimately, integrated assessment ecosystems advance beyond disjointed assessments to a holistic model where learning is not merely assessed but also cultivated, enhanced, and changed. This methodology guarantees that assessment evolves into an integral component of higher education—embedded, adaptive, and conducive to profound, lifelong learning.

5.2. Policy Implications and Institutional Readiness

The shift to a comprehensive, integrated assessment framework in higher education is not merely an educational initiative; it is also a question of institutional policy and strategic coherence. For assessment innovation to be significant, durable, and egalitarian, it must be supported by strong policy frameworks and institutional preparedness at all levels of governance, infrastructure, and culture (Lee et al., 2023; Tai et al., 2022).

Policy consequences necessitate a reevaluation of assessment criteria, quality assurance processes, and regulatory expectations. Conventional policy frameworks frequently emphasize summative metrics, uniformity, and accountability-focused evaluation methods. Although these characteristics are crucial for benchmarking and accrediting, over dependence on them can stifle innovation, diversity, and genuine learning. Progressive policy must broaden its reach to acknowledge and incentivize formative, learner-centered, and competency-based methodologies, while guaranteeing systems for transparency, equity, and academic integrity (Romanowski, 2022; Spowart & Turner, 2021).

Formulating good policy necessitates the involvement of stakeholders—faculty, students, administrators, and policymakers—in a collaborative policy creation process. Collaborative governance improves relevance, validity, and engagement, promoting a collective understanding of assessment as a developmental rather than solely evaluative process. Policies must address the ethical aspects of data gathering, learner consent, accessibility, and cultural responsiveness in assessment systems.

Institutional preparedness denotes the capability of universities and colleges to execute and maintain assessment change. This encompasses investment in professional development to enhance assessment literacy among academic personnel; allocation of resources for digital infrastructure that facilitates e-assessment, learning analytics, and portfolio systems; and the formation of cross-functional teams to integrate curriculum, pedagogy, and evaluation (Hoare et al., 2024; Xia et al., 2024).

Leadership is an essential facilitator. Institutional leaders must advocate for assessment reform as an integral component of comprehensive strategic initiatives aimed at academic achievement, equity, and student success. Readiness also involves cultivating an organizational culture of inquiry and reflection, wherein assessment findings are utilized constructively rather than punitively to guide choices and enhance practices.

Institutions must be adaptable and sensitive to change. The post-pandemic period, characterized by rapid digitalization, has demonstrated that inflexible frameworks can swiftly become outdated. Institutions require policy adaptability and strategic insight to respond to developing technology, evolving learner expectations, and global educational trends. In conclusion, developing a future-ready assessment framework requires cohesive policies and institutional ecosystems that are inclusive, adaptive, and consistent with the objectives of comprehensive higher education.

5.3. The Future of Assessment

The future of assessment in higher education is influenced by swift technological improvements, changing student requirements, and an increasing need for inclusive, significant, and lifelong education. As knowledge economies evolve to be more dynamic, global, and interdisciplinary, assessment systems must surpass conventional limitations and become adaptable, learner-centered, and future-oriented (Barty et al., 2024; Li et al., 2024).

A prominent trend is the emergence of competency-based and mastery learning models, wherein assessment is not limited by rigid timetables but is matched with demonstrable abilities and comprehension. Students advance upon achieving mastery, with evaluations incorporated into repetitive cycles of practice, feedback, and reflection. This method prioritizes depth over rapidity and promotes individualized learning trajectories that cater to varying tempos, modalities, and settings.

Technology-enhanced assessment will persist in its expansion, driven by artificial intelligence, virtual simulations, learning analytics, and blockchain credentialing. These instruments provide instantaneous diagnostics, immersive experience evaluations, and secure digital validation of competencies. Although these technologies provide unparalleled scale and accuracy, their deployment must adhere to ethical standards to guarantee privacy, transparency, and equity.

Micro-credentialing and digital badges are increasingly recognized as alternate methods of assessment and acknowledgment, particularly in light of the changing work market. They offer modular and stacking proof of learning, enabling students to construct portable and verifiable records of accomplishment across both formal and informal educational settings (Chang & Kabilan, 2022; Dahal et al., 2022).

The future of assessment involves adopting holistic and real metrics of student development, such as creativity, resilience, teamwork, and ethical reasoning, which are frequently neglected by standardized testing. Multimodal evaluations, reflective practices, and project-based learning will become increasingly significant as higher education transitions from content delivery to transformative learning (Xia et al., 2024).

The democratization of assessment is equally significant. Students will progressively assume roles as co-designers of assessment criteria, co-assessors of peer work, and self-regulated learners. This interactive methodology improves assessment literacy, ownership, and agency, enabling students to actively influence their educational paths.

Ultimately, the future of evaluation transcends mere methods or measures; it necessitates a redefinition of its purpose and philosophy. It should be reconceptualized as a developmental, inclusive, and empowering practice that aids learners in evolving into critical thinkers, ethical citizens, and adaptable professionals in a complex environment.

CONCLUSION

As higher education adapts to the exigencies of a swiftly transforming, digital, and heterogeneous environment, evaluation methodologies must be radically redefined. Assessment can no longer be confined to summative evaluations or standardized testing based on obsolete positivist frameworks. It must evolve into a dynamic, inclusive, and responsive process that embodies the varied character of learning and equips students for intricate, real-world difficulties.

This chapter has emphasized how the incorporation of philosophical foundations—behaviorism, cognitivism, constructivism, and critical theory—can enhance assessment design and execution. It has demonstrated the efficacy of learner-centered methodologies, including Assessment for Learning (AfL) and authentic assessment, in promoting critical thinking, agency, and substantive learning. The implementation of Universal Design for Learning (UDL) principles guarantees that evaluations are accessible and fair, while ethical technology utilization provides scalable and individualized solutions via AI and learning analytics.

Furthermore, establishing integrated assessment ecosystems that synchronize curriculum, pedagogy, and evaluation allows institutions to convert assessment from discrete occurrences into comprehensive learning experiences. This transition requires institutional preparedness, policy innovation, and a culture shift towards collective accountability and ongoing introspection.

The future of assessment will focus on facilitating knowledge acquisition, personal development, civic responsibility, and professional proficiency. When anchored in inclusivity, justice, and ethical stewardship, assessment transcends mere measurement; it serves as a catalyst for educational equity, change, and lifetime empowerment.

REFERENCES

Almumen, H. A. (2020). Universal Design for Learning (UDL) Across Cultures: The Application of UDL in Kuwaiti Inclusive Classrooms. *SAGE Open*, *10*(4). Advance online publication. DOI: 10.1177/2158244020969674

Anumanthan, S., & Hashim, H. (2022). Improving the Learning of Regular Verbs through TikTok among Primary School ESL Pupils. *Creative Education*, *13*(3), 896. DOI: 10.4236/ce.2022.133059

Baker, L., Phelan, S., Woods, N. N., Boyd, V., Rowland, P., & Ng, S. (2021). Re-envisioning paradigms of education: Towards awareness, alignment, and pluralism. *Advances in Health Sciences Education : Theory and Practice*, *26*(3), 1045. DOI: 10.1007/s10459-021-10036-z

Barty, G., Boyer, N., Chrysikos, A., Griffith, M. L., House, K., Laughlin, T., Ossiannilsson, E., Ward, R., & Zanville, H. A. (2024). *Developing a More Granular and Equitable Approach to the Learner-Earner Journey. The Role of Badging*. Micro-Credentials and Twenty-first Century Skills Within Higher Education to Enable Future Workforce Development. In Zukunft der Hochschulbildung., DOI: 10.1007/978-3-658-42948-5_23

Binhammad, M. H. Y., Othman, A., Abuljadayel, L., Mheiri, H. A., Alkaabi, M., & Almarri, M. (2024). Investigating How Generative AI Can Create Personalized Learning Materials Tailored to Individual Student Needs. *Creative Education*, *15*(7), 1499. DOI: 10.4236/ce.2024.157091

Blundell, C. (2021). Teacher use of digital technologies for school-based assessment: a scoping review [Review of Teacher use of digital technologies for school-based assessment: a scoping review]. Assessment in Education Principles Policy and Practice, 28(3), 279. Routledge. https://doi.org/DOI: 10.1080/0969594x.2021.1929828

Bourke, R. (2020). Assessment to Incite and Reconceptualize Learning. In Oxford Research Encyclopedia of Education. https://doi.org/DOI: 10.1093/acrefore/9780190264093.013.1213

Chang, S. L., & Kabilan, M. K. (2022). Using social media as e-Portfolios to support learning in higher education: A literature analysis. *Journal of Computing in Higher Education*, *36*(1), 1. DOI: 10.1007/s12528-022-09344-z

Chinta, S. V., Wang, Z., Yin, Z., Hoang, N. N. M., Gonzalez, M., Quy, T. L., & Zhang, W. (2024). FairAIED: Navigating Fairness, Bias, and Ethics in Educational AI Applications. arXiv (Cornell University). https://doi.org//arxiv.2407.18745DOI: 10.48550

Chiziwa, W., & Kunkwenzu, E. D. (2021). Investigating Teacher Assessment Practices in the Teaching of Social Studies in Malawian Primary Schools. *Open Journal of Social Sciences*, *9*(7), 480. DOI: 10.4236/jss.2021.97035

Choudhary, K. (2024). An Approach to Enhancing Continuous Evaluation through Self-Reflection among Students of the Foundation Program in Design Course. *Creative Education*, *15*(6), 1003. DOI: 10.4236/ce.2024.156061

Cossette-Lefebvre, H., & Maclure, J. (2022). AI's fairness problem: Understanding wrongful discrimination in the context of automated decision-making. *AI and Ethics*, *3*(4), 1255. DOI: 10.1007/s43681-022-00233-w

Dahal, N., Luitel, B. C., Pant, B. P., & Rajbanshi, R. (2022). Enhancing Student-Teachers Assessment Skills: A Self-and Peer-Assessment Tool in Higher Education. *International Journal of Education and Practice*, *10*(4), 313. DOI: 10.18488/61.v10i4.3173

Dakkaki, J., Drouri, S., Dhoum, S., Mayou, R., & Jabri, M. (2021). Evaluation Grids for Endodontics Preclinical Practical Activities. *Education Research International*, *1*. Advance online publication. DOI: 10.1155/2021/8829119

Dieterle, E., Dede, C., & Walker, M. E. (2022). The cyclical ethical effects of using artificial intelligence in education. *AI & Society*, *39*(2), 633. DOI: 10.1007/s00146-022-01497-w

Do, H., Bich, N., & Nguyen, M. H. (2023). 3How do constructivism learning environments generate better motivation and learning strategies? The Design Science Approach. *Heliyon*, *9*(12). Advance online publication. DOI: 10.1016/j.heliyon.2023.e22862

Elangovan, N., & Sundaravel, E. (2021). Method of preparing a document for survey instrument validation by experts. *MethodsX*, *8*, 101326. DOI: 10.1016/j.mex.2021.101326

Evans, T., & Jeong, I. (2023). Concept maps as assessment for learning in university mathematics. *Educational Studies in Mathematics*, *113*(3), 475. DOI: 10.1007/s10649-023-10209-0

Feuerriegel, S., Hartmann, J., Janiesch, C., & Zschech, P. (2023). Generative AI. *Business & Information Systems Engineering*, *66*(1), 111. DOI: 10.1007/s12599-023-00834-7

Giray, L., Silos, P. Y. D., Adornado, A., Buelo, R. J. V., Galas, E. M., Reyes-Chua, E., Santiago, C. S., & Ulanday, Ma. L. (2024). Use and Impact of Artificial Intelligence in Philippine Higher Education: Reflections from Instructors and Administrators. *Internet Reference Services Quarterly, 28*(3), 315. DOI: 10.1080/10875301.2024.2352746

Gouseti, A., James, F., Fallin, L., & Burden, K. (2024). The ethics of using AI in K-12 education: A systematic literature review. *Technology, Pedagogy and Education, 1*. Advance online publication. DOI: 10.1080/1475939x.2024.2428601

Herzog-Punzenberger, B., Altrichter, H., Brown, M., Burns, D., Nortvedt, G. A., Skedsmo, G., Wiese, E., Nayır, F., Fellner, M., McNamara, G., & O'Hara, J. (2020). Teachers responding to cultural diversity: Case studies on assessment practices, challenges and experiences in secondary schools in Austria, Ireland, Norway and Turkey. *Educational Assessment, Evaluation and Accountability, 32*(3), 395. DOI: 10.1007/s11092-020-09330-y

Hickey, D. T., & Harris, T. (2021). Reimagining online grading, assessment, and testing using situated cognition. *Distance Education, 42*(2), 290. DOI: 10.1080/01587919.2021.1911627

Hoare, A., Hondzel, C. D., Wagner, S. L., & Church, S. (2024). A course-based approach to conducting program review. *Discover Education, 3*(1). Advance online publication. DOI: 10.1007/s44217-023-00085-4

Hosseini, M., & Nimehchisalem, V. (2021). Self-Assessment in English Language Teaching and Learning in the Current Decade (2010-2020): A Systematic Review [Review of Self-Assessment in English Language Teaching and Learning in the Current Decade (2010-2020): A Systematic Review]. Open Journal of Modern Linguistics, 11(6), 854. Scientific Research Publishing. https://doi.org/DOI: 10.4236/ojml.2021.116066

Joh, J. (2021). Implementing Peer Assessment for Optimal Effects : Learners' Voice. *The Journal of AsiaTEFL, 18*(1), 1. DOI: 10.18823/asiatefl.2021.18.1.1.1

Karunanayaka, S. P., & Naidu, S. (2021). Impacts of authentic assessment on the development of graduate attributes. *Distance Education, 42*(2), 231. DOI: 10.1080/01587919.2021.1920206

Kurniawan, E. S., & Sofyan, H. (2020). Application of problem based learning model to improve problem solving ability of student of XI science grade in chemistry. *Journal of Physics: Conference Series, 1440*(1), 12014. DOI: 10.1088/1742-6596/1440/1/012014

Lee, M., Horii, C. V., Austin, A. E., Avery, L., DeSanctis, M., Finkelstein, N. D., Miller, E., & Schaal, B. A. (2023). An Instructional-Workforce Framework for Coordinated Change in Undergraduate Education. *Change The Magazine of Higher Learning*, *55*(1), 54. DOI: 10.1080/00091383.2023.2151809

Lewis, P. R., & Sarkadi, Ş. (2024). Reflective Artificial Intelligence. *Minds and Machines*, *34*(2). Advance online publication. DOI: 10.1007/s11023-024-09664-2

Li, B., Bonk, C. J., Wang, C., & Kou, X. (2024). Reconceptualizing Self-Directed Learning in the Era of Generative AI: An Exploratory Analysis of Language Learning. *IEEE Transactions on Learning Technologies*, *17*, 1515. DOI: 10.1109/tlt.2024.3386098

Lippmann, M. (2021). Inquiry-Based Learning in Psychology. In *Springer international handbooks of education* (p. 1). Springer Nature., DOI: 10.1007/978-3-030-26248-8_59-2

Lodhia, S., Kaur, A., & Williams, B. (2020). Integrated reporting in the public sector. In *Routledge eBooks* (p. 227). Informa., DOI: 10.4324/9780429279621-15

Masuwai, A., Zulkifli, H., & Hamzah, M. I. (2024). Evaluation of content validity and face validity of secondary school Islamic education teacher self-assessment instrument. *Cogent Education*, *11*(1). Advance online publication. DOI: 10.1080/2331186x.2024.2308410

Mowling, C. M., & Sims, S. (2021). The Metacognition Journey: Strategies for Teacher Candidate Exploration of Self and Student Metacognition. *Strategies (La Jolla, Calif.)*, *34*(2), 13. DOI: 10.1080/08924562.2020.1867268

Mudhol, A. C. (2024). Innovative Assessment Methods for Measuring Practical Skills in Higher Education. In Advances in economics, business and management research/Advances in Economics, Business and Management Research (p. 78). Atlantis Press. https://doi.org/DOI: 10.2991/978-94-6463-374-0_8

Ndawo, G. (2022). The development of self skills in an authentic learning environment: A qualitative study. *Curationis*, *45*(1). Advance online publication. DOI: 10.4102/curationis.v45i1.2198

Nguyen, H. M., & Goto, D. (2024). Unmasking academic cheating behavior in the artificial intelligence era: Evidence from Vietnamese undergraduates. *Education and Information Technologies*. Advance online publication. DOI: 10.1007/s10639-024-12495-4

Nicholas, M., Veresov, N., & Clark, J. C. (2021). Guided reading – Working within a child's zone of proximal development. *Learning, Culture and Social Interaction, 30*, 100530. DOI: 10.1016/j.lcsi.2021.100530

Novak, K. (2023). How UDL Creates an Equitable Environment for Students. https://www.edutopia.org/article/universal-design-learning-promotes-equity

Palada, B., Chandan, V. S., & Gowda, C. P., & Nikitha, Prof. (2024). The Role of Augmented Reality (AR) in Education. *International Journal for Research in Applied Science and Engineering Technology, 12*(3), 1400. DOI: 10.22214/ijraset.2024.59079

Plummer, R., Blythe, J., Gurney, G. G., Witkowski, S., & Armitage, D. (2022). Transdisciplinary partnerships for sustainability: An evaluation guide. *Sustainability Science, 17*(3), 955. DOI: 10.1007/s11625-021-01074-y

Qu, X., & Cross, B. (2023). UDL for inclusive higher education—What makes group work effective for diverse international students in UK? *International Journal of Educational Research, 123*, 102277. DOI: 10.1016/j.ijer.2023.102277

Romanowski, M. H. (2022). Controlling higher education from a distance: Using foucault's governmentality to better understand accreditation. *Cogent Education, 9*(1). Advance online publication. DOI: 10.1080/2331186x.2022.2073631

Roshanaei, M., Olivares, H., & Lopez, R. R. (2023). Harnessing AI to Foster Equity in Education: Opportunities, Challenges, and Emerging Strategies. *Journal of Intelligent Learning Systems and Applications, 15*(4), 123. DOI: 10.4236/jilsa.2023.154009

Sheppard-Jones, K., Goldstein, P., Leslie, M., Singleton, P., Gooden, C., Rumrill, P. D., Mullis, L., & Bard, C. E. (2020). Reframing workplace inclusion through the lens of universal design: Considerations for vocational rehabilitation professionals in the wake of COVID-19. *Journal of Vocational Rehabilitation, 54*(1), 71. DOI: 10.3233/jvr-201119

Smith, B., & Wyness, L. (2024). What makes professional teacher development in universities effective? Lessons from an international systematised review. *Professional Development in Education, 1*. Advance online publication. DOI: 10.1080/19415257.2024.2386666

Spowart, L., & Turner, R. (2021). Institutional Accreditation and the Professionalisation of Teaching in the HE Sector. In *IntechOpen eBooks*. IntechOpen., DOI: 10.5772/intechopen.99805

Stoll, L. (2020). Creating capacity for learning: Are we there yet? *Journal of Educational Change, 21*(3), 421. DOI: 10.1007/s10833-020-09394-z

Swiecki, Z., Khosravi, H., Chen, G., Martínez-Maldonado, R., Lodge, J. M., Milligan, S., Selwyn, N., & G sević, D. (2022). Assessment in the age of artificial intelligence. *Computers and Education Artificial Intelligence*, *3*, 100075. DOI: 10.1016/j.caeai.2022.100075

Swist, T., Shum, S. B., & Gulson, K. N. (2024). Co-producing AIED Ethics Under Lockdown: An Empirical Study of Deliberative Democracy in Action. *International Journal of Artificial Intelligence in Education*, *34*(3), 670. DOI: 10.1007/s40593-023-00380-z

Tai, J., Ajjawi, R., Bearman, M., Boud, D., Dawson, P., & Jorre, T. J. de S. (2022). Assessment for inclusion: Rethinking contemporary strategies in assessment design. *Higher Education Research & Development*, *42*(2), 483. DOI: 10.1080/07294360.2022.2057451

Ünal, N. Ü., Karal, M. A., & Tan, S. (2020). Developing Accessible Lesson Plans with Universal Design for Learning (UDL). *International Journal of Disability Development and Education*, *69*(4), 1442. DOI: 10.1080/1034912x.2020.1812539

Varoquaux, G., & Colliot, O. (2023). Evaluating Machine Learning Models and Their Diagnostic Value. In Neuromethods (p. 601). Humana Press. https://doi.org/ DOI: 10.1007/978-1-0716-3195-9_20

Voulgarides, C. K., Etscheidt, S., & Hernández-Saca, D. I. (2023). Educational inequality and the paradox of dis/Ability rights in a schooled society: Moving towards an intersectional discursive, material, and emotive approach*. *Educational Review*, *76*(1), 181. DOI: 10.1080/00131911.2023.2181313

Wahyuni, L. G. E., Dewi, N. L. P. E. S., & Paramartha, A. A. G. Y. (2021). Authentic Assessment Practice. Advances in Social Science, Education and Humanities Research. *Advances in Social Science, Education and Humanities Research*. Advance online publication. DOI: 10.2991/assehr.k.210407.258

Xia, Q., Weng, X., Ouyang, F., Lin, T., & Chiu, T. K. F. (2024). A scoping review on how generative artificial intelligence transforms assessment in higher education [Review of A scoping review on how generative artificial intelligence transforms assessment in higher education]. International Journal of Educational Technology in Higher Education, 21(1). Springer Nature. https://doi.org/DOI: 10.1186/s41239-024-00468-z

ADDITIONAL READING

Holmes, W., Bialik, M., & Fadel, C. (2019). *Artificial intelligence in education: Promises and implications for teaching and learning*. Center for Curriculum Redesign. https://curriculumredesign.org

Luckin, R. (2017). Towards artificial intelligence-based assessment systems. *Nature Human Behaviour*, *1*(3), 1–3. DOI: 10.1038/s41562-017-0055

Popenici, S. A. D., & Kerr, S. (2017). Exploring the impact of artificial intelligence on teaching and learning in higher education. *Research and Practice in Technology Enhanced Learning*, *12*(22), 1–13. DOI: 10.1186/s41039-017-0062-8

Trust, T., & Whalen, J. (2021). K-12 teachers' experiences and challenges with using artificial intelligence tools in classrooms. *Contemporary Issues in Technology & Teacher Education*, *21*(1), 1–22. https://citejournal.org/volume-21/issue-1-21/general/k-12-teachers-experiences-and-challenges-with-using-artificial-intelligence-tools-in-classrooms/

Zawacki-Richter, O., Marín, V. I., Bond, M., & Gouverneur, F. (2019). Systematic review of research on artificial intelligence applications in higher education – where are the educators? *International Journal of Educational Technology in Higher Education*, *16*(39), 1–27. DOI: 10.1186/s41239-019-0171-0

KEY TERMS AND DEFINITIONS

Adaptive Learning Systems: Educational platforms employing AI to tailor learning materials according to individual student performance and preferences.

AI Literacy: The expertise and competencies required to comprehend, engage with, and critically assess the influence and significance of artificial intelligence on society and education.

Artificial Intelligence (AI): The emulation of human cognitive functions by machines, namely in the educational sector to improve learning, automate evaluation, and customize instruction.

Collaborative Learning: A pedagogical approach in which students collaborate to address challenges or accomplish objectives, frequently augmented by technology.

Critical Thinking: The capacity to analyze, assess, and integrate information to make informed and rational decisions—an crucial skill in AI-augmented education.

Digital Pedagogy: A pedagogical method that integrates digital technologies and platforms to facilitate interactive, learner-centered educational experiences.

Ethical AI in Education: The implementation of artificial intelligence in educational settings that upholds privacy, fairness, transparency, and equity.

Human-Centered AI: A design methodology that guarantees artificial intelligence systems emphasize ethical, inclusive, and user-centered solutions, especially within educational settings.

Instructional Innovation: The use of innovative tactics, instruments, or technologies into education to enhance learning results and engagement.

Teacher Professional Development: An ongoing process whereby educators refine their instructional abilities, technical proficiencies, and pedagogical expertise to meet the changing requirements of the classroom.

Chapter 2
Navigating Challenges and Seizing Opportunities in AI-Driven Assessment:
Insights From ChatGPT

Munir Ahmad
http://orcid.org/0000-0003-4836-6151
Survey of Pakistan, Pakistan

Ma Joan M. Delda
http://orcid.org/0009-0000-3678-9339
Biliran Province State University, Philippines

ABSTRACT

The integration of Artificial Intelligence (AI) into education is transforming traditional approaches to teaching, learning, and assessment. This chapter explores the evolving landscape of AI-driven assessment, with a particular focus on ChatGPT, a generative AI language model developed by OpenAI, and its growing role in educational settings. Unlike conventional tools, ChatGPT enables dynamic, interactive engagement, supporting both students and educators in tasks ranging from essay writing to instructional design. The chapter critically examines how such tools challenge conventional assessment paradigms while offering new opportunities for personalized, scalable, and formative evaluation. It also addresses key concerns related to academic integrity, ethical use, and algorithmic bias.

DOI: 10.4018/979-8-3373-7057-6.ch002

INTRODUCTION

AI use in education is bringing about a major change in how knowledge is shared, obtained, and examined. Moreover, AI in education has resulted in the creation of helpful tools that make learning better, make lessons personal, and ease the process of assessment (Kamalov et al., 2023; Vieriu & Petrea, 2025). Out of these, AI-based assessment has attracted a lot of attention because it can make evaluation quicker, customized to each learner, and broad in scope. Since educational institutions face challenges brought by new kinds of learners and technology, AI can help them transform the way teaching is done (Ahmad et al., 2025; Alamäki et al., 2024; Ali et al., 2024; Hopfenbeck et al., 2023; Kamalov et al., 2023; Owan et al., 2023).

The lead in this transformation can be seen with ChatGPT, by OpenAI, which allows learners and educators to use AI functions. LLMs such as ChatGPT help learning stand out from usual educational tools because they respond to users, hold conversations, and assist in various creative and critical activities. Ever since ChatGPT was made public, it has been frequently used by students in academic work to prepare essays, work on math, and think through tough subjects, and also by teachers as a tool for helping students, creating course content, and scheduling educational activities (Adeshola & Adepoju, 2023; Albadarin et al., 2024; Elbanna & Armstrong, 2024; Michel-Villarreal et al., 2023; Monib et al., 2024).

Since AI now has the power to create advanced academic content, how can we make certain assessments are genuine? Can ChatGPT open up new chances for thinking about formative assessment, self-evaluation, and giving students more responsibility? Which protections are necessary to handle issues of academic integrity, bias in algorithms, and ethical use? It is the aim of this chapter to carefully explore the obstacles and benefits related to AI-based assessments, paying special attention to what is learned from using ChatGPT in education. It gives an overview of using AI tools to assess students, explains how generative AI is changing this field, discusses the benefits for teaching practices and universities, outlines possible risks and questions of ethics and lists recommendations for everyone who would use ChatGPT for assessment. Placing ChatGPT together with the methods it is used in learning, this chapter shows how AI is impacting assessment now and what is required for these changes to follow the principles of equity, transparency, and real learning.

TRADITIONAL ASSESSMENT

With traditional assessment, students are evaluated using standard test questions, exercises, and commands given by teachers. Testing these assessments has formed the main basis of past educational evaluation, choosing to focus more on end-of-term results than day-to-day suggestions. Although still useful in some situations, these traditional ways of assessing fail to meet the needs of modern, varied, and technology-based learning practices (Koolivand et al., 2024; Meylani, 2024).

Types of Traditional Assessments

Usually, traditional methods of assessment have held the main place in educational evaluation. Although they have similarities, different tests use different ways, reasons, and levels of evaluation. The following includes the prime examples of traditional assessments; each having particular qualities and uses:

Standardized Tests

Such tests are given and handled in the same way for everyone. Generally, such tests are made by national or institutional officials to see how students measure up to certain standards. All students taking similar tests allow for comparing results between populations and over the years. Many times, these assessments are important for university entrance (such as the SAT and GRE), choosing a college or major evaluating the whole education system. Most standardized tests contain multiple-choice items, passages for reading comprehension, math problems, or reasoning tasks, and the process for administering them is very structured to ensure their validity and reliability. Issues with standardized testing include its added focus on cognitive abilities, a rigid set of questions for everyone, and its ability to cause nervousness in students. They also suggest that standardized tests encourage pupils to cram information more than to question or think, and tend to be less fair towards marginalized individuals (Kubiszyn & Borich, 2024).

Written Examinations

They are commonly used as a traditional form of testing. They are often set up with planned or semi-planned questions that are taken during a set time frame, inside the classroom, or as things to do at home. Some forms of multiple-choice, brief-answer, and essay-style questions may be features of these exams. Written tests are used to check students' skills in remembering, analyzing, using, and combining information. To evaluate students' ideas and arguments, essay questions are frequently given in university and college exams. As for school-level tests, they mostly ask students to remember facts and handle easy comprehension questions. Although exams are a reliable form of assessment, they might not reveal how someone will solve job-related problems since they are very different in real life (Huxham et al., 2012; Ortega-Sanchez, 2016).

Quizzes and Objective Tests

They are generally short tests designed to see if a student knows the recent information. Both formative and summative testing situations usually make use of objective tests, where the questions are true/false, matching, fill-in-the-blank, or multiple-choice. Many people like these tests because they are straightforward to carry out, and their scores can be processed instantly with the help of computers. It is common to use them to assess knowledge, terms, and process skills, and include them in daily lessons as a way to check students' understanding. But they do not always measure the learning of analysis, synthesis, or creativity as well as they do other skills. If students can guess the correct answers well, the reliability of the exam results drops in multiple-choice tests (Fitria, 2024; McDaniel et al., 2012; Scouller, 1998).

Assignments and Essays

Students use assignments and essays to look into topics in their way. You are generally expected to research separately, think critically, mix ideas from various areas, and organize your thoughts into a long essay. Most of the time, essays are checked for your level of analysis, the strength of your arguments, and competence in writing. Students might need to solve cases, read relevant texts, reflect on learning experiences, or practice problem-solving, which depends on the course they take. They are considered useful because they check for logical thinking and how a learner manages their work. Still, it can take a lot of time to mark these assignments, there is a risk of cheating, and they must be assessed the same way using complete rubrics (Gombert et al., 2024; Scouller, 1998).

Oral Examination.

Oral exams have the examiner asking questions and the learner answering, mainly to test the student's knowledge of concepts, reasoning powers, and ability to explain solutions. Many people use this approach in medicine, law, and the humanities, especially in more advanced study. Through oral assessments, we are able to test a student's ability to respond in a natural way, express thoughts clearly, and understand well. Because they are interactive, teachers are able to respond right away and ask more insightful questions depending on each student's answer. Still, they rely heavily on what the examiner thinks and how fair they are toward students and this can make students feel nervous, affecting their performance without having anything to do with what they have learned (Huxham et al., 2012).

Classroom Observation and Participation

Being informal, in this assessment teachers talk and observe students as they interact in the classroom. Much of the time, it is favored in young children's education and for evaluating their skills, especially when group work or discussions are important. By using observation, educators are able to check social skills, motivation, speech skills and how much each student participates in class. It provides instructors with immediate responses and makes it easier to change their ways of teaching.

Challenges in Traditional Assessments

Limited Personalization

Most assessments are built in the same way and judge students using the same standards, regardless of their learning styles (Saul & Wuttke, 2013; Shen, 2024). Taking a strict approach often means overlooking the many differences in learners' backgrounds, skills, and choices. Some students may be skilled at explaining things out loud but have a hard time with writing answers on an exam, and they may need extra time or different ways to express their ideas. If an assessment is not changed for each person, it may not accurately measure their abilities. Consequently, numerous learners end up at a disadvantage, which can influence their inspiration and self-assurance. With time, it is required to support many learning pathways, special needs, and inclusivity, and individualized assessment methods.

High Resources and Time Demands

Preparing for grades using essays, projects, and oral exams takes up much of a teacher's time (Meylani, 2024). To grade subjective work fairly and accurately, graders read the work, analyze it, and often check their decisions more than once. Since grading takes much time, sometimes the usefulness of the feedback decreases. Besides, making arrangements for big standardized tests requires booking locations, recruitment, and training of proctors, each of which is challenging and requires a lot of effort and money. Because of these resource shortages, assessments cannot be given frequently or easily adjusted, so it becomes difficult to keep track of each student's advancement.

Delayed and Limited Feedback

Many traditions mean that feedback is given only once the assessment is over, and this might take several days or even weeks to happen (Omorogiuwa, 2012). Because of this delay, students cannot think over their mistakes and correct their study habits in time. Formative assessment needs both quick and continuous feedback to help students improve, not only to check their progress. Too late an intervention can make students believe false ideas, and they may keep repeating mistakes. Most of the time, traditional feedback is basic and boils down to just a final grade, so it fails to provide clear details about student strengths or weaknesses.

Focus on Lower-Order Cognitive Skills

The common approach in assessments is to measure how well each student can recall facts and understand basic ideas instead of using higher-level thinking. Tests that use multiple-choice options are useful for judging specific information, but they usually fail to measure skills like critical thinking, creativity, or the ability to solve problems. Concentrating mainly on memorization and basic skills does not satisfy today's educational requirements since modern education stresses the use of deep-thinking skills. Consequently, some students end up relying on superficial learning, concerned more with their scores in tests than with understanding the core ideas. Therefore, tests should be created that can check people's higher-order thinking and inventive skills.

Test Anxiety and Stress

Placing importance on results from high-stakes exams typically leads to a lot of stress and anxiety for students, which results in poorer performance and general unhappiness. Trying to achieve good results in a set timeframe can increase nervousness, especially when a person does not handle exam situations well. The testing environment tends to reward students who are skilled at taking tests, rather than students who have real knowledge. Moreover, anxiety may have a stronger effect on certain groups, which could make assessment results inaccurate for these individuals. Fair and right evaluation of student learning depends on lessening stress related to tests.

Assessment Bias and Subjectivity

During human grading of essays, presentations, and oral exams, it is possible to include subjective and biased judgments. Some things, like someone's handwriting, their language ability, their culture, or how they look, may influence how a person is judged without the evaluator realizing it. Such differences can make grades inconsistent and make the results of assessments less reliable. Eventually, each human evaluator will interpret the assignment differently based on their personal preferences.

Dealing with bias shows why it's important to ensure criteria are seen and the same by all, and to add extra tools where possible to lessen personal opinions.

Measuring Soft Skills

Nowadays, professionals are valued more if they use collaboration, communication, ethical judgment, and creative thinking. Still, usual methods of assessment do not work well for assessing abilities that depend on context and are complex. Primarily, written exams look at facts and skills, not at communication and emotions. Usually, it's necessary to use observation, reflection, or project examples to assess such abilities, which takes time and may not always be accurate. Since soft skills are sometimes hard to discern, teachers may have trouble providing complete support to students' development.

Equity and Accessibility Issues

Educators may not see learning barriers in students from diverse backgrounds if they only use standardized tests and traditional ways of assessment. Students who need assistive tools or more time may not be able to use formats set in advance or timed exams. Besides, when students from underprivileged backgrounds lack the opportunity to learn from prepared resources, receive tuition or learn in appropriate environments, it affects how well they do at school. Because of these issues, more inclusive ways of assessing students should be used, giving every student an equal chance to show what they can do.

OPPORTUNITIES IN AI-DRIVEN ASSESSMENT

AI is used in assessment to design, deliver, monitor, and analyze different evaluations. The main goal of this approach is to help or automate parts of the assessment process with the aid of computational models ranging from simple rules to advanced learning algorithms. With pressing needs for assessment to adjust to each person, be easy to use, and produce results swiftly, AI plays a key role in looking at how assessments are conducted and applied to promote learning.

AI is being used in many areas of educational assessment, and this use keeps increasing. These programs are commonly used for grading tests made up of multiple-choice and short-answer questions. Some models can now check essays and responses that students write by hand, due to NLP, which assesses grammar, organization, reasoning, and imagination. Students usually get instant, individual advice from artificial intelligence when they use feedback generation systems. AI also supports practice exercises based on what a student already knows and helps with large-scale testing by providing information-rich results on every student's development and achievements.

Generative AI models, one of the latest developments, now include ChatGPT. Where traditional AI is narrow in what it does, ChatGPT can talk and respond flexibly, depending on the situation. In tests, ChatGPT is used to make custom questions, offer feedback, help with rubrics, and help students improve their assignments by reflection. Moreover, it enables teachers to have dialogues with students that guide them through using the prompts, examining the answers, and offering help at the same time. Even though ChatGPT is not an official grading tool, it works as a cognitive aid to support both educators and students in assessments with greater adaptability and attention (Fitria, 2023; Gill et al., 2024; Halaweh, 2023; Mittal et al., 2025; Morjaria et al., 2024; Tossell et al., 2024).

Enhanced Personalization

ChatGPT, an AI tool, responds to every individual's differences by examining their answers and customizing the questions and comments given (Fang, 2024; Ma, 2023). Should a student face difficulties in clearly expressing a concept in writing, ChatGPT will identify the issue and explain it in a simplified way or give more details to help the learner go through the topic one step at a time. This new approach is a step forward since conventional tests are not designed for students' unique learning styles. Since the AI traverses your development all the time, it keeps adjusting the level and kind of tasks to fit your needs, making learning tailored to you.

In addition, learners can use ChatGPT to interact, which encourages a supportive and attentive approach during assessments. If a student is confused, they can get further explanation or see an example by asking their classmates or the teacher, just like they would in private tutoring. Dialogic assessment helps learners manage their education, which makes learning fun and exciting for them. Teachers gain new opportunities to meet students of various needs without using much more time or resources, which supports both inclusion and equity at school.

With AI-assisted assessment, it becomes easier to pinpoint what areas a student knows poorly, which are not always clear in regular exams. By way of example, if a student provides a general answer, the tutor can help them dig deeper and discover small issues their exam would probably overlook. Because of its helpful reporting, teachers can better pinpoint problem points and help students overcome them earlier. Because of this, using personalized AI makes learning better and teaching more effective.

Sample prompt for ChatGPT:

"Explain the concept of photosynthesis as if I am a beginner who has trouble understanding scientific terms. Use simple language and examples."
Follow-up prompt:
"Can you give me a real-life example to help me understand better?"

Improved Efficiency and Scalability

Using AI-driven tools for assessment, like ChatGPT, makes it convenient to grade many responses and deliver outcomes right away (Chang et al., 2024; Wang & Feng, 2023). Normally, grading open-ended responses, essays, or projects requires a lot of time, which makes it hard for teachers to use them very often. Teachers can use ChatGPT to evaluate hundreds or thousands of assignments in just a few minutes, which greatly cuts down their workload. Having more efficient tools makes it possible for teachers to monitor students' growth regularly instead of just depending on infrequent tests.

Besides saving time in grading, scalability helps in other ways as well. AI platforms are capable of processing different exam questions at once, ensuring everything is evaluated nicely and without variation. Being adaptable, AI-driven tools suit big courses, including MOOCs, where personal feedback from people would be challenging. Being cloud-based makes it easy for ChatGPT to handle lots of interactions, so learners receive their assessments as soon as they are ready.

As educators become more efficient, they can pay more attention to activities such as planning the curriculum, guiding students, and upgrading their skills. Because of AI, teachers do not have to devote as much time to grading, leaving more space for activities that involve humans. This helps the teacher by boosting their work, creating a system that can customize learning for any student.

Sample prompt for ChatGPT:
"Review this 500-word student essay on climate change and provide a summary along with a score based on clarity, argument strength, and grammar."
Follow-up prompt:
"List the top three areas where the essay could be improved."

Real-Time, Actionable Feedback

While normal grading can make students wait for feedback for a long time, ChatGPT gives answers right away and lets you know what to work on next (Koraishi, 2023; Li, 2023; Webb, 2023). Being able to get feedback right away is crucial for students since they can correct their errors and misunderstandings as the material is still understood. In biology, a lab report that any student submits will be met with instant comments on vocabulary, interpreting the facts, and how well the explanation is made. This offers the chance for many improvements before submission.

It is also impressive how ChatGPT makes tough feedback easy to grasp. What makes the AI better than a grade is that it describes the strengths and weaknesses in detail, gives examples of the errors, and provides tips on how to improve. It may notice a poor thesis, unclear transitions between paragraphs, or unsubstantiated claims, and use these to push students to think in more detail. By using dialogic feedback, assessment becomes a process where feedback is given and received all the time.

Students are able to use ChatGPT's interactivity to get a clearer understanding of the feedback or look for more sample problems. It is hard to set up this kind of repeated feedback in the typical classroom when there are many students. Being part of this process, students develop traits such as self-control, self-reflection, and independence, which are necessary for learning over a lifetime.

Sample prompt for ChatGPT:

"I wrote this paragraph on the causes of World War I. Please identify any factual errors or unclear sentences and suggest improvements."

Follow-up prompt:

"Can you explain why this sentence is unclear and how I could rephrase it?"

Assessment of Higher-Order Cognitive Skills

Special models like ChatGPT can assess complex mental processes besides simple memorization, these include analysis, synthesis, evaluation, and creativity (Farrokhnia et al., 2024; Kartal, 2024; Zhai et al., 2024). ChatGPT can evaluate an argumentative essay by checking its logical order, if the points are well-connected, and if the evidence presented is adequate, commenting on how well the reasoning works rather than leaving it at simple correctness. It is not like traditional multiple-choice tests that mainly test a person's memory and understanding.

STEM learning with ChatGPT lets students share how they solved certain problems step by step. Such a method reveals how students think, so the assessment can include both their final solutions and the concepts they used to arrive there. In a physics problem, the AI can challenge students to explain their assumptions and explain how different variables work with each other.

Besides, ChatGPT can offer original lesson plans and judge whether students' work is unique, such as writing poetry or finding innovative ways to address ethical challenges. Working on open-ended tasks boosts the ability to invent and think logically which help children achieve success in the 21st century. By assessing various areas of knowledge and abilities, AI advances an educational system that supports the future.

Sample prompt for ChatGPT:

"Evaluate this argument about the ethical implications of artificial intelligence, noting any logical fallacies or weaknesses."

Follow-up prompt:

"Suggest ways to strengthen the thesis and improve the evidence used."

Reduced Test Anxiety and Flexible Timing

Instead of taking timed exams, AI future alignments can give students an easier way to learn, as they can manage their study time at their own pace (AYDIN YILDIZ, 2023). Using its friendly and helpful interface, ChatGPT allows learners to ask questions, experiment with ideas, and repeatedly try new things with no pressure to be judged quickly. As an illustration, language learners are able to talk and write with ChatGPT, getting regular support over days or weeks, not just during an important testing period.

Students who are anxious or have disabilities can move more comfortably since they are allowed flexibility during exams. Due to ChatGPT, learners can work through the process one step at a time, pause as often as needed, and go over tricky subjects whenever they wish. While traditional classroom exams find it hard to offer such convenience, this happens naturally with AI-based systems.

When less worried about tests, students can direct their attention to answering questions with their real knowledge. Because of its conversational style, ChatGPT helps people develop a mindset that treats errors as ways to learn, not as insults. Because of this environment, students are motivated, interested, and confident, which is very important for learning and good assessment.

Sample prompt for ChatGPT:

"Can we practice some common interview questions? I want to improve my answers gradually, and you can give me feedback after each response."

Follow-up prompt:

"Please give me some tips to make my answers sound more confident and natural."

Assessment of Soft Skills and Collaboration

It is very difficult to assess communication, empathy, and ethical reasoning using typical tests. With ChatGPT, it is possible to carry out fictional discussions and role-play situations to check a person's abilities. A social studies AI might give a student a hypothetical problem and ask them to explain their view, the logic behind it, and how it makes them feel. Analyzing the language tone, clarity, and ethics, ChatGPT gives useful information on interpersonal and intrapersonal abilities.

Besides, group discussions, settling disagreements, and reviewing teamwork skills can become easier using ChatGPT. Using AI, it is possible to see how students have collaborated and discussed ideas that would not be caught by just giving a test to each individual. It provides opportunities to evaluate skills that people need in a work setting, including negotiation, leading others, and knowledge of different cultures.

Taking observations from student-AI interactions lets teachers discover more about how the students are developing. This way of testing skills goes along with cognitive assessments and aids learners in dealing with various non-school problems.

Sample prompt for ChatGPT:

"Role-play a customer service scenario where I have to handle an angry client. Provide feedback on my communication style and empathy."

Follow-up prompt:

"Suggest alternative ways to phrase my responses to be more understanding and professional."

Promoting Equity and Accessibility

It can be tailored to help anyone who needs it, so everyone has the chance to learn. With text-to-speech and speech-to-text, students with sight or movement problems can now take assessments more easily. When using simplified language, learners with little English knowledge can better understand what is asked in the prompts. Providing multiple languages makes it possible for non-native speakers to learn, making the learning process more inclusive.

Since AI is flexible, it can change the difficulty or format of questions in real time depending on each learner's needs. If a student has trouble forming complex sentences, they might be provided with simpler teaching materials or more help from visuals. Because of these accommodations, each student can fairly display their understanding. AI's involvement in assessment also allows different aspects of student performance to be evaluated, not only uniform skills. This approach can help students with various backgrounds have a fair opportunity to succeed.

Sample prompt for ChatGPT:

"Explain the process of mitosis using simple sentences suitable for a student with limited English proficiency."

Follow-up prompt:

"Can you translate this explanation into Spanish (or another language)?"

CHALLENGES IN AI-DRIVEN ASSESSMENT

Even with all the benefits it offers, AI-based assessment does present some serious challenges that need to be managed well for its success. All of these challenges involve technical issues, ethics, teaching approaches, and institutions, so they need to be considered with care (Chiu et al., 2023; Kooli, 2023; Sahin et al., 2024).

Data Quality and Bias

ChatGPT and other AI systems depend on huge data collections to train their language skills. Nevertheless, if the training data is poor or biased, AI may produce wrong or biased evaluations. For instance, when data about certain dialects, cultures, or minority groups is missing, the AI may happen to misunderstand their answers or offer feedback that is not useful. As a result, biases in the system might increase and widen the gaps in education. Making sure the data used for training is of good quality and free from bias is very important, but it still takes a lot of resources.

Transparency and Explainability

Another big problem with AI is that its models often work in mysterious ways. These language models are based on neural networks, which makes it hard for educators and students to see how decisions are reached. Since so little is known about the generation of results or getting feedback, it concerns people about how confident they can be in the process. When students are not sure why a particular response received a certain score, they might feel upset or think they are being treated wrongly, which may make educators cautious about using AI for important decisions. For AI to be accepted, it is important to use clear, explainable AI approaches and explain them well.

Ethical and Privacy Concerns

Concerns about ethics in AI assessment centers mostly on the privacy of data and consent. AI can handle students' work, personal records, and interaction information, which might not be safe from being misused or breached. Relying on technology to evaluate students might cause schools to observe their actions too much, which could violate their right to privacy. Have strong security measures in place, ensure students' consent to the use of their data is obvious, and monitor activities by computer while keeping in mind students' need for control and dignity.

Risk of Over-Reliance and De-skilling

Though AI helps with evaluation, there is a chance that educators and students come to lean too much on automated systems. Being too dependent on technology could take away teachers' abilities, allowing them to step back from important selection tasks, and lose their knowledge about students' learning progress. Just like studying with online tutors, relying heavily on AI-generated feedback could reduce a student's skill in critical thinking. Education is best maintained, and learning stays real when there is a fitting combination of AI and human guidance.

Limitations in Understanding Context and Nuance

Natural language processing has improved, but AI models have not yet mastered recognizing tough context, cultural touches, comedy, irony, or emotions. Since ChatGPT might misunderstand detailed arguments, original writing, or references to various cultures, its feedback and judgment may not be right. As a result, AI cannot be trusted to replace people when it comes to subjects that require strong interpretive skills, such as literature, art, or ethics. It is necessary to address these gaps to ensure AI is used in the right way.

Technical and Infrastructure Barriers

In order to carry out AI-driven assessment, a strong infrastructure is necessary, which includes good internet, powerful computers, and knowledgeable staff. Adopting new technologies may be tough for many educational institutions, mainly those with little money or trained staff. Besides, when the system encounters technical issues, breaks down temporarily, or makes errors in calculations, it can frustrate the people taking the tests and reduce their confidence in the assessment. It requires putting money into both building human resources and developing vital infrastructure.

Legal and Regulatory Challenges

AI is being used more widely in education than the current laws and rules can keep up with. It is still a complicated issue to set up intellectual property rights for AI-generated materials, deal with mistakes made during assessments, and ensure compliance with data privacy laws. Government officials should set clear rules that promote new developments without damaging those involved. If the laws are weak, institutions may face charges, while students could receive mistreatment.

IMPROVEMENT IN AI ASSESSMENT

As the artificial intelligence transforms the horizon of educational assessment, various issues, which have remained unaltered, are manifested, i.e., validity, reliability, bias, and transparency. Theoretical integration becomes important in addressing such issues. This section identifies the main theories of assessment science and AI research on these challenges with the purpose of providing a conceptual scaffold toward AI-powered assessment systems evaluation and design.

Evidence-Centered Design (ECD)

Evidence-Centered Design (Mislevy et al., 2003), is an assessment framework of foundations, which focuses on building an assessment of the intended constructs. It is a principled sequence: specify what is to be measured (construct), what would show evidence of proficiency, and conceive tasks that would elicit this evidence.

Validity in the context of AI-driven assessment deals with the issue of the adequacy of the system that judges the targeted level of learning. As an example, in automated essay scoring: suppose the algorithm is told to give marks in response to such superficial aspects of writing as the size of a word count or the correctness of the grammar, but that the arguments are not considered, and no higher-order thinking is consulted, then the assessment can be judged to lack construct validity. An AI scoring engine may score well on long, complicated written essays, even with weak content. Under the influence of ECD, a developer will be able to apply the scoring rubric and other characteristics of the algorithm so that they meet the goals of deeper learning, including logical thinking, coherence, and evidence.

Generalizability Theory (G-Theory)

Generalizability Theory (Brennan, 2010; Shavelson et al., 1992), is an extension of the classical test theory, which takes into consideration several separate sources of measurement errors. It enables a researcher to assess the consistency of the performance of an assessment on other conditions-raters, items, and occasions.

Reliability in AI evaluation refers to generating results in time consistency over and across contexts and people. To check the generalizability of an AI system, G-Theory can inform how it can be tested under different circumstances. A machine that scores short answers could do well with urban students who had been taught standardized formats, but not on interpretations that come out in the countryside, where linguistic features are different. A generalizability study would be able to indicate this dissimilarity and point to the need to retrain or calibrate the model to apply more widely.

Explainable AI (XAI)

Explainable artificial intelligence is a subdiscipline of the field of artificial intelligence that includes design principles and technical techniques to make AI models more interpretable. Suggested by the U.S. DARPA program and expounded by Gunning (Gunning et al., 2019), XAI is proposed to enable users to understand, trust, and manage AI systems effectively.

In education, trust is important, and therefore, the teachers, students, and administration must be able to know how an AI system arrived at a certain score or recommendation. Black-box styles giving you output without explanation destroy trust and reduce their value as an educational ample. Just imagine a tool powered by AI that identifies students as being at-risk due to the performance data. Without XAI, both the learner and the teacher will have no idea what type of data the flag was found on. XAI had the property of pointing out any patterns, e.g., a decline in the rate of assignment completion or participation, which can then be resolved positively.

Algorithmic Fairness Frameworks

Algorithms do have a framework of fairness (Barocas et al., 2021; Dwork et al., 2012), which seeks to identify, measure, and minimize bias in automated decision-making. They involve such methods as disparate impact analysis, counterfactual fairness testing, and bias-aware training.

The problem of bias is a focal area when solutions to inequality are passed to or increased by training data. Fairness structures offer methods of distributing these models to audit and better them to ensure that they do not discriminate based on race, gender, language, or socioeconomic standing. An oral fluency assessment that involved speech recognition may systematically give poor results to non-native English speakers because of the accents and not the fluency. Through fairness models, developers should be able to discover this imbalance and implement bias-fix measures, including accent-independent training data or adjusting fluency scores to a range of norms of speech.

Constructive Alignment

According to the theory of Constructive Alignment (Biggs, 1996), the practical result of high-quality learning conditions is alleged to be the consistency between intended learning outcomes (ILOs), teaching strategies, and assessment duties. Assessment is supposed to directly measure the competencies that students are supposed to come up with.

Artificial intelligence systems need to be modeled to capture what is envisaged in pedagogy. In case one of the courses focuses on collaborative problem-solving, AI must also evaluate the skills of teamwork, communication, and shared reasoning, rather than only individual answers. The fact that an AI-based grading system is only capable of evaluating the end written reports does not reflect collective efforts in a project-based learning course. An AI system may consolidate discussion logs, peer ratings, and contribution schedules to provide more integrative indicators to tie together with course objectives.

POLICY AND PEDAGOGICAL IMPLICATIONS

When AI-powered tools like ChatGPT are used in schools, they greatly influence policies and the ways teachers teach their students. Because more institutions are using technology, there must be policies and strategies put in place to make the best use of its benefits and limit the related problems.

Policy Implications

The authorities in charge of education should pay special attention to data protection rules for AI assessment platforms. Policy compliance should require organizations to collect, save, and use data openly, meeting regulations such as those established by GDPR or FERPA. In addition, making it clear that students can opt out and adding precise rules for consent will help maintain ethical standards and gain trust among parents and learners. When adopting AI, we must create policies to ensure the digital divide is not made worse. Authorities should focus on developing infrastructure and providing resources to ensure that everyone in different areas can use AI tools equally. AI-based assessments will likely lead to new difficulties for those who are already struggling in school. Those creating policies should keep in mind how to make lessons suitable and understandable for students with certain needs.

AI assessment procedures and the decisions made by their algorithms should always be clear when using them. Organizations should create ways to analyze AI tools to find out if they are biased or inaccurate in their results. Accountability measures need to explain what each school, AI vendor, and educator must do to manage the AI system, settle disagreements, and deal with errors. Generative AI tools such as ChatGPT bring up matters concerning ownership and the originality of work. Schools must set specific rules for the usage of AI in projects, making sure students learn creatively without being in danger of plagiarism. Guidelines on how and why to report concerns and what happens if the rules are broken should be provided to motivate honesty in AI-assisted learning spaces.

Pedagogical Implications

Because AI automates some assessment duties, educators get more time to teach critical thinking, give one-on-one help, and mentor students. In addition, teachers must be able to analyze AI feedback, fit it into their overall assessment plans, and help students who have needs that AI does not notice. Programs for teachers should teach them to work with AI, making certain that AI is used to strengthen human understanding instead of replacing it. In learning settings, students are expected to learn how to read, interpret, and evaluate what AI produces, as well as understand its ethical issues. Educators can explain to students how and when to make the best use of AI-based tools. Advising students to look back at their AI feedback plays a part in metacognition and responsible learning, making them more involved with their education.

Assessment should be developed to emphasize types of questions that require creativity, and AI should still be unable to fully deal with these questions. Students should be able to use AI feedback, adjust their studies, and keep revising their projects. AI can help facilitate group-based assessments, providing feedback as the project progresses on how well a team works together. Instructors should make sure they are aware of how AI systems could influence the feelings of their students. Talking openly about how AI tools operate and their weaknesses helps people be more confident and expect the right things. Using AI to help learners should go alongside human understanding to ensure they feel valued and supported. Coming together to understand AI ethics educates students and gives them the chance to consider their actions before using technologies responsibly.

All of these points together guide how to effectively use AI-based assessment tools such as ChatGPT in the classroom. Through connecting regulations with new teaching approaches, people involved in education can take full advantage of AI's value and keep educational goals secure.

CONCLUSION

Thinking of AI-driven assessment as a responsibility for several stakeholders is necessary. Policies should be made practical, coherent, and clear so that AI is applied correctly in education. By using frameworks that care for basic privacy and security involving data, for example, those like GDPR or FERPA, each system must highlight how it manages the information of its users. Equity is crucial because we need to make sure AI systems do not make learning gaps worse. People who create and enforce public policies should support AI designs that help all kinds of learners, including those with disabilities, newcomers to the language, and groups that are not represented enough.

In addition, strengthening educators is important. This means training on AI as well as learning how to connect what AI provides with what is already taught in schools. These programs are valuable when they equip teachers with tools to carefully assess the feedback, spot its issues, and use human experience in addition to it. It will make sure that AI does not replace all the special input from teachers.

Thirdly, we should include lessons on digital literacy and ethical AI use in students' learning programs. Students should be prepared to deal with AI technologies by recognizing their abilities, understanding what they cannot do, and knowing the issues of ethics around their use. This calls for explaining the rules about AI content, supporting responsible habits instead of relying too much, and urging reflective actions to build thinking on one's own.

Next, making sure everyone can use technology by investing heavily in infrastructure is very important. Access to the internet, hardware, and support is usually lacking in various educational settings, especially in remote or less privileged areas, which makes it hard to use AI for assessment. When AI is made accessible to people from various cultures and backgrounds, everyone has a chance to benefit, which is great for equality. Moreover, it is important to model how AI should be used together with human knowledge and skills. AI is a helpful resource for educators and should work with them rather than replace their roles. When responsibilities, accountability and quality are all set out clearly in hybrid assessments, it helps all parties ensure equal evaluation, keeps faith in the process and protects the parts of evaluation that are not duplicated by AI.

Work in this area should advance by pushing for more research and development to solve its current issues and bring new options to education. Further work in AI should focus on explainable AI (XAI), so AI systems can offer simple explanations for what they do. When educators and students can explain how AI generates their assessments, there will be more trust, transparency, and opportunities to change or contest the outcomes. Also, it is essential to minimize bias and guarantee fairness. Since AI models learn from huge datasets, they could result in bias against some social, cultural, or language groups. It is important for future efforts to focus on collecting training data that includes more variety and on designing algorithms that adjust themselves in real time to avoid bias. For this to happen, educators, AI developers, and ethicists should team up and work together.

Another possible approach is to widen how assessments are used to cover both multimodal and soft skills evaluation. With advancing AI, it is possible to assess someone's communication skills, creativity, teamwork, and emotional intelligence through speech, facial expressions, body movements, and social behavior. Even though it's difficult to measure them in the usual ways, these skills are now considered very important for students in today's world. There is a strong requirement for extended studies that investigate the role of AI-driven assessment on students, educators, and motivation as time passes. It can highlight results that were not planned, improve how things are carried out, and provide suggestions for policies and practices. It will be necessary to look at how AI shapes the whole ecosystem of education as it becomes more common in schools and universities.

In the future, more research should be done on ways to blend AI assessment with personalized courses for everyone. If real-time assessment data and customized content are combined, AI could make learning flexible and supportive for every person. AI-based tools such as ChatGPT are making a big change in educational evaluation, offering individual feedback, working on a large scale, and bringing new insights into learning. However, people still need to address problems linked to fairness, transparency, ethics, and infrastructure to successfully use them. Educators can make the most of AI and support human values by forming strong policies, increasing educator qualifications, promoting ethical AI education among students, and encouraging cooperation between people and machines. To ensure a fair, effective, and responsible assessment system, all involved parties should continue discussing and studying AI with educators, policymakers, technologists, and learners.

REFERENCES

Adeshola, I., & Adepoju, A. P. (2023). The opportunities and challenges of ChatGPT in education. *Interactive Learning Environments*. Advance online publication. DOI: 10.1080/10494820.2023.2253858;WEBSITE:WEBSITE:TFOPB;PAGE-GROUP:STRING:PUBLICATION

Ahmad, M., Ho, W. Y., Goyes Robalino, A. P., Maqsood, M., Ahmad, M., Ho, W. Y., Goyes Robalino, A. P., & Maqsood, M. (2025). Theoretical Implications of Generative AI for Content Generation in Geoinformatics Training. In A. Anna A. (Ed.), *Integration Strategies of Generative AI in Higher Education* (pp. 101–130). IGI Global Scientific Publishing. https://doi.org/DOI: 10.4018/979-8-3693-5518-3.CH005

Alamäki, A., Khan, U. A., Kauttonen, J., & Schlögl, S. (2024). An Experiment of AI-Based Assessment: Perspectives of Learning Preferences, Benefits, Intention, Technology Affinity, and Trust. *Education Sciences 2024, Vol. 14, Page 1386, 14*(12), 1386. https://doi.org/DOI: 10.3390/EDUCSCI14121386

Albadarin, Y., Saqr, · Mohammed, Pope, N., & Tukiainen, M. (2024). A systematic literature review of empirical research on ChatGPT in education. *Discover Education 2024 3:1, 3*(1), 1–26. https://doi.org/DOI: 10.1007/S44217-024-00138-2

Ali, M. H., Kainat, M., Maqsood, M., Fernandez, S. F., Ali, S., & Ahmad, M. (2024). Chatbots in Academic Literacy Exploring AI in Education. In *Enhancing Higher Education and Research With OpenAI Models* (pp. 37–59). IGI Global.

AYDIN YILDIZ, T. (2023). The Impact of ChatGPT on Language Learners' Motivation. *Journal of Teacher Education and Lifelong Learning, 5*(2). Advance online publication. DOI: 10.51535/tell.1314355

Barocas, S., Guo, A., Kamar, E., Krones, J., Morris, M. R., Vaughan, J. W., Wadsworth, W. D., & Wallach, H. (2021). Designing Disaggregated Evaluations of AI Systems: Choices, Considerations, and Tradeoffs. *AIES 2021 - Proceedings of the 2021 AAAI/ACM Conference on AI, Ethics, and Society*, 368–378. https://doi.org/DOI: 10.1145/3461702.3462610;CTYPE:STRING:BOOK

Biggs, J. (1996). Enhancing teaching through constructive alignment. *Higher Education, 32*(3), 347–364. DOI: 10.1007/BF00138871/METRICS

Brennan, R. L. (2010). Generalizability Theory and Classical Test Theory. *Applied Measurement in Education, 24*(1), 1–21. DOI: 10.1080/08957347.2011.532417

Chang, C. Y., Yang, C. L., Jen, H. J., Ogata, H., & Hwang, G. H. (2024). Facilitating nursing and health education by incorporating ChatGPT into learning designs. *Journal of Educational Technology & Society*, *27*(1). Advance online publication. DOI: 10.30191/ETS.202401_27(1).TP02

Chiu, T. K. F., Xia, Q., Zhou, X., Chai, C. S., & Cheng, M. (2023). Systematic literature review on opportunities, challenges, and future research recommendations of artificial intelligence in education. In *Computers and Education* (Vol. 4). Artificial Intelligence., DOI: 10.1016/j.caeai.2022.100118

Dwork, C., Hardt, M., Pitassi, T., Reingold, O., & Zemel, R. (2012). Fairness through awareness. *ITCS 2012 - Innovations in Theoretical Computer Science Conference*, 214–226. https://doi.org/DOI: 10.1145/2090236.2090255;JOURNAL:JOURNAL:ACMCONFERENCES;PAGEGROUP:STRING:PUBLICATION

Elbanna, S., & Armstrong, L. (2024). Exploring the integration of ChatGPT in education: Adapting for the future. *Management and Sustainability*, *3*(1). Advance online publication. DOI: 10.1108/MSAR-03-2023-0016

Fang, L. (2024). Exploring the impact of artificial intelligence-based assistants in modern education: The case of ChatGPT. *Applied and Computational Engineering*, *35*(1). Advance online publication. DOI: 10.54254/2755-2721/35/20230379

Farrokhnia, M., Banihashem, S. K., Noroozi, O., & Wals, A. (2024). A SWOT analysis of ChatGPT: Implications for educational practice and research. *Innovations in Education and Teaching International*, *61*(3). Advance online publication. DOI: 10.1080/14703297.2023.2195846

Fitria, T. N. (2023). Artificial intelligence (AI) technology in OpenAI ChatGPT application: A review of ChatGPT in writing English essay. *ELT Forum: Journal of English Language Teaching, 12*(1). https://doi.org/DOI: 10.15294/elt.v12i1.64069

Fitria, T. N. (2024). Choosing Objective and Non-objective Test as Instrument for Assessment of EFL Student Learning Outcomes. *Globish: An English-Indonesian Journal for English. Education and Culture*, *13*(1). Advance online publication. DOI: 10.31000/globish.v13i1.9601

Gill, S. S., Xu, M., Patros, P., Wu, H., Kaur, R., Kaur, K., Fuller, S., Singh, M., Arora, P., Parlikad, A. K., Stankovski, V., Abraham, A., Ghosh, S. K., Lutfiyya, H., Kanhere, S. S., Bahsoon, R., Rana, O., Dustdar, S., Sakellariou, R., & Buyya, R. (2024). Transformative effects of ChatGPT on modern education: Emerging Era of AI Chatbots. *Internet of Things and Cyber-Physical Systems*, *4*. Advance online publication. DOI: 10.1016/j.iotcps.2023.06.002

Gombert, S., Fink, A., Giorgashvili, T., Jivet, I., Di Mitri, D., Yau, J., Frey, A., & Drachsler, H. (2024). From the Automated Assessment of Student Essay Content to Highly Informative Feedback: A Case Study. *International Journal of Artificial Intelligence in Education*. Advance online publication. DOI: 10.1007/s40593-023-00387-6

Gunning, D., Stefik, M., Choi, J., Miller, T., Stumpf, S., & Yang, G. Z. (2019). XAI—Explainable artificial intelligence. *Science Robotics*, *4*(37). Advance online publication. DOI: 10.1126/SCIROBOTICS.AAY7120

Halaweh, M. (2023). ChatGPT in education: Strategies for responsible implementation. *Contemporary Educational Technology*, *15*(2). Advance online publication. DOI: 10.30935/cedtech/13036

Hopfenbeck, T. N., Zhang, Z., Sun, S. Z., Robertson, P., & McGrane, J. A. (2023). Challenges and opportunities for classroom-based formative assessment and AI: A perspective article. *Frontiers in Education*, *8*. Advance online publication. DOI: 10.3389/feduc.2023.1270700

Huxham, M., Campbell, F., & Westwood, J. (2012). Oral versus written assessments: A test of student performance and attitudes. *Assessment & Evaluation in Higher Education*, *37*(1). Advance online publication. DOI: 10.1080/02602938.2010.515012

Kamalov, F., Santandreu Calonge, D., & Gurrib, I. (2023). New Era of Artificial Intelligence in Education: Towards a Sustainable Multifaceted Revolution. *Sustainability (Switzerland)*, *15*(16). Advance online publication. DOI: 10.3390/su151612451

Kartal, G. (2024). The influence of ChatGPT on thinking skills and creativity of EFL student teachers: A narrative inquiry. *Journal of Education for Teaching*, *50*(4). Advance online publication. DOI: 10.1080/02607476.2024.2326502

Kooli, C. (2023). Chatbots in Education and Research: A Critical Examination of Ethical Implications and Solutions. *Sustainability (Switzerland)*, *15*(7). Advance online publication. DOI: 10.3390/su15075614

Koolivand, H., Shooreshi, M. M., Safari-Faramani, R., Borji, M., Mansoory, M. S., Moradpoor, H., Bahrami, M., & Azizi, S. M. (2024). Comparison of the effectiveness of virtual reality-based education and conventional teaching methods in dental education: A systematic review. *BMC Medical Education*, *24*(1). Advance online publication. DOI: 10.1186/s12909-023-04954-2

Koraishi, O. (2023). Teaching English in the Age of AI: Embracing ChatGPT to Optimize EFL Materials and Assessment. *Language Education & Technology Journal*, *3*(1).

Kubiszyn, T., & Borich, G. D. (2024). *Educational testing and measurement : classroom application and practice*. 14.

Li, Y. (2023). The Potential Application of ChatGPT in Higher Education Management. *Lecture Notes in Education Psychology and Public Media*, *25*(1). Advance online publication. DOI: 10.54254/2753-7048/25/20230750

Ma, T. (2023). The Influence of ChatGPT on Autonomous Learning for College Students. *Lecture Notes in Education Psychology and Public Media*, *25*(1). Advance online publication. DOI: 10.54254/2753-7048/25/20230708

McDaniel, M. A., Wildman, K. M., & Anderson, J. L. (2012). Using quizzes to enhance summative-assessment performance in a web-based class: An experimental study. *Journal of Applied Research in Memory and Cognition*, *1*(1). Advance online publication. DOI: 10.1016/j.jarmac.2011.10.001

Meylani, R. (2024). A Comparative Analysis of Traditional and Modern Approaches to Assessment and Evaluation in Education. [WAJES]. *The Western Anatolia Journal of Educational Sciences*, *15*(1), 520–555. DOI: 10.51460/BAEBD.1386737

Michel-Villarreal, R., Vilalta-Perdomo, E., Salinas-Navarro, D. E., Thierry-Aguilera, R., & Gerardou, F. S. (2023). Challenges and Opportunities of Generative AI for Higher Education as Explained by ChatGPT. *Education Sciences*, *13*(9). Advance online publication. DOI: 10.3390/educsci13090856

Mislevy, R. J., Almond, R. G., & Lukas, J. F. (2003). A BRIEF INTRODUCTION TO EVIDENCE-CENTERED DESIGN. *ETS Research Report Series*, *2003*(1), i–29. DOI: 10.1002/J.2333-8504.2003.TB01908.X;PAGE:STRING:ARTICLE/CHAPTER

Mittal, S., Agarwal, R., Bansal, S., & Sharma, A. (2025). ChatGPT in Financial Education: Assessing its Role in Improving Financial Literacy and Investor Knowledge. *International Journal of Electronic Finance*, *1*(1). Advance online publication. DOI: 10.1504/ijef.2025.10062488

Monib, W. K., Qazi, A., & Mahmud, M. M. (2024). Exploring learners' experiences and perceptions of ChatGPT as a learning tool in higher education. *Education and Information Technologies*, *30*(1), 917–939. DOI: 10.1007/S10639-024-13065-4/METRICS

Morjaria, L., Burns, L., Bracken, K., Levinson, A. J., Ngo, Q. N., Lee, M., & Sibbald, M. (2024). Examining the Efficacy of ChatGPT in Marking Short-Answer Assessments in an Undergraduate Medical Program. *International Medical Education*, *3*(1). Advance online publication. DOI: 10.3390/ime3010004

Omorogiuwa, K. O. (2012). *Benefits and challenges of feedback in formative assessment of distance learners*. https://uir.unisa.ac.za/handle/10500/8558

Ortega-Sanchez, C. (2016). Written Exams: How Effectively are We Using Them? *Procedia: Social and Behavioral Sciences, 228*. Advance online publication. DOI: 10.1016/j.sbspro.2016.07.021

Owan, V. J., Abang, K. B., Idika, D. O., Etta, E. O., & Bassey, B. A. (2023). Exploring the potential of artificial intelligence tools in educational measurement and assessment. In *Eurasia Journal of Mathematics, Science and Technology Education* (Vol. 19, Issue 8). https://doi.org/DOI: 10.29333/ejmste/13428

Sahin, A., Thompson, N., & Ercikan, K. (2024). Opportunities and Challenges of AI in Educational Assessment. *Journal of Measurement and Evaluation in Education and Psychology, 15*, 260–262. DOI: 10.21031/EPOD.1607441

Saul, C., & Wuttke, H. D. (2013). E-assessment meets personalization. *IEEE Global Engineering Education Conference, EDUCON*. https://doi.org/DOI: 10.1109/EduCon.2013.6530106

Scouller, K. (1998). The influence of assessment method on students' learning approaches: Multiple choice question examination versus assignment essay. *Higher Education, 35*(4), 453–472. DOI: 10.1023/A:1003196224280/METRICS

Shavelson, R. J., Webb, N. M., & Rowley, G. L. (1992). Generalizability theory. *Methodological Issues & Strategies in Clinical Research.*, 233–256. https://doi.org/DOI: 10.1037/10109-051

Shen, Y. (2024). Personalised Education: A study on the relationship between student assessment methods and student development. *SHS Web of Conferences, 199*, 01002. https://doi.org/DOI: 10.1051/SHSCONF/202419901002

Tossell, C. C., Tenhundfeld, N. L., Momen, A., Cooley, K., & De Visser, E. J. (2024). Student Perceptions of ChatGPT Use in a College Essay Assignment: Implications for Learning, Grading, and Trust in Artificial Intelligence. *IEEE Transactions on Learning Technologies, 17*. Advance online publication. DOI: 10.1109/TLT.2024.3355015

Vieriu, A. M., & Petrea, G. (2025). The Impact of Artificial Intelligence (AI) on Students' Academic Development. *Education Sciences 2025, Vol. 15, Page 343, 15*(3), 343. https://doi.org/DOI: 10.3390/EDUCSCI15030343

Wang, X., & Feng, Y. (2023). An Experimental Study of ChatGPT-Assisted Improvement of Chinese College Students' English Reading Skills: A Case Study of Dear Life. *ACM International Conference Proceeding Series*. https://doi.org/DOI: 10.1145/3629296.3629300

Webb, J. J. (2023). Proof of Concept: Using ChatGPT to Teach Emergency Physicians How to Break Bad News. *Cureus*. Advance online publication. DOI: 10.7759/cureus.38755

Zhai, X., Nyaaba, M., & Ma, W. (2024). Can Generative AI and ChatGPT Outperform Humans on Cognitive-Demanding Problem-Solving Tasks in Science? *Science and Education*. Advance online publication. DOI: 10.1007/s11191-024-00496-1

Chapter 3
Transforming Assessment: The Role of Technology in Higher Education

Andi Asrifan
https://orcid.org/0000-0002-9934-6129
Universitas Negeri Makassar, Indonesia

Rismawati Sudirman
https://orcid.org/0000-0001-8046-6764
Universitas Muhammadiyah Palopo, Indonesia

Wahira Wahira
Universitas Negeri Makassar, Indonesia

Syamsiarna Nappu
https://orcid.org/0000-0001-7115-7011
Universitas Muhammadiyah Makassar, Indonesia

ABSTRACT

This chapter examines the evolution of assessment in higher education influenced by digital innovation and inclusive teaching methodologies. It analyzes how technology—encompassing AI-driven tools, learning analytics, e-portfolios, and simulations—has transformed assessment into a more learner-centric, adaptable, and instantaneous process. The discourse emphasizes critical aspects such as Universal Design for Learning (UDL), institutional preparedness, student views, and data ethics. Moreover, it rigorously examines the obstacles posed by the digital

DOI: 10.4018/979-8-3373-7057-6.ch003

divide and the ethical ramifications of AI in assessment. The chapter proposes future-oriented assessment environments that are equitable, transparent, and responsive to varied learner needs by integrating inclusive frameworks and strategic strategy.

RETHINKING ASSESSMENT PARADIGMS IN THE DIGITAL ERA

1.1. The Evolution of Assessment in Higher Education

Assessment in higher education has experienced considerable evolution over the past century, transitioning from inflexible, standardized systems to more dynamic and learner-centered approaches. Historically, assessment has predominantly emphasized summative, high-stakes evaluations, including written tests and term papers, which valued memorization and adherence to academic standards (Chiziwa & Kunkwenzu, 2021; Oteng et al., 2023). These evaluations were grounded in positivist traditions that prioritized objectivity, dependability, and the measurement of knowledge. This paradigm frequently overlooked the intricacies of learning processes and the unique requirements of individual students.

Following the emergence of constructivist learning theories in the late 20th century, educational institutions commenced a reassessment of conventional assessment methodologies. There was increasing acknowledgment that learning is an active, contextual, and reflexive endeavor. As a result, formative assessments, peer evaluations, portfolios, and project-based evaluations have arisen as alternative techniques to gauge deeper comprehension and critical thinking (Jeganathan et al., 2024; Naaj et al., 2023; Yao et al., 2020). This paradigm change emphasized not only students' knowledge but also their learning processes and application of knowledge in real-world contexts.

The digitization of education in the early 21st century brought novel tools and platforms for assessment, hence speeding innovation throughout academia. Learning Management Systems (LMS), online assessments, and automated feedback systems have started to augment or supplant conventional evaluation methods, enhancing flexibility and accessibility. The worldwide transition to remote education during the COVID-19 epidemic accelerated the use of technology-enhanced examinations (Dhawan, 2020), revealing the shortcomings of traditional testing and emphasizing prospects for individualized, real-time evaluation.

Currently, evaluation in higher education is characterized by hybridity, integrating in-person, digital, formative, and summative approaches. Institutions are reevaluating assessment not merely as an indicator of academic achievement, but as a crucial component of the learning process, fostering student development, participation, and equity. The evolution signifies a profound philosophical and pedagogical shift:

transitioning from assessment of learning, to assessment for learning, and finally to assessment as learning (Hickey & Harris, 2021; Jeganathan et al., 2024). As higher education transitions into a new epoch influenced by artificial intelligence, big data, and global interconnection, assessment models must evolve to remain inclusive, transparent, and sensitive to the varied and dynamic requirements of learners.

1.2. Drivers of Change: Technology and Pedagogical Shifts

The evolution of evaluation in higher education has been profoundly shaped by two primary factors: swift technical progress and changing educational ideologies. The catalysts of change have transformed both the methods of assessment administration and the core comprehension of what defines effective, equitable, and significant evaluation. Technological innovation, particularly the emergence of digital platforms, mobile learning, artificial intelligence (AI), and learning analytics, has broadened the scope of assessment beyond conventional pen-and-paper examinations. The integration of Learning Management Systems (LMS), cloud-based tools, and AI-driven platforms enables instructors to create exams that are interactive, adaptable, and ongoing. These technologies provide real-time feedback, scalable testing, and individualized learning experiences, fostering a more sophisticated and comprehensive method for assessing student performance (Kumar, 2023; Onesi-Ozigagun et al., 2024).

Concurrently, educational transformations have arisen from criticisms of conventional standardized assessments and the increasing impact of constructivist, socio-cultural, and humanistic learning theories. These frameworks suggest that learning is an active, contextual process in which students generate knowledge through interaction and reflection. Consequently, there has been an increasing focus on formative assessments (Do et al., 2023; Jeganathan et al., 2024), peer collaboration, reflective journaling, and genuine, project-based evaluations. The emphasis has transitioned from evaluating discrete material knowledge to assessing higher-order thinking, creativity, problem-solving abilities, and the potential for lifelong learning.

The COVID-19 pandemic acted as a pivotal moment that expedited technological adoption and educational adaption. Global institutions were compelled to transition to online education, revealing the vulnerabilities of traditional evaluation frameworks and necessitating immediate innovation. This worldwide dilemma heightened the necessity for digital literacy, adaptable evaluation frameworks, and inclusive methodologies (UNESCO, 2020). The dual drivers—technology and pedagogy—are interrelated and mutually reinforcing.

Technological instruments facilitate novel educational opportunities, while advancing pedagogies necessitate more adaptable, learner-focused technologies. This synergy is promoting a transition from evaluation as a fixed conclusion to a dynamic, integrative process incorporated into the learning journey (Mhlongo et al., 2023; Wang, 2023). As higher education evolves in response to the demands of a knowledge-driven, digitally interconnected environment, the interaction of these elements will be pivotal in redefining assessment methodologies that are pertinent, inclusive, and prepared for the future.

1.3. Reconceptualizing Validity and Fairness in the Digital Age

As evaluation methodologies advance in the digital age, conventional concepts of validity and fairness necessitate a radical redefinition. Historically, validity in assessment denoted the extent to which a test accurately evaluated its target construct, frequently within limited psychometric frameworks. Fairness was associated with standardization—guaranteeing that all students were evaluated under same settings, with minimum variation (Jeganathan et al., 2024; Wattoo et al., 2025). Nonetheless, digital transformation has contested these definitions, compelling educators and policymakers to embrace broader and more inclusive interpretations of these concepts.

In digital contexts, validity must consider the dynamic, interactive, and frequently individualized characteristics of learning experiences. Assessments have evolved from static tools to dynamic components integrated inside various technology-enhanced learning environments. Therefore, content validity must be reevaluated to encompass the intricacy of the competencies being evaluated—such as critical thinking, teamwork, and digital literacy—typically measured by performance-based and formative assessment instruments (Kulgemeyer et al., 2023; Singh et al., 2024).

Fairness surpasses uniformity and necessitates a more sophisticated comprehension grounded in equity. While conventional examinations sought equality of conditions, digital evaluations must consider inequities in access to technology, internet connectivity, and digital proficiency (Elnegahy et al., 2021; Wibowo, 2025). Students from underrepresented or marginalized backgrounds may encounter systemic obstacles that hinder their performance in technology-based assessments (Bennett, 2020). Consequently, equity in the digital era necessitates proactive measures to guarantee inclusivity, including adaptive examinations, diverse modes of demonstration, and accessibility features for learners with disabilities.

Furthermore, the implementation of algorithms and artificial intelligence in evaluation systems presents ethical intricacies. Algorithmic bias, transparency deficits, and data privacy concerns must be resolved to maintain fairness and trust in digital evaluation instruments. Educators must consistently assess these technologies to prevent the accidental perpetuation of systemic inequities (Williamson & Piattoeva, 2021).

Ultimately, redefining validity and fairness necessitates a transition from standardization to contextualization and learner-centric approaches. Authentic evaluations must represent actual competencies, whereas equitable assessments must consider varied student requirements and backgrounds (Bennett, 2023; Jankowski, 2022). This transformation necessitates interdisciplinary collaboration, strong policy frameworks, and ethical foresight to guarantee that technology promotes, rather than compromises, the integrity and equity of assessment in higher education.

DIGITAL TOOLS AND PLATFORMS FOR ASSESSMENT INNOVATION

2.1. AI-Powered Assessment Tools and Learning Analytics

Artificial Intelligence (AI) and learning analytics have emerged as transformational elements in the realm of assessment within higher education. These technologies offer unparalleled capacities to gather, analyze, and understand student data, allowing educators to create more personalized, efficient, and significant evaluations (Feuerriegel et al., 2023; Swist et al., 2024). As institutions endeavor to meet the requirements of a swiftly changing digital world, AI-driven tools and learning analytics lead the way in assessment innovation.

AI-driven assessment tools encompass systems that facilitate automated grading, adaptive testing, and the provision of real-time feedback. These tools utilize machine learning algorithms to assess student responses to both objective and open-ended questions with enhanced accuracy and sophistication (Lu et al., 2021). Natural language processing (NLP) enables AI to evaluate essay material, delivering immediate scoring and qualitative input on syntax, coherence, and content alignment. This not only alleviates the faculty's workload but also expedites the feedback loop, hence facilitating formative learning.

Simultaneously, learning analytics denotes the application of data mining and visualization methodologies to observe student activities, discern patterns, and guide instructional decision-making. Platforms integrated inside Learning Management Systems (LMS) monitor various student interactions—including time allocated to activities, login frequency, quiz attempts, and peer collaboration—providing valuable information into learner engagement and advancement (HOUNGUE et al., 2022). These insights enable teachers to act promptly, customize learning pathways, and enhance assessment strategies in real time.

AI and learning analytics provide adaptive exams that modify difficulty levels according to student responses, thus fostering personalized learning experiences. They furthermore facilitate predictive analytics, enabling the anticipation of student outcomes and the identification of at-risk learners prior to academic failure (Rincón-Flores et al., 2024; Yaseen et al., 2025).

Nonetheless, although these tools present significant potential, their deployment prompts critical inquiries regarding ethics, privacy, and openness. Clear governance mechanisms are necessary to prevent data misuse and to guarantee that algorithmic outcomes are explicable and equitable. As higher education undergoes digital transformation, the incorporation of AI-driven assessment tools and learning analytics must adhere to pedagogical norms and ethical accountability. When judiciously applied, these tools can transform the function of assessment—from just quantifying learning to actively influencing and improving it.

2.2. Online Quizzing, E-Portfolios, and Simulation-Based Testing

Digital tools have broadened the assessment capabilities of higher education institutions, facilitating a transition from inflexible, time-constrained tests to adaptable, genuine, and ongoing evaluation models. Prominent advances include online quizzing, e-portfolios, and simulation-based testing, each providing distinct advantages in improving student engagement, monitoring learning progression, and fostering higher-order thinking (Filho et al., 2023; Jeganathan et al., 2024).

Online quizzing systems, incorporated into Learning Management Systems (LMS), enable educators to provide low-stakes, formative exams that offer rapid feedback and facilitate student self-monitoring of their learning progress. These quizzes may be randomized, time-limited, and adaptive to cater to diverse learning levels and mitigate academic dishonesty. They evaluate memory and comprehension, and when intentionally structured, can provide spaced repetition and active retrieval techniques that are demonstrated to improve retention (Kumar, 2023; Plooy et al., 2024).

E-portfolios provide a comprehensive method of evaluation by allowing students to compile digital artifacts that showcase their learning over time. These may encompass research papers, multimedia projects, reflective journals, and peer reviews, offering a more comprehensive depiction of student development than standardized assessments. E-portfolios promote metacognition, creativity, and the synthesis of multidisciplinary knowledge (Chang & Kabilan, 2022; Jeganathan et al., 2024). They function as essential instruments for continuous education and career advancement, enabling students to record abilities and display talents to prospective employers.

Simulation-based testing signifies a pioneering advancement in assessment methodologies, especially in fields necessitating the practical application of information, like medical, engineering, and business. Simulations emulate real-world situations within secure, regulated digital environments, enabling students to make decisions, resolve issues, and obtain prompt, immersive feedback. These evaluations are optimal for assessing critical thinking, decision-making under duress, and procedural competence (Samaras et al., 2021; Sharoff, 2022). With the advancement of virtual and augmented reality technology, simulations are increasingly accessible and influential, revolutionizing the assessment of practical skills on a large scale.

Notwithstanding their advantages, these technologies require digital infrastructure, pedagogical training, and meticulous design to guarantee alignment with educational objectives and equitable access. Institutional preparedness and faculty assistance are essential to prevent shallow execution.

The incorporation of online quizzing, e-portfolios, and simulation-based testing signifies a comprehensive transition towards genuine, learner-centered evaluation. These technologies accommodate various learning styles, enhance engagement, and align evaluations with the competencies necessary in today's intricate, international environment (HOUNGUE et al., 2022; Karunanayaka & Naidu, 2021)

2.3. Integrating LMS and Assessment Frameworks

The amalgamation of Learning Management Systems (LMS) with comprehensive assessment frameworks constitutes a fundamental aspect of revolutionizing higher education. LMS platforms, like Moodle, Canvas, Blackboard, and Google Classroom, have transitioned from mere content delivery systems to holistic ecosystems that facilitate education, assessment, feedback, and analytics. When deliberately matched with assessment frameworks, Learning Management Systems (LMS) can serve as potent tools for enhancing both educational results and institutional efficacy (Binhammad et al., 2024; Jeganathan et al., 2024).

A primary advantage of LMS integration is its capacity to organize and optimize assessment design. Educators may integrate quizzes, assignments, discussion forums, peer reviews, and rubrics directly into course modules, guaranteeing alignment with intended learning outcomes (ILOs). This structural coherence improves transparency for students and facilitates ongoing feedback loops, which are crucial for formative learning. Moreover, LMS-based rubrics and grading instruments enhance uniformity and equity in assessment while minimizing grading duration and subjectivity (Jeganathan et al., 2024; Nkhoma et al., 2020).

Moreover, LMS solutions facilitate data-driven decision-making via integrated analytics dashboards. These instruments furnish educators with immediate insights about student performance, engagement trends, and assessment completion rates. By early identification of at-risk students and assessment of instructional strategies' efficacy, instructors and administrators can implement evidence-based enhancements to curriculum and pedagogy (Ifenthaler & Yau, 2020).

The incorporation of assessment frameworks—such as Bloom's Taxonomy, SOLO Taxonomy, or outcomes-based education models—into LMS platforms strengthens educational intent. Educators can align each assessment activity with distinct cognitive levels or competencies, guaranteeing that exams measure not only knowledge retention but also higher-order thinking, creativity, and problem-solving abilities. This alignment enhances accreditation and quality assurance processes by offering digital evidence that demonstrates how assessments comply with institutional and national standards (Kulgemeyer et al., 2023; Mudhol, 2024).

Successful integration involves more than mere technological infrastructure. It necessitates faculty development, explicit institutional policies, and continuous instructional design assistance. Inadequate training may lead instructors to utilize LMS in a manner that merely mimics conventional techniques, so constraining the transformative capabilities of digital tools.

In conclusion, the integration of LMS with structured assessment frameworks converts digital platforms into purposeful learning environments that promote fairness, personalization, and reflective teaching methodologies. When employed effectively, LMS can surpass mere administrative convenience and emerge as a pivotal catalyst for academic excellence and student success in the digital age (Binhammad et al., 2024).

INCLUSIVITY AND ACCESSIBILITY IN TECHNOLOGY-ENHANCED ASSESSMENT

3.1. Universal Design for Learning (UDL) in Digital Assessment

Universal Design for Learning (UDL) provides a revolutionary framework for creating digital assessments that are inclusive, adaptable, and attuned to the varied requirements of learners. Grounded on the tenets of justice and accessibility, Universal Design for Learning (UDL) contests the conventional "one-size-fits-all" educational approach by prioritizing diverse methods of involvement, representation, and expression (CAST, 2018). In the context of digital assessment, Universal Design for Learning (UDL) guarantees that all students—irrespective of ability, background, or learning style—can effectively exhibit their knowledge and competencies (Millikin, 2023; Söken, 2023).

Digital settings offer distinct advantages for the application of Universal Design for Learning in assessment development. For example, various forms of representation can be attained using multimedia content, including films, diagrams, and text-to-speech systems that accommodate different cognitive preferences and sensory requirements. Diverse modes of expression allow students to exhibit their learning in several formats—written responses, audio recordings, infographics, or interactive simulations—thus mitigating the obstacles presented by conventional, text-centric assessments (Lawrence & Mathis, 2020).

Equally significant are many methods of interaction, which promote student autonomy, choice, and motivation. By providing diverse assessment forms and individualized approaches, educators can augment learner autonomy and mitigate the anxiety frequently linked to high-stakes, standardized testing (Swiecki et al., 2022). Gamified assessments, interactive quizzes, and reflective digital journals exemplify tactics that adhere to UDL principles and promote enhanced involvement.

Furthermore, Universal Design for Learning (UDL) in digital assessment aids students with disabilities by incorporating assistive technologies—such as screen readers, captioning, customizable timing, and keyboard navigation—into the assessment platform. These attributes foster equitable engagement and demonstrate a dedication to inclusive excellence. Significantly, these adjustments advantage not only students with verified requirements but also improve the experience for a wider demographic, encompassing multilingual learners and neurodiverse persons (Dogucu et al., 2023; Elfman, 2023; Estefan et al., 2023).

Implementing Universal Design for Learning in assessment necessitates institutional dedication to inclusive pedagogy, professional development, and infrastructural investment. Faculty should receive support in re-evaluating assessment design via a Universal Design for Learning (UDL) perspective and be equipped with tools and training to incorporate accessibility into their digital content from the beginning. Incorporating UDL into digital evaluation is not solely a matter of compliance, but a moral and educational necessity. It represents a forward-thinking perspective on higher education, ensuring that all learners can succeed, flourish, and be equitably evaluated in a progressively technological academic environment.

3.2. Assessment for Students with Disabilities and Diverse Needs

In the quest for inclusive education, assessment processes must be rigorously evaluated to guarantee they fairly accommodate students with disabilities and varied needs. Technology-enhanced assessment presents both challenges and potential in overcoming the obstacles usually encountered by learners with physical, sensory, cognitive, or learning impairments. When intelligently applied, digital tools can enhance accessibility, customize assessment, and maintain the notion that all students are entitled to equitable and significant methods of demonstrating their learning (Flanagan & Morgan, 2021).

Historically, standardized assessment formats have frequently marginalized students with disabilities by demanding consistent response methods, imposing restricted time limits, or providing inaccessible testing facilities. Conversely, technology-enhanced evaluation can integrate features that facilitate personalized accommodations, like adjustable timing, screen readers, text-to-speech, keyboard navigation, closed captioning, and variable font sizes and contrast levels. These elements enable students to interact with assessment content in accordance with their needs and strengths (Jeganathan et al., 2024; Srivastava et al., 2021).

In addition to technical accessibility, evaluations must also honor the cultural, linguistic, and neurodiverse aspects of student identities. For instance, English language learners may gain advantages from bilingual glossaries, streamlined instructional language, or visual aids. Students with autism spectrum condition may necessitate explicit structure, diminished sensory inputs, and consistent navigation within the digital environment. The integration of multi-modal assessment methods—such as oral presentations, visual projects, or interactive simulations—offers varied avenues for learners to demonstrate their comprehension (Gronseth, 2023).

Effective evaluation for students with disabilities relies cooperative collaboration among academics, disability support services, and instructional designers. Institutions should transcend mere retrofitting of adjustments and adopt proactive design strategies that anticipate diversity from the beginning. This entails adherence to accessibility standards (e.g., WCAG 2.1), ongoing user testing, and the incorporation of assistive technologies into mainstream platforms (Creed et al., 2023).

Significantly, inclusive digital assessment procedures not only advantage students with disabilities but also improve learning settings for everyone. Flexible submission methods, extended deadlines, and scaffolded feedback enhance student autonomy and alleviate performance anxiety universally. This method adheres to the fundamental idea that inclusion enhances quality for all, not alone for the most vulnerable (Olanipekun, 2025; Tai et al., 2022). Fundamentally, creating evaluations for kids with disabilities and varied needs is not an exception, but a dedication to educational equity.

3.3. Bridging the Digital Divide: Infrastructure and Literacy Challenges

Although technology-enhanced assessment offers potential for innovation and inclusivity, it may also intensify educational disparities if the digital divide is not remedied. The digital divide denotes inequalities in access to technological infrastructure, dependable internet connectivity, and digital literacy—elements that profoundly influence students' capacity to engage in and gain advantages from digital examinations. Closing this gap is crucial to prevent technological progress in evaluation from perpetuating systemic exclusion (Jeganathan et al., 2024; Mustafa et al., 2024).

Infrastructure deficiencies are especially evident in rural, isolated, and economically disadvantaged regions. Students in these situations frequently encounter restricted or unreliable internet connectivity, insufficient personal devices, and communal household resources, rendering synchronous and high-bandwidth evaluations problematic (UNESCO, 2021). Within metropolitan centers, socio-economic status can influence access to computers, data plans, or conducive locations for evaluations. These discrepancies significantly influence students' performance and engagement, frequently remaining undetected in conventional assessment criteria (Jankowski, 2022; Jeganathan et al., 2024).

In addition to physical access, digital literacy constitutes a secondary layer of difficulty. Digital literacy comprises not only the proficiency in using technologies but also the comprehension of navigating platforms, interpreting digital directives, submitting assignments, and safeguarding one's data privacy. Students with little prior exposure to digital settings may experience exam anxiety, technological mistakes, or misreading of questions—elements that compromise the validity and fairness of assessment results (Singh et al., 2024; Timotheou et al., 2022).

Addressing this gap necessitates a multifaceted institutional approach. Higher education institutions must provide resources for infrastructure enhancements, including device lending programs, subsidized internet access, and campus hotspots. The introduction of digital literacy training for students and faculty is equally essential, ensuring that all users can effectively engage with assessment tools. Collaborations between governmental and corporate entities may be essential to enhance connection in underprivileged areas (Johnson et al., 2023; Ntorukiri et al., 2022).

Furthermore, the design of assessments must accommodate diverse digital competencies. This encompasses providing low-bandwidth options (e.g., downloading evaluations), asynchronous formats, and explicit, jargon-free directions. Educators should refrain from presuming uniform digital preparedness and instead implement adaptable, robust assessment frameworks that cater to varied learning environments. Technology-enhanced assessment may realize its inclusive potential only if the underlying injustices of the digital divide are effectively confronted. Guaranteeing fair access and digital empowerment is fundamental to a just and revolutionary higher education system.

STUDENT ENGAGEMENT AND FEEDBACK MECHANISMS IN TECH-BASED ASSESSMENT

4.1. Gamification and Interactive Assessment Formats

Gamification and interactive assessment methods have emerged as revolutionary ways for improving student engagement and motivation in higher education. Unlike conventional assessment methods that frequently induce stress, disengagement, and mechanical memorization, gamified and interactive examinations promote active involvement, intrinsic drive, and a feeling of achievement. These methodologies correspond with modern educational frameworks that prioritize experiential learning, learner independence, and emotional engagement with the material (Alsadoon et al., 2022; James et al., 2024).

Gamification denotes the incorporation of game design elements—such as points, badges, leaderboards, stages, and challenges—into non-gaming environments, including academic evaluation. Incorporating game aspects into examinations enables instructors to foster environments that encourage students to embrace intellectual risks, persevere through intricate challenges, and obtain quick feedback on their performance (Bonefont et al., 2022). A computerized quiz that grants badges for precision and swiftness can convert a mundane activity into an engaging experience that fosters mastery learning.

In addition to gamification, interactive assessment formats including simulations, virtual laboratories, interactive case studies, and branching scenarios enable students to apply knowledge in dynamic, real-world situations. These tools transcend static question-and-answer formats by allowing students to make judgments, monitor outcomes, and refine their responses. Interactive evaluations are especially efficacious in fields necessitating practical skills, ethical reasoning, or systems thinking, including business, health sciences, and environmental studies (Heim et al., 2022; Swiecki et al., 2022).

These methods facilitate formative evaluation, offering students continuous feedback and the chance to learn through experimentation. The incorporation of multimedia—audio, video, animation, and drag-and-drop features—accommodates diverse learning styles and improves cognitive engagement. Furthermore, using storytelling and character-driven tales can personalize evaluations, enhancing emotional engagement and retention (Abdulrahaman et al., 2020; Harris & Greer, 2020).

The execution of gamified and interactive assessments must be rooted in pedagogical principles. Inadequately conceived gamification may result in superficial engagement or competition that estranges specific students. Consequently, educators must guarantee that game features correspond with learning objectives, accommodate varied learners, and are integrated within a cohesive educational framework. Gamification and interactive assessments signify a transition towards student-centered, engaging, and feedback-rich educational environments. When executed with consideration, they can convert evaluation from a passive evaluative instrument into a potent catalyst for motivation, creativity, and profound learning in higher education.

4.2. Real-Time Feedback and Formative Learning Pathways

The use of real-time feedback systems in technology-enhanced assessment has transformed student engagement in learning and instructor support for academic development. In contrast to conventional feedback models that typically take place post-assessment—frequently too late to facilitate significant change—real-time feedback offers instantaneous insights, allowing students to reflect, adapt, and enhance their learning strategies throughout their progression (Al-Haddad et al., 2024; Zheng et al., 2022).

Digital platforms, including Learning Management Systems (LMS), intelligent tutoring systems, and adaptive assessment tools, provide immediate feedback to student input. These technologies provide specific explanations, hints, or structured corrections immediately upon identifying a misunderstanding, promoting formative learning experiences that emphasize development rather than evaluation. This methodology fosters metacognition, enabling students to recognize their strengths and flaws and assume responsibility for their learning (Jeganathan et al., 2024; Yu, 2024).

Real-time feedback is particularly effective when integrated into formative assessment pathways—organized sequences of low-stakes evaluations intended to track student progress and guide training. For instance, online quizzes featuring automated explanations, interactive concept maps, or self-directed learning modules enable students to obtain constructive feedback in a non-punitive environment. These pathways facilitate mastery learning, wherein students are motivated to learn from mistakes and repeat activities until competency is attained (Kumar, 2023; Winget & Persky, 2022).

Furthermore, data visualization dashboards—displaying progress bars, performance trends, and skill mastery levels—can augment motivation by rendering learning visible and concrete. These visual instruments assist students in monitoring their accomplishments, establishing objectives, and maintaining engagement, while simultaneously providing educators with real-time data to customize interventions and personalize assistance (Ifenthaler & Yau, 2020).

The efficacy of real-time feedback is contingent upon the quality of the input provided. It must be precise, constructive, and associated with explicit learning objectives. Excessively generic or automated responses threaten to undermine the educational value of feedback and may inundate learners. Educators must meticulously construct feedback mechanisms that harmonize automation with human insight, guaranteeing that pupils obtain supportive and developmentally suitable advice (Jeganathan et al., 2024; Wattoo et al., 2025).

In summary, real-time feedback and formative learning pathways signify a transition from summative assessment to ongoing, adaptive learning. These improvements strengthen the function of assessment not only as an evaluative instrument but as a fundamental component of the learning process—one that fosters agency, reflection, and academic resilience within the contemporary heterogeneous higher education environment.

4.3. Student Perceptions and Attitudes Toward Digital Assessments

Student opinions and attitudes toward digital assessments significantly influence the efficacy and acceptance of technology-enhanced evaluation in higher education. Although digital technologies provide flexibility, interactivity, and prompt feedback, their efficacy is predominantly contingent upon students' experiences and interpretations of these innovations. Comprehending learners' viewpoints yields essential insights for enhancing assessment design, encouraging engagement, and cultivating a constructive learning atmosphere (Martín-Sómer et al., 2023; Parwoto et al., 2024).

A multitude of students value the convenience and accessibility of digital evaluations. Online methods facilitate asynchronous engagement, prolonged timeframes, and the convenience of completing tests in familiar settings. These attributes are particularly advantageous for non-traditional learners, individuals with disabilities, and those managing academic obligations with employment or caregiving (Laamanen et al., 2021)(Jopp & Cohen, 2020). The capacity to obtain immediate feedback and monitor performance over time enables students to exert enhanced control over their learning.

Nonetheless, student perceptions are not consistently favorable. Concerns remain surrounding technological concerns, including platform instability, internet access, and device compatibility, which might induce anxiety and hinder assessment performance. Additionally, several students express unease with automated grading methods, viewing them as impersonal or unjust, especially in the evaluation of open-ended responses or creative assignments (Buchanan, 2020).

A further factor affecting student perceptions is digital literacy. Students with insufficient expertise or confidence in utilizing online resources may experience feelings of overload or disadvantage, leading to disengagement or diminished performance. Language obstacles, cultural expectations, and previous experiences with assessments influence students' responses to digital formats (Chen & Singh, 2025; Singh et al., 2024).

Furthermore, students' views are intricately connected to the transparency and clarity of assessments. When evaluation standards, expectations, and feedback systems are explicitly conveyed, students are more inclined to view digital examinations as equitable and advantageous. In contrast, ambiguous instructions, new interfaces, or unclear scoring systems may result in dissatisfaction and diminished trust.

To improve student experiences, instructors should implement co-design approaches by seeking student feedback in the creation and enhancement of digital exams. Conducting orientation workshops, offering technical help, and supplying scaffolding tools can alleviate adverse views and enhance digital confidence. Student perspectives are integral to assessment innovation. Significant involvement of learners' perspectives guarantees that digital assessment is both technologically sophisticated and pedagogically compassionate, while also being psychologically supporting, in accordance with the overarching objectives of inclusive, student-centered higher education.

POLICY, ETHICS, AND THE FUTURE OF ASSESSMENT IN HIGHER EDUCATION

5.1. Data Privacy, Integrity, and AI Ethics in Student Evaluation

With the growing integration of digital technologies in higher education assessment, significant issues have arisen regarding data privacy, academic integrity, and the ethical application of artificial intelligence (AI) in student evaluation. These difficulties transcend technical or procedural concerns; they embody essential inquiries on trust, fairness, and institutional accountability in the digital era (Gouseti et al., 2024; Swidan et al., 2025).

Data privacy is a critical issue as online assessment platforms gather and analyze substantial amounts of student information, encompassing performance indicators, behavioral data, and biometric identifiers, particularly in remote proctoring scenarios. The possibility of misuse, illegal access, or breaches may jeopardize student confidentiality and institutional integrity (Dakakni & Safa, 2023; Gouseti et al., 2024). Institutions must adhere to data protection requirements, including the General Data Protection Regulation (GDPR), and ensuring that data acquisition is purposeful, transparent, and based on consent (Selwyn, 2020).

Concurrently, upholding academic integrity in digital contexts presents persistent obstacles. Although AI-driven plagiarism detection, browser lockdown applications, and remote proctoring software seek to prevent academic dishonesty, they also provide ethical challenges about monitoring, false positives, and the assumption of mistrust (Balalle & Pannilage, 2025; Boutros et al., 2023). Excessive dependence on invasive monitoring can diminish student autonomy and foster high-stress environments, especially for marginalized or neurodiverse learners (Robertson et al., 2021). Ethical evaluation necessitates the equilibrium of honesty with regard for dignity and the welfare of students.

The implementation of AI in student assessment adds further complication. Machine learning algorithms are progressively utilized to evaluate writings, deliver feedback, and forecast academic achievement. Nonetheless, these systems' fairness is contingent upon the quality of the data and the assumptions underlying their construction. Algorithmic bias, insufficient transparency, and the likelihood of perpetuating systemic inequities are significant concerns (Nandini et al., 2024;

Roshanaei et al., 2023) (Eubanks, 2018). In the absence of explainability and human supervision, AI-driven judgments may erode trust and responsibility.

Confronting these ethical dilemmas necessitates strong institutional frameworks based on principles of equity, inclusion, and accountability. This include the formulation of explicit data governance policies, engaging students in dialogues regarding digital rights, doing impact assessments, and ensuring human oversight in all AI-facilitated evaluations. In the future of evaluation in higher education must be technologically advanced and ethically sound. Safeguarding privacy, upholding integrity, and integrating AI ethics are fundamental components of a sustainable and equitable digital learning environment.

5.2. Institutional Readiness and Faculty Development

The effective execution of technology-enhanced assessment in higher education is significantly contingent upon institutional preparedness and faculty advancement. The efficacy of digital platforms and tools in addressing contemporary assessment concerns depends on the institutions' readiness to incorporate these technologies in a strategic, ethical, and sustainable manner. This necessitates more than infrastructure; it demands cultural, pedagogical, and organizational reform (Swiecki et al., 2022; Xia et al., 2024).

Institutional preparedness denotes the capability of universities and colleges to implement and sustain digital assessment methods on a large scale. This encompasses access to dependable technology infrastructure, cybersecurity measures, and digital policy frameworks that guarantee quality, inclusivity, and adherence to regulatory norms. Institutions must formulate strategic plans that integrate digital assessment with overarching objectives of academic quality, equity, and innovation (Johnson et al., 2016). Furthermore, governance frameworks must possess the agility to adapt to swift technological advancements and changing student expectations (MacDonald et al., 2021; Xia et al., 2024).

Faculty growth is equally essential, functioning as the catalyst for educational innovation. Numerous educators possess expertise in their fields yet may be deficient in digital fluency or instructional design competencies required to develop effective online assessments. Continuous professional development activities, including seminars, mentorship, microcredentialing, and digital learning communities, are vital for enhancing teacher confidence and competence (Brown et al., 2020).

Faculty require training not only in the utilization of digital tools but also in reevaluating assessment philosophy. This encompasses comprehension of formative assessment principles, feedback mechanisms, universal design, and ethical data utilization. Faculty must possess the capability to examine and modify evaluation processes that prioritize students, are culturally attuned, and correspond with learning objectives.

Support frameworks, including instructional design teams, assessment offices, and educational technologists, ought to be integrated into institutional systems to provide continuous consultation and technical support. Moreover, cultivating a culture of experimentation, peer exchange, and reflective practice might assist faculty in managing the intricate transition from traditional to digital assessment models (Angeioplastis et al., 2024; Ceallaigh & Connolly, 2024; Zhang, 2023).

Institutional readiness is not a fixed condition; it is a continuous process of adaptation, learning, and development. Institutions that prioritize faculty development and policy coherence are more equipped to succeed in a future characterized by dynamic, data-informed, and equity-driven evaluation (Assefa & Zenebe, 2024; Lee et al., 2023). In conclusion, the absence of institutional commitment and empowered educators will prevent the realization of transformative assessment. A future of digital assessment relies not alone on technology, but also on individuals, vision, and a collective dedication to significant learning.

5.3. Visioning Future-Ready Assessment: Trends and Projections

As higher education undergoes unparalleled transformations due to globalization, digitalization, and societal changes, the future of assessment must adapt correspondingly. Future-ready assessment anticipates a system that is adaptable, learner-focused, ethically principled, and technologically advanced—equipped to prepare students for intricate, uncertain futures. This vision is influenced by many emerging trends and forecasts that are expected to characterize evaluation processes in the coming decades (Allen et al., 2020; Philippe et al., 2020).

A prominent trend is the enhanced personalization of evaluation via artificial intelligence (AI) and adaptive technologies. AI-driven tools will persist in their evolution, facilitating evaluations that adapt in real time to learners' performance, speed, and preferences. These systems aim to enhance engagement and mastery-based learning while mitigating bias using context-sensitive evaluation models (Nandini et al., 2024; Olanipekun, 2025).

Another forecast is the proliferation of genuine, real-world evaluations, including project-based learning, digital portfolios, and simulations. These formats more accurately represent the competencies essential in the contemporary workforce—collaboration, problem-solving, ethical reasoning, and creativity. Assessment will progressively extend outside the classroom, aligning with industry norms and professional expectations to offer a more comprehensive and career-relevant evaluation (Jeganathan et al., 2024; Perišić et al., 2023).

Blockchain-based credentialing and micro-credentials are increasingly recognized as methods for securely, verifiably, and decentralizing the documentation of learning. These innovations contest conventional degree-centric paradigms and provide detailed acknowledgment of competencies gained through both official and informal educational avenues. As students pursue increased autonomy and mobility, institutions must integrate assessment systems with emerging credentialing paradigms (Barty et al., 2024).

There is an increasing demand for assessments that are transparent, inclusive, and led by students. Students are progressively seeking a role in their assessment processes, encompassing the co-creation of rubrics, goal-setting, and self-reflection on their progress. This participatory approach will serve as a fundamental element of equitable and empowering educational practice (Tai, Ajjawi, et al., 2022; Tai, Dollinger, et al., 2022).

To actualize this vision, institutions must allocate resources towards progressive policies, ongoing capacity development, and interdisciplinary partnerships. Future-ready assessment focuses on harmonizing technology, pedagogy, and ethics to facilitate lifelong learning and societal significance, rather than merely pursuing the latest tools. The future of assessment is not fixed; it is being influenced by contemporary decisions. Through the adoption of innovation, inclusivity, and integrity, higher education may establish an assessment ecosystem that is robust, adaptive, and deeply humanistic.

CONCLUSION

The evolution of evaluation in higher education is now a current necessity rather than a future goal. This chapter illustrates that using technology into assessment procedures presents significant opportunities for innovation, customisation, and inclusivity. AI-driven grading systems, simulation-based assessments, adaptive learning analytics, and e-portfolios have transformed the measurement, monitoring, and development of academic achievement.

Nonetheless, the shift to digital evaluation necessitates more than merely the implementation of technology instruments. It requires a reevaluation of essential educational principles such as equity, transparency, and learner autonomy. Inclusive design frameworks, such as Universal Design for Learning (UDL), guarantee that examinations accommodate the requirements of all students, especially those with disabilities or varied learning experiences. Correspondingly, ethical concerns about data privacy, algorithmic bias, and student autonomy necessitate resolution via comprehensive governance, institutional regulations, and continuous faculty development.

Student opinions and attitudes significantly influence the efficacy of digital assessment. Involving learners in the planning and evaluation process fosters trust and guarantees that assessment is a significant component of the learning experience rather than merely a point of judgment.

A future-oriented assessment environment in higher education must be adaptable, focusing on human needs, and ethically principled. Institutions must adopt ongoing adaptation, interdepartmental cooperation, and progressive leadership. By doing so, assessment can evolve from its traditional function as a gatekeeper to serve as a catalyst for transformative learning, social mobility, and educational equity in the digital age.

REFERENCES

Abdulrahaman, M. D., Faruk, N., Oloyede, A. A., Surajudeen-Bakinde, N. T., Olawoyin, L. A., Mejabi, O. V., Imam-Fulani, Y. O., Fahm, A. O., & Azeez, A. L. (2020). Multimedia tools in the teaching and learning processes: A systematic review [Review of Multimedia tools in the teaching and learning processes: A systematic review]. Heliyon, 6(11). Elsevier BV. https://doi.org/DOI: 10.1016/j.heliyon.2020.e05312

Al-Haddad, S., Chick, N., & Safi, F. (2024). Teaching Statistics: A Technology-Enhanced Supportive Instruction (TSI) Model During the Covid-19 Pandemic and Beyond. *Journal of Statistics and Data Science Education: An Official Journal of the of the American Statistical Association*, *32*(2), 129. DOI: 10.1080/26939169.2024.2315939

Allen, K., Donoghue, G. M., Pahlevansharif, S., Jimerson, S. R., & Hattie, J. (2020). Assessment practices in Philippine higher STEAM education. *Journal of University Teaching & Learning Practice*, *17*(5). Advance online publication. DOI: 10.53761/1.17.5.18

Alsadoon, E., Alkhawajah, A., & Suhaim, A. B. (2022). Effects of a gamified learning environment on students' achievement, motivations, and satisfaction. *Heliyon*, *8*(8). Advance online publication. DOI: 10.1016/j.heliyon.2022.e10249 PMID: 36042749

Angeioplastis, A., Papaioannou, N., Tsimpiris, A., Kamilali, A., & Varsamis, D. (2024). Predicting student specializations: a Machine Learning Approach based on Academic Performance.

Assefa, E. A., & ZENEBE, C. K. (2024). Fostering inclusive excellence: Strategies for effective diversity management in schools. *International Journal of Research in Education Humanities and Commerce*, *5*(2), 189. DOI: 10.37602/ijrehc.2024.5216

Balalle, H., & Pannilage, S. (2025). Reassessing academic integrity in the age of AI: A systematic literature review on AI and academic integrity. *Social Sciences & Humanities Open*, *11*, 101299. DOI: 10.1016/j.ssaho.2025.101299

Barty, G., Boyer, N., Chrysikos, A., Griffith, M. L., House, K., Laughlin, T., Ossiannilsson, E., Ward, R., & Zanville, H. A. (2024). *Developing a More Granular and Equitable Approach to the Learner-Earner Journey. The Role of Badging*. Micro-Credentials and Twenty-first Century Skills Within Higher Education to Enable Future Workforce Development. In Zukunft der Hochschulbildung., DOI: 10.1007/978-3-658-42948-5_23

Bennett, R. E. (2023). Toward a Theory of Socioculturally Responsive Assessment. *Educational Assessment*, *28*(2), 83. DOI: 10.1080/10627197.2023.2202312

Binhammad, M. H. Y., Othman, A., Abuljadayel, L., Mheiri, H. A., Alkaabi, M., & Almarri, M. (2024). Investigating How Generative AI Can Create Personalized Learning Materials Tailored to Individual Student Needs. *Creative Education, 15*(7), 1499. DOI: 10.4236/ce.2024.157091

Bonefont, V., Carbino, B., & Zakerzadeh, R. (2022). Addressing Test Anxiety Using Game-Based Assessment. *Biomedical Engineering Education, 2*(2), 319. DOI: 10.1007/s43683-022-00082-3 PMID: 35856077

Boutros, M.-B. F., Jawad, D., & Ghanimeh, S. (2023). The Implementation of Enterprise Resource Planning Systems for Roads and Infrastructure Construction Companies in Developing Countries. International Conference on Civil Infrastructure and Construction/Proceedings of the ... International Conference on Civil Infrastructure and Construction, 269. https://doi.org/DOI: 10.29117/cic.2023.0038

CEALLAIGH, T. Ó., & Connolly, C. (2024). Navigating transformative assessment and feedback in teacher education: Unveiling challenges and innovative practices. *European Journal of Teacher Education, 47*(2), 197. DOI: 10.1080/02619768.2024.2352816

Chang, S. L., & Kabilan, M. K. (2022). Using social media as e-Portfolios to support learning in higher education: A literature analysis. *Journal of Computing in Higher Education, 36*(1), 1. DOI: 10.1007/s12528-022-09344-z PMID: 36405240

Chen, Z., & Singh, C. (2025). Opportunities and Challenges in Harnessing Digital Technology for Effective Teaching and Learning. *Trends in Higher Education, 4*(1), 6. DOI: 10.3390/higheredu4010006

Chiziwa, W., & Kunkwenzu, E. D. (2021). Investigating Teacher Assessment Practices in the Teaching of Social Studies in Malawian Primary Schools. *Open Journal of Social Sciences, 9*(7), 480. DOI: 10.4236/jss.2021.97035

Creed, C., Al-Kalbani, M., Theil, A., Sarcar, S., & Williams, I. (2023). Inclusive AR/VR: Accessibility barriers for immersive technologies. *Universal Access in the Information Society, 23*(1), 59. DOI: 10.1007/s10209-023-00969-0

Dakakni, D., & Safa, N. (2023). Artificial intelligence in the L2 classroom: Implications and challenges on ethics and equity in higher education: A 21st century Pandora's box. *Computers and Education Artificial Intelligence, 5*, 100179. DOI: 10.1016/j.caeai.2023.100179

Do, H., Bich, N., & Nguyen, M. H. (2023). 3How do constructivism learning environments generate better motivation and learning strategies? The Design Science Approach. *Heliyon, 9*(12). Advance online publication. DOI: 10.1016/j.heliyon.2023.e22862 PMID: 38125439

Dogucu, M., Johnson, A. A., & Ott, M. Q. (2023). Framework for Accessible and Inclusive Teaching Materials for Statistics and Data Science Courses. *Journal of Statistics and Data Science Education: An Official Journal of the of the American Statistical Association, 31*(2), 144. DOI: 10.1080/26939169.2023.2165988

Elfman, L. (2023). Crafting Equitable Access and Engagement. *Women in Higher Education, 32*(12), 6. DOI: 10.1002/whe.21345

Elnegahy, S., Jin, H., & Kim, H. (2021). Fairness, Justice, and Language Assessment. *Language Assessment Quarterly, 19*(1), 102. DOI: 10.1080/15434303.2021.1922412

Estefan, M., Selbin, J. C., & MacDonald, S. (2023). From Inclusive to Equitable Pedagogy: How to Design Course Assignments and Learning Activities That Address Structural Inequalities. *Teaching Sociology, 51*(3), 262. DOI: 10.1177/0092055x231174515

Feuerriegel, S., Hartmann, J., Janiesch, C., & Zschech, P. (2023). Generative AI. *Business & Information Systems Engineering, 66*(1), 111. DOI: 10.1007/s12599-023-00834-7

Filho, R. L. C. S., Brito, K., & Adeodato, P. J. L. (2023). Leveraging Causal Reasoning in Educational Data Mining: An Analysis of Brazilian Secondary Education. *Applied Sciences (Basel, Switzerland), 13*(8), 5198. DOI: 10.3390/app13085198

Flanagan, S., & Morgan, J. J. (2021). Ensuring Access to Online Learning for All Students Through Universal Design for Learning. *Teaching Exceptional Children, 53*(6), 459. DOI: 10.1177/00400599211010174

Gouseti, A., James, F., Fallin, L., & Burden, K. (2024). The ethics of using AI in K-12 education: A systematic literature review. *Technology, Pedagogy and Education, 1*. Advance online publication. DOI: 10.1080/1475939x.2024.2428601

Gronseth, S. (2023). Strategically Inclusive E-Learning Design. *Journal of Technology-Integrated Lessons and Teaching, 2*(1), 68. DOI: 10.13001/jtilt.v2i1.7673

Harris, H. S., & Greer, M. (2020). Using Multimedia for Instructor Presence in Purposeful Pedagogy-Driven Online Technical Writing Courses. *Journal of Technical Writing and Communication, 52*(1), 110. DOI: 10.1177/0047281620978360

Heim, A. B., Duke, J., & Holt, E. A. (2022). Design, Discover, and Decipher: Student-Developed Escape Rooms in the Virtual Ecology Classroom. *Journal of Microbiology & Biology Education, 23*(1). Advance online publication. DOI: 10.1128/jmbe.00015-22 PMID: 35784618

Hickey, D. T., & Harris, T. (2021). Reimagining online grading, assessment, and testing using situated cognition. *Distance Education*, *42*(2), 290. DOI: 10.1080/01587919.2021.1911627

HOUNGUE, P., HOUNTONDJI, M., & DAGBA, T. (2022). An Effective Decision-Making Support for Student Academic Path Selection using Machine Learning. *International Journal of Advanced Computer Science and Applications*, *13*(11). Advance online publication. DOI: 10.14569/ijacsa.2022.0131184

James, W., Oates, G., & Schönfeldt, N. (2024). Improving retention while enhancing student engagement and learning outcomes using gamified mobile technology. *Accounting Education*, *1*. Advance online publication. DOI: 10.1080/09639284.2024.2326009

Jankowski, N. (2022). Reframing Assessment to Center Equity: A Resource to Inform Practice. *Assessment Update*, *34*(2), 6. DOI: 10.1002/au.30294

Jeganathan, S., Raj, L. A., Parthasarathy, S., Khan, A. A. A., & Sathick, K. J. (2024). OptCatB: Optuna Hyperparameter Optimization Model to Forecast the Educational Proficiency of Immigrant Students based on CatBoost Regression. *Journal of Internet Services and Information Security*, *14*(3), 111. DOI: 10.58346/jisis.2024.i2.008

Johnson, S. L., Allen, J., Fernandez, L., Garikiparthy, V., Renovato, L., Land, M., Favela, L., Becerra, K., Belmares, R., Holland, N., & Chacon, J. (2023). Closing the digital divide: Developing a platform to conduct training, outreach, and education for employment skills. *Digital Health*, *9*. Advance online publication. DOI: 10.1177/20552076231154383 PMID: 36756645

Karunanayaka, S. P., & Naidu, S. (2021). Impacts of authentic assessment on the development of graduate attributes. *Distance Education*, *42*(2), 231. DOI: 10.1080/01587919.2021.1920206

Kulgemeyer, C., Riese, J., Vogelsang, C., Buschhüter, D., Borowski, A., Weißbach, A., Jordans, M., Reinhold, P., & Schecker, H. (2023). How authenticity impacts validity: Developing a model of teacher education assessment and exploring the effects of the digitisation of assessment methods. *Zeitschrift für Erziehungswissenschaft*, *26*(3), 601. DOI: 10.1007/s11618-023-01154-y PMID: 37359180

Kumar, P. S. (2023). Transformative Role of ICT in 21st Century Learning: Enhancing Educational Effectiveness and Equitability. *International Journal for Research in Applied Science and Engineering Technology*, *11*(12), 91. DOI: 10.22214/ijraset.2023.57028

Laamanen, M., Ladonlahti, T., Uotinen, S., Okada, A., Bañeres, D., & Koçdar, S. (2021). Acceptability of the e-authentication in higher education studies: Views of students with special educational needs and disabilities. *International Journal of Educational Technology in Higher Education*, *18*(1). Advance online publication. DOI: 10.1186/s41239-020-00236-9 PMID: 34778518

Lawrence, W. J., & Mathis, J. (2020). Multimodal assessments: Affording children labeled 'at-risk' expressive and receptive opportunities in the area of literacy. *Language and Education*, *34*(2), 135. DOI: 10.1080/09500782.2020.1724140

Lee, M., Horii, C. V., Austin, A. E., Avery, L., DeSanctis, M., Finkelstein, N. D., Miller, E., & Schaal, B. A. (2023). An Instructional-Workforce Framework for Coordinated Change in Undergraduate Education. *Change The Magazine of Higher Learning*, *55*(1), 54. DOI: 10.1080/00091383.2023.2151809

MacDonald, C., Backhaus, I., Vanezi, E., Yeratziotis, A., Clendinneng, D., Seriola, L., Häkkinen, S., Cassar, M., Mettouris, C., & Papadopoulos, G. A. (2021). European Union Digital Education quality standard framework and companion evaluation toolkit. *Open Learning*, *39*(1), 85. DOI: 10.1080/02680513.2021.1936476

Martín-Sómer, M., Casado, C., & Gómez-Pozuelo, G. (2023). Utilising interactive applications as educational tools in higher education: Perspectives from teachers and students, and an analysis of academic outcomes. *Education for Chemical Engineers*, *46*, 1. DOI: 10.1016/j.ece.2023.10.001

Mhlongo, S., Mbatha, K., Ramatsetse, B., & Dlamini, R. (2023). Challenges, opportunities, and prospects of adopting and using smart digital technologies in learning environments: An iterative review. *Heliyon*, *9*(6). Advance online publication. DOI: 10.1016/j.heliyon.2023.e16348 PMID: 37274691

Millikin, C. C. (2023). Future-Proof your Instructional Design with Universal Design for Learning and Translanguaging. *Literacy Information and Computer Education Journal*, *14*(1), 3709. DOI: 10.20533/licej.2040.2589.2023.0488

Mudhol, A. C. (2024). Innovative Assessment Methods for Measuring Practical Skills in Higher Education. In Advances in economics, business and management research/Advances in Economics, Business and Management Research (p. 78). Atlantis Press. https://doi.org/DOI: 10.2991/978-94-6463-374-0_8

Mustafa, F., Nguyen, H. T. M., & Gao, X. (2024). The challenges and solutions of technology integration in rural schools: A systematic literature review. *International Journal of Educational Research*, *126*, 102380. DOI: 10.1016/j.ijer.2024.102380

Naaj, M. A., Mehdi, R., Mohamed, E. A., & Nachouki, M. (2023). Analysis of the Factors Affecting Student Performance Using a Neuro-Fuzzy Approach. *Education Sciences, 13*(3), 313. DOI: 10.3390/educsci13030313

Nandini, N., Indora, P., & Singh, R. (2024). Artificial Intelligence in Journalism: An Overview of its Applications and Uses. *Journal of Communication Management (London), 3*(3), 237. DOI: 10.58966/jcm2024337

Nkhoma, C., Nkhoma, M., Thomas, S., & Le, N. Q. (2020). The Role of Rubrics in Learning and Implementation of Authentic Assessment: A Literature Review [Review of The Role of Rubrics in Learning and Implementation of Authentic Assessment: A Literature Review]. Informing Science and IT Education Conference, 237. Informing Science Institute. https://doi.org/DOI: 10.28945/4606

Ntorukiri, T. B., Kirugua, J. M., & Kirimi, F. (2022). Policy and infrastructure challenges influencing ICT implementation in universities: a literature review [Review of Policy and infrastructure challenges influencing ICT implementation in universities: a literature review]. Discover Education, 1(1). Springer Science+Business Media. https://doi.org/DOI: 10.1007/s44217-022-00019-6

Olanipekun, S. O. (2025). Ethical frameworks for AI in journalism: Balancing technological innovation and journalistic integrity. *World Journal of Advanced Research and Reviews, 25*(1), 1342. DOI: 10.30574/wjarr.2025.25.1.0187

Onesi-Ozigagun, O., Ololade, Y. J., Eyo-Udo, N. L., & Ogundipe, D. O. (2024). Revolutionizing education through ai: a comprehensive review of enhancing learning experiences [review of revolutionizing education through ai: a comprehensive review of enhancing learning experiences]. International Journal of Applied Research in Social Sciences, 6(4), 589. Fair East Publishers. https://doi.org/DOI: 10.51594/ijarss.v6i4.1011

Oteng, B., Mensah, R. O., Babah, P. A., & Swanzy-Impraim, E. (2023). Social studies and history curriculum assessment in colleges of education in Ghana: Reflective practices of teacher educators. *Cogent Education, 10*(1). Advance online publication. DOI: 10.1080/2331186x.2023.2175515

Parwoto, P., Ilyas, S. N., Bachtiar, M. Y., & Marzuki, K. (2024). Fostering creativity in kindergarten: The impact of collaborative project-based learning. *South African Journal of Childhood Education, 14*(1). Advance online publication. DOI: 10.4102/sajce.v14i1.1462

Perišić, A., Perisic, I., Lazić, M., & Perišić, B. (2023). The foundation for future education, teaching, training, learning, and performing infrastructure - The open interoperability conceptual framework approach. *Heliyon*, *9*(6). Advance online publication. DOI: 10.1016/j.heliyon.2023.e16836 PMID: 37484382

Philippe, S., Souchet, A. D., Lameras, P., Petridis, P., Caporal, J., Coldeboeuf, G., & Duzan, H. (2020). Multimodal teaching, learning and training in virtual reality: a review and case study. In Virtual Reality & Intelligent Hardware (Vol. 2, Issue 5, p. 421). Elsevier BV. https://doi.org/DOI: 10.1016/j.vrih.2020.07.008

Plooy, E. du, Casteleijn, D., & Franzsen, D. (2024). Personalized adaptive learning in higher education: a scoping review of key characteristics and impact on academic performance and engagement [Review of Personalized adaptive learning in higher education: a scoping review of key characteristics and impact on academic performance and engagement]. Heliyon, 10(21). Elsevier BV. https://doi.org/DOI: 10.1016/j.heliyon.2024.e39630

Rincón-Flores, E. G., Castano, L., Solis, S. L. G., Lopez, O. O., Rodríguez-Hernández, C. F., Lara, L. A. C., & Aldape, P. (2024). Improving the learning-teaching process through adaptive learning strategy. *Smart Learning Environments*, *11*(1). Advance online publication. DOI: 10.1186/s40561-024-00314-9

Roshanaei, M., Olivares, H., & Lopez, R. R. (2023). Harnessing AI to Foster Equity in Education: Opportunities, Challenges, and Emerging Strategies. *Journal of Intelligent Learning Systems and Applications*, *15*(4), 123. DOI: 10.4236/jilsa.2023.154009

Samaras, S., Adkins, C. L., & White, C. D. (2021). Developing critical thinking skills: Simulations vs. cases. *Journal of Education for Business*, *97*(4), 270. DOI: 10.1080/08832323.2021.1932703

Sharoff, L. (2022). Student's Perception of vSim for Nursing® using the Simulation Effectiveness Tool—Modified. *Clinical Simulation in Nursing*, *68*, 1. DOI: 10.1016/j.ecns.2022.04.006 PMID: 36718189

Singh, N., Misra, R., Quan, W., Radić, A., Lee, S.-M., & Han, H. (2024). An analysis of consumer's trusting beliefs towards the use of e-commerce platforms. *Humanities & Social Sciences Communications*, *11*(1). Advance online publication. DOI: 10.1057/s41599-024-03395-6

Söken, A. (2023). Universal Design for Learning: Increasing Inclusive Teaching for Graduate Students. *Journal of Technology-Integrated Lessons and Teaching*, *2*(1), 60. DOI: 10.13001/jtilt.v2i1.7675

Srivastava, S., Varshney, A., Katyal, S., Kaur, R., & Gaur, V. (2021). A smart learning assistance tool for inclusive education. *Journal of Intelligent & Fuzzy Systems, 40*(6), 11981. DOI: 10.3233/jifs-210075

Swidan, A., Lee, S. Y., & Romdhane, S. B. (2025). College Students' Use and Perceptions of AI Tools in the UAE: Motivations, Ethical Concerns and Institutional Guidelines. *Education Sciences, 15*(4), 461. DOI: 10.3390/educsci15040461

Swiecki, Z., Khosravi, H., Chen, G., Martínez-Maldonado, R., Lodge, J. M., Milligan, S., Selwyn, N., & G sević, D. (2022). Assessment in the age of artificial intelligence. *Computers and Education Artificial Intelligence, 3*, 100075. DOI: 10.1016/j.caeai.2022.100075

Swist, T., Shum, S. B., & Gulson, K. N. (2024). Co-producing AIED Ethics Under Lockdown: An Empirical Study of Deliberative Democracy in Action. *International Journal of Artificial Intelligence in Education, 34*(3), 670. DOI: 10.1007/s40593-023-00380-z

Tai, J., Ajjawi, R., Bearman, M., Boud, D., Dawson, P., & Jorre, T. J. de S. (2022). Assessment for inclusion: Rethinking contemporary strategies in assessment design. *Higher Education Research & Development, 42*(2), 483. DOI: 10.1080/07294360.2022.2057451

Tai, J., Dollinger, M., Ajjawi, R., Jorre, T. J. de S., Krattli, S., McCarthy, D., & Prezioso, D. (2022). Designing assessment for inclusion: An exploration of diverse students' assessment experiences. *Assessment & Evaluation in Higher Education, 48*(3), 403. DOI: 10.1080/02602938.2022.2082373

Timotheou, S., Miliou, O., Dimitriadis, Y., Villagrá-Sobrino, S., Giannoutsou, N., Cachia, R., Martínez-Monés, A., & Ioannou, A. (2022). Impacts of digital technologies on education and factors influencing schools' digital capacity and transformation: A literature review [Review of Impacts of digital technologies on education and factors influencing schools' digital capacity and transformation: A literature review]. Education and Information Technologies, 28(6), 6695. Springer Science+Business Media. https://doi.org/DOI: 10.1007/s10639-022-11431-8

Wang, X. (2023). How can technology leverage university teaching & learning innovation? A longitudinal case study of diffusion of technology innovation from the knowledge creation perspective. https://link.springer.com/article/10.1007/s10639-023-11780-y

Wattoo, M. U., Du, J., Shahzad, F., & Kousar, S. (2025). Shaping E-commerce Experiences: Unraveling the Impact of Service Quality on Youth Customer Behavior in a Developing Nation. *SAGE Open*, *15*(1). Advance online publication. DOI: 10.1177/21582440241311786

Wibowo, H. A. (2025). An explication of how website design actually shapes online customer loyalty: Incorporating sem and person-items map analysis. *International Journal of Social Service and Research*, *5*(1), 123. DOI: 10.46799/ijssr.v5i1.1190

Winget, M., & Persky, A. M. (2022). A Practical Review of Mastery Learning [Review of A Practical Review of Mastery Learning]. American Journal of Pharmaceutical Education, 86(10). Elsevier BV. https://doi.org/DOI: 10.5688/ajpe8906

Xia, Q., Weng, X., Ouyang, F., Lin, T., & Chiu, T. K. F. (2024). A scoping review on how generative artificial intelligence transforms assessment in higher education [Review of A scoping review on how generative artificial intelligence transforms assessment in higher education]. International Journal of Educational Technology in Higher Education, 21(1). Springer Nature. https://doi.org/DOI: 10.1186/s41239-024-00468-z

Yao, K., Huang, W., Hsu, L.-C., Yang, C.-K., & Lai, J.-Y. (2020). Evaluation of the Established IoT Smart Home Robot Teaching Module Based on Embedded Thematic-Approach Strategy. *Mathematical Problems in Engineering*, *1*. Advance online publication. DOI: 10.1155/2020/6696155

Yaseen, H., Mohammad, A. S., Ashal, N., Abusaimeh, H., Ali, A. A. A., & Sharabati, A. A. (2025). The Impact of Adaptive Learning Technologies, Personalized Feedback, and Interactive AI Tools on Student Engagement: The Moderating Role of Digital Literacy. *Sustainability*, *17*(3), 1133. DOI: 10.3390/su17031133

Yu, H. (2024). Enhancing creative cognition through project-based learning: An in-depth scholarly exploration. *Heliyon*, *10*(6). Advance online publication. DOI: 10.1016/j.heliyon.2024.e27706 PMID: 38533042

Zhang, X. (2023). How can technology leverage university teaching & learning innovation? A longitudinal case study of diffusion of technology innovation from the perspective of knowledge creation. https://link.springer.com/content/pdf/10.1007/s10639-023-11780-y.pdf

Zheng, X., Luo, L., & Liu, C. (2022). Facilitating Undergraduates' Online Self-Regulated Learning: The Role of Teacher Feedback. *The Asia-Pacific Education Researcher*, *32*(6), 805. DOI: 10.1007/s40299-022-00697-8

ADDITIONAL READING

Al-Haddad, S., Chick, N., & Safi, F. (2024). Teaching statistics: A technology-enhanced supportive instruction (TSI) model during the COVID-19 pandemic and beyond. *Journal of Statistics and Data Science Education: An Official Journal of the of the American Statistical Association, 32*(2), 129. DOI: 10.1080/26939169.2024.2315939

Barty, G., Boyer, N., Chrysikos, A., Griffith, M. L., ... (2024). Developing a more granular and equitable approach to the learner-earner journey. In *Zukunft der Hochschulbildung* (p. 457). https://doi.org/DOI: 10.1007/978-3-658-42948-5_23

Bennett, R. E. (2023). Toward a theory of socioculturally responsive assessment. *Educational Assessment, 28*(2), 83–97. DOI: 10.1080/10627197.2023.2202312

Chang, S. L., & Kabilan, M. K. (2022). Using social media as e-Portfolios to support learning in higher education: A literature analysis. *Journal of Computing in Higher Education, 36*(1), 1–25. DOI: 10.1007/s12528-022-09344-z PMID: 36405240

Creed, C., Al-Kalbani, M., Theil, A., Sarcar, S., & Williams, I. (2023). Inclusive AR/VR: Accessibility barriers for immersive technologies. *Universal Access in the Information Society, 23*(1), 59–78. DOI: 10.1007/s10209-023-00969-0

Jeganathan, S., Raj, L. A., Parthasarathy, S., Khan, A. A. A., & Sathick, K. J. (2024). OptCatB: Optuna hyperparameter optimization model to forecast the educational proficiency of immigrant students based on CatBoost regression. *Journal of Internet Services and Information Security, 14*(3), 111–123. DOI: 10.58346/jisis.2024.i2.008

Kulgemeyer, C., Riese, J., & Vogelsang, C.. (2023). How authenticity impacts validity: Developing a model of teacher education assessment and exploring the effects of digitisation. *Zeitschrift für Erziehungswissenschaft, 26*(3), 601–622. DOI: 10.1007/s11618-023-01154-y PMID: 37359180

Swiecki, Z., Khosravi, H., & Chen, G.. (2022). Assessment in the age of artificial intelligence. *Computers and Education: Artificial Intelligence, 3*, 100075. DOI: 10.1016/j.caeai.2022.100075

Tai, J., Ajjawi, R., & Bearman, M.. (2022). Assessment for inclusion: Rethinking contemporary strategies in assessment design. *Higher Education Research & Development, 42*(2), 483–496. DOI: 10.1080/07294360.2022.2057451

Xia, Q., Weng, X., Ouyang, F., Lin, T., & Chiu, T. K. F. (2024). A scoping review on how generative artificial intelligence transforms assessment in higher education. *International Journal of Educational Technology in Higher Education, 21*(1). Advance online publication. DOI: 10.1186/s41239-024-00468-z

KEY TERMS AND DEFINITIONS

Adaptive Assessment: A digital assessment method that adaptively modifies the difficulty or topic of questions according to a learner's immediate performance.

Assessment as Learning: A method that prioritizes student reflection and self-assessment during the evaluation process to enhance learning depth.

Constructivist Pedagogy: A learning theory that perceives knowledge as actively generated by learners through experience, interaction, and reflection, hence impacting assessment design.

Digital Divide: A discrepancy in access to technology, internet connectivity, and digital literacy abilities that impairs pupils' capacity to engage in technology-enhanced exams.

E-Portfolio: A digital compilation of student work that showcases learning advancement, accomplishments, and reflections over time, frequently utilized for realistic evaluation.

Formative Assessment: Continuous, low-stakes assessments employed to track student learning and furnish input for enhancement rather than conclusive evaluation.

Learning Analytics: The procedure of gathering, quantifying, and evaluating student data from digital platforms to guide instructional choices and tailored feedback.

Simulation-Based Testing: A digital assessment method that simulates real-world tasks or surroundings, enabling students to exhibit applicable knowledge and decision-making skills.

Universal Design for Learning: A framework that facilitates the development of inclusive educational settings through diverse methods of involvement, representation, and expression.

Validity: The degree to which an assessment effectively evaluates its intended construct, particularly significant in the appraisal of higher-order abilities inside digital environments.

Chapter 4
Conceptualizing a Novel Generative Maritime Learning Management System: G-Maritime

Vedat Dogancan
https://orcid.org/0009-0009-0534-5693
Department of Maritime Transportation & Management Engineering, Istanbul Technical University, Istanbul, Turkey

Kadir Cicek
Department of Marine Engineering, Istanbul Technical University, Istanbul, Turkey & Industrial Data Analytics and Decision Support Systems Center, Azerbaijan State University of Economics (UNEC), Baku, Azerbaijan

Metin Celik
https://orcid.org/0000-0003-0107-1380
Department of Basic Science, Istanbul Technical University, Istanbul, Turkey & Industrial Data Analytics and Decision Support Systems Center, Azerbaijan State University of Economics (UNEC), Baku, Azerbaijan

ABSTRACT

The maritime industry is undergoing a transformation process along with the sustainable development goals. In this cycle, continuous maritime skill transition has become essential to ensure that seafarers and shore-based professionals remain future-ready. It is clearly stated that conventional training solutions are no longer sufficient in developing the maritime workforce. This book chapter introduces G-Maritime as

DOI: 10.4018/979-8-3373-7057-6.ch004

a novel Learning Management System (LMS) founded on Large Language Models (LLM). Conceptualizing the G-Maritime LMS, a retrieval-augmented generation (RAG) system supported with a maritime-specific LLM is provided. Moreover, the system is guided by well-established instructional design techniques (SJT, ADDIE, Bloom) that maximize the benefits of AI integration into learning and assessment environment. Therefore, G-Maritime is fundamentally capable of delivering personalized learning and assessments. In addition to conceptual proposal, the study addresses probable challenges such as compliance, certification, and accessibility. A pilot implementation roadmap is also proposed to test the system. The study offers a valuable insight for trainers, policymakers, industry professionals, and investors seeking to understand and support maritime skill transition with generative LMS solutions. By integrating domain-specific AI capabilities with personalized content delivery, G-Maritime LMS represents a scalable model for future maritime learning ecosystems. G-Maritime has potential to become an accelerator for human-centred digital transformation in global shipping.

1. INTRODUCTION

The maritime industry is undergoing a profound transformation. It has driven by rapid technological advancements, environmental sustainability imperatives, and changing operational demands (Yi, Jung, & Lee, 2025). The growing complexity of maritime systems, increased regulatory requirements, and the global shortage of qualified maritime professionals demand more efficient and innovative learning solutions. The traditional approaches often fall short in addressing the dynamic needs of maritime professionals. There is a need for advanced and effective solutions to support workforce development in an era of rapid digital and green transformation. For instance, the comprehensive review of the STCW Convention, initiated by the IMO, clearly highlights the growing need to redefine and expand the competencies required for future seafarers (IMO, Report of the Working Group, 2024). The upcoming STCW'2026 amendments will also introduce new competencies that require innovative training modules. Furthermore, the requirements of the third-party inspection regimes (i.e. SIRE 2.0, TMSA 3, Rightship) highly requires an adaptable and skill-oriented learning framework. The third-part requirements with very high compliance expectations will drive a human-centric approach in the near future. At this insight, it is necessary to align competency acquisition and assessment methods with these changing requirements. It ensures the readiness and adaptability of maritime workforce.

Ensuring human competence is vital for ensuring safety, resilience and reliability aspects of sustainable maritime transportation industry. STCW-based formal assessments are mainly based on classical exams and tests to identify knowledge gaps (Emad & Roth, 2008). However, the practical demonstrations are still conducted under limited conditions. Research highlights critical shortfalls in conventional training models. Just to name few issues, outdated methods, incomplete feedback, and overemphasis on theoretical knowledge were pinpointed (Smith, 2018; Johnson et al., 2019; Wang, 2020). The main interest on the existing model is to fail addressing individual learning styles and evolving maritime regulations (Lee & Choi, 2017; El Mekkaoui et al., 2023; Hanzu-Pazara et al., 2008). For existing solutions, the other constraint is to predict actual seafarer competencies (Patel & Kumar, 2019). Given these limitations, the industry is shifting toward dynamic assessment and learning models that integrate technical and soft skills, personalized learning, and continuous feedback. The rapid change in the market has triggered the demands and needs in this manner.

In addition to the core studies in literature, various projects have been carried out in maritime education and training. As a complementary action to current efforts, notable projects and initiatives include EU SKILLSEA'2023, MET-NET'2023, i-MASTER'2023, MINE-EMI'2022, MATES'2022, BLUEGENERATION'2022, SEAMAP'2022, iSOL-MET'2020, IAMU GMP'2019, INTERTANKO BCAV'2018, SeaTALK'2015, and KNOW-ME'2014. These projects have contributed to shaping the maritime learning landscape. For instance, SKILLSEA and MATES concentrate on digitalization and green shipping through forecasting future skills. Both projects basically underline the need for dynamic educational models that can respond to rapidly changing maritime technologies. The initiatives have great potential to contribute sustainability measures. However, a highly critical concern is the lack of skill acquisition tools/platforms that align with the skill frameworks developed in these projects. On the other hand, MET-NET and i-MASTER demonstrate the international collaboration synergy in creating harmonized and transferable maritime curricula. Here, the distinguish efforts for the unification are so valuable. Beyond, the projects such as MINE-EMI and SEAMAP explore the role of immersive learning, simulations, and blended education approaches. The project demonstrations illustrated both soft and technical skills acquisition in order to improve operational excellence and resilience. The BLUEGENERATION initiative highlights the importance of youth participation in blue careers, while IAMU GMP and INTERTANKO BCAV offer strategic guidance on integrating industry expectations into seafarer training pathways. Meanwhile, SeaTALK and KNOW-ME provide early response for diversity competency via promoting Maritime English standardization. These initiatives have consensus on a shared perspective through future-oriented, inclusive, and technology-enabled maritime learning strategies. Indeed, it is expected that the solutions should be modular, scalable, and capable of lifelong upskilling. It supports that both new entrants and experienced professionals remain competent.

The variety of the recent projects emphasizes digital transformation, skill transition, and competency-based frameworks. Still more, the efforts to explore new instructional technologies have been continued. The new proposals target to add value by incorporating dynamic content generation and assessment functions. Market actors expect these initiatives to be more practical and customized to enhance workforce modernization by addressing skill gaps effectively. In particular, there is growing interest in advanced systems that support new generation features (i.e. real-time performance analytics, adaptive feedback loops, AI-centred mentoring capabilities, personalized learning).

This ongoing skill transition highlights the urgent need for interactive and novel solutions such as Learning Management Systems (LMSs). The recent expectations on such kind of systems prioritizes regulatory and operational dynamics. The artificial intelligence (AI) will make it possible to deliver such high-level expectations sought in an LMS. A domain-specific LMS, powered by large language models (LLMs), offers a scalable and intelligent solution. This integration has capability to generate personalized, context-aware training pathways tailored to the evolving realities of the maritime industry. In doing so, the chapter emphasizes how AI can offer adaptive, context-aware, and role-specific learning pathways. The proposed system aims to bridge the widening gap between traditional learning systems and the evolving demands of industry. Additionally, the model is fine-tuned with well-established instructional design frameworks and thematic contents (i.e. SIRE 2.0 inspection, management of change, etc).

The primary objectives of this book chapter are: i) To examine the potential of LLMs to create a maritime learning ecosystem. ii) To identify key requirements to design a generative LMS. iii) To investigate the adaption of instructional methodologies into generative LMS. iv) Conceptualize an LLM based maritime LMS framework. Achieving these objectives requires a multidisciplinary approach that bridges the gap between artificial intelligence, instructional design, and maritime domain expertise jointly. The proposed framework aims to facilitate a more agile learning environment tailored to maritime terminology. Indeed, it concentrates on the diverse learning needs. It also remains responsive to the maritime change management. Hence, this promotes continuous skill development, operational excellence, and workforce readiness.

The book chapter is organized as follows: The introduction section provides an overview of the technological changes and growing maritime skill transition gap correspondingly. The literature review on the scientific studies on LLMs integration into LMS is conducted in second section. In the third section, the conceptual framework of the G-Maritime, integration potential, pilot study plan, probable limitations and challenges are introduced in detail. Final section concludes the impact of the LLMs in learning and assessment and further issues.

2. LITERATURE REVIEW

The literature review of this study is mainly concentrated on two key aspects; i) The studies criticize the background of maritime skill transition, ii) The potential of LLMs integration into LMS. Then, the gaps to be fulfilled is identified.

When maritime skill transition examined in detail, it clearly seems that technological innovations (i.e. maritime autonomous surface ships, alternative fuels, cybersecurity threats, etc.) are fundamentally altering the skill landscape (Bogusławski et al., 2022; Karim, 2022). As marine technologies keep evolving, skill demands have been risen accordingly. So, it requires seafarers to operate, manage, monitor, and control the emerging technologies (Nguyen, 2018). Nevertheless, existing learning mechanisms are often misaligned with these rapidly shifting technological demands (Kim et al., 2023). Fundamentally, the compliance with the STCW requirements is another issue. The traditional approaches still leave a growing gap between industry requirements and gained competencies (Renganayagalu et al., 2022; Ravi, 2020; Lau & Ng, 2015; Yadav, 2014). In detail, the key aspects such as training programs, infrastructures, and instructional strategies are still arguable. The current program frameworks have weaknesses such as outdated curricula, limited integration of digital literacy, and insufficient attention to diversity competencies (Veldkamp et al., 2022; Österman & Boström, 2021). Development of training programs on alternative-fuel-powered vessels can be recognized as another example. Despite the several attempts, comprehensive and continuous skill transition frameworks are still lacking. The modernization process requires preparing seafarers for hybrid roles combining soft, technical, cognitive domains (Lokuketagoda et al., 2018). The maritime workforce may struggle to meet future challenges without rethinking of maritime learning systems (Molinari & Sandri, 2024; Kim & Mallam, 2020; Haleem et al., 2021). For instance, marine simulators, ranging from bridge/engine systems to safety and firefighting modules, have vulnerabilities such as unvalidated scenarios, limited interactivity, and inadequate exposure time for cadets (Kumar & Rajini, 2024; Hjelmervik et al., 2018). Despite high-fidelity, the adaptation is constrained by licence, maintenance and update costs. The insufficient instructor adaptation is another shortcoming (Ali, 2006; Muirhead, 2004; Cwilewicz & Tomczak, 2008). As another technology, e-learning platforms are a scalable alternative to which adaptive content generation, feedback mechanisms, and personalization are the critical features (Manuel, 2017; Basak, 2017). Promoting learner presence and scenario realism (Mallam et al., 2019; Baldauf & Procee, 2014; Vaughan et al., 2016), the integration of immersive technologies such as AR, VR, and MR were considered. However, the effective use of these technologies requires both pedagogical alignment and institutional readiness (Mallam et al., 2018; Hontvedt & Arnseth, 2013). Collectively, the initial review calls for the design and development of next-generation maritime learning ecosystems. The expectations highlight key features such as domain-adaptive, modular, dynamic, role-specific, and performance-oriented. The existing studies mainly cited these features as critical limitations of different maritime training technologies.

From futuristic perspective, the transition towards maritime society 5.0 marks another paradigm shift. Driving sustainable operations and enhance human well-being (Autsadee et al., 2025), AI, robotics, and the Internet of Things (IoT) are recently utilized advanced technologies. This transformation requires a fundamental redefinition of workforce competencies, insufficient to meet the demands of a highly digitalized maritime industry (Carayannis & Morawska-Jancelewicz, 2022). Adaptability, critical thinking, and digital fluency (Jagannathan, Ra, & Maclean, 2019) are the new skill sets to adapt technological advancements. Therefore, the majority of the studies cited the growing skill transition gap faced by maritime industry. Since it directly affects to operational resilience, safety, and sustainability goals, an AI-supported learning ecosystem is a genius way ensuring that maritime professionals remain future-ready (Mourtzis, Angelopoulos, & Panopoulos, 2023).

The integration of LLMs into an LMS represents a transformative opportunity for educational technology. It provides more personalized and adaptive learning experiences. The early stage studies have demonstrated that traditional LMS architectures are primarily based on relational databases and modular course designs. This concept limits the potential of AI-driven functionalities (Molinari & Sandri, 2024). To remedy this issue, Baker (2016) emphasized that AI can empower LMS platforms with dynamic learning pathways and personalized content tailored to individual needs. Similarly, Kose and Deperlioglu (2020) explored the incorporation of AI to develop intelligent learning systems sensitive to learner behaviour. In this era, the number of studies has been increased. Zawacki-Richter et al. (2019) studied a systematic review highlighting how AI applications contribute to LMS platforms. The functional improvements are determined as personalization, content generation, and intelligent tutoring. Meanwhile, Holmes et al. (2019) provided a critical perspective (i.e. ethical considerations) AI adoption in educational technologies. In addition, Kumar and Vivek (2021) demonstrated potential of LLMs in educational feedback, interactive content, and learning dialogues within LMSs.

In advance, the integration of LLMs into educational ecosystems marks a transformative shift that requires new understanding to the era. Fundamentally, the models have great potential in the design, deployment, and delivery of learning experiences adapted into specialized training domains. In limited fields such as healthcare, programming, legal, and maritime operations, domain-adapted AI systems have demonstrated in recent years (Dong, 2024; Manley et al., 2024). The implementations in adaptive LMS underscore how fine-tuned LLMs supported with Retrieval-Augmented Generation (RAG). Furthermore, advance vector embedding techniques enable real-time context-sensitive response generation to minimize knowledge decay (Spriggs et al., 2024; Jiang et al., 2023). Besides supporting learners, these models integrates instructional workflows such as scenario creation, error tracking, and adaptive quizzes through just-in-time guidance (Kim & Kim, 2020; Cutumisu et al., 2019). In parallel, the evolution of instructional design has moved toward modular. AI-enhanced frameworks cover several phases from design iterations to learner analytics. These models enable content personalization while taking the advantage of learning taxonomies (i.e. Bloom) and instructional techniques (i.e. ADDIE) (Martin et al., 2024; McMillan, 2023). Herein, fine-tuning strategies, domain-specific data injection, and multi-agent orchestration are increasingly utilized to align LLM outputs (Zhang & Aslan, 2021; Mizrahi et al., 2024). However, achieving effective instructional integration also requires attention to ethical dimensions and learner trust. For instance, the consistency is so critical for LLMs that are especially deployed in high-stakes training domains (Yao et al., 2024; Cai et al., 2024). Successful implementations often balance the instructional planning, lecturer engagement, and iterative testing. Collectively, the existing researches indicates that AI-integrated instructional systems can yield measurable gains if they are pedagogically aligned with real-world needs.

Beyond the insights, Dillenbourg et al. (2022) discussed the future direction of AI-LMS integration while Alvarez and Conati (2020) illustrated how adaptive AI systems could reshape learning. The core studies (Popenici and Kerr, 2017; Gonzalez and de Vicente, 2021; Roschelle and Teasley, 2023) collectively indicate that the full potential of LLM-powered LMS platforms still remains underdeveloped. Particularly, there is an urgent need for developing LMS architectures to fully conceptualize domain specific (i.e. maritime) LLM capabilities. This study targets to overcome this challenge to enable an interactive learning ecosystem for maritime professionals.

Despite a growing body of interdisciplinary literature addressing maritime skill transition, several research gaps limit the realization of AI integration. It is a great milestone to realize domain-specific LMS in industrial basis (Zawacki-Richter et al., 2019; Dong, 2024). Through a critical synthesis of the core studies (Manley et al., 2024; Spriggs et al., 2024; Gonzalez & de Vicente, 2021; McMillan, 2023; Mallam et al., 2019; Kumar & Rajini, 2024; Holmes et al., 2019; Yao et al., 2024; Kim & Kim, 2020; Zhang & Aslan, 2021) in the literature, the following key research gaps are identified: i) Limited domain adaptation of LLMs for maritime training purposes, ii) Insufficient integration of instructional design principles into AI-driven learning systems, iii) Absence of modular and role-specific LMS architectures tailored to seagoing and shore-based maritime professionals, iv) Lack of empirical or conceptual frameworks demonstrating how LLMs can be systematically aligned with international maritime regulations, v) Neglect of ethical, operational, and instructional risks on AI-generated content, vi) Limited personalization and formative assessment in current systems.

To address the mentioned gaps, the current study proposes an innovative conceptual framework that explores the integration of domain-adapted LLMs into a generative LMS tailored to the specific needs of the maritime industry. The expected contributions from this book chapter are as follows: This chapter is provided several contributions to AI-enabled maritime learning field. First, it conceptually proposed maritime-specific LLM integration into LMS. Second, it operationalizes instructional design within AI workflows. Then, it incorporates cognitive, behavioural, and procedural learning objectives respectively. Third, the study develops role-based LMS that alternatively offers separate learning paths for cadets, seafarers and shore-based managers. Fourth, it introduces tools to ensure regulatory compliance, such as competency checklists and automated rubric mapping aligned with STCW standards. Finally, the system uses LLM-generated insights to enable personalized feedback, continuous assessment, and performance tracking. These features aim to build a more adaptive, safe, and future-ready maritime workforce. By addressing key gaps in current research and practice, the study offers a structured framework for the next generation of maritime learning systems.

3. PROPOSED G-MARITIME LMS

3.1 Prerequisites

The successful design and implementation of the G-Maritime LMS requires a clear understanding of the contextual, technical, and pedagogical prerequisites that shape maritime training environments. This section outlines the foundational elements needed to ensure that the system is relevant, scalable, and aligned with both operational realities and educational standards. First, technical readiness is considered to operate the system in environments with limited or unstable internet access. Therefore, shipboard deployment requires minimal hardware dependency. Compatibility with existing software systems is important for integration. Cybersecurity measures must be in place to protect sensitive operational and personal data. Second, organizational conditions must support integration and adaptation. The system is expected to comply with the existing process in the organization. There may be resistance from potential end-users and training and personnel department managers. To overcome this, change management strategies should be developed. Stakeholder engagement is critical. Managing smooth transition, system administrators must also be prepared to manage AI components and updates. Third, pedagogical foundations must be strong. The LMS should follow proven instructional design models. Frameworks like ADDIE, Bloom's Taxonomy, and SJT provide useful structure. The techniques enable the robust content supporting with various learning styles. As a contemporary approach, scenarios must reflect real-life maritime operations. Personalization is key aspect to manage individual learning needs and progress. Feedback should be timely and relevant. Microlearning modules can help users focus on short, actionable skills. Fourth, regulatory compliance must be considered from the conceptualization phase. The system should reflect international standards, especially the STCW Code and other third-party requirements. It is so critical task to achieve system approval by a prestigious classification society. Moreover, any AI-generated content must be verifiable. Competency checklists might assist to compliance monitoring while auditable learning records are necessary for certification and reporting. The system must also be flexible enough to adapt to future regulatory changes. Fifth, human-centred design must guide system development. The interface should be simple, intuitive, and accessible. Language support is critical, especially for multinational crews. Content should be inclusive and relevant to diverse user profiles. The platform should promote trust in AI. Users need to understand how decisions are made and how to provide feedback. Ethical guidelines should guide how AI content is presented and used. Finally, scalability and sustainability should be addressed. The LMS must grow with organizational needs. It should support updates, new modules, and analytics over time. Open standards and modular design will help with long-term use. Cost-effectiveness is important, especially for smaller maritime operators. Partnerships with training providers, technology manufacturers, crewing agencies, ship operators, and other regulatory authorities may support broader adoption. Overall, a successful G-Maritime LMS must be secure, adaptive, inclusive, and standards-aligned. These prerequisites provide the foundation for a system that supports future-ready maritime learning across roles and environments.

3.2 Requirement Analysis

In a broad perspective, designing an AI-enhanced LMS for the maritime domain necessitates a comprehensive requirement analysis. The following key factors highlight why such a G-Maritime LMS is essential for the maritime industry: 1) The frequent updates to international maritime regulations, such as STCW amendments and SIRE 2.0, create a continuous need for competency renewal and regulatory alignment. 2) New compliance frameworks and inspection regimes demand more specialized, role-specific knowledge that traditional training methods cannot adequately address. 3) The increasing use of digital technologies on board ships requires seafarers to develop new technical and IT-related skills. 4) The integration of AI and automation in ship operations reshapes job roles, requiring hybrid skill sets that combine operational and digital expertise. 5) Maritime professionals must now engage with real-time data systems, necessitating skills in data interpretation and decision support. 6) Environmental regulations and the shift to green shipping technologies require knowledge in energy efficiency, emissions control, and sustainability strategies. 7) The generational shift in the workforce brings new expectations for flexible, technology-enabled, and personalized learning environments. 8) Growing workforce shortages, especially among experienced seafarers, highlight the need for accelerated and scalable upskilling solutions. 9) The increasing complexity of shipboard systems demands continuous learning across mechanical, digital, and regulatory domains. 10) The influence of Industry 4.0 and Society 5.0 introduces human-centric, smart operational paradigms that require lifelong learning and adaptive competencies. Hence, there is a need for a new learning ecosystem enables continuous skill transition arising from maritime industry transformation.

This analysis must also take the unique operational constraints of maritime environments into account. Data privacy, cybersecurity, and regulatory compliance are critical in both onboard and shore-based settings. Physical and digital infrastructure limitations (i.e. low bandwidth, hardware variability, and lack of system interoperability) pose significant barriers to implementation. Furthermore, the system must be scalable and cost-effective to perform service for ship fleets and different type of maritime organizations.

3.2 Background

3.2.1 Large Language Models (LLM)

AI has led to breakthroughs in the modern world for both daily life and applications in businesses. Machine Learning (ML) is a subfield of the AI technology that has enabled the development of Natural Language Processing (NLP) field. Deep Learning (DL) field has emerged as a result of the advancements in ML and has paved the way for the development LLMs. LLMs are a subset of language models that are trained with massive text data with self-supervised learning approach, leveraging deep neural networks with billions of parameters (Raiaan et al., 2024). Neural network architectures have been developed over time and form the foundation of LLM training. These architectures are Recurrent Neural Network (RNN), Long Short-Term Memory (LSTM), Gated Recurrent Unit (GRU) and Transformer architecture. LSTM and GRU architectures were developed with a motivation to address the limitations of RNN architecture (Korkmaz, 2025; Pascanu et al., 2013). In 2017, Vaswani et al. (2017) developed the Transformer architecture, which is a revolutionary attempt for LLM trainings. It has enabled the rise of modern LLMs such as GPT, BERT, Llama, PaLM, Grok, Gemini or DeepSeek (Naveed et al., 2023).

LLMs are capable of performing a wide range of NLP tasks such as text generation, question answering, text classification, summarization, language translation, or sentiment analysis (Moradi et al., 2025). In more detail, LLMs can understand natural language, generate human-like text based on prompts, provide detailed and context-aware answers to user queries, classify documents, or e-mails according to predefined labels, summarize extensive documents, perform translations across various languages, analyse the sentiment behind sentences, and generate code in various programming languages. Besides, Multimodal Large Language Models (MM-LLMs) can perform not only text-based NLP tasks, but also understand and generate images, audio, and video.

These capabilities make LLMs a powerful tool that offers modern solutions for a wide range of needs. From this perspective, LLM-based systems are being developed to improve efficiency, facilitate routine tasks, and save time. LLMs are widely used across various domains, such as assisting with code generation for software developers, enabling content creation and recommendation systems for social media, powering chatbots for customer service, supporting decision-making in medical diagnosis in the healthcare sector, facilitating personalized learning, providing recommendations on agricultural practices, offering financial advice for businesses, analysing legal documents, and enabling real-time language translation (Korkmaz, 2025 ; Moradi et al., 2025 ; Naveed et al., 2023 ; Raiaan et al., 2024).

Despite the outstanding performance of LLMs in NLP tasks, they have faced several key challenges over time. For instance, LLMs can confidently generate hallucinations, in which a response appears plausible but is factually incorrect (Huang et al., 2023). Lack of domain-specific knowledge can result in poor LLM performance in specialized fields, or generating outputs based on outdated information can lead to misinformation, potentially misguiding users. Another key challenge, overfitting, occurs when the model becomes overly dependent on its training data while generating responses. This issue reduces the model's generalization capability, which is critical for producing coherent and reasonable outputs. The training and local usage of LLMs require high computational power, resulting in significant computational costs that limit both model training and deployment. Security and privacy are another issue when it comes to use of LLMs since the possibility of generating false, harmful, biased, unfair, or private personal information (Han et al., 2024; Naveed et al., 2023).

Since LLM challenges require state-of-the-art solutions, adaptation methods have been developed to address these needs. Model adaptation methods, or model optimization methods, have been developed for maximizing the efficiency of LLM utilization across a wide range of tasks in various domains. Adaptation methods include RAG, Fine-tuning and In Context Learning (ICL). The RAG method consists of two main components: a retrieval model and a generation model. The retrieval model extracts information from an external knowledge base, while the generation model produces outputs by utilizing both the user prompt and the retrieved information. As a result, the RAG system is capable of generating context-aware, domain-specific, verifiable and up-to-date responses, while minimizing hallucinations and outdated information (Gupta et al., 2024 ; Gu u & Popescu, 2024). On the other hand, fine-tuning is a training method that is used for model adaptation with a supervised learning approach with annotated datasets. It enhances the performance of language models by adapting them to specific domains or tasks using specialized training data. There are significant fine-tuning strategies such as instruction tuning, transfer learning, and parameter-efficient fine-tuning (PEFT) (Singh et al., 2025). The performance of LLMs can also be enhanced through the in-context learning (ICL) method. ICL is a prompt engineering approach in which prompts are optimized by providing examples to improve the model's task understanding. It involves various techniques such as Few-Shot Learning (FSL) and Chain-of-Thought (CoT) prompting (Jain et al., 2024).

Improvements in the main architectures of language models have resulted in immense advancements in the AI field. Most notably, the development of the Transformer architecture has paved the way for modern LLMs, which demonstrate outstanding performance in NLP tasks. AI-powered systems with LLMs are now used in various sectors, facilitating routine tasks and enhancing the quality and efficiency of business practices. From the perspective of this study, it can be concluded that LLMs offer great opportunities in the field of education, with a potential to support the development of AI-based solutions to enhance the efficiency of training content, enable individualized learning experiences, accelerate time-consuming tasks, and contribute to the continuous improvement of the education.

3.2.2 Maritime-specific LLM under development

The maritime-specific LLM currently under development constitutes a foundational component of the G-Maritime LMS architecture. The model is being fine-tuned using large maritime documentary. The model particularly focuses on key operational domains such as upskilling, operational excellence, compliance management, change management, etc. This domain-adapted LLM will serve as the core intelligence layer of the G-Maritime LMS. Its development is strategically aligned with LMS functions. Once fully integrated, maritime-specific LLM will enhance learning environment (i.e. terminology, dynamic content generation, consistent assessment, adaptive instructional responses, etc.). It enhances the LMS's capability for the end users.

3.2.3 Instructional Techniques & Concepts

The proposed G-Maritime LMS is guided by well-established instructional design techniques and concepts that maximize the benefits of AI integration. Adopting AI capabilities, the system ensures adaptive learning, personalized feedback, and data-driven instructional improvements. The following instructional frameworks are integrated into the G-Maritime LMS: ADDIE, SJT and Bloom's Taxonomy. The ADDIE model structures the design and development of e-learning modules in an iterative manner. AI assists in; i) Analysing learner performance through data-driven insights, ii) Designing and developing adaptive content based on individual progress, iii) Implementing personalized learning paths using AI-driven recommendations, iv) Evaluating course effectiveness through automated assessment tools and real-time analytics. SJT is used to assess maritime professionals' decision-making skills under realistic conditions. AI enhances this process in the following aspects; i) Simulating real-world maritime scenarios using generative models, ii) Providing instant feedback and explanations to learners based on their responses, iii) Adjusting difficulty levels dynamically to match learner competency levels. AI supports content generation aligned with Bloom's Taxonomy, ensuring a progression from basic knowledge acquisition to advanced analytical and creative thinking. AI-driven functionalities include; i) Automated content curation that aligns with different cognitive skill levels, ii) Adaptive quizzes and assessments tailored to the learner's progression, iii) AI-generated scenario-based exercises that encourage higher-order problem-solving skills.

In practical manner, the integration of these instructional frameworks within the G-Maritime LMS allows for relevant, contextualized and systematic learning experiences. For example, a cadet performing ballast operations can receive step-by-step scenario guidance. Monitoring of the cadet performance for each task is aligned with Bloom's taxonomy. As another example, a deck officer preparing for enclosed space entry drills may be proactively evaluated through dynamic SJT-based modules under different operating environment. For instance, an engineering officer learning fuel changeover procedure during manoeuvring can interact with AI-generated procedural compliance scenario including unexpected failure modes and time pressure. Similarly, a second officer can enhance his/her competency in voyage planning by using microlearning modules that dynamically address the effects of different weather patterns, vessel traffic densities, situational awareness, regulatory requirements, and other critical parameters. An Electro-Technical Officer (ETO) can strengthen her/his fault diagnosis skills through interactive assessment modules. The system presents real-time electrical failure scenarios, allowing the ETO to practice accurate troubleshooting steps in a controlled environment. A Chief Engineer (C/E) can use the system to prepare the engine room team for SIRE 2.0

inspections. The system simulates inspection conditions, enabling crew members to practice procedural compliance, documentation readiness, and critical communication during engine room inspection.

The system uses learner performance data to improve the instructional content and delivery. It adapts training materials based on individual progress and learning gaps. Instructors can access real-time dashboards to monitor each learner's progress. The feedback loop between learning outcomes and real operations becomes stronger. It supports better skill development via timely response to training needs. The instructional strategies employed in G-Maritime LMS also reinforce personnel behaviour.

3.3 Conceptual Framework

This study conceptualizes a framework, namely G-Maritime LMS, to develop an AI-powered LMS integrated with LLMs in order to support maritime skill transition. The system aims to combine generative AI capabilities with instructional design techniques to ensure the quality and consistency of the learning mechanism. In line with this purpose, the system aims to create personalized training contents and learning paths using generative AI capabilities, dynamically track the performance of learners through data analysis, analyse the effectiveness of provided trainings to ensure continuous improvement, creating scenarios in which necessary professional or cognitive skills are supposed to be used to solve problems, creating quizzes and assessments that focus on learners' skills and competencies.

To achieve this aim, a RAG-based architecture is proposed as a framework since the RAG systems demonstrate remarkable performance in generating domain-specific, context-aware and up-to-date information. Additionally, a domain-specific LLM which is obtained through domain-adaptive pretraining and fine-tuning with task-specific datasets is deployed in the framework as a generation model, having a great potential to increase the performance of generation tasks with a higher adaptation to the maritime domain. This integration ensures that the system can provide accurate, relevant, and regulation-aligned learning content for diverse maritime training needs.

Figure 1 demonstrates the proposed framework, a RAG system with a maritime domain-specific LLM currently under development. The proposed framework consists of the following RAG system components tailored for the maritime education purposes: i) Maritime knowledge base containing domain-specific, up-to-date, and high-quality maritime documents. ii) Vector database that stores the vector embeddings of the texts extracted from the knowledge base. iii) Retrieval model that extracts the most relevant data from the knowledge base through the vector database. iv) Maritime-specific LLM, as a generation model, that performs generative AI tasks. v) Content repositories that store training and assessment contents.

Figure 1. The proposed framework for RAG-based system with maritime specific LLM.

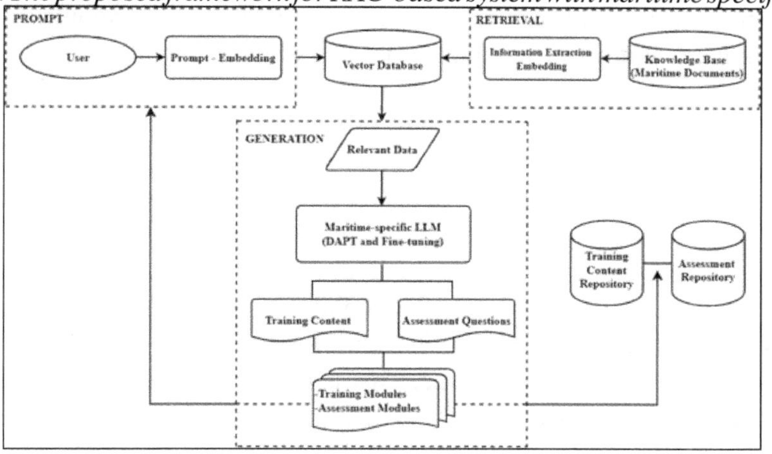

The proposed framework enables a maritime LMS to perform tasks and functions supported with generative AI. The workflow of the proposed system is explained as follows: First, a user prompt is entered into the system. Second, the retrieval model extracts the most relevant information from the knowledge base through embeddings in the vector database based on the user's prompt. Third, the maritime-specific LLM uses the combination of the prompt and retrieved data to create maritime training contents, assessment questions, maritime-related realistic scenarios tailored for specific needs, provide personalized recommendations for learning or evaluate performance of learners. Lastly, training and assessment modules are stored in the content repository to form a learning library.

G-Maritime LMS is designed to enhance learning environment and to facilitate maritime skill transition through a set of intelligent, adaptive, and learner-centric functions as follows; i) It delivers personalized learning pathways. ii) It offers adaptive assessments to monitor skill transition gap. iii) AI-powered mentoring provides real-time guidance. iv) Scenario-based learning modules simulate real-life challenges for practical skill development. v) The system ensures dynamic content remains current with regulatory and technological changes. These intelligent features are interconnected through a unified AI-driven learning framework. In practical implementations, personalized learning pathways are developed based on initial diagnostic assessments, learner profiles, and job-role competencies. These allow seafarers to progress at their own pace while focusing on specific areas for improvement. The system dynamically adjusts the learning content and sequencing. It refers performance data and learner interaction patterns to optimize knowledge retention. Adaptive assessments are conducted by analysing behavioural indicators, response time, and error patterns to identify underlying competency gaps. This enables both learners and instructors to better understand personalized solutions progress. AI-powered mentoring serves as a real-time support mechanism. It simulates the presence of an instructor by answering learner queries, offering hints during complex exercises, and redirecting users toward additional resources (i.e. digital library). This mentoring functionality is especially critical for remote learners onboard ships. Scenario-based learning modules are designed to replicate operational situation awareness. This enables learners to apply theoretical knowledge in various realistic maritime contexts such as maintenance planning, drill implementations, oil spill response, incident handling, pre-inspection preparedness, etc. The scenarios can be customized based on the operational conditions in different complexity levels. Moreover, the system is continuously updated through automated regulatory scanning and content refreshment mechanisms. That is one of the critical shortcomings of the existing LMS solutions. It integrates both the regulatory changes and emerging industry practices along with the tasks. This ensures that both training materials and assessment tools remain updated. For instance, G-Maritime LMS supports a continuous learning environment where maritime professionals can develop their competencies in alignment with the emerging concepts such as smart and green shipping transition.

3.4 Integration & Pilot Study Plan

While the chapter offers a conceptual roadmap for AI integration into maritime training, an extended effort is required to strength practical relevance. First, there is a need for concrete case studies that illustrate the operational demands. For example, the recent SIRE 2.0 vetting findings might highlight the lack of behavioral safety awareness, cyber preparedness, and environmental compliance. Furthermore, the theoretical background of the key topics such as cyber-physical systems, predictive analytics, and real-time decision-making has onerous importance for skill transition. It means that the areas insufficiently addressed by legacy training models. The experiences from operational level highlighted that many seafarers lack the confidence to respond to emergencies involving digital systems or advanced navigation equipment, indicating systemic training gaps. The industrial report published by key authorities mentioned serious shortfalls in crew digital competencies and inadequate understanding of emissions regulations among seafarers. These gaps have direct operational implications. This might lead to regulatory non-compliance. Moreover, the challenges of maritime training are not globally uniform. Regional differences in updated content, instructor readiness, and infrastructures are seemed.

Therefore, any proposed AI integration must be sensitive to geographic, economic, and institutional diversity, offering scalable and adaptable solutions.

Most importantly, the integration of AI should move beyond generic promises of personalization and efficiency. Instead, implementation should focus on problem-based alignment. Just to name a few cases: Example-1) How does AI concretely reduce the time to competency in ballast operations? Example-2) How does it mitigate human error in ECDIS use? Example-3) Can it improve knowledge retention in safety drills under stress? Example-4) How can AI-assisted feedback loops improve procedural accuracy during enclosed space entry operations? Example-5) Can generative AI create real-time, role-specific responses for engine room fault diagnostics to support junior engineers? Example-6) How does scenario-based AI simulation help in preparing crew for handling cyber incidents onboard? Example-7) How can AI personalize emergency response training based on prior performance metrics of each individual? Example-8) How does AI-generated content enhance compliance training for MARPOL Annex VI emission control requirements? Example-9) Can AI integration reduce cognitive overload during multi-alarm bridge navigation scenarios? Example-10) How does AI-supported multilingual instruction help reduce misunderstandings in multi-national crew safety briefings? Example-11) How does AI support proactive risk identification by analysing near-miss reports and generating targeted safety drills? Example-12) Can AI-driven adaptive quizzes accelerate familiarization with newly installed equipment, such as scrubbers or BWTS units? Example-13) How can AI simulate communication breakdowns in emergency scenarios to enhance crew coordination under pressure? Example-14) How does AI-powered content generation help align onboard training with rapidly changing international regulations like STCW amendments? Example-15) How can AI analyse patterns in learners' decision-making during simulation exercises to identify latent competency gaps before they manifest in real operations? Example-16) How does AI assist in continuous competency tracking for shipboard emergency response teams by automatically analysing drill performance logs? Example-17) Can AI simulate complex cargo handling scenarios for chemical tankers to accelerate decision-making under uncertainty? Example-18) How can AI-generated situational judgement tests help assess and improve soft skills like leadership and teamwork during crisis simulations? Example-19) How does AI enable early identification of training gaps in port state control (PSC) preparedness by analysing inspection data trends? Example-20) How can AI-driven procedural exercises/simulations help marine engineering cadets master critical routines like fuel changeover during manoeuvring, reducing reliance on real-engine time?

These are the kinds of targeted questions that G-Maritime must address to validate its pedagogical effectiveness. The questions also give idea about differences with the conventional e-learning platforms. Future iterations of this framework should therefore include adaptive learning pathways tailored to role-specific maritime tasks. To evaluate the feasibility, effectiveness, and scalability of the G-Maritime LMS, a structured pilot study is planned. The pilot application will involve cadets, maritime instructors, and technical managers, crewing and training managers aiming to test the system. The test covers microlearning modules, assessment tools, scenario generations. Data collection will focus on user experience with several metrics. The pilot study is expected to provide empirical insights into usability. The outcomes will inform iterative design improvements, guide industrial conformity mapping, and support policy recommendations.

3.5 Extended Discussion

While the G-Maritime LMS presents a novel concept, several critical dimensions remain underexplored and need further elaboration for real-world implementation. In this kind of system, one of the most prominent omissions involves the issue of data privacy and security. Since the maritime industry operates under strict confidentiality norms, G-Maritime must incorporate robust cybersecurity mechanisms, including encrypted data handling, secure API gateways, and authentication protocols. Another significant oversight pertains to the technical infrastructure requirements needed to operationalize G-Maritime. Unlike shore-based educational platforms, G-Maritime must contend with low-bandwidth environments and limited onboard hardware capacity. This raises the necessity of designing a lightweight, modular, and partially offline-capable LMS architecture. Furthermore, the economic feasibility of the system must be evaluated. While AI technologies promise long-term cost savings, the initial investment in hardware and software customization, might be a strict barrier for a SME. A cost-benefit analysis is furtherly required. Cultural and organizational dimensions also represent another major challenge. Considering the probable resistance to rapidly evolving digital technologies in maritime industry, encompassing stakeholder engagement has vital importance. Therefore, successful adoption of G-Maritime will require a robust change management strategy. Comparing to experienced professionals, younger seafarers may exhibit high adaptability to AI-powered systems. G-Maritime should therefore integrate adaptive user interfaces in order to ensure inclusivity and effectiveness across diverse user profiles. Conducting a benchmark study is another key aspect. Comparisons with current maritime e-learning platforms, such as Videotel, Seagull, or Marlins, would also provide valuable to clarify the system's relative value and innovation potential. Lastly, given the operational constraints of seagoing environments, G-Maritime must address the requirement for offline functionality. The ability to store, update, and synchronize content without continuous internet access is essential for onboard training facilities.

In summary, G-Maritime offers a promising vision for AI-assisted maritime training. Managing an industry-accepted solution, the following key areas must be addressed to ensure successful real-world implementation and long-term sustainability: i) G-Maritime must incorporate strong cybersecurity measures to protect sensitive training and operational data in compliance with maritime standards. ii) A detailed cost analysis is needed to assess economic feasibility, including implementation, maintenance, and long-term value. iii) The system should be scalable across different maritime organizations (shipping companies, training institutions, administrative authorities, etc.) with varying digital readiness. iv) Full alignment with STCW requirements and other maritime regulations is essential to ensure legitimacy and certification. v) Effective change management strategies must address resistance to AI adoption and support user engagement across generations. vi) Offline usability must be prioritized to ensure core functionalities remain available during low or no connectivity at sea. vii) Human-centred design should guide user interface development to ensure accessibility, simplicity, and minimal cognitive load. viii) Integrated analytics and feedback tools are needed to track progress, personalize learning, and support real-time adaptation. ix) Pilot studies in real-world training settings are necessary to validate system effectiveness and guide iterative improvement. x) The platform should be future-proofed to adapt to emerging technologies, regulations updates, and dynamic learning needs over time.

4. CONCLUSION

This book chapter fundamentally presents a G-Maritime LMS tailored to the maritime industry. The conceptual proposal of the G-Maritime LMS provides a generative and forward-thinking response to the increasing demands for novel maritime learning solutions. By integrating LLM, RAG, and instructional techniques (e.g., ADDIE, Bloom, SJT), the proposed system has potential to promote effective maritime skill transition. The chapter explores the pedagogical, technical, and operational dimensions of AI-assisted maritime learning system. It also identifies a roadmap for implementation, validation, and scalability.

The following highlights of this study outline how the proposed G-Maritime LMS is recognized as a novel solution for the maritime community: i) Identifying fundamental gaps in traditional maritime training practices that hinder the development of future-ready competencies. ii) Proposing an AI-powered LMS architecture based on maritime-domain adapted LLM and RAG systems. iii) Aligning AI-generated learning and assessment content with STCW standards and evolving international maritime regulations. iv) Incorporating established instructional design frameworks such as ADDIE, Bloom's Taxonomy, and SJT to enhance learning effectiveness and instructional quality. v) Enabling personalized, adaptive learning pathways that respond to individual learner profiles, performance data, and operational roles. vi) Supporting usability in low-bandwidth and offline shipboard conditions through resilient system design. vii) Addressing key operational concerns such as cybersecurity, digital trust, and responsible AI usage in maritime education environments. viii) Outlining a pilot study plan for empirical validation of system functionality, end-user feedback, and learning outcomes. ix) Offering organizational strategies for overcoming resistance to digital transformation in conservative maritime institutions. x) Contributing to the global smart and green shipping transition by equipping maritime professionals with future-oriented, AI-enhanced competencies.

Moreover, the chapter conducts a comprehensive literature review on maritime skill transition and AI integration into learning management process. Besides, cross-sectoral benchmarking among aviation, health, defence, and energy were investigated to clearly understand the background of domain-specific initiatives. Particular to maritime domain, traditional maritime e-learning platforms were also reviewed. Since the traditional approaches for maritime learning mechanisms (formal, continuous, inhouse, onboard) fail to meet modern expectations, a need for innovative solutions have emerged. With this perspective, this chapter addresses the importance of the maritime skill transition to maintain a workforce equipped with required skills and appropriate competency. Besides, it was emphasized that the state-of-the-art technologies, especially AI-based systems, have a great capacity to offer modern solutions in the new era. It is visible that LLMs are actively used in a diverse range of sectors, facilitating processes and improving the quality of business practices. Therefore, it is a remarkable point that the potential use of LLMs in maritime education field presents a great opportunity to develop cutting-edge solutions within the scope of maritime skill transition goals. In addition, it is also a significant point that the instructional design techniques form a basis for designing and developing training and assessment. The proposed framework presents an AI-powered LMS with a RAG system that includes a maritime-domain specific LLM. The system enables the LMS to perform generative AI tasks, aligning with the principles of instructional design techniques, such as creating personalized training contents, short quizzes, formal evaluations, self-assessments, providing personalized recommendations, or simulating real world maritime scenarios for training purposes. This study provides meaningful insight into how generative LMS solutions can support maritime skill transition, offering practical value for trainers, policymakers, industry professionals, and investors. Indeed, potential contributions of this study may be offering a foundational approach for AI-based industry implementations related to maritime training, providing knowledge on LLM domain adaptation methods that can be utilized for

AI-based systems in maritime industry, or providing an insight for the integration of instructional design techniques with AI solutions for the education field.

In this chapter, the proposed G-Maritime LMS presents an AI-centred learning management solution while several aspects of the system design and implementation need further development given as follows; i) The system requires pilot testing in real maritime environments to validate its practical effectiveness and usability. ii) A detailed technical architecture must be developed to ensure system transparency, replicability, and integration feasibility. iii) Scalability across diverse organizational and institutional infrastructures needs to be addressed for broader industry adoption. iv) Formal regulatory approval processes and certification pathways should be integrated into the system design. v) User interface and experience must be refined to accommodate varying digital literacy levels and cultural contexts.

Finally, the long-term success of the G-Maritime LMS depends on the industry tendencies to restructuring maritime industry in the near future. It brings a new understanding to support lifelong learning in maritime domain. In this circumstance, G-Maritime has the potential to become not only a model for maritime AI education systems but also an accelerator for human-centred digital transformation in global shipping. Future research may aim to investigate advanced RAG-based systems, explore alternative model adaptation approaches to obtain domain-specific LLMs, or reporting industry applications that highlights the strengths and weaknesses of the AI-powered LMS systems.

REFERENCES

Ali, A. (2006). Role and importance of the simulator instructor (Master's thesis). World Maritime University, Malmö, Sweden.

Alvarez, A. I., & Conati, C. (2020). Towards using artificial intelligence for adaptive learning in online learning environments. *Journal of Educational Technology & Society*, *23*(4), 33–45.

Autsadee, Y., Jeevan, J., Othman, M. R. B., & Salleh, N. H. B. M. (2025). Maritime Society 5.0: A global transition on human economy and civilisation for maritime sustainability. *Australian Journal of Maritime and Ocean Affairs*, *17*(1), 1–26. DOI: 10.1080/18366503.2023.2287872

Baker, R. S. (2016). Staying in control: Automated education with learning management systems and artificial intelligence. *Journal of Educational Data Mining*, *8*(1), 12–25.

Baldauf, M., & Procee, S. (2014). Augmented reality in ships bridge operation. *Isis*, *2014*, 170–178.

Basak, S. K. (2017). A framework on the factors affecting to implement maritime education and training system in educational institutions: A review of the literature. *Procedia Engineering*, *194*, 345–350.

Bogusławski, K., Gil, M., Nasur, J., & Wróbel, K. (2022). Implications of autonomous shipping for maritime education and training: The cadet's perspective. *Maritime Economics & Logistics*, *24*(2), 327–343. DOI: 10.1057/s41278-022-00217-x

Cai, H., Lin, Z., Zhan, Y., Li, Y., Gong, R., Zhou, Y., Zhang, J., & Wang, B. (2024). SciAssess: Benchmarking LLM proficiency in scientific literature analysis. arXiv. https://arxiv.org/abs/2403.01976

Carayannis, E. G., & Morawska-Jancelewicz, J. (2022). The futures of Europe: Society 5.0 and Industry 5.0 as driving forces of future universities. *Journal of the Knowledge Economy*, *13*(4), 3445–3471. DOI: 10.1007/s13132-021-00854-2 PMID: 40477679

Cutumisu, M., Chin, D. B., & Schwartz, D. L. (2019). A digital game-based assessment of feedback-seeking behavior and its relation to academic achievement. *British Journal of Educational Technology*, *50*(6), 2977–3003. DOI: 10.1111/bjet.12832

Cwilewicz, R., & Tomczak, L. (2008). Improvement of ship operational safety as a result of the application of virtual reality engine room simulators. *WIT Transactions on Information and Communication Technologies*, *39*, 535–544.

Dillenbourg, P., Schneider, D., & Synteta, P. (2022). Virtual learning environments: Integrating AI tools for effective collaboration and learning. *AI and Education Journal*, *39*(3), 56–78.

Dong, C. (2024). How to build an AI tutor using LLM and RAG. arXiv. https://arxiv.org/abs/2311.17696

El Mekkaoui, S., Benabbou, L., Caron, S., & Berrado, A. (2023). Deep learning-based ship speed prediction for intelligent maritime traffic management. *Journal of Marine Science and Engineering*, *11*(1), 1–18. DOI: 10.3390/jmse11010191

Emad, G., & Roth, W. M. (2008). Contradictions in the practices of training for and assessment of competency: A case study from the maritime domain. *Education + Training*, *50*(3), 260–272. DOI: 10.1108/00400910810874026

Gonzalez, M. A., & de Vicente, M. J. (2021). Generative AI in learning management systems: Opportunities and challenges. *AI and Learning Sciences Review*, *7*(1), 41–58.

Gupta, S., Ranjan, R., & Singh, S. N. (2024). *A Comprehensive Survey of Retrieval-Augmented Generation (RAG)*. Evolution, Current Landscape and Future Directions.

Gu u, B. M., & Popescu, N. (2024). Exploring Data Analysis Methods in Generative Models: From Fine-Tuning to RAG Implementation. In *Computers* (Vol. 13, Issue 12). Multidisciplinary Digital Publishing Institute (MDPI). https://doi.org/DOI: 10.3390/computers13120327

Haleem, A., Javaid, M., Vaishya, R., & Deshmukh, S. G. (2021). Areas of applications of Artificial Intelligence (AI) in maritime industry: A review. *Ocean Engineering*, *234*, 109276. DOI: 10.1016/j.oceaneng.2021.109276

Han, S., Wang, M., Zhang, J., Li, D., & Duan, J. (2024). A Review of Large Language Models: Fundamental Architectures, Key Technological Evolutions, Interdisciplinary Technologies Integration, Optimization and Compression Techniques, Applications, and Challenges. In *Electronics (Switzerland)* (Vol. 13, Issue 24). Multidisciplinary Digital Publishing Institute (MDPI). https://doi.org/DOI: 10.3390/electronics13245040

Hanzu-Pazara, R., Lupu-Dima, L., & Vasilache, S. (2008). The impact of the new learning models on the development of e-learning systems. *Informações Econômicas*, *12*(2), 34–39.

Hjelmervik, K., Nazir, S., & Myhrvold, A. (2018). Simulator training for maritime complex tasks: An experimental study. *WMU Journal of Maritime Affairs*, *17*(1), 17–30. DOI: 10.1007/s13437-017-0136-7

Holmes, W., Bialik, M., & Fadel, C. (2019). *Artificial intelligence in education: Promises and implications for teaching and learning*. Center for Curriculum Redesign.

Hontvedt, M., & Arnseth, H. C. (2013). On the bridge to learn: Analysing the social organization of nautical instruction in a ship simulator. *International Journal of Computer-Supported Collaborative Learning*, *8*, 89–112. DOI: 10.1007/s11412-013-9167-6

Huang, L., Yu, W., Ma, W., Zhong, W., Feng, Z., Wang, H., Chen, Q., Peng, W., Feng, X., Qin, B., & Liu, T. (2023). *A Survey on Hallucination in Large Language Models: Principles*. Taxonomy, Challenges, and Open Questions., DOI: 10.1145/3703155

International Maritime Organization (IMO). (2024). *Report of the Working Group on the Comprehensive Review of the 1978 STCW Convention and Code* (HTW 10/WP.3).

Jagannathan, S., Ra, S., & Maclean, R. (2019). *Education and skills for inclusive growth, green jobs and the greening of economies in Asia: Case study summaries*. Springer.

Jain, A., Maleki, A., & Saade, N. (2024, August 7). *Methods for adapting large language models.* ai.meta.com. https://ai.meta.com/blog/adapting-large-language-models-llms/

Jiang, Z., Zhang, H., & Ni, J. (2023). Active Retrieval Augmented Generation for knowledge-intensive tasks. arXiv. https://arxiv.org/abs/2305.06983

Johnson, A., Smith, B., & Thomas, L. (2019). Challenges in Maritime Education: Bridging Theory and Practice. *Journal of Marketing Education*, *42*(3), 115–128.

Karim, M. S. (2022). Maritime cybersecurity and the IMO legal instruments: Sluggish response to an escalating threat? *Marine Policy*, *143*, 105138. DOI: 10.1016/j.marpol.2022.105138

Kim, D., & Mallam, S. (2020). Human factors considerations for the design and implementation of autonomous ships. *Journal of Marine Science and Engineering*, *8*(5), 308. DOI: 10.3390/jmse8050308

Kim, J., Lee, C., Jeong, M., Cho, E., & Lee, Y. (2023). Identifying optimal approaches for sustainable maritime education and training: Addressing technological, environmental, and epidemiological challenges. *Sustainability, 15*(10), 8092. DOI: 10.3390/su15108092

Kim, W.-H., & Kim, J.-H. (2020). Individualized AI tutor based on developmental learning networks. *IEEE Access: Practical Innovations, Open Solutions, 8*, 176594–176607. DOI: 10.1109/ACCESS.2020.3026359

Korkmaz, N. (2025). *Büyük Dil Modelleri ve İstem Mühendisliği.* https://bilgem.tubitak.gov.tr/yte/

Kose, U., & Deperlioglu, O. (2020). Intelligent learning systems: Integration of AI into LMS for personalized education. *International Journal of Artificial Intelligence in Education, 30*(2), 183–203.

Kumar, N., & Rajini, G. (2024). Reimaging maritime education and training using latest technologies. Salud, Ciencia y Tecnología – Serie de Conferencias, 3, 895. https://doi.org/.DOI: 10.56294/sctconf2024895

Kumar, V., & Vivek, S. (2021). AI in education: Application of natural language processing (NLP) in learning management systems. *International Journal of Learning Analytics and Artificial Intelligence for Education, 4*(1), 45–67.

Lau, Y. Y., & Ng, A. K. (2015). The motivations and expectations of students pursuing maritime education. *WMU Journal of Maritime Affairs, 14*, 313–331. DOI: 10.1007/s13437-015-0080-5

Lee, J., & Choi, H. (2017). What affects learner's higher-order thinking in technology-enhanced learning environments? The effects of learner factors. *Computers & Education, 115*, 143–152. DOI: 10.1016/j.compedu.2017.06.015

Lokuketagoda, M. G., Miwa, T., Jayasinghe, S., & Dev Ranmuthugala, P. (2018). Training engineers for remotely operated ships of the future. In *Proceedings of the 19th Annual General Assembly (AGA), International Association of Maritime Universities (IAMU)* (pp. 17–19). Barcelona, Spain.

Mallam, S. C., Nazir, S., Renganayagalu, S. K., Ernstsen, J., Veie, S., & Edwinson, A. E. (2019). Design of experiment comparing users of virtual reality head-mounted displays and desktop computers. In *Proceedings of the 20th Congress of the International Ergonomics Association (IEA 2018)* (pp. 240–249). Springer. https://doi.org/DOI: 10.1007/978-3-319-96071-5_28

Manley, E. D., Urness, T., Migunov, A., & Reza, M. A. (2024). Examining student use of AI in CS1 and CS2. *Journal of Computing Sciences in Colleges, 39*(6), 41–51.

Manuel, M. E. (2017). Vocational and academic approaches to maritime education and training (MET): Trends, challenges and opportunities. *WMU Journal of Maritime Affairs, 16*(3), 473–483. DOI: 10.1007/s13437-017-0135-8

Martin, F., Zhuang, M., & Schaefer, D. (2024). A systematic review of the use of artificial intelligence in K–12 education (2017–2022). Computers & Education. *Artificial Intelligence*, *6*, 100195. DOI: 10.1016/j.caeai.2023.100195

McMillan, J. H. (2023). *Classroom assessment: Principles and practice for effective standards-based instruction* (8th ed.). Pearson.

Mizrahi, M., Mazor, Y., Goldberg, Y., & Berant, J. (2024). State of what art? A call for multi-prompt LLM evaluation. arXiv. https://arxiv.org/abs/2401.00595

Molinari, A., & Sandri, S. (2024). Evolution of LMS design and implementation in the age of AI and large language models. In *Proceedings of the 2nd International Workshop on Artificial Intelligence Systems in Education (AIxEDU 2024)*. CEUR Workshop Proceedings.

Moradi, M., Yan, K., Colwell, D., Samwald, M., & Asgari, R. (2025). A Critical Review of Methods and Challenges in Large Language Models. In *Computers, Materials and Continua* (Vol. 82, Issue 2, pp. 1681–1698). Tech Science Press. https://doi.org/DOI: 10.32604/cmc.2025.061263

Mourtzis, D., Angelopoulos, J., & Panopoulos, N. (2023). Smart manufacturing and Industry 5.0: Human-centered approaches and skill development strategies. *Journal of Manufacturing Systems*, *68*, 162–174. DOI: 10.1016/j.jmsy.2023.02.003

Muirhead, P. M. (2004). New technology and maritime training in the 21st century: Implications and solutions for MET institutions. *WMU Journal of Maritime Affairs*, *3*, 139–158.

Naveed, H., Khan, A. U., Qiu, S., Saqib, M., Anwar, S., Usman, M., Akhtar, N., Barnes, N., & Mian, A. (2023). *A Comprehensive Overview of Large Language Models*. https://arxiv.org/abs/2307.06435

Nguyen, L. (2018). 9 experts discuss the skills seafarers need in the future. *Informa Connect*. Retrieved September 21, 2024, from https://knect365.com/shipping/article/c17e1ac8-6e3a-4e33-855c-5adbb3bad9aa/

Osterman, C., & Boström, M. (2021). Workplace bullying and harassment at sea: A structured literature review. *Marine Policy*, *136*, 104910. DOI: 10.1016/j.marpol.2021.104910

Pascanu, R., Mikolov, T., & Bengio, Y. (2013). *On the difficulty of training recurrent neural networks.*

Popenici, S., & Kerr, S. (2017). Exploring the impact of artificial intelligence on teaching and learning in higher education. *Research and Practice in Technology Enhanced Learning, 12*(1), 1–14. PMID: 30595727

Raiaan, M. A. K., Mukta, M. S. H., Fatema, K., Fahad, N. M., Sakib, S., Mim, M. M. J., Ahmad, J., Ali, M. E., & Azam, S. (2024). A Review on Large Language Models: Architectures, Applications, Taxonomies, Open Issues and Challenges. *IEEE Access: Practical Innovations, Open Solutions, 12*, 26839–26874. DOI: 10.1109/ACCESS.2024.3365742

Ravi, L. (2020). Maritime education in India—The "theory–practice" conundrum. *IIRE Journal of Maritime Research and Development, 4*(2), 15–22.

Renganayagalu, S. K., Mallam, S. C., & Hernes, M. (2022). Maritime education and training in the COVID-19 era and beyond. TransNav. *International Journal on Marine Navigation and Safety of Sea Transportation, 16*(1), 59–69. DOI: 10.12716/1001.16.01.06

Roschelle, J., & Teasley, S. D. (2023). Collaborative learning with AI: Integrating GPT in learning management systems for enhanced educational outcomes. *Journal of Learning Analytics, 10*(2), 75–92.

Singh, K., Deshpande, S., & Patwardhan, S. (2025). Refining the Giants: A Comprehensive Review of Fine-Tuning Strategies for Large Language Models. *Lecture Notes in Networks and Systems, 1144*, 65–82. DOI: 10.1007/978-981-97-7839-3_5

Smith, B. A. C. (2018). *DP sea time validation: An in-depth review of the commonly utilized DP validation practices and suggestions for how the industry can improve.* Dynamic Positioning Committee.

Vaswani, A., Shazeer, N., Parmar, N., Uszkoreit, J., Jones, L., Gomez, A. N., Kaiser, L., & Polosukhin, I. (2017). *Attention Is All You Need.* https://arxiv.org/abs/1706.03762

Vaughan, N., Gabrys, B., & Dubey, V. N. (2016). An overview of self-adaptive technologies within virtual reality training. *Computer Science Review, 22*, 65–87. DOI: 10.1016/j.cosrev.2016.10.001

Veldkamp, E. L., Bygvraa, D. A., Dawicki, H. E., Dawicki, M. G., & Center for Ocean Policy & Economics (COPE) Working Group. (2022). Psychological safety, bullying, sexual assault and harassment in the maritime sector. *Medical Sciences Forum, 13*(1), 25. https://doi.org/DOI: 10.3390/msf2022013025

Wang, L. (2020). Evaluating Competency-Based Maritime Training Programs. *International Maritime Journal*, *36*(2), 77–90.

Yao, Y., Zhang, Y., Ma, Y., & Zhao, Y. (2024). A survey on large language model security and privacy. *High-Confidence Computing*, *4*(2), 100211. DOI: 10.1016/j.hcc.2024.100211

Yi, S.-Y., Jung, M., & Lee, S.-I. (2025). *Adapting to change: International maritime education and training for future seafarers – focusing on the comprehensive review of the STCW convention and code. Journal of International Maritime Safety*. Environmental Affairs, and Shipping., DOI: 10.1080/25725084.2025.2464486

Zawacki-Richter, O., Marín, V. I., Bond, M., & Gouverneur, F. (2019). Systematic review of research on artificial intelligence applications in higher education: Where are the educators? *International Journal of Educational Technology in Higher Education*, *16*(1), 1–27. DOI: 10.1186/s41239-019-0171-0

Chapter 5
Immersive Reality Technology-Based Gamification on Sustainable Education

Matthew Abiola Oladipupo
https://orcid.org/0000-0002-5984-6217
University of Salford, UK

David Taiwo Oyekunle
https://orcid.org/0009-0007-3994-1712
University of Salford, UK

Amaonwu Onyebuchi
https://orcid.org/0000-0002-6954-4853
Hussaini Adamu Federal Polytechnic, Nigeria

Ogechukwu Nkiruka Onyedibe
https://orcid.org/0009-0000-4452-5894
Federal University of Technology, Nigeria

Ugochukwu Okwudili Matthew
https://orcid.org/0000-0003-0828-9710
Federal University of Lavras, Brazil

Mgbike Francisca Chinenye
https://orcid.org/0009-0008-3244-2598
Federal College of Education (Technical), Umunze, Nigeria

Morgan Nwaiku
https://orcid.org/0009-0001-8984-8387
Teesside University, UK

Godwin Nse Ebong
https://orcid.org/0000-0002-9899-8838
University of Salford, UK

ABSTRACT

The Industry 5.0 concept for emerging sustainable education involves transforming every lesson into an interactive Virtual Reality (VR), Augmented Reality (AR), and Mixed Reality (MR) experimental gamification. By producing immersive and engaging experiences that were previously unthinkable, Extended Reality (XR) technology is transforming a number of sectors, including education. The present

DOI: 10.4018/979-8-3373-7057-6.ch005

study investigated the domain of simulation-based learning, shedding light on its significance, challenges, and boundless possibilities in the context of health technology education. The paper advanced hi-tech educational technology adoption in the development of interactive educational pedagogy in Society 5.0 and Education 5.0 by describing the technological underpinnings, guiding principles, essential values, and key components of Industry 5.0 in education. The study adopted Actor-Network Theory (ANT) model to explore the implication of technological pedagogy content knowledge (TPCK) model instruction design for immersive education technology.

INTRODUCTION

The rapid evolution of digital technologies have transformed the educational landscape, yet many institutions continue to rely on traditional, didactic teaching methods that fail to meet the needs of 21st-century learners(Ugochukwu Okwudili Matthew, Kazaure, Kazaure, Hassan, et al., 2022). While immersive technologies such as Extended Reality(XR), Virtual Reality (VR), Augmented Reality (AR), and Mixed Reality (MR) offer promising avenues for experiential and personalized learning, their integration into mainstream education remains fragmented and under-theorized(D. Oyekunle, Claude, Waliu, Adekunle, & Matthew, 2024). This disconnect between technological potential and pedagogical practice presents a critical problem: how can immersive tools be meaningfully embedded into educational systems to enhance learning outcomes, foster ethical awareness, and support sustainable development?. One of the most pressing issues is the lack of a cohesive framework that links immersive technologies with established educational theories and assessment models. Educators often struggle to align these tools with curriculum goals, resulting in isolated or superficial applications that fail to leverage their full potential. Moreover, existing pedagogical models are not always equipped to handle the dynamic, interactive nature of immersive environments, leading to challenges in instructional design, learner engagement, and outcome measurement. Another significant problem lies in the assessment of learning within immersive contexts. Traditional evaluation methods such as standardized tests and static rubrics are ill-suited to capture the depth of understanding, emotional intelligence, and real-time decision-making that immersive experiences can cultivate. Without adaptive, competency-based assessment tools, educators are unable to measure the true impact of immersive learning or provide meaningful feedback to students(Qin, 2024).

Accessibility and inclusivity also remain major concerns, in addition to high costs, technical complexity, and limited infrastructure that prevent equitable access to immersive technologies, particularly in under-resourced educational settings(Jat-to & Aladesusi, 2025). This digital divide risks exacerbating existing inequalities and undermines the goal of inclusive, human-centered education as envisioned by Education 5.0 and Industry 5.0 in Society 5.0 extreme automation(Ugochukwu Okwudili Matthew, Kazaure, et al., 2024). The goal of Education 5.0, Society 5.0, and Industry 5.0, is centered on creating a human-centric, ethical, and inclusive learning ecosystem powered by advanced technologies. These paradigms emphasize the integration of artificial intelligence (AI), generative AI, and tools like ChatGPT to personalize learning, foster emotional intelligence, and support lifelong education(Ugochukwu Okwudili Matthew, Oyekunle, et al., 2024). Education 5.0 promotes adaptive, immersive, and collaborative learning environments using AI-driven analytics and virtual tools to enhance engagement and creativity. Society 5.0 envisions equitable access to education through digital inclusion, using generative AI to democratize knowledge and bridge social gaps(Ramkissoon, 2024). Industry 5.0 aligns educational technology with human-machine collaboration, where ChatGPT and similar tools act as intelligent partners in learning, enabling real-time feedback, ethical reasoning, and workforce readiness. Together, these frameworks advocate for a future-ready education system that leverages AI not just for efficiency, but to cultivate empathy, innovation, and sustainability in learners across all contexts.

Furthermore, there is a lack of empirical research that systematically evaluates the long-term effects of immersive learning on student performance, motivation, and ethical development. While anecdotal evidence and pilot studies suggest positive outcomes, comprehensive, theory-driven investigations are needed to validate these claims and guide best practices. This research addresses these problems by proposing a computational model that integrates immersive technologies with Actor-Network Theory (ANT), Technological Pedagogical Content Knowledge (TPCK), the SAMR model, and Design Science Research Methodology (DSRM). The goal is to create a scalable, adaptive, and ethically grounded framework for immersive education that supports personalized learning and real-time assessment. By doing so, the study aims to bridge the gap between innovation and implementation, offering practical solutions to the complex challenges facing modern education. This research work is structured into introduction, background of the study, research questions, objective of the study, theoretical framework, literature review, system flow diagram, and methodology of implementation, discussion of findings, study limitations and conclusion.

BACKGROUND OF THE STUDY

Immersive technologies revolutionize medical education by enhancing hands-on learning, improving knowledge retention, and enabling realistic simulations for safer skill acquisition. They democratize access to high-quality training, foster deeper clinical understanding, and prepare students for real-world challenges, transforming traditional teaching into an engaging, experiential, and globally accessible educational paradigm. By integrating immersive technologies like VR/AR with gamification, it enables realistic simulations of clinical scenarios, enhancing decision-making, procedural skills, and emotional intelligence. AI-driven feedback supports personalized learning and competency-based assessment, while Actor-Network Theory ensures dynamic interaction among learners, tools, and educators. This approach addresses limitations of traditional methods by offering safe, repeatable, and ethically sound training environments. It also fosters collaboration, adaptability, and sustainability key pillars of Education 5.0 and Industry 5.0. Ultimately, it redefines medical training to be more inclusive, experiential, and future-ready. Together, Industry 5.0 and Education 5.0 redefine the role of technology not as a replacement for human effort, but as a partner in creativity, empathy, and sustainable development. Immersive technologies serve as the connective tissue between these paradigms, enabling transformative experiences that prepare individuals for a future where innovation is both intelligent and humane. Industry 5.0 and Education 5.0 represent a paradigm shift toward human-centric innovation, emphasizing collaboration between humans and intelligent technologies. Unlike Industry 4.0, which focused on automation and efficiency, Industry 5.0 integrates emotional intelligence, creativity, and sustainability into industrial ecosystems(Aheleroff, Huang, Xu, & Zhong, 2022). It envisions a future where humans and machines work in synergy, enhancing productivity while preserving human agency and well-being. Education 5.0 mirrors this evolution by moving beyond digital transformation to prioritize personalized, ethical, and emotionally intelligent learning(Adel, 2024). It promotes adaptive instruction, lifelong learning, and the development of holistic competencies such as empathy, critical thinking, and social responsibility. This model supports inclusive and equitable education, aligning with the goals of Society 5.0, a vision for a super-smart society where technology serves human welfare and environmental sustainability. In Education 5.0, immersive technologies transform learning into an experiential, interactive process. Students can explore historical events, conduct virtual experiments, or collaborate in simulated environments that adapt to their learning styles and emotional states. XR fosters deeper engagement, improves retention, and supports inclusive education by bridging geographic and physical barriers. Immersive technologies VR, AR, MR, XR, play a pivotal role in actualizing these paradigms.

In Industry 5.0, XR enables personalized training, real-time feedback, and safe simulation of complex tasks, fostering human-machine collaboration and reducing operational risks. Workers can engage with digital twins, cobots, and spatial interfaces that enhance decision-making and procedural accuracy. Immersive learning environments, powered by technologies like VR, AR and MR, are grounded in foundational educational psychology theories that emphasize learner engagement, experience, and cognitive processing(Asoodar, Janesarvatan, Yu, & de Jong, 2024). The ANT and DSRM together form a robust interdisciplinary framework for advancing immersive reality technology-based gamification in sustainable education. ANT treats technologies like VR/AR, educators, learners, and AI agents as co-equal "actors," mapping their interactions to understand how knowledge and technology interventions circulate within the learning ecosystem. When grounded in educational psychology, particularly constructivist learning and cognitive load theories, this fusion ensures that technological innovations are not only technically functional but pedagogically meaningful, adaptive, and capable of scaling across diverse learning contexts(Waliu, Matthew, et al., 2025). The intersection of ANT and DSRM provides a rich, interdisciplinary framework to analyze and construct immersive reality technology-based gamification systems within sustainable educational practice. In the context of immersive learning, the student interacts not only with the instructor but also with simulation environments, virtual rewards, real-time adaptive systems, and learning analytics dashboards. These non-human actors contribute actively to knowledge construction, which aligns with the tenets of constructivist learning theory emphasizing active engagement, situated cognition, and social interaction. DSRM supports the iterative development of immersive learning environments through structured cycles of problem identification, artifact design, testing, and refinement. First, a pedagogical gap is identified: limited engagement and transferability of knowledge in traditional educational models.

Drawing on comparative studies, immersive tools have consistently shown superior results in student motivation, retention, and application of concepts, particularly in science, technology, engineering, mathematics (STEM) and medical education(Bunmi et al., 2024). These empirical insights justify the need for immersive technology-based gamified interventions. During artifact design, immersive applications are conceptualized to leverage gamified simulations, problem-solving quests, and collaborative virtual spaces that prioritize active learning. Cognitive load theory is central during this phase, ensuring the design minimizes extraneous cognitive load while maximizing germane and intrinsic load (Gumel et al., 2019). Visual cues, multimodal feedback, and adaptive scaffolding are embedded to support deep learning without overwhelming working memory. ANT informs the ecosystemic layout, identifying actors (learners, content, AI engines, VR platforms), tracking their interactions, and understanding the negotiation of technology assistances and knowledge within the network(Ugochukwu Okwudili Matthew, Kazaure, Kazaure, Nwamouh, & Chinonso, 2022). For example, a VR simulation's success is contingent on how well the software (non-human actor) aligns with the instructor's pedagogy (human actor) and the learner's cognitive readiness. Implementation and testing phases use feedback from student performance, engagement metrics, and cognitive assessments to iteratively refine the artifact. The final deployment phase includes dissemination across varied contexts, enabling scalability and transferability while maintaining adaptability to local educational cultures. The ANT and DSRM fusion, framed by constructivist and cognitive load theories, offers a holistic, learner-centered model for designing sustainable immersive learning systems that are technically robust, psychologically sound, and educationally transformative(Luo, 2024).

RESEARCH QUESTIONS

There are five thoughtfully crafted research questions to guide the current study on Immersive Reality Technology-Based Gamification in Sustainable Education:

i. How does the integration of immersive technologies (VR/AR) gamification enhance student engagement and learning outcomes in sustainability-focused curricula?
ii. What are the cognitive and emotional impacts of immersive gamified environments on learners compared to traditional instructional methods within sustainability education?
iii. In what ways can ANT and DSRM support the co-construction of knowledge and stakeholder collaboration in immersive education ecosystems?
iv. How do AI-driven adaptive feedback mechanisms within immersive gamified platforms contribute to personalized learning experiences that foster sustainability competencies?
v. What are the key design considerations and limitations in implementing immersive, gamified learning solutions that align with the educational principles of Education 5.0, Industry 5.0, and Society 5.0?

OBJECTIVE OF THE STUDY

By providing students with immersive learning experiences that are interesting, memorable, and productive, AR and VR technologies have the potential to revolutionize education. Lesson-specific information and instructional text can be displayed using AR over the user's actual environment, while VR can make academic subjects more relatable by giving learners new viewpoints and insights. The general field of education have undergone modification due to simulation based technology that have been used to substitute practical resource deficiency. With the use of cutting-edge technology gamification like VR, AR and XR instructors may now tailor their classroom instruction to meet the needs of every student through immersive instructional pedagogy. The development of virtual reality-based educational applications provides new avenues for topical exploration. As innovative methods are developed to improve new pedagogic components in the teaching, among other fields, VR has the potential to be an experience learning tool.

The current paper presented technology approach to education by developing AI integrated cloud-adaptive learning environments with VR and AR gamifications using an ANT model to reinforce TPCK framework for immersive educational technology. The principal aim is to thoroughly investigate the educational use of VR and AR technology as pedagogy tools. In light of its potential to revolutionize healthcare professional training, the study illustrates how VR and AR are affecting collaborative medical education. The study supports the expanding significance and revolutionary potential of VR and AR technologies in the medical field by highlighting their pedagogical advantages, difficulties, and future prospects in health education.

THEORETICAL FRAMEWORK

The integration of XR technology in educational settings is intended to enhance students' learning engagement as active methodologies are at the heart of wide spreading educational gamification on the account that game designs leverages psychological environments to effect learning(Lampropoulos & Kinshuk, 2024). Because of its nature, XR gamification can inspire students to obtain higher academic results by increasing their interest in the subjects they are studying, as well as their involvement, motivation and focus. Medical education and nursing training have demonstrated the value of VR, AR, MR, XR are composed of instructional aids in the evolving digital environment characterized by extreme automation(Jagatheesaperumal, Ahmad, Al-Fuqaha, & Qadir, 2024),(Foster, Moroney, Phillips, & Lilienthal, 2024). VR is a versatile tool that can be used to replicate arthroscopy surgeries and enhance ophthalmologic tests(Ong, Tan, Lam, & Koh, 2021). Medical professionals and nurse educators can benefit from immersive technology-based training that emphasizes skill transferability into the clinical field and offers a rich, dynamic, engaging, and safe learning environment(Tang, Chau, Kwok, Zhu, & Ma, 2022). It encourages learning by doing, closes the theory-practice gap, and enhances the transfer and acquisition of digital proficiencies. At the moment, researchers frequently use VR, AR, and MR technologies as teaching tools to enhance, replace, or supplement conventional teaching techniques in medical education and training(Barteit, Lanfermann, Bärnighausen, Neuhann, & Beiersmann, 2021). The growing importance of extended reality in medicine has led to the creation of platforms that instruct basic topics like human anatomy and educate physicians on intricate surgical techniques(Herur-Raman et al., 2021). With the help of gadgets like Microsoft HoloLens and Google Glass, surgeons may be able to better visualize intraoperative procedures and diagnostic pictures, thereby increasing procedure success and safety(Ong et al., 2021). The advent of Industry 5.0 heralds not only a revolution in technology but also a radical change in the way intelligent machines and people work together to address the need for human centeredness. In order to ensure that employees are capable of meeting the demands of their jobs, training has always been an essential part of the industrial sector and occupational fitness.

With AR, learners can receive step-by-step guidance with instructions projected right into the equipment, as opposed to merely reading procedures or watching someone else completing the task(Bryant & Hemsley, 2024). This interactive method guarantees improved task recall and comprehension while also accelerating the learning process. Because AR can replicate a wide range of scenarios, from routine operations to emergency situations, personnel can be ready for a variety of eventualities. Under AR's careful supervision, individuals can rehearse their responses, polish their abilities, and become skilled at operating machinery, guaranteeing that they are not merely trained but also competent(Bryant & Hemsley, 2024). Even although AR is a disruptive technology on its own, it becomes much more potent when paired with other state-of-the-art technologies like Internet of Things (IoT) which allows for real-time data collection and analysis(Rane, Choudhary, & Rane, 2023c). Imagine an AR-glasses-wearing technician inspecting machines, due to the inbuilt IoT sensors, the glasses can display data instantly, including temperature, pressure, and other operational details. This provides the user with an overall view of the machine's condition and its digital environment. The integration of AR technology and AI algorithms not only let operators monitor real-time data, but they can also suggest maintenance schedules, foresee potential issues, and even recommend operational tweaks for increased efficiency(Savaglio et al., 2020). According to(Tang et al., 2022), medical and clinical workers can benefit from rich, dynamic, safe, and engaging learning experiences through immersive technology-based training that emphasizes the transferability of skills into the clinical setting. It enhances the transfer and development of skills, closes the theory-practice gap, and promotes learning-by-doing(van As & Cooke, 2024). Scholars now frequently use VR, AR, and MR technologies as teaching tools to augment, enhance, or even replace conventional teaching techniques in medical education and training which prompted medical students' anatomy education to use of technology(Yang, 2023).

On the other hand, medical and healthcare practices typically require a wide range of practical abilities which had induced technology such as VR, AR, and MR to be used to improve procedural and practical teaching(Navarro-Parra & Chiappe, 2024). In order to foster technological agility in medical and nursing education, the impacts of simulated training interventions are currently being extensively explored. Studies using randomized controlled trials show that training based on immersive technology may enhance students' acquisition of digital knowledge. Immersive technology is thought to give students a fresh approach to learning and make it easier for them to pick up crucial medical concepts and procedures. VR in particular can be used to produce an accurate and highly interactive operative simulation with opportunities for recording and analyzing findings, especially with the growing usage of virtual training for practitioners and students in the healthcare or medical areas(Barteit et al., 2021). The precision and workflow of clinical abilities including surgery, diagnosis, image reconstruction, and intra-operative viewing could be completely transformed by AR and MR technology. The VR and AR have grown in importance as surgical technology becomes more integrated. This technology has a lot of potential for orthopaedics since it allows users to superimpose digital images on their vision of the real world. The current study looked into how immersive technology might be used in nursing and medical education. According to(Lungu et al., 2021), who evaluated the efficacy of AR in surgical oncology training and procedures, noting that AR can enhance surgical outcomes as well as all other clinical explorations. Examining the psychological consequences of simulation training, it was shown that AR can create training scenarios that are both realistically achievable and emotionally authentic(Kaplan et al., 2021).

According to(Liu et al., 2024), immersive technology in promoting empathy in medical education by showcasing how VR may effectively reduce the emotional and cognitive divide between patients and healthcare practitioners. VR's capacity to enhance retention of complicated anatomical knowledge, complements the empathic approach, examining how these technologies might greatly improve instructional results and learner performance/engagement while synthesizing their many contributions(Barteit et al., 2021). This aspect of the educational revolution that VR and AR are driving is crucial because these technologies help people communicate and comprehend medical concepts more deeply. Furthermore, the creation of virtual reality training programs tailored to medical procedures and anatomy instruction highlighted how effective these programs are at enhancing procedural competencies and learning objectives(Gupta et al., 2023). Enhancing the visibility of anatomical features through the practical applications of AR is a crucial aspect for surgical planning and educational objectives. While AR training will not, at least not anytime soon, replace traditional medical schools, it will augment classroom instruction with 24/7, location-independent access to standardize digital content(Jiang et al., 2022). By using AR platforms, information can be gathered, progress can be monitored, and updates can be done easily as new materials become available. Healthcare applications of augmented reality include complete anatomy, which offers an inside-the-body experience, shoulder arthroscopy, which educates users about arthroscopy procedures(Zuñiga-Aviles & Cruz-Martinez, 2024). A vast array of other professions that are vital to the running of healthcare are also trained in the medical area, in addition to physicians and nurses: midwives, emergency medical technicians, medical assistants, therapists, technicians, and related professions. The VR environment's generative imagination makes it one of the most important components of immersive learning, increasing positive pedagogic encounters(D. Lee, Bathish, & Nelson, 2024). Through the use of virtual reality headgear or goggles, student-nurses can immerse themselves completely in a personalized virtual environment as though they were physically present(Barteit et al., 2021). They can engage with their environment and gain knowledge inside an engaging and educational digital environment. VR may be used to create incredibly realistic simulations that allow trainee nurses to practice problem-solving skills without really putting themselves in danger. Industry 5.0's use of AR and VR is a thorough reference source that will offer customized, easily accessible, and well-thought-out experiences.

The overall effectiveness and experience of education can be improved and applied in a variety of subject matter, contexts, and participants by incorporating design principles that make use of gesture, voice, and hand controls in virtual environments, enabling students to interact with multimedia lessons and learn materials quickly and intuitively, and combining different teaching methods(Lampropoulos & Kinshuk, 2024). Therefore, compared to instructor-led teaching alone, VR and AR can result in higher learning results because of its immersiveness and interactivity depending on the role of teachers. Programs for teacher education are enhanced by VR and AR, which also offers prospects for future educational technology development. This study aims to assess virtual reality's revolutionary potential and its implications for enhancing nursing education through the provision of dynamic and engaging learning environments. Large language model advances and the creation of more potent and lightweight AR glasses have recently being developed. As (H. Lee et al., 2023)points out, with the advancements in big language models and the creation of more lightweight and potent AR glasses, VisionARy is the first system that incorporates ChatGPT into AR glasses to enhance oral language proficiency and offer a contextualized learning environment. In comparison to conventional learning approaches, the evaluation results indicate that VisionARy is highly accepted and has the potential to be effective in enhancing oral language abilities(H. Lee et al., 2023). The paper offered significant new information for the development of language learning systems in the future in a manner that stimulated clinical federated learning paradigms. In order to create a unique intelligent agent for teaching foreign languages to young children, (Topsakal & Topsakal, 2022) presented a framework for creating a language learning software program that uses voicebots AR and ChatGPT, an AI that uses the Large Language Model. The intelligent agent will employ AR and voicebots to create a fun and engaging learning environment(Topsakal & Topsakal, 2022).

According to(Pitura, Kaplan-Rakowski, & Asotska-Wierzba, 2025), exposing pre-service teachers to a variety of teaching and learning scenarios and settings and allowing them to practice and define their skills in completely safe and regulated settings where VR and AR can assist them close training gaps. The use of VR in various educational contexts and levels, as well as the usage of AR head-mounted displays in educational activities, have been the subject of numerous recent systematic literature reviews, overviews, scientific mapping, meta-analyses, and bibliometric studies. Through the hands-on experiences it provides, VR supports effective learning experiences in both K–12 and higher education environments(Waliu, Muojekwu, et al., 2025),(Esseme et al., 2025). It provides new opportunities to enhance students' learning, support diverse teaching approaches, and boost students' motivation and comprehensive scientific indoctrination. VR can also result in positive learning behaviors and attitudes in diverse pedagogic contexts. Because of this, VR and AR can be effectively applied in a variety of educational situations and subject areas, such as science, technology, engineering, art, and mathematics (STEAM) in developing technology for medical and healthcare vocational education(Belbase et al., 2022). The metaverse future digital gamification being a multidisciplinary field of research that has applications in many educational technology contexts(Jibril et al., 2022). In non-gaming situations, gamification applies the game components, techniques, and ideas that make games fun, challenging, fascinating, and engrossing in order to improve end users' motivation, engagement, and experiences while stimulating straightforward pedagogic connections. Since gamification is based on active designs, the theories leverage the psychological principles of learning, it is expected that gamification would be adopted and integrated into educational settings to enhance students' learning experiences and outcomes. By its very nature, gamification may make the educational process more engaging and dynamic, which will increase students' interest in the main subjects and motivate them to perform better academically(Ansar & George, 2022).

According to (Neerupa, Naveen Kumar, Pavithra, & John William, 2024), gamification's motivational components can lead to improved psychological states and desired student academic actions. By emphasizing digital gamification and prompt editing, generative AI also makes it easier to create multimedia learning content, bridging the gap between novice and expert creators. The process effectively prepare the data for the software application by utilizing ChatGPT's functionalities, creating interactive dialogues that was hosted at Google DialogFlow using ChatGPT features. In addition, (Nguyen, Cao, & Trương, 2023) provided a proposal for integrating ChatGPT with VR/AR technology into the biology curriculum of Vietnamese high schools. The framework includes the subsequent steps: (i) Curriculum alignment and lesson planning,(ii) creation and selection of VR/AR resources,(iii) integration of ChatGPT as a virtual tutor,(iv) immersive and interactive learning environments, and(v) mechanisms for evaluation and feedback focus. The systematic approach to effectively integrating ChatGPT with VR/AR technology is provided for educators by this innovative pedagogical interpretation(D. O. Oyekunle et al., 2025). Utilizing ChatGPT in conjunction with VR/AR technologies to teach biology has significant implications for Vietnamese high schools(Rane, Choudhary, & Rane, 2023b). Students' understanding, retention, and enthusiasm in biological topics could all be enhanced by this teaching approach. It also prepares students for future careers in fields that rely heavily on science and technology. It is recommended that future research investigate the efficacy of this approach, its impact on students' learning outcomes, and strategies for overcoming implementation challenges. According to (Villegas-Ch, García-Ortiz, & Sánchez-Viteri, 2024), students can access an extensive library of biological knowledge and resources by integrating ChatGPT with VR/AR technology. ChatGPT may provide comprehensive explanations, retrieved pertinent data from reliable sources, and multimedia content, including interactive simulations and 3D models that enhances students' learning experiences(Oriakhi et al., 2024).

LITERATURE REVIEW

The convergence of immersive technology with the paradigms shift to Education 5.0, Industry 5.0, and Society 5.0 marks a transformative shift in the pursuit of sustainable education(Supriya et al., 2024),(Ugochukwu Okwudili Matthew, Kazaure, et al., 2024). Immersive technologies such as VR, AR, and MR are increasingly recognized for their potential to foster experiential, learner-centered environments that align with the goals of sustainable development(Papanastasiou, Drigas, Skianis, Lytras, & Papanastasiou, 2019). These technologies enable students to engage in contextualized, interactive learning experiences that promote critical thinking, empathy, and real-world problem-solving key competencies for addressing global challenges. Education 5.0 builds upon the digital foundations of Education 4.0 but shifts the focus toward human-centered, value-driven learning(Rane, Choudhary, & Rane, 2023a). It emphasizes emotional intelligence, ethical reasoning, and sustainability as core educational outcomes. This paradigm supports the integration of immersive technologies to personalize learning pathways, enhance engagement, and cultivate lifelong learning habits. According to (Carayannis & Morawska, 2023), Education 5.0 also aligns with the demands of Industry 5.0 by preparing learners to collaborate with intelligent systems in adaptive, creative, and socially responsible ways. Industry 5.0, as envisioned by the European Commission, prioritizes the synergy between human creativity and advanced technologies to foster inclusive and sustainable industrial ecosystems(Costa, 2024). In educational contexts, this translates to the use of AI-enhanced immersive platforms that support skill development, innovation, and ethical decision-making. However, (Carayannis, Kostis, Kafka, & Valvi, 2024) argue that Industry 5.0's emphasis on personalization and human-machine collaboration necessitates educational models that are flexible, interdisciplinary, and technologically enriched.

Society 5.0 extends this vision by advocating for a super-smart, inclusive society where digital transformation serves human welfare and environmental stewardship. It calls for educational reforms that integrate technological literacy, ethics, and sustainability into curricula(De Villiers, 2024). Immersive learning environments, when aligned with Society 5.0, democratize access to quality education and empower learners to become agents of change in their communities(Mobo, 2024). Empirical studies support the efficacy of immersive technologies in enhancing learning outcomes, particularly in STEM and environmental education. According to (Damaševičius & Sidekerskienė, 2024), highlights how virtual field trips and digital storytelling tools can bridge the gap between theoretical knowledge and real-world application, fostering deeper understanding and civic engagement. However, sustainability concerns such as device lifecycle, energy consumption, and digital equity must be addressed to ensure responsible implementation(Goel, Masurkar, & Pathade, 2024). As a matter of fact, the integration of immersive technology within the frameworks of Education 5.0, Industry 5.0, and Society 5.0 offers a holistic approach to sustainable education. It not only enhances pedagogical effectiveness but also aligns learning with broader societal and environmental goals, paving the way for a more equitable, resilient, and future-ready global education system. According to(Li & Duan, 2025), Industry 5.0 enhances AI by encouraging ethical innovation in education and human-AI collaboration. Society 5.0 extends these goals by ensuring equitable access and aligning education with social sustainability(Ugochukwu Okwudili Matthew, Oyekunle, et al., 2024). Together, these paradigms create a transformative ecosystem where technology enhances pedagogy, equity, and lifelong learning for a resilient future. Highlighting some important areas where AI is having a big impact on fine tuning the Education 5.0 and Society 5.0 modern civilization include:

i. **Gamification and Multimedia Simulation-Based Learning:** The ability of game-based learning to interest students in a manner that traditional classroom instruction may not is a critical component of Education 5.0(Oberer & Erkollar, 2022). Game-based learning has the potential to improve learning outcomes, motivation, and engagement. Assessing the efficacy of gamification in education is crucial in order to ascertain its influence on the learning outcomes of students. A variety of indicators are available for evaluating the efficacy of game-based learning with respect to task accomplishments. Student engagement, which measures students' drive, enthusiasm, and participation in learning activities using multimedia simulation as a curriculum pedagogy tool, is one crucial indicator(D. Oyekunle, Matthew, Waliu, & Fatai, 2024). Game-based learning has been shown in numerous studies to boost motivation and student participation in computer science classes. According to, (J. J. Xu, Sun, Liu, Zhang, & Zhou, 2025)game-based learning can boost student interest and engagement in science classes, which will increase academic accomplishment. Another crucial indicator is student feedback, which sheds light on how well students believe game-based learning activities work.

ii. **Federated Learning**: Federated learning is a novel approach to AI training that is quickly taking the lead in complying with a number of new privacy requirements on digital information assemblage(Mathew, Rodriguez, Rosa, Ayub, & Adasme, 2024). With the analysis of large amounts of data, AI systems in Education 5.0 are able to recognize the distinct learning styles, preferences, and strengths of each student, allowing for the customization of learning experiences to the individual(Alam, 2022). Students will be provided with content and activities that are tailored to their individual needs, which makes the design of individualized learning paths easier. Intelligent AI-driven adaptive learning platforms dynamically modify the level of difficulty and speed of lessons according to each student's progress, maximizing comprehension and retention(Gligorea et al., 2023). The federated learning will provides a method to accessing the raw data coming from distributed data warehouse repositories, sensors on satellites, machines and an increasing number of smart gadgets at home and on our bodies by processing data at their source(W. Xu et al., 2023).Federated learning provides a mechanism to unlock information to fuel new AI applications by training AI models without attempting to manipulate data, making it possible for AI to be widely used in products like chatbots, spam filters, and recommendation engines.

iii. **Smart Tutoring Applications**: AI-powered intelligent tutoring programs provide real-time, personalized assistance to students. These systems offer additional resources, coaching, and feedback based on each student's achievement. Intelligent teaching systems adapt to learning speeds and continuously assess knowledge, making learning more engaging and effective. This can be accomplished by utilizing machine learning and artificial intelligence to develop individualized lesson plans and modify education in real time in response to student success. Personalized learning is a key component of Education 5.0, which seeks to adapt the educational process to the unique requirements and skills of every student(Supriya et al., 2024). In addition to the flexibility of the training to adjust to each student's unique needs and talents, evaluation metrics that gauge the success of personalized learning may include student engagement, motivation, and achievement.

iv. **Expanded Curriculum Creation**: Large-scale educational data is analyzed by AI to find patterns, gaps, and places where courses need to be improved(D. O. T. Oyekunle, Okwudili Matthew, Preston, & Boohene, 2024). Teachers are able to create more effective and relevant lesson plans because to this data-driven methodology. The AI systems also evaluate the effectiveness of various teaching approaches and suggest modifications to improve overall learning results.

v. **Interactive Education & Context Gamification**: Students' motivation and engagement are increased by AI in educational games and interactive learning platforms. For the reason that AI algorithms customize gaming scenarios and challenges based on individual player achievement, learners are immersed in an engaging and pleasurable environment. Gamification and AI turn traditional learning into a dynamic, participatory educational process(Matthew & Kazaure, 2020). AI in Education 5.0 smoothly incorporates gamification features and simulations into the learning process. Educational platforms encourage students and make learning fun by adding multimedia game-like aspects. For courses like biology and engineering that need real-world application, simulations offer useful, hands-on experiences in virtual environments.

vi. **VR and AR immersive technology:** By enabling immersive and interactive settings, AR and VR technologies have the potential to completely transform the educational process. By tailoring virtual experiences to each user's unique learning preferences and styles, AI can improve these technologies in Industry 5.0 human eccentricity(Zafar, Langås, & Sanfilippo, 2024). To develop immersive learning experiences, AI in Education 5.0 combines VR and AR. With the use of these cutting-edge technology, students can now connect with instructional materials in three dimensions multimedia presentation, increasing their comprehension and assimilations.

vii. **NLP & Conversational ChatGPT**: In terms of language models, generative artificial intelligence (GenAI) and ChatGPT in particular are significant technological developments that can revolutionize NLP and change the educational landscape(Ugochukwu Okwudili Matthew, Bakare, Ebong, Ndukwu, & Nwanakwaugwu, 2023). The educational landscape of the twenty-first century will be significantly impacted by the recommendations provided by ChatGPT users, which have the potential to enhance instruction and learning. Due to a number of factors, educational robots that harness the power of conversational interaction are becoming more accessible. In the future, excessive digital automation will probably also become commonplace, leading to possible uses of GenAI for NLP synthesis. This is in addition to the scientific advancements made in industry 5.0 through human-robot collaboration. Students receive fast feedback from NLP systems with AI capabilities that automatically interpret written assignments. Additionally, it facilitates continuous improvement by expediting the grading process and providing insightful feedback on students' writing skills. With NLP, linguistic learning programs that provide personalized practice and feedback may also be created. A strong and adaptable AI language model that could assist with a variety of tasks, including data analysis, translation, text production, and codification, was the goal behind the creation of ChatGPT(Oriakhi et al., 2024).

SYSTEM FLOW DIAGRAM

Figure 1. The system flow diagram for the Immersive pedagogy Paradigms

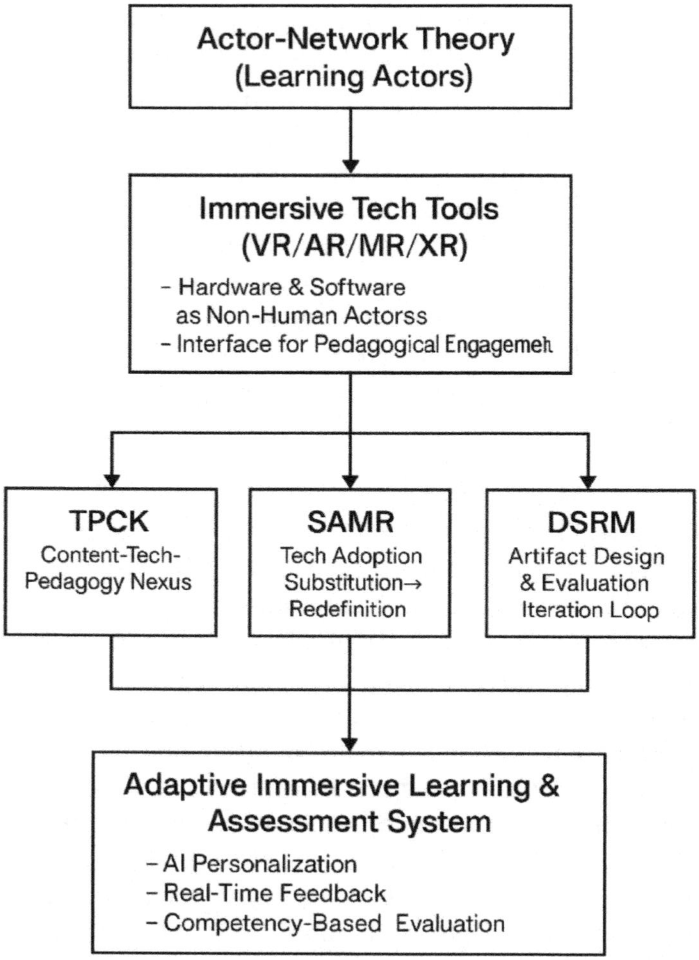

The Figure 1 thoughtfully connects key theoretical frameworks, ANT, TPCK, SAMR, and DSRM, with immersive technologies (VR/AR/MR/XR), presenting a layered model for educational innovation. ANT anchors the network, recognizing both human and technological actors. The immersive technology layer is not just visual but interactive, serving as the medium through which learners engage and co-create knowledge. TPCK ensures balanced integration of content, pedagogy, and technology, while SAMR tracks the depth of transformation. DSRM's iterative loop promotes continuous refinement of digital learning artifacts. The final layer, an adaptive learning and assessment system, translates these interactions into measurable outcomes like skill proficiency and emotional growth. In practice, this model supports the development of immersive lesson plans, AI-enabled assessments, and collaborative simulations. Educators can track student progression across SAMR levels, refine instructional design via DSRM, and personalize learning using TPCK. ANT's network mapping helps identify key actors and barriers in implementation, facilitating scalable, context-sensitive strategies aligned with Education 5.0 goals.

METHODOLOGY OF THE STUDY

The study utilizes a hybrid methodology integrating ANT, TPCK, Substitution, Augmentation, Modification, Redefinition (SAMR), and DSRM, positioning learners, educators, and VR/AR tools as co-actors in a dynamic educational network. Immersive technologies are applied through iterative artifact design, guided by pedagogical coherence and transformative tech integration. Assessment is embedded using AI-driven feedback, competency-based evaluations, and emotionally intelligent simulations. The approach aligns with Education 5.0 and Industry 5.0 values, emphasizing ethical, personalized, and sustainable learning. Research questions examine engagement, personalization, and authentic skill transfer, with outcomes demonstrating enhanced participation, adaptability, and measurable learner growth through immersive experience. This foundation supports a dynamic, interdisciplinary approach where immersive VR/AR tools co-evolve with educational goals. Combined with DSRM, TPCK, and SAMR model, the methodology enables iterative artifact development, adaptive learning design, and transformative educational experiences rooted in sustainability and personalization. This integration ensures that technological innovations are pedagogically meaningful, contextually grounded, and dynamically scalable. At the core, ANT serves as the ontological foundation by positioning both human and non-human actors students, instructors, VR headsets, AR content, AI systems, and learning platforms as network participants that continuously negotiate meaning, functionality, and educational outcomes. In an immersive environment, ANT enables the analysis of how technologies do not merely support education but actively shape pedagogical processes, learner engagement, and knowledge construction. The technology becomes an autonomous actor, co-creating learning experiences through interactions and feedback loops. Complementing ANT, DSRM provides a pragmatic framework for artifact development.

It begins with identifying a relevant educational problem, such as low learner retention or limited experiential learning in traditional models. Based on this, a VR/AR-based educational artifact is iteratively designed, demonstrated, evaluated, and refined. DSRM supports the innovation cycle by testing how immersive environments can be practically integrated into instructional systems and by measuring their effectiveness using user feedback, learning analytics, and achievement data. The TPCK framework grounds the methodology pedagogically. It guides educators and designers in ensuring that content (subject matter), pedagogy (teaching strategies), and technology (VR/AR) are harmonized(D. Oyekunle, B. E. A. Claude, et al., 2024). This triad ensures that immersive solutions are not technologically driven for novelty's sake but are designed to promote content mastery through pedagogical logic. For example, in a biology class, an AR model of a heart must not only be accurate but also accompanied by interactive instruction that aligns with learning objectives. The SAMR model offers evaluative scaffolding to gauge how deeply immersive technologies transform the educational experience. At lower levels, VR/AR may serve as substitutes or augmentations for example, replacing textbook diagrams with 3D models. At higher levels, these tools can modify or redefine tasks, allowing students to engage in exploratory dissections, virtual surgeries, or collaborative problem-solving simulations that were previously impossible. Together, these frameworks interact symbiotically. ANT maps the socio-technical relationships that define the learning environment; DSRM structures the iterative process of system development; TPCK ensures educational coherence; and SAMR assesses the transformative impact of immersive technologies. This integrated methodology is vital for advancing immersive education as a sustainable, adaptive, and research-driven field.

Figure 2. Technological pedagogy content knowledge (TPCK) model: Author Illustration.

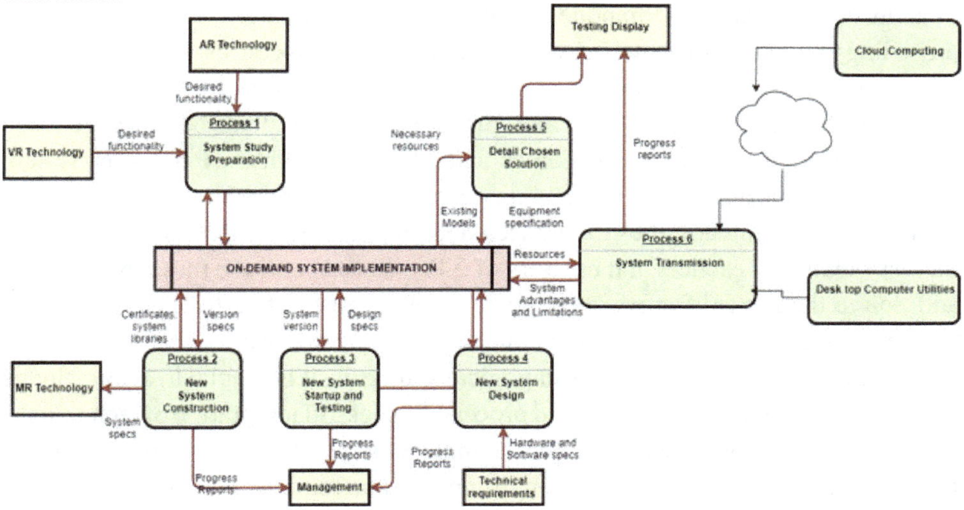

TPCK development pipelines and incremental process techniques are illustrated in Figure 2, which also provides theoretical frameworks that emphasize the educational and psychological underpinnings of integrating VR and AR technology in medical education. Innovative answers to long-standing problems in the profession can be found by utilizing the immersive, interactive potential of VR and AR to improve medical education and training. **Process 1: System Study Planning** — choosing and implementing VR or AR technologies based on criteria that can be used for the technology or learning objectives. **Process 2: New System** — calculating the impacts or results of the educational project in a realistic way, considering the likelihood or viability of each result, such as if we have the required technical personnel on hand. Through gamified components and real-time feedback, this method not only improves physical results by encouraging the recovery of motor skills and boosting strength and flexibility, but it also increases motivation and adherence to pedagogy procedures and services. Applications for AR enhance physical therapy and cognitive rehabilitation by superimposing therapeutic exercises on the patient's surroundings, which makes the process more engaging and pleasurable. Using AR, for instance, individuals recovering from stroke or traumatic brain injury might be encouraged to practice spatial reasoning, memory, and problem-solving skills by projecting cognitive exercises. **Process 3: Startup and Experimental Testing on the new system** — this entails comparing the results to the chosen criteria for the new system for sustained impact of VR and AR on pedagogy processes, providing valuable insights for their integration into education systems as TPCK component.

Process 4: Design of the New System- where the TPACK model concentrates on the integration of technology inside particular content areas, the best approach to address the pedagogy component transmission is ultimately determined by the preceding processes. **Process 5:** Designated Solution in Specifics- the last action to take is communicating the process's results, where the carefully organized project process is demonstrated to provide an explanation of the rationale behind the chosen challenge, design, technology, outcomes, and evaluation methods. **Process 6:** System Communication/ Broadcast- Depending on the sending and receiving protocol, the local computer protocol, the cloud-based delivery process, or both may have basic delivery feature. Teachers and creators of XR materials can use these examples in addition to theoretical frameworks and concepts to ensure that their designs result in memorable and readily available educational opportunities.

To develop a new method in pedagogical synthesis, it is crucial to acknowledge that learning is a socially complicated process. Successful integration of technology-enabled teaching approaches requires an understanding of the individual characteristics of each student as well as the environmental factors that may impact learning results(Alamri, Watson, & Watson, 2021). Each case study's main flaw was that it wasn't made or supported for a broad curriculum or long-term incorporation into the university system. Technology serves as a straightforward replacement for teaching aids in the classroom setting while enhancing educational activities through GenAI augmentation(Yadav, 2025). When technology is used appropriately, it significantly redesigns instruction and totally transforms the conventional method of teaching. Among the instructional enhancement techniques are substitution and augmentation, whereas the pedagogy transformation tools are redefinition and modification(Son, 2024). The substitution and augmentation approaches are usually associated with the first three levels of Bloom's taxonomy of education which include knowledge, comprehension, and application for educators who are more familiar with Bloom's Taxonomy, whereas the modification and redefinition approaches are thought to be equivalent to the top three learning stages that comprised of analysis, synthesis, and evaluation(Rothe & Snyder, 2024). The SAMR model, introduced by Ruben Puentedura, is a framework that helps educators evaluate how technology is used in teaching(Adeshina, 2024). It outlines four levels of integration. The first two Substitution and Augmentation enhance traditional tasks. Substitution involves replacing a traditional tool with a digital one without changing the task's function, while Augmentation adds functional improvements. The next two Modification and Redefinition—are transformative. Modification allows significant redesign of tasks using technology, while Redefinition enables creation of entirely new tasks that were previously inconceivable. The model encourages educators to move beyond basic integration and leverage technology to transform learning experiences meaningfully(Buledi & Badariah, 2024). It's critical to keep in mind, that SAMR model is an effective reflecting tool for evaluating the extent of technological integration, it is not a foolproof answer to all problems in education. Within this framework, ANT has also been applied to investigate the dynamics of drift in digital processes and to build AI that can collaborate with specialists in human fields.

Information system research has demonstrated that ANT can be used to create a distinctive contribution by enhancing comprehension of educational methodology in the distributed social context(Castañeda, Marín, & Villar-Onrubia, 2024). According to(Ellinger, Mini, Gregory, & Widjaja, 2021), who proposed a theory in which humans assign duties and rights to an agentic information system to carry out a task. The foundation of our research lies in the socio-technical viewpoint, which emphasizes the cognitive synthesis of clinical artifacts as a means of enhancing nursing and medical education. The paper looked at how simulation artifacts affected users' ability to reason in clinical and medical assignments. Our assumption is that the interaction between human and technology based reasoning is steering conversation around cognitive reasoning from the standpoint of clinical and medical story-making. We contend that the incorporation of immersive technology (VR and AR) into medical education causes cognitive shift. It is important to comprehend the cognitive shift that occurs between case-based and model-based thinking in order to fully recognize the active influences simulation models have on people's understanding of complex systems and challenges it present. Forming assumptions, conducting experiments, and drawing comparisons all involve cognitive shifts in both deductive (model-based) and inductive (case-based) reasoning(Kapsali, Bayer, Brailsford, & Bolt, 2022).

Figure 3. VR and AR-integrated cloud-adaptive learning environments, author illustration

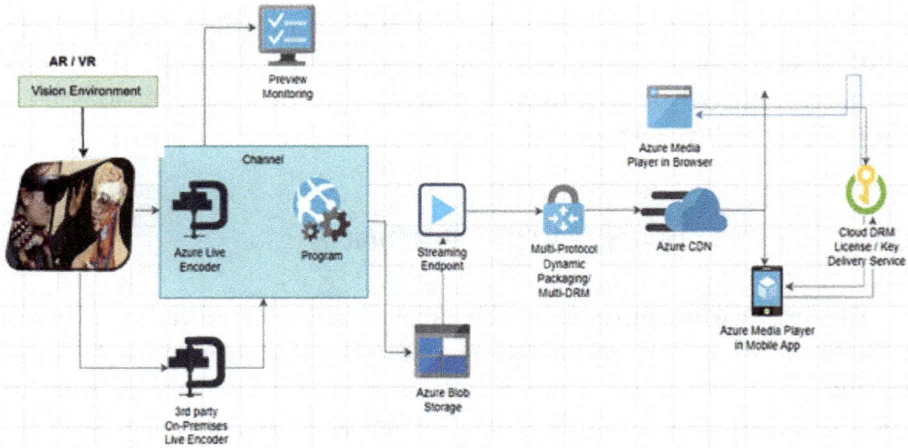

Refer to **Figure 3**, the aim of the study was to illustrate situations in which the technology actor actively participates in the process of resource integration and service exchange with the user and other relevant actors, leading to interactive and context-aware VR and AR mobile gamification. AI is significantly contributing to the development of VR and AR systems, particularly in the area of clinical and medical education. These interactive, realistic training scenarios are made possible by these immersive technologies, and they can be very similar to actual healthcare operations. AI algorithms are used to create distinct patient-based anatomical models and intricate, dynamic environments, giving trainees a safe and regulated environment in which to practice a range of surgical approaches and methods. In order to provide a more effective and interesting learning experience, AI can also enable real-time customization of the VR and AR scenarios based on the trainee's performance. The goal of the multidisciplinary field of AI in computer science is to develop intelligent agents and platforms that can carry out tasks that normally demand cognitive abilities similar to those of humans. In order to perceive, reason, learn, and adapt to new information, AI systems use techniques including machine learning, deep learning, natural language processing, computer vision, and expert systems. This research aims to identify the main players in ANT, elucidate their recruiting process and demonstrate their impact on educational problem-solving. Through the integration of numerous AI approaches, scholars can create intelligent agents capable of addressing intricate issues and revolutionizing multiple facets of human existence, such as healthcare and education instruction. The specialized use of AR and VR in easing communication and information processing inside clinical training environments is growing, with the goal of providing improvements in AI-driven medical training sites. A vital component of medical education is effective communication, and by using VR and AR to translate and transcribe trainer comments to trainees, learning outcomes and experiences can be substantially enhanced. In addition to exploring VR and AR's potential uses in transcription, translation, feedback data summarization, and real-time corrections and recommendations for instructors, the research also attempts to emphasize how these technologies can help close this communication gap.

DISCUSSION OF RESEARCH FINDINGS

The empirical findings in Table 1 highlight the superior performance of immersive education across multiple domains engagement, cognitive retention, skill acquisition, and inclusivity. While these benefits underscore the transformative potential of VR/AR, the analysis must consider limitations such as accessibility gaps, device costs, and cognitive overload risks. Though immersive environments offer personalization and real-time feedback, their long-term pedagogical impact and scalability require further evaluation. The contrast with traditional methods reveals promise, but also calls for nuanced integration and contextual adaptation.

Table 1.

Dimension	Immersive Education (VR/AR/Gamification)	Traditional Learning Methods
Engagement & Motivation	Highly engaging due to interactive, gamified, and sensory-rich experiences; fosters intrinsic motivation and learner curiosity(Yeganeh, Fenty, Chen, Simpson, & Hatami, 2025).	Often passive; relies on lectures and textbooks; may result in lower attention and motivation.
Cognitive Impact	Enhances higher-order thinking, critical reasoning, and spatial skills through simulation and real-time feedback(D. Oyekunle, Ugochukwu, Rosa, Rodriguez, & Fatai, 2024).	Emphasizes memorization and factual recall; limited opportunities for experiential or spatial learning.
Personalization & Adaptability	AI-driven systems tailor content to individual pace, performance, and learning style; supports inclusive, differentiated learning(D. Oyekunle, B. E. A. Claude, et al., 2024).	One-size-fits-all approach; minimal adaptation to learner differences.
Skill Transfer & Practicality	High transferability to real-world scenarios; especially effective in technical and clinical fields using simulations(Waliu, Muojekwu, et al., 2025).	Often abstract; practical application may be limited to labs or external settings.
Emotional & Social Learning	Encourages collaboration, empathy, and emotional engagement through role-playing and scenario-based learning(Lavanya, Somu, & Mishra, 2024).	Focuses on individual tasks and rote learning; less emphasis on emotional or collaborative development.
Instructional Feedback	Immediate and data-driven feedback through AI and game mechanics enhances reflection and learning(Jibril et al., 2022).	Often delayed or generalized; dependent on teacher availability.
Accessibility & Reach	Expands access via mobile and cloud-based XR platforms; supports remote and underrepresented learners(Sharma, Channa, Malhotra, Jain, & Kumar, 2025).	Tied to physical classrooms; accessibility limited by geography and infrastructure.
Cognitive Load Management	Uses multimodal delivery, but requires careful design to avoid overload(Ugochukwu O Matthew & Kazaure, 2020).	Generally linear and less cognitively demanding; may under-stimulate advanced learners.
Assessment & Evaluation	Real-time analytics and adaptive assessments provide ongoing performance tracking and formative insights.	Standardized tests dominate; limited formative or process-based feedback mechanisms.
Sustainability & Future Alignment	Aligns with Education 5.0, Industry 5.0, and Society 5.0 principles, promotes lifelong learning, ethical reasoning, and skill readiness for evolving societies(Ajani, Gamede, & Bansal, 2024).	Rooted in 20th-century paradigms; slower to adapt to technological and societal shifts.

Table 2. Linking Theoretical Concepts to Practice in Immersive Education

Theoretical Framework	Practical Implementation	Measurable Outcomes
Actor-Network Theory (ANT)	Treats VR/AR tools, students, educators, and pedagogical strategies as co-actors in a learning network.	Network analysis showing interaction density; stakeholder mapping; collaboration levels.
TPCK Framework	Guides the integration of technology with content and pedagogy ensuring tech use is contextually relevant.	Pre/post lesson evaluations; teacher proficiency rubrics; instructional effectiveness scores.
SAMR Model	Classifies tech integration from substitution to redefinition of learning tasks.	Task complexity ratings; student-created artifacts showing transformed learning processes.
Design Science Research Methodology (DSRM)	Facilitates iterative development of immersive learning artifacts aligned with educational goals.	Prototype usability testing; learning gains from simulation; student satisfaction surveys.
Education 5.0 Principles	Emphasizes emotional intelligence, ethics, and human-centered design in education.	SEL (Social-Emotional Learning) metrics; ethical decision-making simulations; learner reflection scores.
Industry 5.0 Values	Promotes collaboration between humans and intelligent systems in real-world task simulations.	Workplace-readiness assessments; performance in XR-based training environments.

The **table 2** effectively bridges theoretical models with real-world application in immersive education, showcasing measurable outcomes for each framework. Its strength lies in clarifying abstract concepts like ANT and TPCK through tangible metrics such as collaboration levels and instructional effectiveness. However, some outcome indicators like student satisfaction surveys and ethical decision-making simulations may oversimplify complex learning processes or lack standardized validation. In addition, scalability and contextual adaptability across diverse learning environments are not addressed. The table could benefit from linking data sources and specifying how indicators are measured. Overall, it offers a strong foundation for design but needs refinement for longitudinal, empirical validity.

LIMITATIONS OF THE STUDY

While this study offers a comprehensive framework for integrating immersive technologies and AI into education, several limitations must be acknowledged. First, the implementation of VR/AR/MR tools is resource-intensive, requiring significant financial investment, technical infrastructure, and ongoing maintenance. This may limit scalability and accessibility, particularly in under-resourced or rural educational settings, potentially reinforcing existing digital divides. Second, the study's reliance on emerging technologies introduces challenges related to usability, interoperability, and rapid obsolescence. As platforms and devices evolve quickly, maintaining consistency in research outcomes and ensuring long-term applicability of findings can be difficult. Additionally, the immersive nature of these tools may lead to cognitive overload or physical discomfort (e.g., motion sickness), especially with prolonged use, which could affect learner engagement and performance.

Third, while AI and generative tools like ChatGPT offer personalized feedback and adaptive learning, they also raise ethical concerns regarding data privacy, algorithmic bias, and the potential for over-reliance on machine-generated content. These issues require careful governance and transparent design. Furthermore, the study's theoretical integration—combining ANT, TPCK, SAMR, and DSRM while innovative, may present complexity in practical application. Educators may require extensive training to navigate and implement the model effectively, which could hinder adoption. Lastly, the study's findings may be context-specific, particularly in fields like medical education, and may not generalize across all disciplines or cultural settings without adaptation. Future research should explore longitudinal impacts, cross-disciplinary applications, and strategies for inclusive, ethical scaling of immersive educational technologies.

FUTURE RESEARCH FOCUS

Future research on immersive reality technology-based gamification in sustainable education should explore adaptive and emotionally intelligent learning systems that leverage AI to personalize VR/AR experiences. Investigations should assess long-term learning outcomes, environmental impacts of immersive tech deployment, and inclusive design for diverse learners. Cross-disciplinary approaches, blending neuroscience, educational psychology, and sustainability science, will be essential in optimizing cognitive engagement and real-world skill transfer. Emphasis should be placed on scalable, low-resource solutions that ensure global access and align with the goals of Education 5.0 and Society 5.0. Since games and gamification components are inherently fulfilling, they can also have a beneficial effect on students' emotions, which are crucial components of education since they have the power to either support or undermine learning as well as students' focus and involvement. The constructivist and contextual learning theories, which contend that students are more likely to learn and attain superior learning outcomes when they actively engage in the learning activities, are thus supported by augmented reality and gamification. Therefore future applications of gamified augmented reality should have the potential to influence students' social, emotional, and cognitive development. As a result, a lot of considerations should be made when creating these instructional applications.

Because both gamification and augmented reality are multimodal, special care should be taken to create learning activities that don't overwhelm students' cognitive capacities. Therefore, the many gamification components that are employed to create a constructive and engaging learning environment and encourage students to participate more actively and for longer periods of time ought to concentrate on addressing certain educational contexts and activities.

CONCLUSION

This study underscores the transformative potential of integrating VR, AR, and gamified learning approaches into education systems aligned with the frameworks of Education 5.0, Industry 5.0, and Society 5.0. These immersive tools are not only technological enhancements but active pedagogical agents that reshape how learners interact with content, instructors, and one another. They support constructivist and experiential learning principles, enabling students to explore, experiment, and apply knowledge in realistic virtual environments that mirror complex real-world scenarios. The study emphasizes that gamified immersive environments significantly improve engagement, learner motivation, and cognitive and behavioral outcomes. Real-time feedback, simulation-based practice, and adaptive learning pathways powered by AI promote personalization and inclusivity, particularly in fields like healthcare, technical education, and sustainability education. The emotional and social dimensions of learning are also enriched, as gamification fosters collaboration, persistence, and curiosity. Using ANT and DSRM, the research maps the human and non-human actors, students, technologies, AI systems, educators and their co-constructed roles in building effective learning ecosystems.

Meanwhile, frameworks like TPCK and SAMR ensure that immersive learning designs are pedagogically coherent, content-specific, and reflective of transformative change. The findings call for continued research, policy development, and cross-disciplinary collaboration to ensure immersive education contributes meaningfully to global educational sustainability and prepares learners for complex, interconnected future societies. It emphasizes ethical, adaptive learning with AI-driven assessment. Objectives include promoting sustainability, personalization, and competency-based evaluation. The research questions ask how immersive tools enhance engagement, align with personalized ethical learning, and support real-time assessment. Findings show VR/AR increase learner motivation, enable differentiated instruction through AI feedback, and facilitate authentic, task-based assessments reflecting future-ready educational paradigms. Ultimately, the study concludes that immersive reality technology and gamification should not be considered optional digital enhancements but vital components of sustainable, inclusive, and future-oriented education. These tools serve as catalysts for shifting from passive to active learning, from standardized to personalized instruction, and from teacher-centered delivery to student-driven exploration. To realize this vision, educational stakeholders must invest in inclusive design, teacher training, policy alignment, and infrastructure that supports broad access and long-term adoption.

CONFLICT OF INTEREST

There is no conflict of interest regarding this publication.

REFERENCES

Adel, A. (2024). The convergence of intelligent tutoring, robotics, and IoT in smart education for the transition from industry 4.0 to 5.0. *Smart Cities*, *7*(1), 325–369.

Adeshina, A. E. (2024). From Theory to Practice: A Framework for Inclusive Technology Integration in Education. *International Journal of Instructional Technology and Educational Studies*, *5*(1), 1–6.

Aheleroff, S., Huang, H., Xu, X., & Zhong, R. Y. (2022). Toward sustainability and resilience with Industry 4.0 and Industry 5.0. *Frontiers in Manufacturing Technology*, *2*, 951643.

Ajani, O. A., Gamede, B. T., & Bansal, R. (2024). Challenges and Opportunities of Integrating Industry 5.0 and Emerging Technologies in Higher Education for Enhancing Employability Skills. *Industry 5.0 and Emerging Technologies: Transformation Through. Technology and Innovation*, •••, 217–230.

Alam, A. (2022). Employing adaptive learning and intelligent tutoring robots for virtual classrooms and smart campuses: Reforming education in the age of artificial intelligence *Advanced computing and intelligent technologies* [Springer.]. *Proceedings of ICACIT*, *2022*, 395–406.

Alamri, H. A., Watson, S., & Watson, W. (2021). Learning technology models that support personalization within blended learning environments in higher education. *TechTrends*, *65*(1), 62–78.

Ansar, M., & George, G. (2022). Gamification in education and its impact on student motivation—a critical review. *Emerging IT/ICT and AI Technologies Affecting Society*, 161-170.

Asoodar, M., Janesarvatan, F., Yu, H., & de Jong, N. (2024). Theoretical foundations and implications of augmented reality, virtual reality, and mixed reality for immersive learning in health professions education. *Advances in Simulation (London, England)*, *9*(1), 36. PMID: 39252139

Barteit, S., Lanfermann, L., Bärnighausen, T., Neuhann, F., & Beiersmann, C. (2021). Augmented, mixed, and virtual reality-based head-mounted devices for medical education: Systematic review. *JMIR Serious Games*, *9*(3), e29080. PMID: 34255668

Belbase, S., Mainali, B. R., Kasemsukpipat, W., Tairab, H., Gochoo, M., & Jarrah, A. (2022). At the dawn of science, technology, engineering, arts, and mathematics (STEAM) education: Prospects, priorities, processes, and problems. *International Journal of Mathematical Education in Science and Technology*, *53*(11), 2919–2955.

Bryant, L., & Hemsley, B. (2024). Augmented reality: A view to future visual supports for people with disability. *Disability and Rehabilitation. Assistive Technology, 19*(3), 800–813. PMID: 36149835

Buledi, M. H., & Badariah, T. A. T. (2024). Exploring Digital Technology Usage among English Language Instructors at a Saudi Higher Education Institution and Validating a Hierarchical Structure of Usage Based on the SAMR Model. *IIUM Journal of Educational Studies, 12*(1), 90–111.

Bunmi, E. E., Esegbona-Isikeh, O. M., Oriakhi, V. N., Akiotu, C. A., Emakporuena, D., & Matthew, U. O. (2024). STEM application in education: Implication of STEM computational paradigm on employment prospects. *HAFED POLY Journal of Science. Management and Technology, 6*(1), 131–148.

Carayannis, E. G., Kostis, P. C., Kafka, K. I., & Valvi, T. (2024). *Toward Industry 6.0 and Techno-Centric vs Human-Centric Smart Balancing: The Journey from Industry and Society 4.0 toward Industry and Society 5.0 and Beyond Sustainable Economic Development*. Routledge.

Carayannis, E. G., & Morawska, J. (2023). *University and education 5.0 for emerging trends, policies and practices in the concept of industry 5.0 and society 5.0 Industry 5.0: Creative and Innovative Organizations*. Springer.

Castañeda, L., Marín, V. I., & Villar-Onrubia, D. (2024). Relational topologies in the learning activity spaces: Operationalising a sociomaterial approach. *Educational Technology Research and Development, 72*(5), 2793–2815.

Costa, E. (2024). Industry 5.0 and SDG 9: A symbiotic dance towards sustainable transformation. *Sustainable Earth Reviews, 7*(1), 4.

Damaševičius, R., & Sidekerskienė, T. (2024). Virtual worlds for learning in metaverse: A narrative review. *Sustainability, 16*(5), 2032.

De Villiers, C. (2024). The Impact of Society 5.0 on Curriculum Development in Higher Education. *Journal of Ethics in Higher Education*, (4), 1–25.

Ellinger, E., Mini, T., Gregory, R., & Widjaja, T. (2021). Facilitating Collective Action in Agentic IS Platforms: The Case of Decentralized Autonomous Organizations. *University of Miami Business School Research Paper*(3938489).

Esseme, A. C. B., Oladipupo, M. A., Ogechukwu, O. N., Andrew-Vitalis, N., Akpan, E. E., Oseni, V. E., & Matthew, U. O. (2025). Healthcare Applications of Augmented Reality (AR) and Virtual Reality (VR): Immersive Simulation in Medical-Clinical Education. In Mazhar Hussain, S., & Nawaz Hakro, A. (Eds.), *Creating Immersive Learning Experiences Through Virtual Reality (VR)* (pp. 201–238). IGI Global.

Foster, T. C., Moroney, W. F., Phillips, H. L., & Lilienthal, M. G. (2024). Human Factors in Simulation and Training: An Overview. *Human Factors in Simulation and Training*, 1-64.

Gligorea, I., Cioca, M., Oancea, R., Gorski, A.-T., Gorski, H., & Tudorache, P. (2023). Adaptive Learning Using Artificial Intelligence in e-Learning: A Literature Review. *Education Sciences*, *13*(12), 1216.

Goel, A., Masurkar, S., & Pathade, G. R. (2024). An Overview of Digital Transformation and Environmental Sustainability: Threats, Opportunities, and Solutions. *Sustainability*, *16*(24), 11079.

Gumel, A. A., & Abdullahi, A. B., & O, U. M. (2019). *The Need for a Multimodal Means of Effective Digital Learning through Data Mining and Institutional Knowledge Repository: A Proposed System for Polytechnics in Northern Nigeria.* Paper presented at the Proceedings of the 2019 5th International Conference on Computer and Technology Applications.

Gupta, S., Wilcocks, K., Matava, C., Wiegelmann, J., Kaustov, L., & Alam, F. (2023). Creating a Successful Virtual Reality–Based Medical Simulation Environment: Tutorial. *JMIR Medical Education*, *9*, e41090. PMID: 36787169

Herur-Raman, A., Almeida, N. D., Greenleaf, W., Williams, D., Karshenas, A., & Sherman, J. H. (2021). Next-generation simulation—Integrating extended reality technology into medical education. *Frontiers in Virtual Reality*, *2*, 693399.

Jagatheesaperumal, S. K., Ahmad, K., Al-Fuqaha, A., & Qadir, J. (2024). Advancing education through extended reality and internet of everything enabled metaverses: Applications, challenges, and open issues. *IEEE Transactions on Learning Technologies*.

Jatto, E. O., & Aladesusi, G. A. (2025). *Empowering Pre-Service Teachers for Inclusive Education Through Technology: Strategies, Tools, and Innovations Empowering Pre-Service Teachers to Enhance Inclusive Education Through Technology*. IGI Global Scientific Publishing.

Jiang, H., Vimalesvaran, S., Wang, J. K., Lim, K. B., Mogali, S. R., & Car, L. T. (2022). Virtual reality in medical students' education: Scoping review. *JMIR Medical Education*, *8*(1), e34860. PMID: 35107421

Jibril, A. U., Abdullahi, N. M., Ali, A. S., Abdulkadir, H., Matthew, U. O., & Haruna, K. (2022). Motivational aspects of digital games in learning process. *Science in Information Technology Letters*, *3*(1), 1–9.

Kaplan, A. D., Cruit, J., Endsley, M., Beers, S. M., Sawyer, B. D., & Hancock, P. A. (2021). The effects of virtual reality, augmented reality, and mixed reality as training enhancement methods: A meta-analysis. *Human Factors*, *63*(4), 706–726. PMID: 32091937

Kapsali, M., Bayer, S., Brailsford, S., & Bolt, T. (2022). The agency role of simulation models in model-building groups. *The Journal of the Operational Research Society*, *73*(7), 1423–1443.

Lampropoulos, G., & Kinshuk. (2024). Virtual reality and gamification in education: A systematic review. *Educational Technology Research and Development*, *72*(3), 1691–1785.

Lavanya, K., Somu, L. K., & Mishra, S. K. (2024). Effectiveness of Scenario-based Roleplay as a Method of Teaching Soft Skills for Undergraduate Medical Students. *International Journal of Applied & Basic Medical Research*, *14*(2), 78–84. PMID: 38912358

Lee, D., Bathish, M. A., & Nelson, J. (2024). Transforming Nursing Education: Developing Augmented Reality Procedural Training. *Cyberpsychology, Behavior, and Social Networking*. PMID: 38407873

Lee, H., Hsia, C.-C., Tsoy, A., Choi, S., Hou, H., & Ni, S. (2023). *VisionARy: Exploratory research on Contextual Language Learning using AR glasses with ChatGPT.* Paper presented at the Proceedings of the 15th Biannual Conference of the Italian SIGCHI Chapter.

Li, L., & Duan, L. (2025). Human centric innovation at the heart of industry 5.0–exploring research challenges and opportunities. *International Journal of Production Research*, •••, 1–33.

Liu, J. Y. W., Mak, P. Y., Chan, K., Cheung, D. S. K., Cheung, K., Fong, K. N., & Maximo, T. (2024). The Effects of Immersive Virtual Reality–Assisted Experiential Learning on Enhancing Empathy in Undergraduate Health Care Students Toward Older Adults With Cognitive Impairment: Multiple-Methods Study. *JMIR Medical Education*, *10*, e48566. PMID: 38358800

Lungu, A. J., Swinkels, W., Claesen, L., Tu, P., Egger, J., & Chen, X. (2021). A review on the applications of virtual reality, augmented reality and mixed reality in surgical simulation: An extension to different kinds of surgery. *Expert Review of Medical Devices*, *18*(1), 47–62. PMID: 33283563

Luo, H. (2024). *Instructional Design with Emerging Technologies: Theory, Practice, and Research.* Taylor & Francis.

Mathew, U. O., Rodriguez, D. Z., Rosa, R. L., Ayub, M. S., & Adasme, P. (2024). *Advancing healthcare 5.0 through federated learning: Opportunity for security enforcement using blockchain*. Paper presented at the 2024 International Conference on Software, Telecommunications and Computer Networks (SoftCOM).

Matthew, U. O., Bakare, K. M., Ebong, G. N., Ndukwu, C. C., & Nwanakwaugwu, A. C. (2023). Generative Artificial Intelligence (AI) Educational Pedagogy Development: Conversational AI with User-Centric ChatGPT4. *Journal of Trends in Computer Science and Smart Technology*, *5*(4), 401–418.

Matthew, U. O., Kazaure, A. S., Kazaure, J. S., Hassan, I. M., Nwanakwaugwu, A. C., & Okafor, N. U. (2022). Educational Technology Adaptation & Implication for Media Technology Adoption in the Period of COVID-19. *Journal of Trends in Computer Science and Smart Technology*, *4*(4), 226–245.

Matthew, U. O., & Kazaure, J. S. (2020). Multimedia e-learning education in nigeria and developing countries of Africa for achieving SDG4. [IJICTHD]. *International Journal of Information Communication Technologies and Human Development*, *12*(1), 40–62.

Matthew, U. O., Kazaure, J. S., Kazaure, A. S., Nwamouh, U. C., & Chinonso, A. (2022). ICT Policy Implementation as Correlate for Achieving Educational Sustainability: Approaching Development in Multi ICT Dimensions. *Journal of Information Technology*, *4*(4), 250–269.

Matthew, U. O., Kazaure, J. S., Ndukwu, C. C., Ebong, G. N., Nwanakwaugwu, A. C., & Nwamouh, U. C. (2024). *Artificial Intelligence Educational Pedagogy Development: ICT Pedagogy Development for Education 5.0 Educational Perspectives on Digital Technologies in Modeling and Management*. IGI Global.

Matthew, U. O., Oyekunle, D. O., Akpan, E. E., Oladipupo, M. A., Chukwuebuka, E. S., Adekunle, T. S., & Onumaku, V. C. (2024). *Generative Artificial Intelligence (AI) on Sustainable Development Goal 4 for Tertiary Education: Conversational AI With User-Centric ChatGPT-4 Impacts of Generative AI on Creativity in Higher Education*. IGI Global.

Mobo, F. D. (2024). *Education 5.0: Navigating the Future of Learning Preconceptions of Policies, Strategies, and Challenges in Education 5.0*. IGI Global.

Navarro-Parra, S. L., & Chiappe, A. (2024). Simulated Learning Environments as an Interdisciplinary Option for Vocational Training: A Systematic Review. *Simulation & Gaming*, *55*(2), 135–158.

Neerupa, C., Naveen Kumar, R., Pavithra, R., & John William, A. (2024). Game on for learning: A holistic exploration of Gamification's impact on student engagement and academic performance in educational environments. *Management Matters, 21*(1), 38–53.

Nguyen, P., Cao, L., & Trương, H. (2023). Integrating ChatGPT with Virtual Reality and Augmented Reality Technology in Teaching Biology at High Schools in Vietnam.

Oberer, B., & Erkollar, A. (2022). *Education 5.0: the effectiveness of game based learning strategies on post-pandemic educational competences.* Paper presented at the The International Symposium for Production Research.

Ong, C. W., Tan, M. C. J., Lam, M., & Koh, V. T. C. (2021). Applications of extended reality in ophthalmology: Systematic review. *Journal of Medical Internet Research, 23*(8), e24152. PMID: 34420929

Oriakhi, V. N., Esegbona-Isikeh, O. M., Esseme, B., Claude, A., Emakporuena, D., Nwanakwaugwu, A. C., & Matthew, U. O. (2024). Generative artificial intelligence in education: ChatGPT-4 experiences to anticipated ChatGPT-5. *HAFED POLY Journal of Science. Management and Technology*, *6*(1), 149–169.

Oyekunle, D., Claude, B. E. A., Waliu, A. O., Adekunle, T. S., & Matthew, U. O. (2024). Cloud based adaptive learning system: virtual reality and augmented reality assisted educational pedagogy development on clinical simulation. *Journal of Digital Health*, 49-62.

Oyekunle, D., Matthew, U. O., Waliu, A. O., & Fatai, L. O. (2024). Healthcare applications of Augmented Reality (AR) and Virtual Real-ity (VR) simulation in clinical ceducation. *Journal of Clinical Images and Medical Case Reports*, *5*(6), 3141.

Oyekunle, D., Ugochukwu, O. M., Rosa, R. L., Rodriguez, D. Z., & Fatai, L. O. (2024). Novel Approaches in Clinical Simulation: Immersive Educational Technology to Enhance Nursing Education. *INFOCOMP Journal of Computer Science, 23*(1).

Oyekunle, D. O., Nwaiku, M., Matthew, U. O., Ogechukwu, O. N., Nwanakwaugwu, A. C., Adebola, N. T., & Olawoyin, O. O. (2025). *Transition to Sustainable Human-Centric Education in Emerging Artificial Intelligence Industry 5.0: Conversational AI With User-Centric ChatGPT-5 Higher Education and Quality Assurance Practices*. IGI Global Scientific Publishing.

Oyekunle, D. O. T., Okwudili Matthew, U., Preston, D., & Boohene, D. (2024). Trust beyond technology algorithms: A theoretical exploration of consumer trust and behavior in technological consumption and AI projects. *Journal of Computer and Communications, 12*(06), 10.4236.

Papanastasiou, G., Drigas, A., Skianis, C., Lytras, M., & Papanastasiou, E. (2019). Virtual and augmented reality effects on K-12, higher and tertiary education students' twenty-first century skills. *Virtual Reality (Waltham Cross)*, *23*(4), 425–436.

Pitura, J., Kaplan-Rakowski, R., & Asotska-Wierzba, Y. (2025). The VR-AI–Assisted Simulation for Content Knowledge Application in Pre-Service EFL Teacher Training. *TechTrends*, *69*(1), 100–110.

Qin, C. (2024). Discussion on the Curriculum Design and Implementation of Competency-Based Vocational Education. *Journal of Modern Educational Theory and Practice*, *1*(2).

Ramkissoon, L. (2024). AI: Powering Sustainable Innovation in Higher Ed *The Evolution of Artificial Intelligence in Higher Education* (pp. 203-229): Emerald Publishing Limited.

Rane, N., Choudhary, S., & Rane, J. (2023a). Education 4.0 and 5.0: Integrating artificial intelligence (AI) for personalized and adaptive learning: Nov.

Rane, N., Choudhary, S., & Rane, J. (2023b). Education 4.0 and 5.0: Integrating Artificial Intelligence (AI) for personalized and adaptive learning. *Available at SSRN* 4638365.

Rane, N., Choudhary, S., & Rane, J. (2023c). Enhanced product design and development using Artificial Intelligence (AI), Virtual Reality (VR), Augmented Reality (AR), 4D/5D/6D Printing, Internet of Things (IoT), and blockchain: A review. *Virtual Reality (VR), Augmented Reality (AR) D, 4.*

Rothe, L., & Snyder, C. K. (2024). Using Bloom's taxonomy to visualise antiracist teaching strategies. *Whiteness and Education*, •••, 1–19.

Savaglio, C., Ganzha, M., Paprzycki, M., Bădică, C., Ivanović, M., & Fortino, G. (2020). Agent-based Internet of Things: State-of-the-art and research challenges. *Future Generation Computer Systems*, *102*, 1038–1053.

Sharma, A., Channa, A., Malhotra, P., Jain, A., & Kumar, S. (2025). *Leveraging XR for Environmental Communication and Behavior Change: A Media Perspective Exploring the Impact of Extended Reality (XR) Technologies on Promoting Environmental Sustainability*. Springer.

Son, T. (2024). Intelligent Tutoring Systems in Mathematics Education: A Systematic Literature Review Using the Substitution, Augmentation, Modification, Redefinition Model. *Computers*, *13*(10), 270.

Supriya, Y., Bhulakshmi, D., Bhattacharya, S., Gadekallu, T. R., Vyas, P., Kaluri, R., & Mahmud, M. (2024). Industry 5.0 in smart education: Concepts, applications, challenges, opportunities, and future directions. *IEEE Access: Practical Innovations, Open Solutions*.

Tang, Y. M., Chau, K. Y., Kwok, A. P. K., Zhu, T., & Ma, X. (2022). A systematic review of immersive technology applications for medical practice and education-trends, application areas, recipients, teaching contents, evaluation methods, and performance. *Educational Research Review*, *35*, 100429.

Topsakal, O., & Topsakal, E. (2022). Framework for a foreign language teaching software for children utilizing AR, voicebots and ChatGPT (large language models). *The Journal of Cognitive Systems*, *7*(2), 33–38.

van As, J., & Cooke, R. (2024). *Immersive Virtual Community Engagement: Unleashing the Potential of AI Avatars and Virtual Reality in Education to Enhance Learning Excellence Integrating Cutting-Edge Technology Into the Classroom*. IGI Global.

Villegas-Ch, W., García-Ortiz, J., & Sánchez-Viteri, S. (2024). Educational advances in the metaverse: Boosting learning through virtual and augmented reality and artificial intelligence. *IEEE Access: Practical Innovations, Open Solutions*.

Waliu, A. O., Matthew, U. O., Oseni, V. E., Oyekunle, D. O., Oladipupo, M. A., Adekunle, T. S., & Esseme, A. C. B. (2025). *Immersive Educational Pedagogy Development: Cloud-Based Adaptive System for Higher Education Generative AI Approaches to Sustainable Development in Higher Education*. IGI Global Scientific Publishing.

Waliu, A. O., Muojekwu, E. E., Matthew, U. O., Kazaure, J. S., Oseni, V. E., Ononiwu, C. C., & Haruna, K. (2025). *Clinical Simulation in nursing education: Immersive Educational Tech for nurses and midwives Creating Immersive Learning Experiences Through Virtual Reality (VR)*. IGI Global.

Xu, J. J., Sun, X. F., Liu, Y. N., Zhang, S. Y., & Zhou, Q. (2025). Effects of Game-Based Learning on Students' Motivation in Chemistry: A Meta-analysis. *Journal of Chemical Education*.

Xu, W., Yang, Z., Ng, D. W. K., Levorato, M., Eldar, Y. C., & Debbah, M. (2023). Edge learning for B5G networks with distributed signal processing: Semantic communication, edge computing, and wireless sensing. *IEEE Journal of Selected Topics in Signal Processing*, *17*(1), 9–39.

Yadav, S. (2025). *Leveraging AI to Enhance Teaching and Learning in Education: The Role of Artificial Intelligence in Modernizing Classroom Practices Optimizing Research Techniques and Learning Strategies With Digital Technologies*. IGI Global Scientific Publishing.

Yang, J. (2023). *Technology-Enhanced Preclinical Medical Education (Anatomy, Histology and Occasionally, Biochemistry): A Practical Guide Biomedical Visualisation: Volume 17–Advancements in Technologies and Methodologies for Anatomical and Medical Education*. Springer.

Yeganeh, L. N., Fenty, N. S., Chen, Y., Simpson, A., & Hatami, M. (2025). The Future of Education: A Multi-Layered Metaverse Classroom Model for Immersive and Inclusive Learning. *Future Internet*, *17*(2), 63.

Zafar, M. H., Langås, E. F., & Sanfilippo, F. (2024). Exploring the synergies between collaborative robotics, digital twins, augmentation, and industry 5.0 for smart manufacturing: A state-of-the-art review. *Robotics and Computer-integrated Manufacturing*, *89*, 102769.

Zuñiga-Aviles, L. A., & Cruz-Martinez, G. M. (2024). *Designing Exoskeletons*. CRC Press.

Chapter 6

The Use of Rasch Analysis to Enhance Measurement Instruments in Education

Sinethemba Mthimkhulu
https://orcid.org/0000-0002-7852-1258
University of Pretoria, South Africa

ABSTRACT

Constructing a valid and reliable measurement instrument is essential in education and research to ensure that all respondents are evaluated on the same scale. Validity and reliability ensure that inferences made from the instrument are trustworthy. This chapter discusses the Rasch analysis as a practical method for improving assessments to promote fair and inclusive practices. Consequently, this chapter aims to demonstrate the viability of Rasch analysis as a valuable tool for establishing validity, while also highlighting aspects that prospective Rasch analysis users should carefully consider when applying Rasch analysis to improve assessments. Rasch analysis appears to be a vital method for validating instruments because the model provides outputs that enable the designer to evaluate the dimensionality of the instrument, test hypotheses, and verify the instrument's internal consistency. The model offers statistics that can be used to assess the goodness-of-fit of the instrument items and to identify items that may function differently for respondents. However, Rasch analysis users are advised to carefully select the sample size, pay attention to misfitting items, and address issues related to missing data. Rasch analysis can be recommended as a practical approach for enhancing assessments.

DOI: 10.4018/979-8-3373-7057-6.ch006

INTRODUCTION AND BACKGROUND

Developing fair and valid measurement instruments has become a prerequisite in modern-day life. Instruments are now developed and translated across languages and cultures to measure varying personality traits, attitudes, and cognitive abilities. The main concern is ascertaining the validity and fairness of an instrument to ensure that each respondent taking the assessment is measured on the same scale. Rasch's analysis offers a variety of statistical models that can be used to ascertain the fitness of the items and their functioning in slightly varying groups. This is because Rasch item analysis provides evidence of how well the item's content yields useful data about the abilities of the respondent (Othman et al., 2012). Use of the Rasch analysis provides designers with a better chance of improving the assessment from pilot testing data before it can be administered to the full sample.

The Rasch model analyses categorical data that include responses from instruments such as a competency assessment and survey questionnaires. Rasch Measurement Theory (RMT) is a model that plots persons and the items of the test on a straight line and thereafter calculates the scores of the respondents to determine where the item might have functioned differently for the respondents or whether the item is a misfit (Combrinck, 2018). This allows the designers to revise the assessment if items show signs of Differential Item Functioning (DIF). Using programs such as the Rasch Unidimensional Measurement Models 2030 (RUMM2030), and Winsteps Software, scholars and assessment designers can validate a measurement instrument and check for DIF using the outputs produced by the programs after running the Rasch analysis (Mthimkhulu, 2023; Roux, 2020; Souza et al., 2017). This chapter examines the literature on the viability of Rasch analysis as a method used to enhance measurement instruments while accounting for the shortfalls that accompany the model. It is important to note that there are a variety of statistical models housed under the RMT, such as multidimensional and unidimensional models. The user must select the appropriate model for their data, and this requires a basic understanding of the principles of measurement.

The Rasch analysis is grounded in the fact that the predictor of a construct lies in the relationship between item difficulty and the ability of the person taking the test (Boone, 2016; Linacre, 1994). Subsequently, it becomes mandatory to first articulate what is measured (Combrinck, 2020), and Rasch analysis will then provide sufficient statistics to determine how well it is measured. Researchers and organisations design instruments to measure various traits across disciplines; however, the method of ascertaining the validity and the fairness of the instrument is often not considered or given the attention it deserves. This chapter, therefore, contributes to the scientific instrument design literature by arguing for the feasibility of the Rasch analysis as a method of validating a measurement instrument for enhanced practices in assessments. This chapter serves as a readily available guide aimed at advocating for fair and valid assessment practices in education.

This chapter explores Rasch analysis as a viable method to consider when enhancing instruments, although it is not universally beneficial. This chapter may be useful to novice researchers and assessment designers (Yu, 2020) looking to validate their instruments using Rasch measurement. It is important to understand that there are other psychometric theories, such as Classical Test Theory (CTT) and Item Response Theory (IRT) models, that can be used to enhance measurement instruments. Rasch measurement emerged in response to the shortfalls of the other models, although it also has its limitations, as discussed in the literature and this chapter. The debate between Rasch vs IRT has been going on for decades, and the issues around them remain contentious (Yu, 2020). It is therefore crucial to note that the user needs to have a conceptual understanding of their instrument and the nature of their data before choosing a theory that can best help to validate their instrument.

Aims and Objectives of the Chapter

This chapter argues that Rasch analysis, which stems from Rasch's (1960) development of a model that can assess the internal functioning of items and measurement instruments (Andrich, 2004; Bond & Fox, 2015), can be a useful method for improving assessments. The assessment designer can enhance an instrument by validating the instrument and detecting item functioning. Rasch analysis is useful when identifying measurement problems such as item local independence and item bias (Muller, 2020). RMT enhances the quality and usefulness of instruments, and despite the extensive application of Rasch analysis, Rasch models are still being explored and discovered (Combrinck, 2018). This chapter contributes to the ongoing discussion around the use of Rasch analysis in education and also pays attention to the aspects that instrument designers need to be aware of when using RMT. Rasch analysis is used across disciplines such as behavioral psychology, medicine, and education. Examples and studies from various disciplines will be used in this chapter. Integrating the literature from various disciplines enables this chapter to address the following two objectives:

- *Explaining the use of Rasch analysis in education to enhance assessment practices*
- *Describing the aspects to consider when using Rasch analysis to enhance assessments*

QUALITY MEASUREMENT

Measurement Invariance

An important assumption in the use of instruments, especially when comparing scores, is that the items of the instrument are measurement invariant; that they measure the latent trait in the same way across the respondents (Verhagen et al., 2016). To ascertain measurement invariance in instruments, assessment designers can make use of several quality control or statistical procedures to ensure that the assessment items are fair (Alavi & Bordbar, 2018) and unbiased for all respondents. This is important because the design and development of fair and unbiased instruments are now a prerequisite in modern-day testing. Therefore, it is essential to examine and ascertain that the instrument used has evidence of psychometric properties (validity and reliability) (Stolt et al., 2022).

If an instrument is measurement variant, it raises concerns about the validity of the instrument (Verhagen et al., 2016), and inferences made from the results of the instrument may be erroneous and misleading. That can have serious implications for decision-making in policy, practice, and research. The assumption is that if the instrument is measurement variant, the instrument may no longer be fair across the respondents, and is potentially biased, therefore requiring investigation.

Reducing Bias and Enhancing Fairness in Instruments

The use of psychometric theories such as IRT and Rasch analysis has the potential to highlight and address the issues of bias and fairness in assessments (Alavi & Bordbar, 2018). These theories can assess items that might function differently for the test takers, thus alerting the assessment designer about the items that might be biased and unfair and/or perform poorly in the instrument. The use of Rasch and IRT models to enhance and ensure quality in the instruments used to measure a person's ability is recommended. To enhance fairness and reduce bias in instruments, it is advisable to keep an open mind about the strengths and the limitations of each psychometric theory. This is because different problems in different settings require different solutions (Yu, 2020). The user needs to carefully consider different factors when choosing a model to provide evidence of the psychometric properties of their instruments.

Measurement Terminology

Table 1 presents frequently used terminology in the chapter.

Table 1. Frequently used terminology in this chapter

Key term	Description
Construct	The latent trait or idea that is measured by the instrument. It cannot be directly observed and is therefore measured with an instrument.
Difficulty	Refers to how difficult or easy the item is (the number of respondents who correctly responded to the item and agree with the item).
Dimension	Refers to a set of items measuring one construct that may be made up of sub-constructs.
Discrimination	The extent to which the items of the instrument can be differentiated between upper/ lower-class respondents.
Persons	Refers to the respondents taking the test.
Measurement instrument	Refers to a tool, such as a checklist, questionnaire, or test, that is used to measure a construct.
Item	It is a statement that is worded in a way that elicits information. It is usually referred to as a question.

(Compiled by the author)

UNDERSTANDING THE RASCH ANALYSIS AMID OTHER PSYCHOMETRIC THEORIES

Different types of psychometric theories include CTT, Rasch Measurement and IRT (Alavi & Bordbar, 2018). The CTT has long been used as a psychometric theory for testing instruments. Theories such as Rasch and IRT emerged in response to the limitations of CTT (Yu, 2020). A well-known limitation of CTT is that it does not offer invariant measurement because it fails to separate person and item parameters (Combrinck, 2020; Hobson, 2015). Furthermore, the CTT assumes that there is a linear relationship between the raw scores and the latent trait, which may be erroneous. By implication, CTT uses correlations between items to select the items that are measuring the latent trait (Medvedev & Krageloh, 2022).

Rasch measurement separates the parameters and accounts for item difficulty as a parameter (Boone & Rogan, 2005) by applying a statistical model that predicts the precise mathematical relationship between the item and the measured construct (Medvedev & Krageloh, 2022). The limitations of the CTT do not mean the theory does not offer useful information in understanding the properties of an instrument. The CTT is well documented in the literature (Yu, 2020). CTT can be used in conjunction with IRT and Rasch to obtain a wide range of information to enhance the instruments (Stolt et al., 2022).

IRT is a method used to test item function and is favoured in research because the item parameter estimates derived from IRT are less confounded and influenced by sample-specific characteristics. IRT has the feature of producing person parameter invariance when the model fit is valid, and test information reflects the measurement precision of the assessment on the scale of the construct of interest (Junker, 2015; Zanon et al., 2016). This feature is achievable when the IRT model fits the available test data. IRT is an extension of CTT with mathematical roots in psychology, as its basis is embedded in psychological measurement (Alavi & Bordbar, 2018). IRT offers more accurate statistical properties of items to determine where the item functions differently, in terms of discrimination, difficulty, or pseudo-guessing, than other methods such as CTT (Diaz et al., 2021; Zanon et al., 2018).

Typically, in educational assessments and social surveys, data are generated in the form of a two-way array of discrete response data for *N* subjects[1] and *J* probes[2], (Junker, 2015). The respondent's responses to the items may be seen as fallible measures of one or more underlying constructs, represented generically by a scalar or vector-valued index, which may sometimes be referred to as the latent variable. When the response variables are discrete valued (Junker, 2015), IRT and its variants provide a set of modelling and estimation tools for making inferences about the relationships between the test items, respondents' responses to the items and the respondent's location in the latent structure.

IRT and RMT are both models used to analyse measurement data; however, they differ in terms of model-specific assumptions. The key differences between the two are that Rasch analysis focuses on measurement rather than statistical modelling. Rasch models require the data to fit the model to produce invariant measures (when the data do not fit the model, then the model is not appropriate), whereas IRT models are flexible and allow for variations in item discrimination. IRT allows for the modelling of a second parameter, implying item discrimination, and also allows the Item Characteristic Curve (ICC) to cross when more information is incorporated into the estimation of the person's ability. However, the measurement scale is no longer guaranteed to have the same meaning across the examinees (Diaz et al., 2021). Instruments designers are cautioned about the flexibility of IRT in item discrimination because it can lead to inconsistencies in meaning across the different respondents in the assessment (Diaz et al., 2021). Rasch measurement assumes that item discrimination powers should be the same across the items.

A REVIEW OF RMT

A variety of statistical methods are generally used to develop test instruments in research methods; these include point biserial correlations, Cronbach's alpha, and Rasch analysis. The focus of this chapter is Rasch analysis. Combrinck (2018) explained Rasch analysis as a model that plots persons and the items on a linear scale starting from less difficult to more difficult; thereafter, the items and the persons are aligned. The logic behind this model is that at the centre of the model is the proposition that the person's responses to the items lie in the item's difficulty and the person's abilities. The initial Rasch 1960 model was built under the assumption that the probability of the person correctly answering a dichotomous item lies in the relationship between two parameters (person's ability and the difficulty of the item) (Fischer et al., 2021; Muller, 2020). Therefore, the probability of correctly responding to the item is a mathematical function of the difference between item difficulty and the ability of the respondent. The following equation, provided by Fischer et al. (2021), describes the notion of how items are analysed in the initial Rasch model.

$$P\left(X_{ni} = 1 \,|\beta_n, \delta_i\right) = \frac{\exp(\beta_n - \delta_i)}{1 + \exp(\beta_n - \delta_i)} \tag{1}$$

Combrinck (2020) shares a rather simpler overview of the Rasch item analysis equation.

Figure 1. Rasch equation

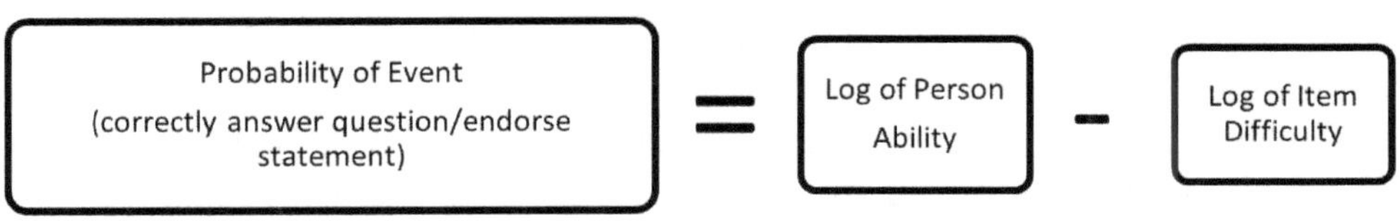

(Source: Combrinck, 2020, p. 12)

A total sum of the respondents' achievement scores cannot be used to accurately determine their achievement (Boone, 2016) because test items are not equal in difficulty; hence, the need for Rasch analysis, which accounts for item difficulty simultaneously with the abilities of the respondents (Andersen, 1977). The raw scores are minimal sufficient statistics and are insufficient to infer an individual's achievement (Andersen, 1977), thus necessitating the use of Rasch analysis, which has logistic ICC and equal item-discrimination powers (Boone & Rogan, 2005). RMT has the power to determine the item difficulty and the item's discriminating power. What is interesting is that for each person and item, RMT can estimate exactly where the items function differently (Hagel, 2014).

The Rasch analysis is a psychometric technique that was developed to improve the precision with which researchers can construct an instrument, monitor the instrument's quality, and compute the respondent's performance (Boone, 2016). At the core of RMT are three fundamental features. Stemler and Naples (2021) listed them as follows: First, Rasch analysis assumes that the construct under investigation is normally distributed, implying that the distribution of knowledge based on the respondent's achievement score follows a normal distribution curve. Second is the proposition that the derived measures should be test-free and person-free, meaning that the rank ordering of the item difficulty remains the same regardless of the present subset of more difficult or less difficult items from the same scale. The ordering of the items and traits assists in understanding the meaning of the underlying data and provides the basis for further analysis. Third is the belief that the objective of the RMT is to construct a unidimensional scale and then test how well the data fit that model through the notion of fit statistics. Fit statistics allow the determination of whether the items the respondent answered proceed in the order anticipated based on the scale developed. The degree to which a parameter estimate is valid is measured by statistics quantifying the fit of the data to the measurement model (Linacre, 1994).

Starting from the raw scores, RMT creates linear, objective measurements that are known as precision measurements (standard error and quality/fit), freed as far as statistically possible from the local details of the raters (Linacre, 1994). The models provide fit statistics that indicate that the aberrations in the data do not affect the substantive meaning of the measures. Subsequently, RMT measures each respondent's performance level, qualified by its standard error and quality control fit statistics. The concept of linearity is fundamental in the Rasch analysis (Boone, 2016) because it helps provide objective measurement. The person's abilities are placed in a straight line, and the items are also placed along the same line according to their level of difficulty; the analysis can then begin. The RMT works under the assumption that the probability of a certain item response is a logistic function of the difference between the level of the measured construct represented by the item and the ability of the person (See Figures 1 & 2). Figure 2 illustrates the linearity of the Rasch analysis model (Linacre, 2010).

Figure 2. Illustrating the linearity of the RMT model

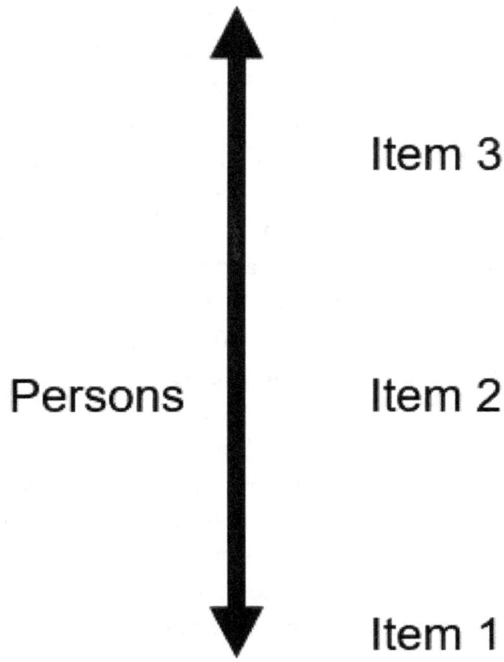

(Source: Boone 2016, p. 3)

When the analysis is conducted, the first point to look at is the variable measured, second, the person, and third, the item difficulty. Instrument designers must first describe the variable to be measured before the analysis (Boone, 2016). The line represents the variable measured. The person represents the respondent taking the test, located at some point along the measured variable. The items range from easy to difficult. Item one is easy, item two is medium easy/difficult, and item three is difficult. Therefore, the variable is measured by a variety of items ranging from easy to difficult. The Rasch analysis then assumes that the possibility of the respondent correctly answering the items depends on their abilities and the difficulty of the items. The indication is that this model accounts for the unequal item difficulty in the instrument and the difference in the persons' abilities. These two parameters (item difficulty and person's ability) are taken into account during the analysis of the respondent's scores. The Rasch analysis can detect assessment bias relating to any specific items and/or group of examinees (Linacre, 1994).

The Rasch Family of Models

Rasch models are a family of measurement models that can be used to describe latent traits where items from an instrument and the person's scores are plotted on the same scale of the measured variable (See Figure 2). The Rasch model houses a variety of mathematical models, such as the Partial Credit Model (PCM), Rating Scale Model (RSM), Polytomous Rasch Model (PRM), and Many-facet Rasch Model (MRM), among others.

The RMS is often used in Likert-type data sets. It describes the probabilistic relationship between the item's difficulty and the person's ability. The relationship is based on the assumption that the person's abilities increase as item difficulty increases (Boone & Rogan, 2005; Boone, 2016). It is frequently used in survey-type data where the same responses are present (Combrinck, 2024; Yu, 2020). The PCM is a modification of the RSM where the threshold estimates are free to differ per item within a scale, thus not constrained (Smith et al., 2008; Yu, 2020). The PCM was developed to accommodate data types that can be generated from essay-type questions where the respondents can earn partial credit (Yu, 2020).

One may ask, when does one use the Rasch analysis, and how to select a model? Simply put, assessment designers can make use of the Rasch analysis when they want to provide psychometric evidence of their instrument. In addition, the selection of an appropriate Rasch model depends on the response scale of the instrument (Stolt et al., 2022). Selecting the appropriate Rasch model requires a sound understanding of the kind of data the designer has at the time. For example, if a questionnaire was administered with a 4-point Likert scale, the designer can opt for the RMS model. The rule of thumb in this case is to understand the type of data analysed. Fortunately, the RUMM software selects the appropriate Rasch model based on the data loaded into the software.

Rasch measurement exists as the 1-Parameter Logistic (PL) model of the IRT models[3] (Stolt et al., 2022; Yu, 2020). The 1PL model assumes that the items differ only in difficulty, whereas the 2PL adds the discrimination parameter that allows the items to differ in how well they differentiate between individuals. The discrimination parameter in Rasch measurement is accounted for by the fit statistics, thus rendering the Rasch modelling sufficient when used alone (Yu, 2020). The 3PL model includes the guessing parameter, which accounts for the possibility that a correct answer can be randomly guessed. In Rasch modelling, when guessing occurs, it simply means that the item was poorly formulated; thus, revision and possible exclusion of the item are necessary (Wright, 1995).

RMT has unidimensional and multi-dimensional models (Aryadoust et al., 2021); the user needs to have a sound understanding of whether their instrument is unidimensional or multi-dimensional, so as to choose the correct Rasch model. For example, in education, assessments are often classified as multidimensional (Yu, 2020), which necessitates the use of multidimensional models. The suitability of the model lies in the kind of problem, context, and initial reason for the use of the model.

Developments in Rasch Measurement

Rasch analysis provides a stable foundation for predictive models (Linacre, 2010) because the core intention of Rasch analysis is to produce parameter estimates that are independent as far as possible from the dataset (items and persons). Rasch models were initially designed for dichotomous items; however, with research and the growing popularity of the model, Rasch analysis is now also used for polytomous items (Aryadoust et al., 2021). Dichotomous items have only two possible scores, i.e., correct or incorrect responses (Stolt et al., 2022). The Rasch analysis calculates the success-to-failure odds of the respondents answering the items. The idea is that there is a 50% chance of choosing the correct response and a 50% chance of choosing the incorrect response (Combrinck, 2018). Typically, the dichotomous items are multiple-choice items or true or false items. In contrast, polytomous items are the kind of items that have more than one possible response (Stolt et al., 2022), for example, Likert-type items or items that require constructed responses, where the respondent needs to provide a constructed response.

The arena of assessments has changed from pencil-and-paper versions to Computerised Adaptive Testing (CAT)[4]; it is therefore crucial to ensure that CAT instrument items are valid, fair, and non-biased, thus ensuring measurement invariance. The continued use of Rasch analysis in various fields has enabled the development and validation of CAT. For instance, Hobson (2015), used Rasch measurement to compile evidence of whether the Trait Emotional Intelligence Questionnaire (TEIQue) can be administered as a CAT. The results of the study showed that the instrument can be developed as a CAT. Furthermore, Ebenbeck and Gerbhardt (2022) made use of Rasch analysis to build an item pool for a CAT assessment. The aim was to create a fair and non-biased assessment in special education, focusing on learning, language, and behaviour. The purpose of Rasch measurement in CAT is to enhance measurement quality. Rasch measurement is preferred in CATs because theories such as CTT cannot be applied in CAT (Combrinck, 2020; Hobson, 2015).

Concerns About Rasch Measurement

The results from Rasch analysis can be used to improve instruments, inform policy, and assist in assessment decision-making (Yu, 2020). However, it is also important to consider concerns about the use of Rasch measurement. Rasch measurement is a 1PL model that accounts for item difficulty but not for random variation in the data. The concern around the Rasch analysis is that, when the differences between the data and the model exceed minor random variation, it is assumed that something must have gone wrong in the data collection stage. Modifying the data collection approach might be a plausible remedy to the variation rather than changing the model (Andrich, 2011; Yu, 2020). That creates more work for the assessment designers in revising the administration of the instrument. Because of this concern, the IRT is preferred as it is descriptive (aims to fit the model to the data) whereas Rasch measurement is prescriptive (aims to fit the data to the model) (Aryadoust et al., 2021).

The unidimensionality of Rasch models was not well accepted by scholars because of the complexity of psychological constructs and language proficiency (Aryadoust et al., 2021). As such, the Rasch models were considered inappropriate because of their inability to cater for multi-dimensional instruments. However, over time, Rasch modellers developed multi-dimensional models to accommodate various fields of study (Aryadoust et al., 2021; Yu, 2020). The creation of a set of items that measures one construct, thus loading into a single dimension, may be plausible (Pelton, 2002); however, the concern is with the Rasch requirement that items should have equal uniqueness, which may result in parallel ICCs, and that is unlikely. If the researcher selects and refines items to meet the requirement, there is a possibility that the instrument will be less valid in measuring the intended construct, although it would be more reliable and have minimal error estimates. If this procedure is conducted excessively (removing all misfitting items), that might result in the elimination of all items in the instrument.

THE USE OF RASCH ANALYSIS TO ENHANCE MEASUREMENT INSTRUMENTS

Before conducting a Rasch analysis, the data must be cleaned and prepared for the Rasch analysis programs such as Winsteps and/or RUMM2030. Combrinck (2019) prepared a guide that one can use to prepare the data for the RUMM2030 program. The guide outlines step by step how to prepare the data for Rasch analysis. Literature on how to clean and prepare the data for Rasch analysis (Combrinck, 2020) is available. Clean data are useful because it provides more accurate estimates (Anselmi et al., 2019). Thus, the user needs to ascertain that the data have been cleaned and undergone quality assurance measures before Rasch analysis can take place. It is recommended in this chapter that the user needs to have basic data processing skills that include, but are not limited to, the use of Statistical Software Package for Social Sciences (SPSS), and Microsoft Excel.

The use and reporting of Rasch analysis depend simply on the initial reason why this method was chosen (Stolt et al., 2022). For example, if the initial purpose of the Rasch analysis is to ascertain the item functioning, then the focus should be on the statistics that account for the item functioning. However, it is important to note that with Rasch analysis, some statistics, such as the goodness-of-fit statistics, should always be reported. This section of the chapter addresses the first objective of the chapter:

- *Explaining the use of Rasch analysis in education to enhance assessment practices*

Testing for Unidimensionality in the Instrument

The Rasch model allows the test developers to test whether the instrument used is unidimensional (Linacre, 2010). A unidimensional instrument implies that the instrument only measures one latent trait (Hagel, 2014) with no presence of unknown variance outside the construct (Rosli et al., 2020). For instance, if the instrument is constructed to measure the reading abilities of Grade 6 learners, the scores obtained from the instrument should reflect the reading abilities of Grade 6 learners. The instrument should measure the intended construct (Roux, 2020), and the scores retrieved from the instrument should be solely based on the trait/construct measured. Unidimensionality is not absolute but a relative matter; there is no standardised version of testing for it. However, in psychometric instruments, it is advised that unidimensionality be tested if the instrument is intended to measure one common trait.

Using the Principal Components Analysis (PCA) (Linacre, 2010) of the model residuals and local independence of the items, the designer can test for the instrument's dimensionality. Local independence refers to an item not correlating highly with the others, resulting in item redundancy. Local independence can be investigated using standardised residual correlation values (Rosli et al., 2020). If the $r > .70$, the assumption of local independence might be violated; items should therefore be investigated (Combrinck, 2020).

The commonly used approach to test for unidimensionality in Rasch models is to "identify the two item sets from a PCA of residuals, estimate separate person measures based on the two item sets, compare the two estimates on a person-by-person basis" (Hagel, 2014, p. 456). This can be done by using t-tests and by determining the number of cases that differ significantly at the 0.05 level. Hagel (2014) further argues that unidimensionality can be strictly inferred if ≤5% of the tests are significant or the lower bound of the binomial 95% confidence interval of the examined ratio overlaps 5%. If the above cannot be observed in the PCA of residuals, then the measurement scale is multidimensional.

Combrinck (2020) and Caronni et al. (2023) presented the idea that eigenvalues >2.0 signify that items could be forming another dimension; therefore, potential multidimensionality should be examined after removing the Rasch construct (item difficulty). In a study by Makhubela (2019), some of the items of the different constructs of the instruments displayed signs of multidimensionality. In the instrument, the PCA residuals accounted for 52.8% of the variance; however, the unexplained variance of the eigenvalue (4.7, above the recommended 2.0 eigenvalue) suggested the total scale was not unidimensional (Makhubela, 2019). Another dimension might have formed. In the same instrument, the sub-construct that covered dissociation, it was observed that the PCA residuals indicated the construct was unidimensional because the eigenvalue was below 2.0 (eigenvalue 1.5) (Makhubele, 2019). It lies with the instrument designer, informed by the construct/s measured, to choose the correct model (unidimensional/multidimensional) to validate the instrument.

Transforming Ordinal Scales

Unlike other theories, RMT can transform ordinal data (ratings with unequal intervals) into linear (Boone & Rogan, 2005; Boone et al., 2014; Souza et al., 2017; Muller, 2020) measures that have equal interval units referred to as logits (Combrinck, 2024). Logits account for the abilities of the test takers and the difficulty of the item. The transformation of raw scores into abstract linear logit scales and probability scales allows the researcher to infer the probability of a person choosing a certain response (Souza et al., 2017; See Figure 3). For example, in an instrument that has a yes or no answer, Rasch analysis provides data that show the probabilities of the respondent choosing a yes or a no answer.

Statistics such as tests of significance and effect sizes can be calculated on interval measures (Caronni et al., 2023). Rasch analysis is endorsed because it can transform the ordinal scores to interval measures; thus, significance testing and effect size can be calculated. The Rasch analysis can generate linear scores, enabling it to meet the assumptions of parametric statistical tests such as the t-test and Analysis of Variance (ANOVA) (Boone & Rogan, 2005). Furthermore, the interval measures produced by Rasch analysis increase the chances of making correct inferences about the measured trait; thus, the Rasch analysis is preferred in instrument validation.

Individual Item-fit Statistics

Individual item-fit statistics are an indication of the items and persons and how they link to fit the Rasch model. Fit statistics help inform the researcher about how well the items of the instrument fit a unidimensional measured variable (Smith et al., 2008). The Rasch model assumes that as the ability of the person increases, the probability of correctly responding to more difficult items should also increase (Boone & Rogan, 2005; Boone, 2016; Combrinck, 2018). However, if the fit statistics show item misfit, that simply implies that the specific item/s have violated the model's assumption and thus should be paid attention to. That means that the person's ability did not increase as the item's difficulty increased. Paying attention to the item could mean many things, such as the item's rephrasing, retranslation and/or possibly removal from the instrument.

Equally important are the chi-square values produced after calculating individual item-fit statistics (Linacre, 2010). The chi-square determines the goodness-of-fit of the interaction between the items and the latent trait. Chi-squares indicate the invariance across the measured variable. The chi-square determines whether the hierarchical ordering of items is consistent across the increasing levels of the measured variable (Combrinck, 2018; Roux, 2020). A significant chi-square means that the data and the Rasch model are significantly different from one another (Combrinck, 2020), whereas a small chi-square that is not significant ($p > 0.05$) is acceptable and indicates that the data fit the model well.

Table 2 shows fit statistics from a reading comprehension passage investigated in two languages (English and isiZulu language groups). From Table 2, five of the 15 items show signs of misfitting (overfit/underfit). Items 3 and 4 were overfit (residual values above +2.5). The items were too discriminating between the two language groups that took the assessment. Items 7, 9 and 10 were underfit (residual values were below -2.5). That simply means that the items discriminated a little between the two language groups. What can be gathered from this finding is that the five items in the instrument need to be investigated.

Table 2. Example of item fit statistics produced by RUMM2030

Item	Difficulty	SE	Fit Residual	Chi-Square	Probability
Z03	-0,260	0,133	2,651*	12,88	0,025
Z04	-0,895	0,124	2,855*	14,44	0,013
Z08	-0,727	0,130	1,688	13,84	0,017
Z13	-0,517	0,145	2,170	2,89	0,717
Z02	-1,090	0,120	-1,262	12,10	0,034
Z05	1,978	0,199	-1,441	4,46	0,485
Z07	-0,965	0,124	-3,253*	33,62	0,000**
Z09	1,678	0,187	-2,911*	14,54	0,013
Z10	0,922	0,168	-3,503*	19,59	0,001
Z11	-0,275	0,140	-1,622	8,64	0,124

continued on following page

Table 2. Continued

Item	Difficulty	SE	Fit Residual	Chi-Square	Probability
Z15	0,899	0,173	-2,286	9,56	0,089
Z01	-0,363	0,081	1,839	12,72	0,026
Z06	-0,540	0,083	-2,458	11,58	0,041
Z12	0,265	0,107	-2,057	13,47	0,019
Z14	-0,110	0,083	-0,525	10,86	0,054

* Fit residuals are shown if below -2.5 or above +2.5.

** Bonferroni adjustment is 0.000667 for all the items. Items that are smaller than the Bonferroni adjustment are highlighted, and they are significant.

(Source: Examining PIRLS 2021: Differential item function across English and isiZulu language groups, Mthimkhulu (2023, p. 95), University of Pretoria, Copyright 2023 by University of Pretoria).

The identification and evaluation of misfitting items is crucial in the development of a unidimensional instrument (Smith et al., 2008); therefore, the use of reliable fit statistics is recommended. The identification and removal of items showing signs of misfit can reduce the burden on the respondent of responding to redundant items and may also improve the person-measure assessment (Pallant et al., 2006). Subsequently, the fit statistics produced by Rasch analysis are viable in instrument development, especially if the aim is to develop a unidimensional instrument. Fit statistics can also be used for hypothesis testing.

Hypothesis Testing

The item-fit statistics allow the Rasch analysis user to partially accept/reject the null hypothesis. In educational measurements, a hypothesis is used to determine whether there is a variation in the mean scores of the examinees. For instance, the null hypothesis states that the mean scores of the different groups of examinees are equal, while the alternative hypothesis states that the mean scores of the different groups of examinees are not equal (See Mthimkhulu, 2023; Roux, 2020). Using fit statistics, one can determine whether the items are a misfit and thus accept/reject the null hypothesis based on the number of items showing signs of misfit. For instance, Mthimkhulu (2023) examined two language groups that completed the same passage in their respective languages. From the fit statistics that displayed the number of items that were misfits, the null hypothesis was partly rejected. Further analysis, such as the calculation of DIF, is required to provide further evidence to reject or accept the null hypothesis of the investigation.

Persons' Reliability

Person's reliability is often referred to as summary statistics. Statistics such as Cronbach's Alpha and person separation reliability are considered measures of the internal consistency of the instrument. These statistics indicate the reliability of the instrument. An instrument cannot be regarded as valid when there is no evidence of reliability (Ismail et al., 2015). Anything that might threaten the reliability of the instrument is also a threat to the validity of the instrument. Subsequently, it is crucial to ascertain the reliability of an instrument.

This kind of statistic shows whether the items of the instrument were able to adequately differentiate between the different types of test takers (Combrinck, 2018; Rosli et al., 2020). Simply put, summary statistics indicate whether the instrument items were able to sufficiently distinguish between examinees with high abilities and examinees with low abilities (Bond & Fox, 2015). When using RUMM2030 to calculate summary statistics, a variety of categories are produced; the focus should be on the power of analysis of fit and Person Separation Index (*PerSepInx)* (See Table 3). The *PerSepInx* displays how adequately the instrument items were able to separate between the persons measured (Wright & Stone, 1999). Fisher's (1992) table for interpreting *PerSepInx* is useful when dealing with this kind of statistic. It is noteworthy to mention that if the separation is narrow, the indication is that the items were redundant and thus unable to adequately differentiate between the examinee's abilities, whereas if the separation is wide, the implication is that there is a gap between the item difficulty and the persons abilities and as such the instrument was inaccurate (Roux, 2020). From the example in Table 3, instrument items were able to adequately distinguish between high- and low-ability learners in English and Afrikaans, whereas they could not do so for the isiZulu language.

Table 3. Example of summary statistics produced by RUMM2030

Analysis Name	Power of Analysis of Fit	PerSepIdx with extremes	PerSepIdx no extremes	Coefficient Alpha with extremes	Coefficient Alpha no extremes
PearlRhino [a]	Reasonable	0.53986	0.53596	N/A	N/A
English Only	Good	0.68384	0.67271	0.76884	0.75525
Afrikaans Only	Good	0.66821	0.65360	0.77425	0.75263
isiZulu Only	Too Low	0.30891	0.24412	0.53673	0.48474

[a] The analysis file *PearlRhino* included all languages.

(Source: Examining the equivalence of the PIRLS 2016 released texts in South African three language groups, Roux, 2020, p. 130) University of Pretoria, Copyright 2020 by University of Pretoria)

Detecting DIF

DIF is a term that implies that the probability of a correct response in equally able respondents is different due to various reasons that might make the respondents different from each other (Strobl et al., 2015). Such differences may include race, gender, and language. The presence of items that display signs of DIF in instruments may make the instrument biased against one group and favour the other. It is essential to ascertain that these items are identified and dealt with. Item equivalence can be ascertained using Rasch analysis.

It is crucial to note that item bias can take place in different forms. Item bias, and item impact are related, but they are not identical (Zumbo, 1999). Item impact takes place when groups simply differ in performance on an item, and the impact continues after controlling for the overall skill on the construct measured, which implies that DIF is present. Item bias occurs when the items favour/discriminate against a particular group. The testing of DIF is prone to false positives and false negatives. Similarly, highly discriminating items can be mistakenly regarded as DIF. Items with high discrimination indices are better used to differentiate between the test takers with high/low levels of the tested traits (Killen, 2010). Therefore, when DIF is investigated, accurate measurements should be used to minimise other aspects that may appear as DIF. Fortunately, Rasch statistical outputs can determine whether the instrument is showing signs of non-uniform or uniform DIF (Combrinck, 2020).

Makhubele's (2019) study found that the instrument items can be used across genders because none of the examined items functioned differently. Therefore, the items of the scale used provide consistent meaning to the different respondents. In a study published by Roux (2020), it was found that some of the items of the instrument had different item functioning and needed some improvement to be used across the languages investigated. Rosli et al. (2020) reported that one item functioned differently, whereas the remaining items measured the same construct. Lastly, Ismail et al. (2015) reported that three items might be problematic; however, they concluded that the instrument validated had adequate psychometric properties and the items were psychometrically fit to be used in the instrument they were validating. From these distinct findings, it can be deduced that the Rasch analysis proves to be a viable method of validating an instrument and checking for DIF across groups with slightly different qualities.

To support the above conclusions, the Rasch analysis provides an ICC graph that can be used to determine the location where the item might have functioned differently in the group of respondents (Andrich, 2004). Below is an example of an ICC graph that displays the probability value (*y-axis* indicates the expected value) and a person's location (*x-axis* indicates the abilities of the examinees). The values -5 to -0.9 indicate the group of respondents who have lower abilities (Lower-class interval) of correctly responding to the item. The values 0 to 5 indicate the group of respondents who have higher abilities (Upper-class interval). Graph a, in Figure 3, shows that at approximately 0.8 logits, boys had a slightly higher chance of correctly responding to the item when compared to girls. Similarly, in the upper-class interval, boys had higher chances of correctly responding to the items than girls. Inferences can therefore be made about the functioning of the items between boys and girls. One clear inference from graph a is that males had higher chances of correctly responding to the items when compared to females. The instrument might have favoured the boys. Graph b shows the ICCs when DIF was resolved.

Figure 3. (a/b): ICC showing the DIF of the item

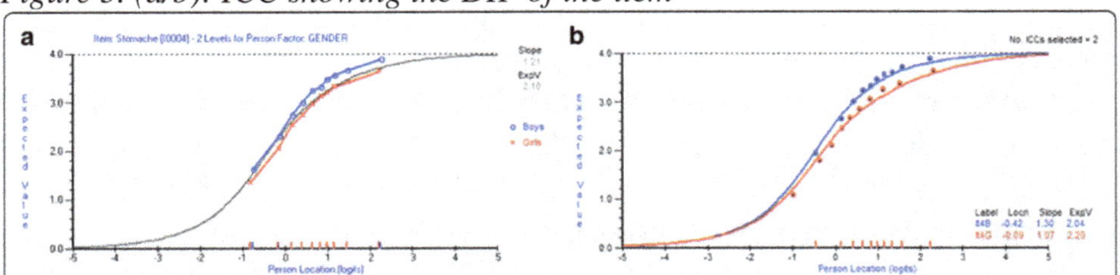

Fig. 2 a-b Item Stomach ache showing DIF, before and after DIF is resolved

(Source: Hagquist and & Andrich, 2017, p. 6).

Aspects to Consider When Using the Rasch Analysis to Enhance Measurement Instruments

This section of the chapter addresses the second objective of this chapter. This section attempts to:

- *Describe the aspects to consider when using Rasch analysis to enhance assessments*

Sample Sizes

The consensus is that 30 is the minimum acceptable sample size in quantitative studies to obtain valid estimates. Having a sample that is representative of the population is mandatory in quantitative studies. Sample sizes are not only crucial for validity and reliability purposes but also for generalising from the sample to the population. Thus, testing sufficient samples allows the researcher to make inferences about the population. The developments in Rasch analysis allow for small sample sizes (Boone & Rogan, 2005). In Rasch analysis, the sample size varies based on the number of parameters estimated, the expected stability of the parameters, and the specific Rasch model used (Combrinck, 2020). Assessment designers should first determine the above before choosing a sample size for Rasch analysis.

Researchers are cautioned to pay attention to sample sizes when they conduct a Rasch analysis. Smith et al. (2008) investigated the relationship between the sample size and fit statistics and concluded that t-statistics are susceptible to sample size, whereas the mean squares statistics are less sensitive to sample size. This conclusion applies to polytomous data. Small sample sizes (>30) can be utilised to derive useful information about the validity of the instrument if there are fewer parameters estimated, and the instrument has been piloted more than once (Babcock & Hogde, 2020; Combrinck, 2020). Users are advised that in small sample sizes, multiple rounds of data are required to provide valid parameter estimates.

Small sample sizes can also be used when the dichotomous Rasch model is used. In a study conducted by Fischer et al. (2021), to investigate the use of limited item pools and model misfit, it was suggested that limited item pools and small to medium sample sizes can be analysed using the sparser Rasch model to provide a valid precision of parameter estimation. Smith et al. (2008) indicated that research showed that mean squares and t-statistics are highly susceptible to the different sample sizes for dichotomous data. Lastly, Wright (1997) shared a table that illustrates the sample sizes required for various calibration precisions and tests of fit. Item calibration is crucial in the improvement of the instrument. Item calibration focuses on eliminating/removing items that might be biased when the instrument is administered.

Misfit and DIF Items

Rasch analysis is used in various disciplines to calibrate instruments. This is done by calculating item-to-person fit so that the non-fitting items can be identified and instruments can be improved (Combrinck, 2018). In the Rasch analysis, misfitting items are often referred to as items that do not fit the model and thus require attention. When an item does not fit the Rasch model, the indication is that the respondents of the instrument had difficulties in comprehending the item (Rosli et al., 2020). The items can either be underfit or overfit. Underfitting items simply imply that the item had little discriminatory power among the group of examinees, while overfit implies that the item had high discriminatory power among the group of examinees.

When using the Winsteps program, the researcher should start by interpreting the Mean Squares (MNSQ) values and can then look at the Z standardised (ZSTD) scores using the acceptable ranges (Combrinck, 2020; Rosli et al., 2020). The ZSTD can be examined if the MNSQ indicates a problem; however, the ZSTD can be ignored if the MNSQ is accepted. In RUMM2030, the researcher can look at the residual values and use the ranges used in Table 2 to interpret their outputs. Additionally, one can consult the literature to find other acceptable ranges of values that can be used to determine items fitting the model (Muller, 2020) or use a rule of thumb.

Equally important is attending to the items that Rasch analysis flags as functioning differently. Andrich and Hagquist (2015) showed that when DIF items are resolved, the functioning of the item also improves (See Figure 3, Graph b). Attending to such items is vital for the improvement of instrument validity. As such, designers are encouraged to pay attention to items that are flagged as problematic. This is because if items are showing signs of misfit and/or DIF, it simply implies that the items are not following the assumption of Rasch measurement.

Missing Data

Missing data is often a problem in research because it may prevent the researcher from making inferences and generalising the findings to the population. Therefore, missing data must be addressed. Data might be missing because respondents respond to items they want to respond to and leave the others out, have insufficient time to complete the items of the instrument, or lack the knowledge to respond to certain items (Hohensinn and Kubinger, 2011; Soysal et al., 2016). Subsequently, data can be missing not at random or missing at random.

Studies have shown that parameter estimation bias increases when missing data increases (Hohensinn & Kubinger, 2011; Soysal et al., 2016). Specifically, a study conducted by Soysal et al. (2016) found that individual-model fit decreased and the ability estimation bias increased as missing data increased. It was also found by Soysal et al. (2016) that in small sample sizes, estimation errors increased as missing data increased by item number. In very large sample sizes, non-imputation of missing data and the use of regression-based estimation provided good results regardless of the increasing volume of missing data (Soysal et al., 2016).

The common way of dealing with missing data is to score the responses as incorrect responses or consider the missing data as items that were not administered at all to the respondents (Hohensinn & Kubinger, 2011). The input of missing data as incorrect responses leads to incorrect estimations (Soysal et al., 2016). Hohensinn and Kubinger (2011) found that these two methods of dealing with missing data led to biased results when looking at the values that determine the fitness of items. When the missing data are marked as incorrect responses or regarded as not administered at all, global and goodness of fit values reveal biased results. These are crucial values that are used to sample the items that will make it to the main instrument; thus, valid estimates should be obtained to make valid inferences about the items and persons.

Combrinck (2018) explored the application of multiple imputations using structural equation modelling and Rasch scores as predictors (Combrinck, 2018) to deal with MNAR dichotomous data. The aim was to model the missing data to best identify a model that can be used for the imputation of missing data. The pairwise deletion method was recommended by Soysal et al. (2016) as a possible way of dealing with missing data. Designers are therefore encouraged to explore a model that can be used to deal with missing data in their studies; this should be done to ensure that the results are not biased and that they reflect the true estimates of the instrument. Missing data treatment can be sought from previous studies similar to the study conducted, or using already existing methods of dealing with missing data that work for that particular study.

CONCLUSION AND RECOMMENDATIONS

In summary, this chapter has argued the viability of Rasch analysis as a method to detect DIF and ascertain the construct validity of the instrument while also outlining aspects that researchers should pay attention to. Rasch analysis is a useful tool for developing and improving an instrument (Caronni et al., 2023). The statistical outputs can be used to inform decision-making and possibly create alternate items should there be a need (Yu, 2020). However, the end users need to be careful of aspects such as sample sizes when using the model. This chapter concludes that Rasch analysis is useful to provide evidence of the psychometric properties of an instrument. The kind of statistics produced in the analysis allows the end user to make informed inferences about the quality of the instrument. The use of Rasch analysis allows the user to improve the items of the instrument, thus increasing adequate measurement of the construct. However, the end user should also be cautious about sample sizes, missing data, items showing signs of misfitting, and DIF. Although the focus of this chapter was on Rasch measurement, as noted in the above discussion, novice users are encouraged to explore all the relevant psychometric theories and choose one that best fits their purpose. The following recommendations were made based on the above discussion.

Recommendations

- To obtain an accurate measurement of the ability tested, a test should have an adequate number of items to measure the ability (Andrich & Hagquist, 2015; Killen, 2010). The greater the number of items in a test, the greater the potential validity and assessment precision (Andrich & Hagquist, 2015). However, unidimensionality and local item independence should be determined.
- Rasch analysis is recommended because it houses many statistical models that one can make use of. Rasch analysis produces PCA residual values that can be used to ascertain the dimensionality of the instrument. The model is useful when one wants to ascertain that the instrument they are developing/ have developed measures a singular construct.
- RMT is effective in ascertaining the reliability and quality of an assessment tool (Caronni et al., 2023; Othman et al., 2012).
- RMT, as a psychometric theory and application, can be taught in social science programmes to enhance the development of high-quality instruments and improve measurements in human sciences (Combrinck, 2018).
- Rasch analysis can be used to create an item bank for a certain construct and ascertain construct-relevant items.
- Rasch analysis can be used for small sample sizes if the data are made up of multiple rounds of testing (Babcock & Hodge, 2020). Instruments can be pilot-tested and analysed using Rasch models until the researcher is satisfied with the results that confirm the validity of the instrument (Combrinck, 2020) before main testing.
- If items cannot be improved, they can be removed. The removal of redundant items can be beneficial because it results in a shorter and more concise measurement of the construct (Makhubele, 2019). Andrich and Hagquist (2015) shared insights on how to resolve DIF in instrument items.
- Rasch models are recommended because they are increasingly used to build new measurement scales, examine already existing scales, and address issues such as cross-cultural validity in instruments (Elhan et al., 2005; Souza et al., 2017). The idea is that the stability of item difficulty can be estimated in

different groups, thereby permitting comparisons of non-overlapping homogenous groups.

REFERENCES

Alavi, S. M., & Bordbar, S. (2018). Differential item functioning analysis of high-stakes test in terms of gender: A Rasch model approach. *MOJES: Malaysian Online Journal of Educational Sciences*, *5*(1), 10–24.

Andersen, E. B. (1977). Sufficient statistics and latent trait models. *Psychometrika*, *42*, 69–81.

Andrich, A. (2004). Controversy and the Rasch Model: A Characteristic of Incompatible Paradigms? *Medical Care*, *42*(1), 1–7. PMID: 14707751

Andrich, D. (2011). *Rasch models for measurement*. Sage.

Andrich, D., & Hagquist, C. (2015). Real and Artificial Differential Item Functioning in Polytomous Items. *SAGE Journals, 75*(2), 185–205. https://doi.org.uplib.idm.oclc.org/10.1177/0013164414534258

Anselmi, P., Colledani, D., & Robusto, E. (2019). A Comparison of Classical and Modern Measures of Internal Consistency. *Frontiers in Psychology*, *10*(2714), 1–10. DOI: 10.3389/fpsyg.2019.02714 PMID: 31866905

Aryadoust, V., Ng, L. Y., & Sayama, H. (2021). A comprehensive review of Rasch measurement in language assessment: Recommendations and guidelines for research. *Language Testing*, *38*(1), 6–40.

Babcock, B., & Hodge, K. J. (2020). Rasch Versus Classical Equating in the Context of Small Sample Sizes. *Educational and Psychological Measurement*, *80*(3), 499–521. DOI: 10.1177/0013164419878483 PMID: 32425217

Bond, T. G., & Fox, C. M. (2015). *Applying the Rasch Model: Fundamental measurement in the human sciences* (3rd ed.). Routledge.

Boone, J. W. (2016). Rasch Analysis for Instrument Development: Why, When, and How? *CBE Life Sciences Education*, *15*(4), 1–7. DOI: 10.1187/cbe.1604-0148 PMID: 27856555

Boone, J. W., & Rogan, J. (2005). Rigour in quantitative analysis: The promise of Rasch analysis techniques, *African Journal of Research in Mathematics. Science and Technology Education*, *9*(1), 25–38. DOI: 10.1080/10288457.2005.10740574

Boone, J. W., Staver, J. R., & Yale, M. S. (2014). *Rasch analysis in the human Sciences*. Springer.

Caronni, A., Ramella, M., Arcuri, P., Salatino, C., Pigini, L., Saruggia, M., Folini, C., Scarano, S., & Converti, R. M. (2023). The Rasch Analysis Shows Poor Construct Validity and Low Reliability of the Quebec User Evaluation of Satisfaction with Assistive Technology 2.0 (QUEST 2.0) Questionnaire. *International Journal of Environmental Research and Public Health, 20*(1036), 1–16. DOI: 10.3390/ijerph20021036 PMID: 36673791

Combrinck, C. (2018). *The use of Rasch Measurement Theory to address measurements and analysis challenges in social science research.* [Doctoral Thesis]. University of Pretoria.

Combrinck, C. (2019). *Rasch unidimensional measurements models: Analysis data in RUMM2030 handout*. University of Pretoria, Centre for Evaluation and Assessment.

Combrinck, C. (2020). Is this a useful instrument? An Introduction to Rasch Measurement Models. In S. Kramer, S. Laher, A. Fynn, & H. H. Janse van Vuuren (Eds.), (pp. 1–48), *Online Readings in Research Methods*. Psychological Society of South Africa: Johannesburg. https://doi.org/DOI: 10.17605/OSF.IO/BNPFS

Combrinck, C. (2024). Not liking the Likert? A Rasch analysis of forced-choice format and usefulness in survey design. *SAGE Open, 14*(4), 1–18. DOI: 10.1177/21582440241295501

Diaz, E., Brooks, G., & Johanson, G. (2021). Detecting Differential Item Functioning: Item Response Theory Methods Versus the Mantel-Haenszel Procedure. *International Journal of Assessment Tools in Education, 8*(2), 376–378.

Ebenbeck, N., & Gebhardt, M. (2022). Simulating computerized adaptive testing in special education based on inclusive progress monitoring data. *Frontiers in Education, 7*(945733), 1–4. DOI: 10.3389/feduc.2022.945733

Elhan, A., Kutlay, Ş., Küçükdeveci, A. A., Cotuk, C., Ozturk, G., Tesio, L., & Tennant, A. (2005). Psychometric properties of the Mini-Mental State Examination in patients with acquired brain injury in Turkey. *Journal of Rehabilitation Medicine, 37*(5), 306–310. DOI: 10.1080/16501970510037573 PMID: 16203619

Fischer, L., Rohm, T., Carstensen, C. H., & Gnambs, T. (2021). Linking of Rasch-Scaled Tests: Consequences of Limited Item Pools and Model Misfit. *Frontiers in Psychology, 12*(633896), 1–9. DOI: 10.3389/fpsyg.2021.633896 PMID: 34295279

Fisher, W. (1992). Reliability Statistics. *Rasch Measurement Transactions, 3*(6), 238.

Hagel, P. (2014). Testing Rating scale Unidimensionality Using the Principal Component Analysis (PCA)/t-test Protocol with the Rasch Model: The Primacy of Theory over Statistics. *Open Journal of Statistics, 4*, 456–459. DOI: 10.4236/ojs.2014.46044

Hagquist, C., & Andrich, D. (2017). Recent advances in analysis of differential item functioning in health research using the Rasch model. *Health and Quality of Life Outcomes, 15*(181), 1–8. DOI: 10.1186/s12955-017-0755-0 PMID: 28927468

Hobson, E. G. (2015). *Using the Rasch model in a computer adaptive testing application to enhance the measurement quality of emotional intelligence*. University of Johannesburg.

Hohensinn, C., & Kubinger, K. D. (2011). On the impact of missing values on item fit and the model validness of the Rasch model. *Psychological Test and Assessment Modeling, 53*(3), 380–393. https://www.proquest.com/scholarly-journals/on-impact-missing-values-item-fit-model-validness/docview/1399684427/se-2

Ismail, R., Noh, M. Z. M., Ismail, N. H., & Tamil, A. M. (2015). A tale of two construct validation analysis: Rasch model and exploratory factor analysis approach for three-factor eating questionnaire (TFEQ-R21) among Malaysian male workers. *The Medical Journal of Malaysia, 70*(3), 169–175. PMID: 26248780

Junker, W. B. (2015). *Factor Analysis and Latent Structure: IRT and Rasch Models* (2nd ed.). International Encyclopedia of the Social & Behavioral Sciences., https://doi.org/https://doi.org/10.1016/B978-0-08-097086-8.24126-4

Killen, R. (2010). *Teaching Strategies Quality Teaching & Learning: Outcome-based assessment.* Juta Publishers.

Linacre, J. M. (1994). *Many-Facet Rasch Measurement* (2nd ed.). Mesa Press.

Linacre, J. M. (2010). Predicting Responses from Rasch measures. *Journal of Applied Measurement, 11*(1), 1–9. PMID: 20351444

Makhubele, M. (2019). Using the Trauma Symptom Checklist for Children-Short form (TSCC-SF) on abused children in South Africa: Confirmatory factor analysis and Rasch models. *Child Abuse & Neglect, 98*(104241), 1–9. DOI: 10.1016/j.chiabu.2019.104241 PMID: 31704542

Medvedev, O. N., & Krägeloh, C. U. (2022). Rasch Measurement Model. In Medvedev, O. N., Krägeloh, C. U., Siegert, R. J., & Singh, N. N. (Eds.), *Handbook of Assessment in Mindfulness Research.* Springer., DOI: 10.1007/978-3-030-77644-2_4-1

Mthimkhulu, S. (2023). *Examining PIRLS 2021: Differential item functioning across English and isiZulu language groups.* [Master's Dissertation]. University of Pretoria.

Muller, M. (2020). Item fit statistics for Rasch analysis: Can we trust them? *Journal of Statistical Distributions and Applications, 7*(5), 1–11. DOI: 10.1186/s40488-020-00108-7

Othman, H., Asshaari, I., Bahaludin, H., Nopiah, Z. M., & Ismail, N. A. (2012). Application of Rasch measurement model in reliability and quality evaluation of examination paper for Engineering Mathematics courses. *Procedia: Social and Behavioral Sciences*, *60*, 163–171. DOI: 10.1016/j.sbspro.2012.09.363

Pallant, J. F., Miller, R. L., & Tennant, A. (2006). Evaluation of the Edinburgh Post Natal Depression Scale using Rasch analysis. *BMC Psychiatry*, *6*(28), 1–9. DOI: 10.1186/1471-244X-6-28 PMID: 16768803

Pelton, T. (2002, April). Where are the limits to the Rasch advantage? In *The International Objective Measurement Workshop*, New Orleans.

Rosli, R., Abdullah, M., Siregar, N. C., Hamid, N. S. A., Abdullah, S., Beng, G. K., Halim, L., Daud, N. M., Bahari, S. A., Majid, R. A., & Bais, B. (2020). Student Awareness of Space Science: Rasch Model Analysis for Validity and Reliability. *World Journal of Education*, *10*(3), 170–177.

Roux, K. (2020). Examining the Equivalence of the PIRLS 2016 Released Texts in South Africa Across Three Languages. [Doctoral Thesis]. University of Pretoria.

Smith, A. B., Rush, R., Fallowfield, L. J., Velikova, G., & Sharpe, M. (2008). Rasch fit statistics and sample size considerations for polytomous data. *BMC Medical Research Methodology*, *8*(33), 1–10. DOI: 10.1186/1471-2288-8-33 PMID: 18510722

Souza, M. A. P., Coster, W. J., Mancini, M. C., Dutra, F. C. M. S., Kramer, J., & Sampaaio, R. F. (2017). Rasch Analysis of the participation scale (P-scale): Usefulness of the P-scale to a rehabilitation service network. *Bio Med Central. Public Health*, *17*(934), 1–3. DOI: 10.1186/s12889-017-4945-9 PMID: 29216914

Soysal, S., Arikan, Ç. A., & Inal, H. (2016). Impact of Missing Data on Rasch Model Estimations. *The Turkish Online Journal of Educational Technology*, (Special issue), 1166–1175.

Stemler, S. E., & Naples, A. (2021). Rasch Measurement vs. Item Response Theory: Knowing when to cross the line. *Practical Assessment, Research & Evaluation*, *26*(11), 1–12. DOI: 10.7275/v2gd-4441

Stolt, M., Kottorp, A., & Suhonen, R. (2022). The use and quality of reporting of Rasch analysis in nursing research: A methodological scoping review. *International Journal of Nursing Studies*, *132*, 104244. PMID: 35635906

Strobl, C., Kopf, J., & Zeileis, A. (2015). Rasch Trees: A new method for detecting differential item functioning in the Rasch model. *Psychometrika*, *80*(2), 289–295. DOI: 10.1007/S11336-013-9388-3 PMID: 24352514

Verhagen, J., Levy, R., Millsap, R. E., & Fox, J. P. (2016). Evaluating evidence for invariant items: A Bayes factor applied to testing measurement invariance in IRT models. *Journal of Mathematical Psychology*, *72*, 171–182.

Wright, B. D. (1995). 3PL IRT or Rasch? *Rasch Measurement Transactions*, *9*, 408.

Wright, D. B. (1997). Solving measurement problems with the Rasch model. *Journal of Educational Measurement*, *14*, 97–116.

Wright, D. B., & Stone, M. H. (1999). Measurement essentials (2nd ed.). Wide range.

Yu, C. H. (2020). Objective Measurement: How Rasch Modeling Can Simplify and Enhance Your Assessment. In Khine, M. (Ed.), *Rasch Measurement*. Springer., DOI: 10.1007/978-981-15-1800-3_4

Zanon, C., Hutz, S. C., Yoo, H. H., & Hambleton, K. R. (2016). An Application of Item Response Theory to psychological test development. *Psicologia: Reflexão e Crítica: Revista Semestral do Departamento de Psicologia da UFRGS*, *29*(18), 1–10. https://doi.org/https://10.1186?s41155-016-0040-x

Zumbo, B. (1999). *A handbook on the theory and methods of differential item functioning: Logistic regression modelling as a unitary framework for binary and Likert-type item scores.* Directorate of Human Resource Research and Evaluation.

ENDNOTES

1 *N* subjects refers to the respondents who took the test/examines/test takers

2 *J* probes means the test, scale, or the items

3 Some scholars dispute this claim (*cf.* Aryadoust et al., 2021, p.8).

4 In CAT, the difficulty of the next item administered to the respondent lies in the previous answer provided by the respondent (Ebenbeck & Gebhardt, 2022)

Chapter 7
Portfolio Assessment in Higher Education:
General Uses and Various Applications

Thaddaeus Dachille
https://orcid.org/0000-0002-2942-729X
Independent Researcher, USA

ABSTRACT

This chapter explores portfolio assessment in undergraduate education, offering practical guidance for students and instructors. It examines three common portfolio formats: websites, USB flash drives, and compact discs. The chapter provides strategies for effective implementation. These strategies include but are not limited to the planning and the selection phase of your portfolio contents and the design considerations needed for enhancing your portfolio's aesthetics to improve self-branding and viewer engagement. Other strategies in the chapter include some sample ideas and adaptable rubrics drawn from several generalizable fields of study, with the goal of providing applicable and adaptable resources for readers. Since the chapter is written for a broad and transferable understanding of the topic of portfolio evaluations, the chapter's material is relevant to students, instructors, and instructional support professionals across a wide range of disciplines in higher education.

INTRODUCTION

This chapter explores portfolio assessment in undergraduate education, offering practical guidance for students and instructors. It examines three common portfolio

DOI: 10.4018/979-8-3373-7057-6.ch007

formats: websites, USB flash drives, and compact discs. The chapter provides strategies for effective implementation. These strategies include but are not limited to the planning and the selection phase of your portfolio contents and the design considerations needed for enhancing your portfolio's aesthetics to improve self-branding and viewer engagement. Other strategies in the chapter include some sample ideas and adaptable rubrics drawn from several generalizable fields of study, with the goal of providing applicable and adaptable resources for readers. Since the chapter is written for a broad and transferable understanding of the topic of portfolio evaluations, the chapter's material is relevant to students, instructors, and instructional support professionals across a wide range of disciplines in higher education.

WHAT IS A PORTFOLIO

Portfolios provide a valuable means for students to demonstrate and gauge their abilities in a field of study (Carpenter, Ray, & Bloom, 1995). Portfolio assessments can be considered a form of inquiry-based learning because this form of evaluation prompts students to respond to a series of questions, determining how and which samples of their documentation best answer those aforementioned questions (Hollins, 2019). A portfolio project is also a dynamically reflexive assignment, because instructors provide feedback directly within the student-created project when they return the assignment to the student. This fosters a collaborative and thought provoking learning environment for both students and instructors.

As a multifaceted examination tool, that showcases work samples, the portfolio's "contents" are often guided towards a specific audience. These samples are gathered over a designated period and compiled into a structured format, which is the portfolio itself. As previously stated, portfolios serve as a form of evaluation, that is increasingly electronic in nature (Syzdykova, Koblandin, Mikhaylova, & Akinina, 2021). Evolving from their origins in the visual arts as an entirely paper-based product, portfolios have transitioned to the digitized format prevalent today (Thomas, 1998; Davis and Ponnamperuma, 2005). The transition and mass adoption of portfolio assignments in diverse fields of study has been hastened by the development of personal computers. While portfolios are often exclusively presented digitally, they can also be simultaneously presented in a traditional, paper-based format. If a paper format is also chosen, it is crucial to ensure a professional presentation through high-quality digital printing and the use of a glossy paper; and, it is recommended to use appropriate packaging solutions that could include a leather binder, or a coil or hardbound binding.

The work samples within a portfolio can encompass a variety of items that can include student writings, speeches, video productions, artwork, and other exemplary sources of documentation that has been self-selected by the student (Carpenter, Ray, & Bloom, 1995; Driessen, 2017). These selections can represent work from a single class, a semester, or an entire academic program. A comprehensive portfolio typically contains ten to twenty exemplary student work samples (Carpenter, Ray, & Bloom, 1995). The diverse nature of portfolio content allows for significant customization by the student. The use of portfolios in higher education spans a wide range of disciplines, including:

- Liberal arts and sciences, general studies, and humanities;
- Fine arts, dance, and theatre;
- Health professions and related programs;
- Business;
- Professional studies in education;
- Engineering;
- Computer and information science;
- And law enforcement and firefighting.

This list represents a selection of fields where portfolios can be utilized for assessment purposes. The broad applicability of portfolio review in higher education suggests its continued and expanding use in the future, particularly with the development of new technologies. For example, wearable heads-up displays could potentially offer innovative ways to present portfolio content – and this will be more widely investigated in the last section of this chapter titled, *Into the future: The hypothetical possibilities of portfolio assessments*. Conclusively, the personal nature of portfolios, often incorporating self-directed and experiential learning approaches are valued in education – contributing to its concurrent value and expanded use within the learning industry.

While portfolio assessments offer a valuable test solution to survey your students' learning gains, they are sometimes underutilized by instructors. While not always the most convenient option, portfolios can be effectively implemented across various fields of study. However, instructors should be mindful that grading a portfolio requires significant time and effort compared to other methods, such as a multiple-choice test (Kuon, Philbrick, & Gill, 2024; Zaabalawi and Zaabalawi, 2024). Multiple-choice tests can be efficiently graded using automated tools like Codio.com, which can quickly assess student responses based on pre-formatted options. Furthermore, multiple-choice tests can be administered and supervised by graduate assistants, reducing the time investment required from the instructor.

When selecting an examination method, it is crucial to carefully weigh the pros and cons of using each process. Importantly, the use of a portfolio evaluation often requires significant time and effort from instructors, while multiple-choice tests can be efficiently graded using automated tools, reducing the instructor's workload. It's important to recognize that portfolio assessment may not be the most appropriate method for every instructor or to use in a large seminar classroom. The choice of assessment method ultimately rests with the instructor, and the adoption of a portfolio method is solely based on the specific objectives and student learning outcomes. The following section will delve further into the various formats of modern portfolios, providing a deeper understanding of their diverse possibilities and modalities.

WHAT FORMAT DO TYPICAL PORTFOLIOS COME IN?

The abundance of choices in modern life, from fast-food menus to educational methodologies, can be both exciting and overwhelming. Just as a fast-food menu presents a wide array of options, educators face a similarly diverse range of portfolio assessment methods. While each portfolio method of delivery has its own set of complexities, many are also relatively straightforward to implement. This section will explore several of the most commonly implemented portfolio assessment methods.

While portfolio assessment originated in the fine arts, primarily for showcasing visual artwork in print form, its modern applications have expanded significantly across higher education, encompassing diverse digital formats (Thomas, 1998; Davis and Ponnamperuma, 2005). Currently, the most common delivery methods for portfolios include: website portfolios, USB Flash drive portfolios, and Compact disc portfolios.

Figure 1. Three types of modern portfolio to choose from

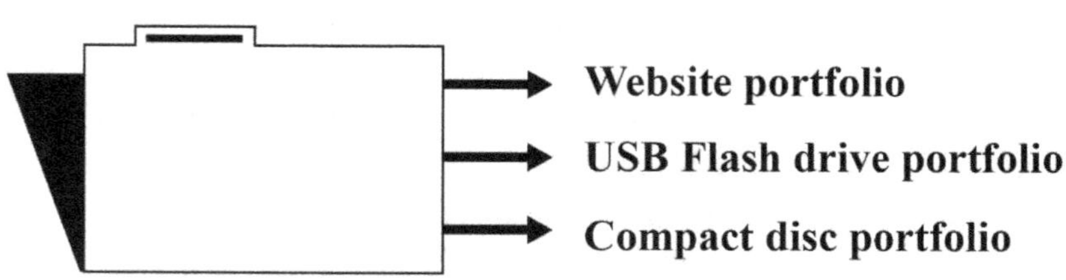

Figure I. Digital portfolios have largely replaced traditional paper versions. Today, they are most commonly found as websites, on USB flash drives, or on compact discs. While a professionally printed and packaged hard copy can serve as a valuable backup in case of technological issues, digital formats are now the standard.

These formats represent the most contemporary and widely applicable means of portfolio delivery. Given the ease of dissemination and the pervasiveness of web-based technology, presenting a paper portfolio in today's environment would be unusual. Among the three digital options, websites offer the greatest accessibility. Due to their user-friendliness in contemporary higher education, a more thorough exploration of the considerations involved in creating a portfolio website is warranted. However, it's important to acknowledge the increased planning required for website portfolios. Students, instructors, and instructional staff developing these websites must consider several factors, including:

a. Whether to purchase a web domain and the associated cost;
b. The availability and expense of hosting for the portfolio website;
c. And, whether the portfolio website should utilize a dynamic or static presentation (definitions of these terms are available in the chapter glossary).

These three considerations are paramount when selecting a modern web-based portfolio delivery method.

Given these factors, it's understandable why some students might opt for a USB Flash drive or compact disc portfolio format. These alternative methods can be easier to produce when facing tight deadlines or budget constraints that limit the planning required for website implementation.

Of the additional choices to make a portfolio, that include a USB flash drive or compact disc, careful attention should be paid to its presentation. Enhancing the visual appeal through creative design is crucial. Equally important is consideration to the user's experience. When planning your portfolio, you should be thinking about how the users will they interact with the content you present them with.

To facilitate this interaction, explore software options within the Adobe Creative Suite. Adobe InDesign is a powerful tool that allows for the creation of both interactive Portable Document Format (PDF) and traditional print layouts. While Adobe Creative Suite can be costly, explore options like student licenses, free trials, or used software to make it accessible. Alternatively, Adobe Animate can be resourced to create interactive presentations with easy-to-use navigation. When choosing how to present your content (if you present your portfolio with something other than a website) the author advises using InDesign because it offers greater flexibility, enabling the simultaneous creation of both interactive and print versions for wider dissemination. If access to Adobe Creative Suite or the individual products mentioned above is unavailable, a well-designed, interactive Microsoft PowerPoint presentation can be a viable alternative for showcasing your portfolio. While it may not offer the same level of sophistication and professional polish as Adobe products, it still allows for the creation of an attractive and presentable portfolio.

Figure 2. Display of your portfolio with its main features

Figure 2. This figure describes some of the main areas you should consider when developing your digital portfolio. These areas are described in the graphic as a clear and consistent header, placing easy to use navigation on your landing page, images that align with the content to reinforce the multimodal statement you are making, and clear, easy to read writing that reinforces your multimodal message of your digital portfolio.

Although this section outlines several portfolio formats to help determine the most suitable option, it's essential to remember that portfolio requirements vary depending on the specific context. Therefore, the most appropriate technology should be selected for each portfolio assessment, and this format should be clearly communicated to students at the student's earliest convenience. The next section will offer practical guidance on incorporating basic design elements into portfolios to improve the readability and visual appeal of student work.

SELECTION OF PORTFOLIO CONTENTS

Selecting content for a portfolio requires careful consideration. Begin by gathering a comprehensive collection of materials and then carefully choose the most impactful examples that align with the portfolio's goals and objectives. To aid in this selection process, consider developing a "mind map" to visualize the main concepts and identify the strongest pieces (Hollins, 2019). A mind map is a brainstorming activity that helps you visualize the main concepts surrounding a topic. So, for a portfolio, the items thoughts surround this focused mind map would include imagery, information, and documentation that you feel would best represent your abilities.

To guide your selection process, utilize the mnemonic "**P.L.A.N.**":

- **P**recise: Ensure your portfolio selections align closely with the provided rubric.
- **L**ayout: Choose a portfolio layout that is visually appealing and appropriate for your field.
- **A**nalyze: Reflect on your professional goals and tailor your portfolio to showcase your strengths and career aspirations.
- **N**etwork: Consider your portfolio as a professional networking tool and explore opportunities to share it online with peers working in your industry of choice and potential future employers.

By following these strategies, you can effectively select the most impactful content for your portfolio and showcase your skills and accomplishments in a professional document.

This section investigated some strategies to help you select content for a portfolio project. The strategies included in this section discussed developing a mind map based on learning strategies identified by Hollins (2019). The section also addressed a memory tool, a mnemonic described as **P.L.A.N.** Armed with these strategies, you should have some ideas about how to select the best content for any portfolio project you undertake. In the next section, the author will talk about designing your portfolio. It takes an approach that assumes not everyone making a portfolio is an art major or even an artist. It just offers some simple strategies to make a visually pleasing portfolio to better enhance the delivery of your material to its respective viewers.

Should you spend time designing your portfolio (even if you are not an art major)?

The answer to whether design matters in a portfolio is a resounding yes. We live in a visual world, and as visual beings, we must apply basic design principles to every product we create, including academic portfolios in fields like mathematics or history. With readily available free tools like Canva, even basic design elements can be incorporated to enhance visual appeal and aesthetics.

Several key factors contribute to a well-designed portfolio:

a.) Consistency
b.) Color choices
c.) Typography
d.) Personal branding
e.) The message
f.) The tone
g.) And the format

Consistency in the design of your portfolio is crucial. Maintaining the same layout and font throughout the portfolio creates a unified and professional look. This principle extends to other design elements as well. Consistent color choices, or a well-chosen color palette, contribute to visual harmony. The overarching goal of consistency is to create a cohesive and visually appealing presentation.

Color choice in your portfolio is equally important. Colors evoke emotions; warm colors (orange, red, yellow, and their combinations) advance, while cool colors (blue, green, purple, and their combinations) recede (Flanagan, n.d.). Consider the emotional impact of your chosen colors. As Joyce Walsh Macario notes in *Graphic Design Essentials: Skills, Software, and Creative Solutions*, "color is a very powerful and provocative design element, but using multiple colors successfully can be challenging." Utilize free online tools, such Adobe Color should be resourced for your design process. This online website helps you select complimentary, analogous, and other color harmonies to use in your portfolio that work well together and make your project look great!

Typography, or the fonts you select in your portfolio also conveys meaning and makes a statement. Readability is the most critical factor when choosing fonts. While design experts might employ unique fonts for artistic expression, it's generally recommended to prioritize readability for broader audiences (Smith, 1993). Just like with color, there are a number of websites available that can offer you free fonts to download and use in your projects. Look for a useful link at the end of the chapter where you can download a number of free fonts.

In today's competitive job market, establishing a **personal brand** early in one's career is highly advantageous (McNally & Speak, 2010). Shaping how others perceive your value, competence, and trustworthiness through strong relationships is a key component of branding. In your portfolio, whether created as an undergraduate or a professional, you can effectively communicate your brand strength. To leverage brand development in your portfolio, maintain a consistent message throughout your example and showcase your professional connections with hyperlinks.

A portfolio, as a designed project, requires careful consideration of its message, tone, and format. As Frank Chimero articulates in *The Shape of Design (2015)*, "All design work seems to have three common traits: there is a message to the work, the tone of that message, and the format that the work takes. Successful design has all three elements working in co-dependence to achieve a whole greater than the sum of the individual parts." A compelling portfolio effectively integrates these interdependent elements throughout its development.

The **message** of a portfolio is its content. It should remain focused on the portfolio's intended purpose. Adhering closely to instructor guidelines and referencing the provided rubric will help maintain this focus.

Tone refers to the way the message is presented. It reflects the level of formality and style. An art student, for example, might have more aesthetic flexibility and could adopt a less traditionally "professional" tone, perhaps experimenting with bolder design choices. A business student, on the other hand, should likely adopt a highly professional tone, ensuring that fonts, colors, and overall design are clear and accessible to any viewer.

The **format** of a portfolio typically falls into one of the three categories discussed earlier: website, USB drive, or compact disc. While these options are often pre-determined, students who have a choice should select the delivery method that best showcases their work while remaining cost-effective. Website portfolios, for example, can incur additional expenses such as domain registration and hosting.

Visual considerations are important, especially for visually inclined students, as portfolio development can uncover hidden talents. Designing and implementing this innovative assessment format also presents exciting challenges. The following section will provide practical examples of how portfolio assessments can be used in various disciplines within higher education.

THE PRACTICAL APPLICATION OF A PORTFOLIO ASSESSMENT IN THE CLASSROOM

As Clive Humby, the renowned mathematician, is often quoted as saying, "data is the new oil" (Talagala, 2022). Like any valuable commodity, data provides key insights into students: their values, work habits, interests, and backgrounds. This data is a crucial resource for educators at all levels. Assessment serves as a tool to extract this valuable information, this "black gold," from students.

Portfolio assessment yields several important data points, including:

a.) A snapshot of student growth, learning gains, and achievements over time (Driessen, 2017);
b.) Insights into students' teamwork and collaborative learning skills;
c.) Identification of procrastination or preparedness;
d.) Discovery of unseen student talents that might be missed by other assessment methods.

Unlike simple paper tests, portfolios often provide a more comprehensive view of student growth, learning, and achievement over time (Driessen, 2017). These are just some of the factors that make portfolios a valuable assessment tool. The longitudinal nature of portfolio use, requiring students to gather materials over time, allows teachers to observe gains (or lack thereof) and understand student progress over a longer period than traditional tests allow. This extended timeframe offers a clearer picture of student success (or struggle).

If the portfolio assessment is collaborative, it can provide insights into students' teamwork and cooperation. Group work often reveals student motivations and can help identify personal challenges that peers may have when working together. For instance, when implementing a group portfolio project, there can be isolated events where certain individuals have a hard time working together with others and this can help someone sense personal prejudices they may have towards certain classmates or peers in the academic program.

Similarly, any longitudinal project, such as a portfolio assignment, can help identify students that struggle with procrastination. The demands of a college semester require students to manage their time effectively, a skill they may not have fully developed previously in high school. Instructors sometimes play a supportive role in helping students improve their time management skills. Identifying procrastination through alternative assessments like portfolios can help students who might otherwise struggle and may not have completely gained these skills earlier in life.

Test anxiety can prevent some students from fully demonstrating their cognitive abilities through traditional assessments. Using a variety of assessment methods, including portfolios, can provide a more complete understanding of the student population. This broader perspective can highlight both student struggles and hidden talents that would or could be unsensed with only in-classroom high pressure testing such as timed scantron tests or essay formats.

While portfolio assessment offers valuable insights, its practical application requires careful consideration. Just as portfolios can uncover hidden talents, they can also obscure student abilities. Group projects, for example, may allow peers to inadvertently mask the performance of an underperforming student. As discussed earlier, instructors should carefully weigh the pros and cons of portfolio assessment and select methods appropriate for their specific classroom context and student population. Building on this discussion, the following section provides additional implementation strategies and prompts key considerations for instructors planning to utilize this non-traditional assessment approach.

HOW SHOULD AN INSTRUCTOR INCLUDE A PORTFOLIO ASSESSMENT IN CLASSROOM?

Continuing this conversation hinted at in the previous section, considering to use a portfolio should be deeply thought-out by every instructor. There are several thoughts that should converge and they are as follows, 1.) if the content is best evaluated using a portfolio format as a summative assessment? And, is this the most appropriate means to evaluate student understanding for the subject being evaluated? Another consideration includes 2.) does the rubric used by the instructor ensure the proper time for students to gather the most appropriate examples of their student work to be evaluated? These considerations are valuable and they are further considered bellow:

1.) The consideration of whether to use a summative portfolio project by an instructor in higher education should begin in the class planning phase prior to the launch of any new class. This is important to give sufficient time to plan for a summative portfolio assessment in order to give the students ample time to consider the criteria needed for an assessment of this nature and to select key work samples needed to showcase their abilities and understanding.
2.) The restated planning phase of considering a summative portfolio assessment by any instructor in higher education is needed because a comprehensive rubric should be established for students at the beginning of the new class when the syllabus is given to students. This way, students can plan all semester for the summative portfolio project and consider the work they produce to better align with the beforementioned criteria established by the instructor.

Thinking, thinking, thinking, you should be always thinking about how to best strategize your students towards the success you anticipate they will have when you give them a portfolio assignment. There is a saying, "the devil is in the details", and in a portfolio assignment, the details you give your students quells their concerns and gives them a broad understanding of what you will expect from them – and - what their portfolio should contain. In order to give you more understanding of how to place detailed directions with the goals and objectives to strategize and help you develop an upcoming portfolio assignment; the next section will work with you to help you develop the goals and objectives you should include in a portfolio assessment.

ALIGNMENT OF PORTFOLIO GOALS AND OBJECTIVES

When planning your portfolio project, it is important to align the portfolio goals with curriculum standards and learning objectives; This will provide strategies to teachers for addressing specific, measurable, and achievable learning objectives with an assessment portfolio. To review, momentarily, when planning a portfolio project, aligning portfolio goals with curriculum standards and learning objectives is crucial for achieving specific, measurable, and achievable learning outcomes. A goal is a broad, overarching aim, while objectives are the specific steps needed to achieve that goal. Think of goals as the desired outcome (e.g., "a delicious cake") and objectives as the necessary ingredients (e.g., flour, sugar, eggs). With this distinction in mind, let's explore how to align portfolio goals with learning objectives.

In order to best align your portfolio goals with the specific learning objectives LinkedIn Advice (n.d.) offers a few utilitarian suggestions to expedite this process, they include:

a.) Start with a rubric or checklist;
b.) Select the context of the content you want the students to include;
c.) Ensure that the evidence you will be gathering (or asking your students to gather) is clear, measurable, and is comparable to the requirements you are asking to be measured;
d.) Go back and review your requirements one more time ensuring that you did not miss anything important and that any revisions you need to make are completed prior to providing this assignment to students.

When instructors carefully align goals and objectives in a portfolio assignment, students gain a clear understanding of the project criteria. This clarity often translates to fewer student questions, as the detailed assignment materials address most potential points of confusion. From an instructor's perspective, anticipating student questions and addressing them proactively in the project description can significantly reduce the workload associated with fielding inquiries later. Thorough planning before assigning the project minimizes the need for clarification afterward.

In the next section, we will see some examples of common portfolio in higher education. This will include some of the specific items that are commonly found in field-specific portfolio assignments from generalizable areas of study, although the author notes that the content taught form program to program is assumed to be delivered in different ways.

THREE COMMON PORTFOLIO USES IN HIGHER EDUCATION

Portfolios are widely used in higher education. This section highlights three popular areas instructors can utilize portfolios to assess student learning. Portfolio examples include traditional art students' portfolios, nursing students' portfolios, and business students' internship portfolios.

An art portfolio, which is typically in a digital format, is used "to collect students' works purposefully in order to understand students' efforts, progress or achievements, and it is an important tool of course assessments" (Lu, 2007, p. 164). Images utilized in an art portfolio should contain a threaded together theme, whether that is similarities with color, design choices, abstractions that have appropriate congruency, and other features that show continuity, planning, and thematically appropriate formulations of imagery that tie the artwork examples together and make them seem like the same art student produced the artworks.

Table 1. Sample art student's portfolio

Categories of the general questions to guide the student when developing the portfolio:	**Aesthetic look and design of the portfolio**	**Portfolio writing**	**Making connections to other examples student has created**	**Materials used in the artwork presented**
These are general questions to guide the student when developing the portfolio:	How is the portfolio designed, has there been effort to emphasize a unique and profound visual look?	Is the writing in the portfolio clear, easy to read, and written to a general audience?	How does the artwork presented in the portfolio relate to other examples the artist has made?	Does the students portfolio use art materials in novel and creative ways?
These are general questions to guide the student when developing the portfolio:	Has the artist incorporated color or symbolism in the portfolio design? How is the typography used in the portfolio, does it add or detract from the message, tone, and format the artist selected?	Does the portfolio contain clear and easy to find contact information for stakeholders to reach the artist?	Is it clearly understood that only one artist has created this portfolio or should the examples be revised?	Are the materials utilized in the portfolio artwork examples consistent with other examples the artist has created and displayed in the portfolio?

This rubric has been adapted from art portfolio rubric research developed by Groenendijk, Kárpáti, and Haanstra (2020). The rubric addresses several areas of visual art such as the design of the portfolio itself to the artwork showcased in the portfolio.

While distinct from an art student's portfolio, a medical student portfolio also serves as a valuable assessment tool (Thomas, 1998; Davis and Ponnamperuma, 2005). Like portfolios across other disciplines, medical portfolios often include specific elements. Medical students can showcase their learning and engagement through various methods incorporated within the portfolio. Written reflections, such as journal or diary entries concisely and clearly describing medical procedures, are one common component (Reed, 2015). Lists of completed readings demonstrate engagement with academic materials. Documenting attendance at relevant talks highlights a student's commitment to expanding their knowledge. Finally, completed student projects provide tangible proof of learning and progress can be captured in a comprehensive medical student portfolio. These diverse formats within the portfolio offer a wide-ranging view of the student's educational journey, contributing valuable insights into their developing medical expertise. This approach to assessment is relevant across various healthcare fields, including nursing.

Table 2. Sample nursing student's portfolio

Categories of the general questions to guide the student when developing the portfolio:	Aesthetic look and design of the portfolio	Portfolio writing	Showcase of learning	Demonstration of sufficient academic ability
These are general questions to guide the student when developing the portfolio:	How is the portfolio designed, has there been effort to emphasize a clean and professional look?	Is the writing in the portfolio clear, easy to read, and written to a general audience? Did the student successfully synthesize complex information?	How does the documentation in the portfolio enhance the credibility of the student as they step into a professional career?	Does the student example provide tangible proof of a comprehensive knowledge of medical content?
These are general questions to to guide the student when developing the portfolio:	Has the nursing student incorporated their personal brand into the portfolio? How is the typography used in the portfolio, does it contribute to a more professional message or detract from it?	Does the portfolio contain clear and easy to find contact information for stakeholders to reach the nursing student?	Is the documentation sufficient to make the case that learning gains have occurred over the course of the nursing students training?	How does the content presented in the portfolio provide a panoramic view of the student's educational journey?

This rubric has been adapted from medical student portfolio literature provided by Reed (2015). The rubric addresses several categories typically included in a nursing students portfolio requirements.

A business student portfolio distinguishes itself from portfolios in other higher education disciplines due to several key characteristics. Often, it's specifically designed to document and track the critical internship phase of a student's academic journey (David and Hein, 2012). This focus on the internship experience means the portfolio's structure is tailored to record the student's time spent in this practical setting. Beyond simply tracking time, the portfolio includes valuable insights from various stakeholders. Tutors who supervise the student's placement contribute their observations and notes on the student's performance. Similarly, it is common practice for all individuals involved in the internship, including supervisors at the internship site, to provide feedback and evaluations. These contributions offer a comprehensive perspective on the student's progress and development. The portfolio, therefore, becomes a repository of information reflecting the student's practical skills and professional growth during the internship. This detailed record serves as a valuable tool for assessment and reflection. Ultimately, the business student portfolio offers a unique snapshot of their transition from academic learning to real-world application.

Table 3. Sample business student's portfolio

Categories of the general questions to guide the student when developing the portfolio:	**Aesthetic look and design of the portfolio**	**Portfolio writing**	**Showcase of learning**	**Demonstration of sufficient academic ability**
These are general questions to to guide the student when developing the portfolio:	How is the portfolio designed, has there been effort to emphasize a clean and professional look?	Is the writing in the portfolio clear, easy to read, and written to a general audience?	How does the documentation in the portfolio provide sufficient evidence that the student is capable of networking with diverse stakeholders in a multi-level organization?	Did the student include stakeholder commentary from their site placement to make the project more collaborative and contain more sources of data?
These are general questions to guide the student when developing the portfolio:	Has the business student incorporated their personal brand into the portfolio? How is the typography used in the portfolio, does it contribute to a more professional message or detract from it?	Does the portfolio contain easy to find contact information for stakeholders to reach the business student?	Does the documentation adequately make the case that the student has made a difference while deployed in their internship setting? Is there additional sources of documentation that further highlight the students experience in the placement?	How does the content presented in the portfolio provide a panoramic view of the student's experience in the placement? Did the writing in the portfolio have a gannet chart to give a timeline for the student's deployment?

This rubric has been adapted from research presented by David and Hein (2012) *discussing how to develop and deploy a business student's portfolio. The rubric addresses several categories often associated with a business student's site internship portfolio project that is a capstone project at some universities to fulfill a student's graduation requirements.*

These examples illustrate the diverse elements that can be incorporated into a portfolio assignment. These elements might include visual images, student reflections, lists of acquired knowledge or skills, and feedback from stakeholders at an internship site. While these suggestions are often associated with specific fields of study, they can be adapted and applied to any discipline in higher education. They represent only a fraction of the possibilities, as instructors have considerable flexibility in customizing portfolio evaluations. In general, instructors assigning portfolios should emphasize the importance of professionalism and demonstrating growth over time. Students should therefore consider including relevant awards, community service experiences, or certifications earned in their chosen field and summarize or list these notable events in their finished portfolio.

The following section outlines the benefits and limitations of portfolio assignments. Given the many factors instructors consider when planning a course and designing instruction to maximize student learning, careful planning is crucial. This next section will help educators determine if portfolio assessment is appropriate for their students and classroom.

THE BENEFITS AND LIMITATIONS OF USING PORTFOLIO ASSESSMENTS IN THE CLASSROOM

Before implementing a portfolio assignment, instructors should carefully weigh its potential benefits and limitations. These considerations should ultimately guide the decision to use any assessment tool, and this section explores key aspects to inform the decision of whether or not to utilize portfolio assessment. The positive attributes will first be discussed in this section, then, negative aspects of portfolio use will be conversed.

Portfolios can foster deeper learning and critical thinking skills among students. This occurs when a student develops a portfolio, they self-analyze their work, considering what examples they have produced are the strongest and what examples are less stellar. This self-analyzation process strengthens the student's inner critic, bolsters their ability to set their own learning priorities, and empowers students with a clearer inner voice, which helps the student develop discernment skills and a deeper more innate personal voice (Kuon, Philbrick, & Gill, 2024; Syzdykova, Koblandin, Mikhaylova, & Akinina, 2021).

Portfolios can empower students to take ownership of their learning and develop essential job specific skills not found in other assessment tools because of the emphasis placed on language. Portfolios, when done correctly, utilize the jargon (vocabulary) of the field of study the portfolio is developed within. This contextual language grounds the learner in the development of the portfolio and helps the student begin to set clear goals and sets forth "a basis of conversations between the teacher and the student" (Hetland, Winner, Veenema, & Sheridan, 2014, p. 88).

When using a portfolio assignment, students can gain enhanced communication skills. This is perhaps due to the tremendous amount of time it takes each student to complete a compressive portfolio assignment. With the lengthy amount of time required to complete a portfolio, there is a process of deep reflection that occurs (Kuon, Philbrick, & Gill, 2024; Syzdykova, Koblandin, Mikhaylova, & Akinina, 2021). Like a ship conducting a sounding exercise to sense the depth of the ocean floor, personal reflection that occurs when developing a portfolio offers a means to sense and feel the depth of learning gained on a topic.

Another source of communication skill development includes learning to write detailed and succinct summaries of information (Reed, 2015). An application of this form of communication development includes the practice of writing summaries of information when sorting out thinking involved over a certain period of time and generating summaries of the learning gained in a particular course.

Other important features of a portfolio assignment include the emphasis on collaboration. When students complete a portfolio, they practice collaboration. The collaborative process can be internal, in a form of self-collaboration, that is often referred to in educational terminology as reflexive learning (Hollins, 2019). The reflexivity that occurs when self-analyzing ones thinking happens whenever a student considers how or why they advanced towards new understandings and new levels of personal development in a particular subject; or they describe the systematic process the student used to gain the cognitive skills they developed on a particular topic. Rodriguez, Martinez-Ulloa, and Flores-Bustos (2022), as cited by Zaabalawi and Zaabalawi (2024), also found that there is almost always a external collaboration that occurs between the teacher and a student when delivering a portfolio. They found that there is often a complete feedback loop that takes place with the development and delivery of a portfolio, because there is a sharing of ideas between the instructor and student(s) whenever the assignment is returned. This collaboration of feedback and ideas occurs more often than on other forms of assessments and so it encourages more collaboration, especially between instructors and students.

One of the most important benefits of using a portfolio examination includes the reduction of text anxiety. As it can be understood that examinations are necessary to capture an accurate understanding of the students' abilities and understanding of content. Sometimes traditional examinations place tremendous pressure on students, who must perform well on the exam day to gain an exemplary grade in a class (Zaabalawi and Zaabalawi, 2024). One of the benefits of using a portfolio assessment is that students have reduced pressure to perform because the assessment takes place over a set period of time and there is no significant test anxiety presented to the learner.

Finally, in order for the portfolio assignment to be successful it must be reliable and valid. In order to be reliable, Deborah Meier, author of *In Schools We Trust* (2003), states that it should have the same criteria used consistently, and that each student is fully aware of this during the examination. So, for a portfolio the criteria being assessed should be very similar from one student to another or from one institution to another. The sense of consistency between portfolios should be noted and visible – for all to see. Another feature that should be contained on every portfolio developed is that each one created should be valid. To be valid, any type of assessment should have a set of predetermined yet mutually agreed upon criteria. These are items that are the same over and over again and these elements remain the same over long periods of time; they hardly change and therefore they can be dependable and reliable. When it comes to a portfolio, and to make it valid, one should always use a rubric.

One potential drawback of portfolio assessment is its inherent subjectivity. Evaluator bias can influence the grading process, particularly when instructors overlook the comprehensive nature of such a substantial assessment. This bias can manifest in several ways, such as neglecting to use a rubric during evaluation or failing to apply consistent rubric criteria and feedback practices across all students, thus compromising grading accuracy and equitable feedback.

A second potential drawback of a portfolio examination includes the time-consuming nature of creating and evaluating student portfolios. It has been said that anything worth doing takes time. This is never truer then when it comes to building a skyscraper. Countless hours of planning go into the research and development of any such large monolithic structure. A portfolio can be seen metaphorically as a personal skyscraper. This large structure is comparative to one's success and achievements completed over a set period of time. With the time it takes time to build a skyscraper, often taking many months just to dig out and set its strong foundation, portfolios are also time consuming when planning and gathering the examples needed for this similarly one-of-a-kind structure. The foundation can be seen as the lengthy set of achievements a student has completed over the semester, or entire time in school. This "foundation of achievements" is then relied upon when a student begins to self-evaluate the items they would like to catalog in their portfolio.

This section discussed some of the benefits and limitations of using a portfolio assessment, which is another name for a non-traditional "test". The areas in this section discussed mostly positive items however there are certain limitations that were also considered in this section. From the minor drawbacks to using this form of assessment, personal bias is an important consideration when choosing this examination method. In the next section, the author will discuss in greater detail the personal bias that can occur when using this assessment method.

THE INFLUENCE OF TEACHER BIAS ON PORTFOLIO-BASED GRADING

We all have bias. Whether we want to admit this or not we all have been shaped by our past experiences and upbringing. This introduces an on-again off-again challenge of sometimes having trouble getting along with or working well with certain other people. Whether they look like someone who was once mean to us or if it was an ingrained hostility towards a person or group of people instilled in us as young children we are influenced by our own biases. Bias is defined by the Oxford dictionary as "prejudice in favor of or against one thing, person, or group compared with another, usually in a way considered to be unfair". Overcoming our bias, in personal life, is one of the most important tasks we as educators need to confront.

When assessing a student portfolio bias can be a problem – just like in our personal lives. Bias takes many forms when assessing a portfolio. It can be outright, where we have a personal feeling of hostility towards another person whether intentional or unintentional. By definition bias is not seeing the whole person or entity because of a preexisting prejudice against that person or a group. Bias can emerge because of one's innate or developmental background that subjugated a person towards feeling hostility towards another person. As a reflexive educator, it is important to continually confront one's bias directly as to not let this become a hinderance in the classroom or when viewing work and giving it a fair evaluation.

Sometimes bias can be minimal and even unintended, even if we are doing our best as an educator to quell our personal biases. In qualitative and mixed-methods research, bias can be a simple mishandling of data. For instance, if a researcher fails to treat each source of data with the same consideration as other sources of data, this identifies a bias (Fink, 2019). Even if the researcher is tiered and just not having the same energy needed to approach each source of data the same as a previous source – this is a form of bias. As a teacher, if we fail to handle the review of each student's portfolio with the same care, consideration, and dedication to giving detailed and yet specific feedback we could be succumbing to bias. Even if it is not intentional or even a personal dislike of a particular student.

Another form of soft bias can occur in any form of self-directed evaluation especially if the rubric has not been evaluated by a third party prior to its implementation (Smith and Noble, 2014). Remember, when someone encounters bias they are unfairly or unjustly evaluated. Sometimes this is not from any outright prejudice against the other person or group of people but simply not following the protocol needed to maintain personal rigor in our evaluation process as educators. Therefore, the inclination of bias is possible and to avoid any unintended bias towards any student, the instructor must utilize the grading rubric, just like the student to avoid any unwanted bias that could hinder the fair and just results.

This section discussed the possibility of bias. Typically, bias considered as not treating a person or group of people fairly based on prejudice. Sometimes, however, bias can be unintended, and this can occur when we do not use the same protocol to grade each student's assignment with the same consistency and rigor. Bias can also occur when we do not have our rubrics double checked by a peer that can help us weed out any unwanted statements, thoughts, or unintended biases that a second "pair of eyes" can help us see as teachers. As the chapter proceeds, in the next section, learn more about the importance of timely and effective feedback.

EFFECTIVE FEEDBACK FOR STUDENT PORTFOLIOS

This section outlines the best practices for providing effective feedback to students on their portfolio assignments. It focuses on three areas: 1.) crafting impactful feedback statements, 2.) giving timely feedback, and 3.) understanding and addressing individual student needs.

1.) **Impactful Feedback Statements:**

Providing praise is crucial, even when a student's work may not be as developed or as comprehensive as others in the class. Recognize the effort that each student has made and highlight all of the positive aspects of their work. Avoid generic, meaningless praise and instead offer specific, genuine compliments focused on the examples and grounded in their work alone. Importantly, remain focused on the subject of the portfolio and the contents therein exclusively.

Praise should be balanced with constructive feedback to guide future improvement. A helpful technique is the "praise sandwich": begin with positive comments, then deliver constructive criticism, and conclude with further positive reinforcement.

For example:

"Your writing demonstrates a professional tone and appropriate language. However, the resume section includes an extracurricular activity that might be perceived as unprofessional. Consider revising this section to maintain a consistent professional image for potential employers. Overall, your portfolio is impressive and contemporary, demonstrating a strong understanding of your field. This minor revision will further enhance its impact."

2.) **Timely Feedback Delivery:**

Using a grading rubric, ideally the same one provided to students at the beginning of the project, ensures consistent and focused feedback. The rubric helps ground your comments in the established criteria. Aim to provide feedback within one to two weeks of the portfolio submission. This way, the feedback is delivered in a timely fashion.

3.) **Addressing Individual Student Needs:**

While efficiency is important, avoid treating students as a group. Recognize and address each student's individuality. Effective feedback requires understanding the nuances of each learner. Building rapport and gaining insight into students' backgrounds and learning styles are essential. Consider using student surveys to gather additional information and develop a more holistic understanding of each individual.

The key takeaways from giving feedback include striving for timely feedback, but prioritize thoughtful and personalized statements in your written feedback. Rubrics are valuable tools for efficient and consistent assessment, but they should not overshadow the importance of individual attention. Invest time into understanding your students; this time and energy will enhance the impact of your feedback because it will personalize your knowledge of the learner and deepen the thoughtfulness of the statements you give each student.

The following section explores the hypothetical future possibilities of portfolio assessments. This section blends emerging technologies with some elements of science fiction to veer into the unknown as this section of the chapter envisions the future potential of this assessment method and how it could change overtime with technological advancements.

INTO THE FUTURE: THE HYPOTHETICAL POSSIBILITIES OF PORTFOLIO ASSESSMENTS

This section explores the potential future scenarios for portfolio assessments in education, acknowledging that predictions are uncertain. However, based on current trends, it is evident that personalized and individualized learning experiences are becoming increasingly important (Redecker et al., 2010). The traditional school setting may evolve into a more "community knowledge center," shifting away from a one-size-fits-all approach. What can be proposed, if students meet in person to attend school in the future is yet to be determined and only time will tell. The take away from what we can assume is that customized, personalized, and individualized learning is what people will strive for; therefore, the educators of the future and the school-based stakeholders will both push for this because the people want customized learning experience. Customized learning, when assessed in a "portfolio" format, will become increasingly digitized and technologized.

Hernandez-de-Menendez, Escobar Díaz, & Morales-Menendez (2020) envision a future where drone technology integrates with field trips. Advancements in technology, such as high-definition head-up displays, could enable students to remotely steer drones, providing an immersive virtual field trip experience. This approach not only fosters a deeper understanding of the world but also encourages students to view themselves as active participants in the learning process.

To adapt this concept to portfolio assessments, students could utilize drones to capture video footage during field trips, creating short documentary films as part of their portfolio projects. This approach leverages the growing popularity of video as a creative medium and the potential for remote access to technology. For example, students could "visit" the Louvre Museum in Paris, France, even from Pittsburgh, Pennsylvania (in the United States of America) by using drone footage captured remotely and include this footage in a documentary-style portfolio. This innovative approach demonstrates how technology can expand learning opportunities and enhance the portfolio assessment process.

In the paper, "The Broken Canvas: Theorized Implications of the Neuralink Invasive Brain-Machine Interface Technology on Artists and Art Production Methods," author Thaddaeus Dachille (2024) explores the potential societal and individual impacts of widespread Neuralink Invasive Brain-Machine Interface Technology adoption. One of his key ideas suggests the emergence of telepathic communication among individuals implanted with the device would become more commonplace in a dystopian scenario involving digital telepathy. This scenario presents a significant challenge to traditional assessment methods, including portfolios. In a future where telepathic communication becomes commonplace, the need for physical or digital portfolios to showcase individual work might diminish. Traditional forms of assessment, which rely on individual expression and the presentation of unique ideas, could become obsolete in a society where thoughts and ideas can be directly shared.

The future-based, hypothesized ideas shared in this section highlight the potential for technology to transform the nature of learning and assessment. Since no one can tell the future, only time will tell if any of these proposed scenarios of the future of portfolio assessment will come true. But it can never be stated enough that current trends in learning are directed towards personalizing the learning experience and with this direction portfolio assessments are likely to evolve. Future based portfolios will most likely continue to incorporate innovative technologies and encourage students to develop their own unique learning journeys through creative and engaging projects and novel video production methods.

This section of the chapter explores some potential future directions for portfolio assessment. The theoretical uses of portfolios in the future are non-conclusive; however, we can assume that personalized learning will continue, and this learning format can be extended into portfolio assessment methods. We can also conclude that some of the new format's portfolios may be found to be as contemporary as any other form of modern technology – and as for now, speculation on future portfolios is as nebulous as any other topic. However, we can assume that evolution will occur, and speculation on this topic is grounded in contemporary learning practices and technology trends. As such, they will continue to evolve as new forms of technology become readily available. In the final section of this chapter, the author will summarize some of the discussion included in this chapter and provide some concluding thoughts on this topic.

CONCLUDING THOUGHTS

In conclusion, this chapter has explored the multifaceted nature of portfolio assessment in higher education, offering practical guidance for students, instructors, and instructional support professionals. Portfolios, evolving from their traditional art-based origins, have become a versatile and increasingly digital tool across diverse disciplines, from the humanities and sciences to professional fields like business and healthcare. This chapter examined common portfolio formats, including websites, USB drives, and CDs, highlighting the design considerations crucial for creating visually appealing and engaging presentations that effectively showcase student work and personal branding. Furthermore, it discussed the benefits of portfolio assessment, such as fostering deeper learning, enhancing communication skills, promoting collaboration, and reducing test anxiety. The chapter emphasized the importance of aligning portfolio goals and learning objectives, providing strategies for effective implementation, including the use of rubrics and clear communication of expectations. It also offered examples of portfolio use in different fields, illustrating the adaptability of this assessment method. While acknowledging the potential drawbacks, such as subjectivity and time investment, the chapter underscored the value of portfolio assessment in providing a more comprehensive understanding of student growth, learning, and achievement. Ultimately, this chapter advocates for the thoughtful and strategic use of portfolios as a valuable tool for enhancing teaching and learning in higher education, empowering students to demonstrate their abilities and preparing them for future success. Careful planning, clear communication, and a focus on both content and presentation are essential for maximizing the effectiveness of portfolio assessments. As technology continues to evolve, the possibilities for innovative portfolio formats and applications are likely to expand, further enriching the educational experience.

QUESTIONS FOR DEEPER REFLECTION:

1. Please list the three common portfolio formats discussed in this chapter:

   ____

2. Describe some of the benefits of using a portfolio assessment in higher education:

___

3. What are some strategies for implementing portfolio assessment?

___

4. How do portfolios serve as a form of guided inquiry-based learning?

___

5. What types of samples should be included in a nursing students' portfolio?

___

6. List at least three disciplines that portfolios be utilized for assessment?

___

7. What are the three most common delivery methods for a modern portfolio?

___

8. What key considerations should be addressed when creating a portfolio website?

___

9. Why is design important in a portfolio, even for non-art majors?

___

10. What are some factors that contribute to a well-designed portfolio?

____
____

11. Describe some of the potential drawbacks of using a portfolio assessment?

____
____

12. What are some key questions instructors should ask themselves before using a portfolio assessment in their classroom?

____
____

ADDITIONAL INFORMATION

Here is a useful checklist for evaluating student portfolios. This checklist can serve as a templates for teachers to adapt to their specific instructional needs:

- ✓ Does the content presented in the portfolio represent the strongest work the student has created?
- ✓ Is there any thing missing in the student's portfolio that was not included? If so, what was this item and why do you recommend its inclusion?
- ✓ Is the tone of the writing in the student's portfolio professional?
- ✓ Does the student use difficult to understand jargon and should the student revise the writing to explain the jargon for a general audience?
- ✓ What is the strongest part/element of the student portfolio?
- ✓ Conversely, what is the weakest part/element of the student portfolio?
- ✓ Could the portfolio benefit from some images?

LIST OF RESOURCES

This list offers some hyperlinks to design tools, portfolio assets, and assessment resources:

Adobe Color: https://color.adobe.com/

This is an excellent resource for selecting off-the-shelf color choices to liven up your portfolio designs!

1001 Free fonts: http://1001freefonts.com

This site provides free fonts you can download and install in your portfolio. Although computers often come preloaded with numerous fonts to choose from, this off-the-shelf resource will make your text pop in your portfolio!

Free images for commercial use: http://unsplash.com

Another great off-the-shelf resource that gives you free high-resolution pictures you can use. Why reinvent the wheel? Use free professional-quality images for your work when possible!

Rubric example: https://www.starkstate.edu/wp-content/uploads/2016/02/REVISED-MASTER-RUBRIC.pdf

This rubric showcases an easy-to-use template that provides detailed guidance for grading a student's work. It is in the category of education however, it can be easily adapted to another field of study.

REFERENCES

Carpenter, C. D., Ray, M. S., & Bloom, L. A. (1995). Portfolio assessment: Opportunities and challenges. *Intervention in School and Clinic*, *31*(1), 34–41.

Chimero, F. (2015). *The shape of design*.

David, L. T., & Hein, M. (2012). Student portfolio–A tool to achieve quality in training. *Bulletin of the Transilvania University of Braşov. Series VII: Social Sciences• Law*, 169-174.

Davis, M. H., & Ponnamperuma, G. G. (2005). Portfolio assessment. *Journal of Veterinary Medical Education*, *32*(3), 279–284. PMID: 16261482

Driessen, E. (2017). Do portfolios have a future? *Advances in Health Sciences Education: Theory and Practice*, *22*, 221–228. PMID: 27025510

Fink, A. (2019). *Conducting research literature reviews: From the internet to paper*. Sage publications.

Flanagan, L. (n.d.). Understanding Warm Colors and Cool Colors: Color Examples and How to Use Color Palettes at Home. Retrieved from: https://www.thespruce.com/understanding-warm-and-cool-colors-1976480

Groenendijk, T., Kárpáti, A., & Haanstra, F. (2020). Self-assessment in art education through a visual rubric. *International Journal of Art & Design Education*, *39*(1), 153–175.

Hernandez-de-Menendez, M., Escobar Díaz, C., & Morales-Menendez, R. (2020). Technologies for the future of learning: State of the art. [IJIDeM]. *International Journal on Interactive Design and Manufacturing*, *14*(2), 683–695.

Hetland, L., Winner, E., Veenema, S., & Sheridan, K. (2014). *Studio thinking 2*. Teachers College Press.

Kuon, T., Philbrick, J., & Gill, D. (2024). Reflections on Implementing an ePortfolio as a Capstone Project for an LIS Master's Degree Program. *Journal of Education for Library and Information Science*, *65*(4), 455–461.

LinkedIn Advice. (n.d.). Student Engagement: How can portfolios align with curriculum standards and learning outcomes? Retried from: https://www.linkedin.com/advice/0/how-can-portfolios-align-curriculum-standards

Lu, P. C. (2007). The integration of blog platform and e-portfolio in art assessment. *The International Journal of Arts Education*, *5*(2), 154–185.

McNally, D., & Speak, K. D. (2010). *Be your own brand: Achieve more of what you want by being more of who you are*. Berrett-Koehler Publishers.

Meier, D. (2003). *In schools we trust: Creating communities of learning in an era of testing and standardization*. Beacon Press.

Redecker, C., Leis, M., Leendertse, M., Punie, Y., Gijsbers, G., Kirschner, P., & Hoogveld, B. (2010). *The future of learning: New ways to learn new skills for future jobs. Results from an online expert consultation. Technical Note JRC60869*. JRC-IPTS.

Reed, S. (2015). Collecting evidence for your portfolio. In Collecting evidence for your portfolio (Second Edition ed., pp. 39-56). SAGE Publications, Inc., https://doi.org/DOI: 10.4135/9781473922419

Rodriguez, R., Martinez-Ulloa, L., & Flores-Bustos, C. (2022). E-portfolio as an evaluative tool for emergency virtual education: Analysis of the case of the University Andres Bello (Chile) during the COVID-19 pandemic. *Frontiers in Psychology, 13*, 1–10. DOI: 10.3389/fpsyg.2022.892278 PMID: 35783798

Smith, J., & Noble, H. (2014). Bias in research. *Evidence-Based Nursing*, *17*(4), 100–101. PMID: 25097234

Smith, R. C. (1993). *Basic graphic design*. Prentice Hall.

Syzdykova, Z., Koblandin, K., Mikhaylova, N., & Akinina, O. (2021). Assessment of E-portfolio in higher education. *International Journal of Emerging Technologies in Learning (Online)*, *16*(2), 120.

Talagala, N. (2022). Data as The New Oil Is Not Enough: Four Principles For Avoiding Data Fires. Retrieved from: https://www.forbes.com/sites/nishatalagala/2022/03/02/data-as-the-new-oil-is-not-enough-four-principles-for-avoiding-data-fires/#:~:text=Generally%20credited%20to%20mathematician%20Clive,entity%20that%20drives%20profitable%20activity

Thomas, D. S. M. (1998). The use of portfolio learning in medical education. *Medical Teacher*, *20*(3), 192–199.

Zaabalawi, R. S., & Zaabalawi, J. (2024). Portfolios versus exams: A study to gauge the better student assessment tool. *Language Testing in Asia*, *14*(1), 28.

KEY TERMS AND DEFINITIONS

Compact Disc formatted Portfolio: A compact disc portfolio is any portfolio that is burned to a CD. The files on this sort of portfolio are only viewable if the recipient has a CD reader that can view the HTML, .doc (Microsoft Word), or Adobe PDF files.

Dynamic portfolio website: Conversely, a dynamic website contains numerous interactive and user-friendly components such as offering users the ability to leave a message or sending a message with a contact form. Dynamic portfolio websites are easier to build now than before with user friendly portfolio website building tools like WordPress.

Longitudinal assessment: A portfolio is a type of assessment that takes place over a set period of time, in other words longitudinally. It is completed outside of the classroom as homework. If it is completed by an administrator in higher education, they may take many weeks to complete the detailed information needed to be evaluated.

Portfolio Goals: A preestablished set of broad and overarching desired outcomes for the successful completion of a portfolio assessment that helps guide the student to complete the needed items required by the instructor.

Portfolio Objectives: The specific, measurable items that the portfolio should accomplish. These measurable items should be listed and or placed in a rubric format for learners to better understand the specific work they are asked to complete.

Portfolio Rubric: This framework offered to the students gives them the precise steps they will need take to complete their portfolio. This includes the documentation they need to gather, the writings they should include, and any and all parameters they need to consider. It is essentially a multifaceted blueprint for the student to accomplish the task of developing a portfolio.

Static portfolio website: has basic information and does not have interactive and user-friendly components such as leaving a message or sending a message with a contact form.

Test anxiety: One of the primary benefits of a portfolio assessment is the fact that the participant taking (or completing) the portfolio assessment is not strained under the tight pressure of taking a traditional examination. Instead of facing "test anxiety", the developer of the portfolio is more of a curator gathering work examples over a pronounced, yet sometimes lengthy, amount of time. Therefore, the portfolio developer is less likely to face test anxiety, or emotional strain associated with other sorts of in-person, short-term assessments.

USB Flash drive portfolio: This type of portfolio is an external USB flash drive that a recipient of the portfolio can plug into a computer and view the contents of the portfolio. With this sort of delivery system, a viewer can make notes and resave the files, or download the files as they see needed.

Website Portfolio: A portfolio of this nature is a website either static or dynamic that users can access after typing in a specific domain name. The portfolio of this site should contain a landing page, an about page identifying the publisher of the portfolio, and the work they wish to showcase. It is also a good idea to include contact information or a contact form for users to connect with the publisher of any website portfolio.

Chapter 8
Scrutinising the Seven Key Pillars of People Analytics and Their Linkage With the Competitive Advantage of Higher Education Institutions (HEIs)

Arushi Handa
https://orcid.org/0009-0004-1827-0698
Amity University, Noida, India

Rashmi Maini
https://orcid.org/0000-0002-8426-3312
Amity University, Noida, India

Vinita Sharma
Amity University, Noida, India

ABSTRACT

We are entering a new dawn where we are making considerable strides in realising value from People Analytics interventions. For over twenty years, researchers and professionals have been scrutinising the role of people analytics in accelerating the efficiency and effectiveness of human resource functions within an organisation. As a result, they advocate for people analytics as a driving force behind HR's strategic

DOI: 10.4018/979-8-3373-7057-6.ch008

partnership. Despite the increasing recognition of People Analytics in driving data-driven decision-making within human resources, current academic literature largely overlooks a structured framework for understanding the role of people analytics and its linkage with the competitive advantage of higher education institutions (HEIs). Previous studies focus broadly on the generic benefits of analytics in HEIs without systematically examining its key functions. The role of the seven crucial pillars of people analytics still needs deeper insights in the context of HEIs. On digging deeper into the field of People Analytics in HEIs, we encounter a significant research gap that persists in our understanding of the key pillars of PA (Workforce Planning, Talent Sourcing, Talent Acquisition and Hiring, Onboarding & Engagement, Performance Management, Talent Retention and Employee Wellness) and their linkage with the competitive advantage of HEIs.

INTRODUCTION TO THE SEVEN PILLARS OF PEOPLE ANALYTICS

With digitalization taking a head start in today's era, the inquisitiveness surrounding the use of big and small data is increasing (Tursunbayeva et al., 2018). Several techniques of data analytics are being adopted to further explore social policies, customising consumer marketing and forecasting votes, in addition to several others (Raguseo, 2018). The term people analytics (PA), alternatively termed HR analytics, encompasses a great deal of analytical tools and techniques to effectively optimise HR functions (Deloitte, 2017) and influence the organisational outcomes (Wang et al., 2023). PA focuses mainly on the improvement of HR management, improves decision-making and efficiently speeds up the overall performance of organisations (Huselid, 1995). PA commits to aid organizations as it helps them gain a better understanding of their workforce. It provides individuals and departments with subsequent data on the characteristics of the employees (Pape, 2016). It claims to result in an 80% rise in the efficiency of the recruiting process, growth in improving productivity of business by 25% and a simultaneous 50% reduction in turnover rates (Mckinsey, 2020).

The past years have witnessed a visible increase in the interest surrounding the applications of HRM strategically in Higher Education Institutions (HEIs) (Falleta, 2014). This sheds light on the shift in the academic field towards more organised approaches. By making use of empirical data from Saudi Universities, Allui and Sahni (2016) points out how valuable data-driven HRM is to the effectiveness of HEIs. Nguyen (2016) emphasises the importance of the betterment of HRM facilities in Vietnamese Universities (Sharif et al., 2024). Several modifications surrounding the funding and management of HEIs imply that there exists a growing need for quantifiable outcomes in HEIs (Rosser et al, 2003:1). The scarcity of resources and a progressively reducing trust in practices of HEIs is the cause of a growing demand in the public towards HEIs for displaying their productivity. The way in which the effectiveness and efficiency of HEIs are viewed is changing. It is now being associated with economic outcomes such as how employable the graduates are (Mansour et al., 2015).

PA is viewed as a growing innovative field whose foundation lies on traditional principles of personnel management, and it is the representative of a tremendous change in the power dynamics of organisations and how they enhance the quality of their workforce (Fitz-Enz and Mattox, 2014). Since the inception of people analytics (PA), innovations have slowly trickled their way into the daily practice of several organisations (Tursunbayeva et al., 2022). When we look at the HR rhetoric in place today, analytics has the underlying potential to not only bring about a seismic shift in the way in which HR functions, but also greatly impact the way in which it affects organisations (Andersen, 2017). PA is considered now a game changer when it comes to the future of HR (van der Togt & Rasmussen, 2017). In spite of this, organisations have not fully embraced HR analytics, since its adoption rate still remains slow in organisations (Boudreau, 2017; Marler and Boudreau, 2017). Cameron (1978, 1986) said that HEIs have long been averse to systems that assess their effectiveness.

When it comes to human resources, despite this, current academic and industry literature, it lacks a formal understanding for comprehending the essential functions of PA in the context of HEIs. Most of the previous studies focus broadly on the generic benefits, challenges, and strategic significance of PA without delving into a systematic examination of its foundational functions. In particular, there is still a dearth of research studies on the seven pillars of PA, which represent the fundamental skills and fields crucial to the application of PA.

Practitioners and scholars lack a formal framework which is foundational for understanding what makes the PA system robust in HEIs. So, there exists a research gap and this chapter tries to bridge the gap. It highlights the role of PA in HEIs and how these pillars can serve as a competitive advantage for HEIs. The same will not only offer clarification but also a path forward for researchers and practitioners. The research questions guiding this study are designed to further explore the fields of PA via the lens of its 7 pillars. Firstly, the study seeks to identify and categorically sort these pillars. It then goes on to explore the importance of PA in HEIs. Finally, the research concludes by studying the overall impact PA has on HEIs and how it helps them gain a competitive adv antage. This all-encompassing strategy broadens our understanding of PA as well as enables businesses to fully utilise it, paving the way for revolutionary business methods.

Seven pillars of people analytics and its application in Higher Education Institutions:

Previous research studies show how low-performing organisations differ from high-performing organisations based on their involvement in data data-driven approach to HR practices (Dessler, 2004). People analytics is expanding its reach to every domain and HEIs are no exception. In HEIs, a data-driven approach ensures institutional effectiveness. High performing HEIs, on an average focus on data driven workforce planning (30%), Recruitment (33%), Hiring (37%), Engagement (34%), Appraisal (95%), Retention (45%) and employee wellness (33%) (Marler & Bordeau, 2017). PA, to a large extent, acts as a one-stop solution for the effective management of HR functions at HEIs, as it offers an evidence-based approach to combat obstacles and challenges and improves overall efficiency. The data-driven functions of HRM are presented in the form of key pillars of Human resource analytics. These pillars are the backbone of managing human resources in organisations. These pillars contribute significantly to the success of HEIs as they act as a competitive advantage. The seven key pillars (Figure 1), namely, Workforce planning, Talent sourcing, Talent acquisition and hiring, Onboarding and engagement, Performance Management, Employee Retention and Employee Wellness are explored in the context of competitive advantage of HEIs.

Figure 1. Seven Key Pillars of People Analytics

1. The first pillar of PA: Workforce Planning

Numbers don't lie, and this evidently points towards the pertinence of workforce planning. "Workforce planning" is the name of the process which makes sure that the organisation is well equipped to serve the needs of the present and the future by way of having the right personnel at the right time, right place and right price (Jacobson, 2010). Workforce planning involves determining roles of interest, establishing the current state, analysing historical trends, determining forecasting scenarios, assessing performance gaps and establishing action plans(Figure 2). It is considered a tedious task, with the problem of planning growing in sync with the size of the company. It points out how and the time at which employees must be hired. It makes a union of decisions revolving around staffing and scheduling (De Bruecker et al., 2015). It occupies a core and central position in the field of HRM because it ensures the company is staffed accurately (Othman et al., 2011). Human resource planning plays a very crucial role in developing strategies for managing people in the organisation, functions such as recruitment and hiring are dependent on sound planning. Workforce planning brings under its umbrella the alignment of human resources i.e, human capital with organisational goals. (Cotten, 2007). Recently, it has been highlighted in a few studies that not just the right person for the right job is enough but rather the right cost of hiring is crucial to understand (Hurst & Kelley Patterson, 2014). Understanding the demand and supply of the workforce requires a data-driven approach to make informed decisions. Evidence-based workforce planning results in effective decisions (Marler & Boudreau, 2013)

Figure 2. Steps and data points of Workforce Planning Analytics

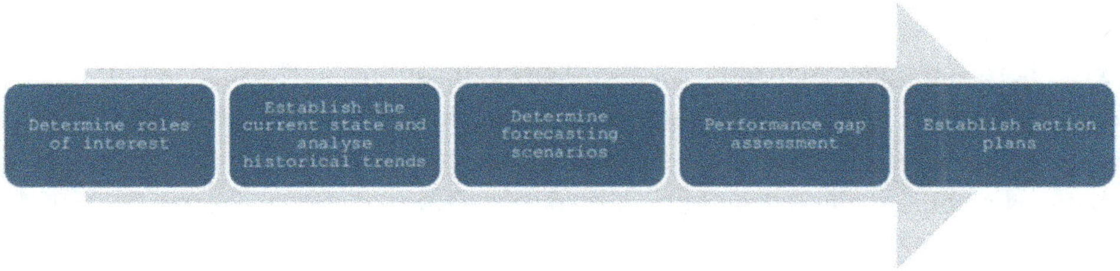

Work is changing when it comes to its nature, specifically pertaining to technological, organizational as well as competitive developments; this implies that both public and private HEIs now struggle to plan effectively their workforce. Evidence-based workforce planning is the saviour of organisations in this dynamic and turbulent environment when it comes to the implementation of hiring strategies (Aral et al., 2012). Human capital is seen as a determinant of an organisation's success and largely depends on the effective planning of Human resources (Armstrong, 2008). Data-driven workforce planning is essential for managing the demand and supply of the workforce in HEIs. It ensures that HEIs are neither overstaffed nor understaffed (Attaran et al., 2018). They are considered the best source for moulding future generations. (Mallillin, 2017). As organisations are growing to understand the importance of human resources, data driven decisions pertaining to workforce planning has been a prerequisite for organisational effectiveness (Ford, 2014).

2. Second Pillar of PA: Talent Sourcing

Talent is often regarded as irreplaceable and rare, but the targeted prescriptions surrounding talent are ambiguous. While the presence of talented people is integral to the organisation, discussions surrounding the contribution of talent in comparison to that of technology are murky. While rarity does possess dimensions of talent, the role talent plays in the creation of hard-to-implicate resources is unclear, as the area of analysis is the organisation as a whole, but not the talent pool. Evidently, the dimension which can be connected to talent is its imitability. The process of talent sourcing involves creating an HR plan, defining ideal candidates, choosing multiple sourcing channels, encouraging employee referrals, establishing relationship with past applicants, creating outreach messages and building an effective employer brand (Figure 3). The sourcing of human capital is the driving force behind organisational effectiveness (Bendickson et al., 2023). In today's time, the skill sets possessed by employees have a limited duration, which is the antecedent driving the increasing technological innovations. A 2019 survey conducted on 3,500 managers showed that merely 29% of new hires possess the complete skill set required for their jobs, leaving behind future scope (Harvard Business Review 2021). This sheds light on the second pillar of PA which is Talent Sourcing. The analysis is proof of the relationship that exists between talent management and the organisation's performance (McKinsey 2023). There are sufficient resource-based theories which tell us that the strategic value of an organization and its subsequent success rest on how the organization manages resources, including human resources (Rumelt, 1991; Wernerfelt, 1984).

Figure 3. Steps and data points of Talent Sourcing Analytics

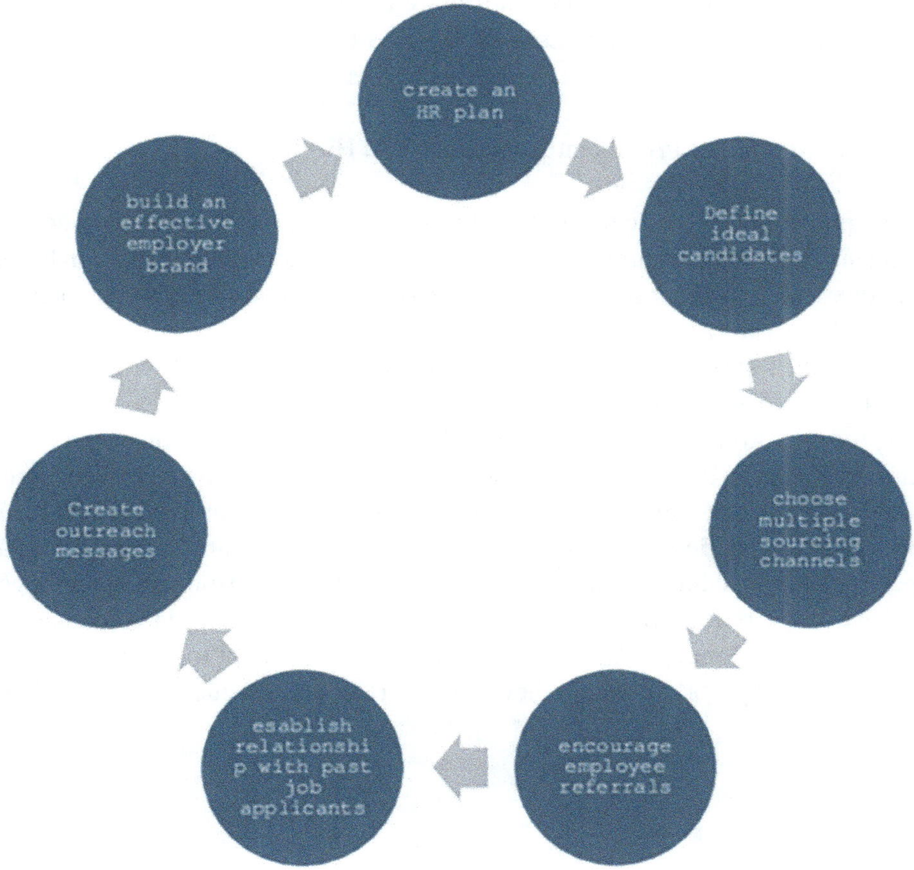

Organisations now encounter several problems such as outsourcing, downsizing, budgetary cuts and an ageing population, by way of globalisation. Hiring therefore, becomes an integral element of appealing, selecting and employing talent (Bussin, 2014). Organizations now take into use the data-driven employee value proposition to attract talent. This is a mix of benefits and qualities that makes a company appealing to potential hires while also encouraging existing employees to stay (Bussin, 2014). Empirical research backs the claim that talent sourcing followed by talent management, when done right, may elevate the existing level of workers in an organisation as it is responsible for the creation of a sound base of employee engagement and performance (Levenson et al., 2005). In HEIs also, sourcing the right talent for the institution is a big challenge. Due to technological advancements and other factors, constant changes are occurring in the environment of these institutions. To meet expectations, we need to make informed decisions regarding efficient talent-sourcing strategies. Talent sourcing is a prerequisite for talent acquisition and hiring and if it is not done based on accurate data, it may lead to spurious results. Data-driven decision on talent sourcing gives productive results.

3. The third pillar of PA: Talent Acquisition and Hiring

The process of talent acquisition and hiring involves the identification and recruitment of qualified incumbents for the organisation. According to modern hiring techniques, the changing needs of the workforce and trends need to be analysed properly for organisational development.

During the last few years, the influence of a shortage of talented people, altering workplace standards and technological breakthroughs is seen in the talent acquisition (TA) process. This is why, the battle for people is now more intense than ever before (Harvard Business Review, 2023). Talent acquisition process involves generation of leads, sourcing of candidates, recruitment, Pre- employment assessment, Interview, reference verification, final hiring decision and onboarding (Figure 4). It has experienced tremendous change over the past several years, from talent shortages that have made it difficult for employers to find and hire the right candidates to new expectations among job seekers regarding how they want to work, whether it involves how they work or whom they work for (Harvard Business Review, 2023).

Figure 4. Steps and data points of Talent Acquisition Analytics

In HEIs, the recruitment of every faculty member provides the organisation with an opportunity to improve itself and build on its prevailing culture to bring out desired change (DiPiro, 2011). HEIs can create a positive brand image and sustain their reputation by using data-driven hiring of top-qualified academics. While hiring the absolute best may be financially unfeasible for most institutions and impossible for all, identifying the relatively best scholars is not overly challenging if evidence-based decisions are made. A pertinent challenge lies in applying this understanding instead of giving priority to other objectives (Dilger, 2009). With every appropriate new hire, the organisation is presented with an opportunity to bring about change to the organisation's culture. Existing faculty members may resist change when an HEI aims to change their research standards and teaching services or bring in innovative approaches in different fields; however, with the help of a data analytics approach, reasons for resistance may be addressed carefully to get the desired results. Based on the data, we need to bring in new individuals with fresh perspectives, as it offers the best chance to drive cultural transformation. Additionally, as faculty with outdated methods or mindsets retire or move on, HEIs can recruit individuals who align with their evolving vision from day one (DiPiro, 2011).

4. The fourth pillar of PA: Onboarding and Engagement

Workers, too, as they are social beings, thrive with trust, social cohesion, and a sense of purpose. They too, feel a need for recognition and want collaborative teams. Clear responsibilities and roles are the driving forces behind their growth (McKinsey, 2021). The fourth pillar of PA, onboarding and engagement focuses on this. According to Deloitte (2023), high-performing organisations recognise the value of treating onboarding as a comprehensive, company-wide initiative that fosters a sense of belonging and boosts productivity (Deloitte, 2020). Onboarding is an intricate process that permeates in every organization, with its sub-processes being given varied preferences across companies. The process starts from the point of hiring in the employee's life cycle and ends at the point at which the employee is transformed into a fully trained employee independently performing duties (Süveges & Kurucz, 2024) (Figure 5). The fact that standard levels of employee commitment and organisational commitment are the driving forces behind employee retention, is backed by research (Gelencsér et al., 2024). The entire onboarding process accelerates commitment, which greatly impacts employee retention rates positively (Stein & Christiansen, 2010). Onboarding and engagement must be conducted with due care. Any loopholes or gaps should be addressed while engaging an individual for better outcomes. In order to achieve suitable outcomes for onboarding and engagement of employees, the inputs from employees should be collected and utilised as important data points for making informed decisions.

Figure 5. Steps and basic data points of Onboarding and Engagement Analytics

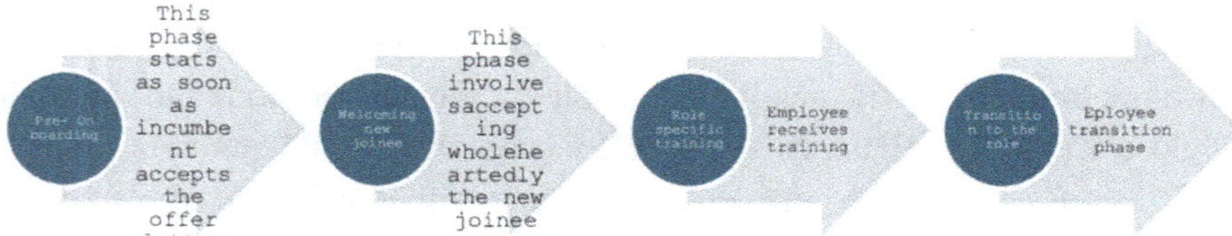

Broadly speaking, onboarding in HEIs is also concerned with all the actions these institutions take to acclimatise their new hires with their institutions (Klein & Polin, 2012). The onboarding process is an accumulation of an array of practices and programs which are executed in the initial days, weeks or even months of a new hire. These practices can be in the form of inductions, training sessions, seminars, provision of information through handbooks or online material and even social gatherings (Armstrong, 2009; Klein and Polin, 2012; Klein et al., 2015). For HEIs also, evidence-based decisions are essential from time to time, they need to understand the changing needs and concerns of HEIs and their employees. The manner in which new employees are introduced and integrated into a company plays a big role in their success, both in the short term and long term. There is high time to introduce a data-driven approach to onboarding and engaging their employees. Still, only about 32% of companies offer a formal onboarding experience (Aberdeen Group, 2017). A well-executed onboarding experience helps new employees adjust to their new environment, get up to speed with their job responsibilities faster, understand the organisations' vision, mission, goals and values to have essential resources and find out how they may add value to the organisation's growth and development. Data-driven decisions for onboarding employees of HEIs help them understand their path towards the company's mission and values. The process clarifies how they can contribute to the organization's growth and success and enhances their performance (Ulrich and Dulebohn, 2015)

5. The fifth pillar of PA: Performance Management

The fifth pillar of PA is performance management. Performance management continues to be difficult to clearly define (McKinsey, 2024). Performance management essentially addresses the challenges that organisations encounter when attempting to define, measure and enhance the performance of an employee with the ulterior aim of improving organizational efficiency. This tells us that performance management is comprised of various levels of analysis and has linkages with matters relating to employees' performance (Den Hartog et al., 2004). The fundamental building blocks of performance management are rather simple, but their integration into the business operating system is a tedious task (McKinsey, 2017). The process of performance management involves visioning, goal setting, strategic planning, institutional planning, analysing results, forecasting, measuring success and awarding employees (Figure 6). Organisational performance has always had an indelible impact on the actions companies take, which makes the means to measure this performance a topic of keen interest in the last few years, making Performance Management a buzzword amongst academics and research scholars of various fields. Identifying the performance of an organisation is becoming increasingly important as it contributes to attracting investment, increasing share value as well as attracting top talent. Consequently, it is pertinent to address how this information related to organizational performance is communicated to potential investors, customers and employees. Since the beginning of this century, the formulation of indicators dealing with the same is in the works.

Figure 6. Steps and basic data points of Performance Management Analytics

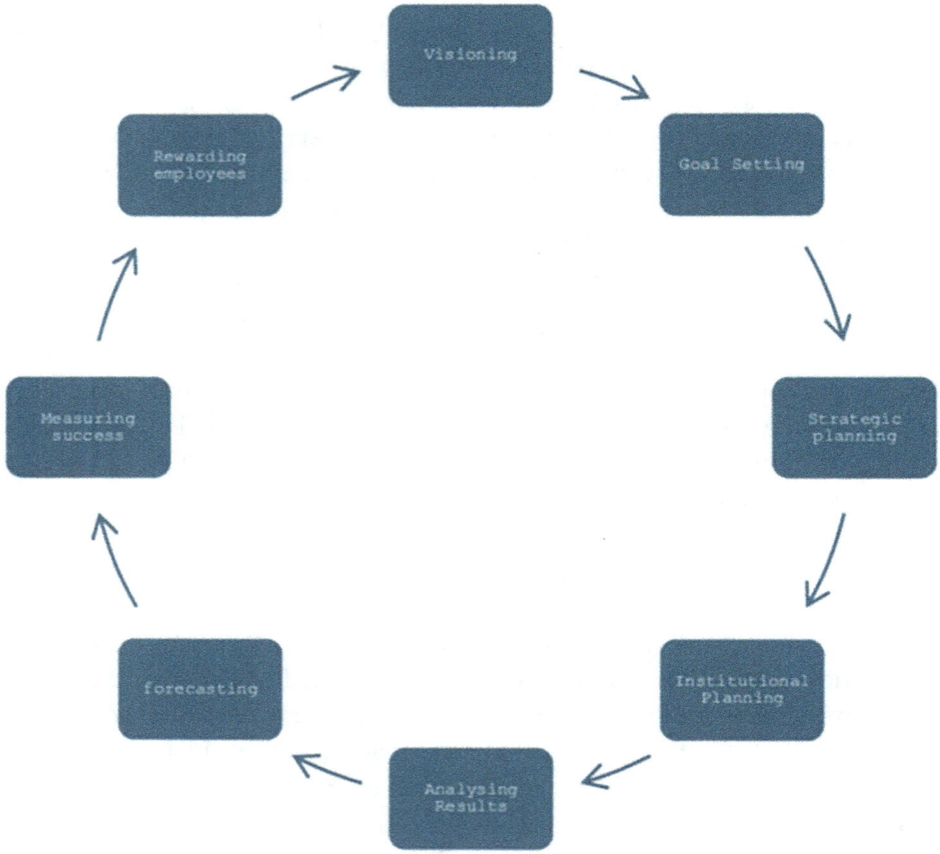

Nowadays, facts and evidence supporting the efficacy and significance of these institutions are sought after by the general public in addition to prospective students. As a result, obtaining funds and drawing in new students secures the position of being the top priority for HEIs. They place a high priority on the calibre of their academic personnel, including their recruiting, training, incentive programs, utilisation, and motivation, to thrive in this competitive environment. These components are deemed to be essential for raising these institutions' overall efficiency. The implementation of the Performance management system is more important than ever, considering these new requirements (Jiang et al., 2012). Performance management as a practice establishes a common knowledge of objectives and strategies for achieving them. It is also regarded as a method for managing and developing personnel in a way that improves the performance of teams, individuals, and the organisation holistically (Armstrong, 2006). A crucial function of human resource management, performance management can be difficult to use successfully in practical contexts because of its intricacy. Institutions must adopt these management strategies to stay competitive and address any accountability or compliance requirements that may come up (Arbo & Benneworth, 2008). In HEIs, control is often limited and inflexible due to the specialisation and rigidity within the faculty. As a result, performance management becomes a crucial practice for any organisation and is often viewed as a weakness if not properly implemented.

6. The sixth pillar of people analytics: Talent Retention

The core aim of the HR system is to appeal, motivate and retain talented employees within the organisation (Katz & Kahn, 1978). The present business environment faces multifaceted challenges, including intensifying competition across borders, disruptive technological breakthroughs, a development in the knowledge era, dynamism and versatility are important elements of the workplace (Catteeuw et al., 2007). The paradigm shift in the present environment focuses on the incremental shift in the competencies and skill sets in business organisations and HEIs are no exception. Therefore, due to changing demographic details, there is a big demand for highly intellectual employees. To address such challenges, we need to focus more on human talent than financial capital (Ewing et al., 2002; Ployhart, 2006).

Hiring is behind discovering untapped potential and ambitions of leadership that previously, may be plagued by a record of underperformance or prioritizing short-term objectives. (Harvard Business Review, 2014). It is understood that the average cost to replace an employee exceeds the employee's annual salary by one and a half to even two times (Deloitte, 2022). Recruitment and retention are two areas which are considered the main areas of concern in the hospitality sector (Powell & Wood, 1999). The best employees of an organisation are its lifeblood. Such employees, with their fresh mindsets and ideas, can bring about drastic changes in even the most conservative firms. However, many organisations continue to struggle to retain such high-performing employees, with special emphasis on the science and engineering domain (Cross et al., 2018). Firms must ensure that the needs of the organisations must be met (Nyambegera et al., 2001). The reason behind the hyperfocus on the retention of employees is the realisation of organisations regarding the huge opportunity and recruitment costs associated with talent leaving an organisation. The basic steps of employee retention are hiring the right candidate, allot responsibilities appropriately, accessible work environment, appreciate great work, appraisal of performance appropriately, worklife balance, appropriate training, cultivate team spirit (Figure 7). When top talent leaves an organisation, it has detrimental effects on the morale of employees left behind as well as takes a toll on the revenue of the organisation (Vigoda, 2000). The intense, highly competitive business environment compels firms to have the ability to retain talent in order to remain competitive in the market (Gallo, 2015).

Employee retention is defined by Kaur (2017) as a process that encourages employees to stay with the organisation for an extended period of time. The efforts aimed at the enhancement of organisational efficiency along with its economic management via the relationship between employer and employee is what Frederick Taylor coined as 'scientific management' (Taylor, 2004).

Figure 7. Steps and data points of Talent Retention

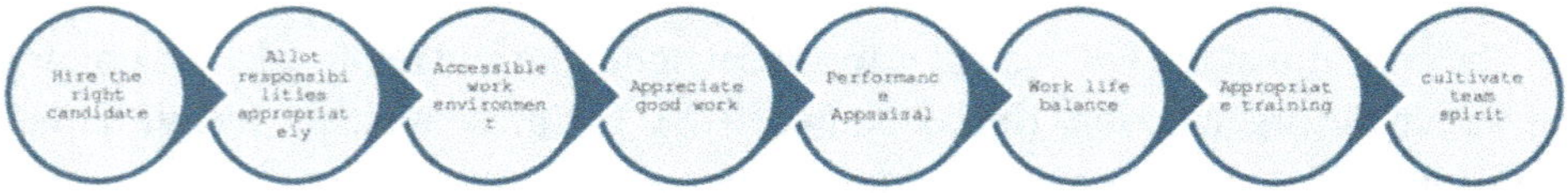

Employee retention is now becoming increasingly crucial for organizations because the replacement and retraining new staff can be expensive (Irshad & Afridi, 2007), particularly when it comes to those who are extremely talented individuals with a distinctive skill set. HEIs are encountered with several dynamic challenges that are a byproduct of changing business environment, disruptive technological innovations, emerging competition, changing productivity, higher education institutions are facing several challenges in the contemporary competitive market environment created by business dynamics, emerging technology, competition, shift in the employment nature and the employees (faculty and staff) turnover. In HEIs, the employees needed to be both sound academics as well as researchers. They are at the forefront of the knowledge-driven economy, gaining sound insights from interdisciplinary domains (Chahar et al., 2021).

7. The seventh pillar of PA: Employee Wellness

Globally, the economy shows signs of growing widespread discontent amongst employees in addition to a rat race for top talent. The trend of quiet quitting and the Great Resignation plagues organisations today like never before (Deloitte, 2023). The World Health Organisation regards employment as a social determinant of health, which has implications so grand it affects our wellbeing at a deeper level (WHO, 2023). At first glance, health is considered an individual matter, all individuals are responsible for maintaining their good health (Roslender et al., 2006). But when we talk of health in regard of employment, it becomes closely associated with the concept of safety (Roslender et al., 2006). Reduced healthcare costs are behind the increasing investment of organisations in wellness programs and employee health. Companies are now increasingly investing in both employee health as well as employee programs (Aral et al., 2012). Currently, growing rates of obesity, diabetes and several other health problems are behind the growing prevalence of wellness programs as well as the implications it has for employer-sponsored insurance and rates of absenteeism (Baicker et al. 2010; Boles et al. 2004).

Figure 8. Steps and data points of Employee Wellness Analytics

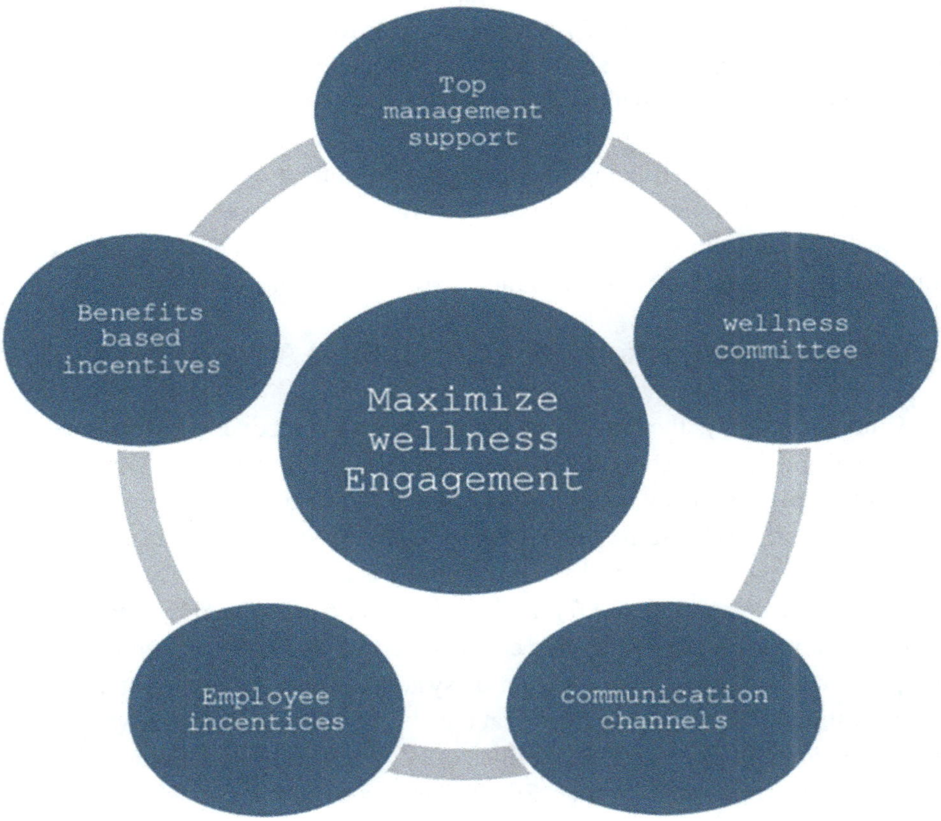

The absence of disease has traditionally been defined as health. However, our expectations for a high-quality life have progressed beyond merely being disease-free.

These days, well-being is viewed as a better standard of health. Generally speaking, wellness entails embracing beliefs and actions that improve one's general quality of life. (Owen, 2002). The non-static, evolving role of academia has raised several requirements for academicians to showcase themselves as the change agents, who are carving the teaching and learning cultures at the individual, department and organisational levels and ultimately changing society at large (Gibbs, 2013; Green and Little, 2016; Kenny et al., 2017).

Today, people enjoy the comforts of advanced technology from the cosy corners of their homes. Despite all the modern conveniences and accomplishments, several people still experience a sense of loss and emptiness. Every element of life, including our work, is affected due to this depressing feeling. In the past, making a living was the main goal of the job, with developing one's inner self, often being neglected. But in the modern world, using spirituality to find a meaningful purpose at work has gained significance. As a result of this, businesses are laying emphasis on "workplace spirituality" (WS), which is to improve workers' "professional well-being" (Paul & Jena, 2022). The scarcity of wellness programs is the reason for a decreasing level of job satisfaction and motivation among workers across several organisations (Spreitzer & Porath, 2012).

The necessity for well-being has been brought to light by the increasing stress in both personal and professional lives. The effective employee wellbeing process involves Top management support, a wellness committee, a communication channel, employee incentives, benefits-based incentives (Figure 8).

Data-driven HR functions as a Competitive Advantage for HEIs

Although initially, the private sector focused on the concept of 'competitive advantage' and theories about it, however, now even public sector organisations are focusing deeply on having an edge over competitors and making decisions based on that (Porter, 1980; Barney and Arikan, 2005; Powell, 2001). In case public and private HEIs, the need to have a competitive advantage is as essential as in corporations (Bryson et al., 2007). In fact, the competition faced by HEIs is quite varied and not just related to private education sector but rather a blend of market competition where conventional education system also exists (Bryson et al., 2007). Previous studies have acknowledged that the element of competitive advantage has not discussed in the context of core pillars of HR and hence need more exploration (Eleyan, 2020; Huisman & Wende, 2005; Marginson, 2007).

In conclusion, the integration of Human Resource Management (HRM) practices aids universitites to boost the performance of both their employees and the organisation (Chen et al., 2009; Fuming & Jiliang, 2007; Lew, 2009) Leadership which is dynamic in nature and effectively employs these three elements in the teaching process, it helps HEIs achieve their organisational goals. Since the employment ecosystem of HEIs forms a core component of the knowledge economy, in the case of education, human capital is regarded as much more important in comparison to other resources, such as physical capital or infrastructure.

The significance of collaboration amongst individuals in HEIs is emphasised by the need for all educators, irrespective of their position, whether in leadership, middle management or other roles, to work together cohesively to achieve shared objectives. This collaborative approach is vital rather than simply focusing on machines and technology (Balyasin and Gebremerkel, 2020; Guest and Clinton, 2007; Ulrich, 2013)

It is within this context that the management of people with the help of accurate data is a prerequisite for the sustainable growth of HEIs (Pellert, 2007; Julius, 2000).

Table 1. HR metrics focusing on the seven key pillars of PA

1.Workforce Planning Metrics
a. Demand forecasting for HEIs
Revenue of HEIs
Revenue per Full Time Employee
Output per Full Time employee
Revenue per Full Time employee
b. **Supply Analysis for HEIs**
Employee turnover rate
Time to fill
Internal Mobility rate
Skill Gap analysis
2.Talent sourcing Analytics and Hiring metrics
Source of hire
Offer acceptance rate
Application to interview ratio
Interview to offer ratio
Application completion rate
3.Talent Hiring
Time to fill
Time to hire
Quality of hire
Cost per hire

continued on following page

Table 1. Continued

1.Workforce Planning Metrics
First year attrition rate
ROI
4.Onboarding and engagement
Onboarding completion rate
Time to Value
Employees satisfaction rate
Pulse surveys
5.Performance metrics
Target achievement rate
Quality of work
Productivity
Competency developed during the year
Attendance record
Punctuality / Delay in delivering work
6.Employee Retention metrics
Retention rate
Cost of turnover
7.Employee wellness metrics
Healthcare cost
Employee stress level
Employees satisfaction rate
Cost of Fringe benefits
Metrics for More Profitable HEIs by focusing on dedicated role of HR
Total HR Staff
HR-to-Employee Ratio
HR Expenses
HR Expense to Operating Expense Ratio
HR Expense to FTE Ratio
Annual Salary Increase
Target Bonus for Non-Executives
Target Bonus for Executives
Maximum Reimbursement Allowed for Tuition/Education Expenses per year
Percentage of Employees Participating in Tuition/Education Reimbursement Programs

continued on following page

Table 1. Continued

1.Workforce Planning Metrics
Time-to-Fill
Cost-Per-Hire
Annual Overall Turnover Rate

1. Workforce planning analytics and competitive advantage:

Workforce planning analytics comprises of various techniques of data analysis, data modelling techniques to optimize the decisions pertaining to human resource planning. Workforce planning analytics goes beyond conventional way of HR planning and gain deeper meanings by leveraging data related to workforce trends, current and future predictions. Additionally, it focuses on prescriptions for future workforce strategies. It supports data driven decisions to plan cost effective and efficient workforce strategies by striking the balance between demand and supply of human resources.

Like in any other organisation, HEIs, also plan their current and future needs by focusing on various data points such as faculty members' voluntary and involuntary turnover, growth of scholars' enrolment and demand for various skill sets. According to Roisseau and Boudreau, (2011), predictive modelling can be applied to understand the historical data for HEIs to better understand the demand and supply of HEIs. Another important technique is scenario planning, this can be used to examine the potential impact of several factors such as cut in budget, change in the demographic profiles of students and many other on workforce planning. This allows HEIs to be highly active and adaptable to environmental and organisational change. What if scenarios can be utilised to unravel student and faculty ratio and ultimately leaves a great impact.

By applying analytics, recruitment needs along with skill gap analysis can be done and based on the analysis, fruitful insights can be fetched to make informed decisions by managers for targeted recruitment and training initiatives. Metrices such as 'Revenue per Full Time Employee', 'Time to fill', 'Skill gap analysis' and many other are relevant to understand the effectiveness of workforce planning (Table1). Workforce planning analytics can help optimise the workforce by analysing employees' workload, efficiency and performance in HEIs. It focuses on data driven allocation of work and resources to enhance the effectiveness of workforce. Allocating budget for faculty and staff in HEIs greatly influences staffing in general and workforce planning in particular. Cost modelling based on data analysis also supports to a large extent to optimise Human Resource Planning.

There are many benefits of applying workforce planning analytics. Data driven informed decisions, proactive planning, improved efficiency, improved talent management and ultimately, it leads to a competitive advantage to HEIs and it provides excellent alignment with strategic objectives of the organisations. Many techniques and tools can assist human resource planning in HEIs. Customised workforce planning software, statistical software packages to analyse data such as Smart PLS, AMOS etc, data visualisation techniques and software such as 'Power BI' and 'Tableau' to name a few and other data warehousing tools for HEIs to strengthen the data infrastructure for effective Human Resource Planning Analytics (Aljawarneh, 2024). According to Tasmin et al., (2022), application of big data and machine learning for more diverse and larger datasets are appropriate for making informed decisions in HEIs to manager workforce. So, evidence-based workforce planning gives an edge over the competitors and serve as a competitive advantage.

2. Talent sourcing analytics and competitive advantage

To improve the process of sourcing incumbents, analytics plays a crucial role. Metrices such as 'cost to internal Sources', 'cost to external sources', 'Offer acceptance rate', 'Application to interview ratio' and many others are important ones to understand the effectiveness of talent sourcing function. Talent sourcing analytics in HEIs utilised various tools and techniques to attract faculty and staff members. Throughout the process of talent sourcing, we make use of the data to make informed and implied decisions. Sourcing largely depends on identifying a qualified pool of people. HEIs make use of data to optimise the process of attracting the eligible incumbent for faculty and staff positions. Paying attention to various sources of recruitment based on the proper analytics yield the maximum number of quality applicants (Marler and Fisher 2013). By optimising internal and external channels of recruitment, talent sourcing can offer the best ROI for the organisation and eventually serves as a competitive advantage. Data analytics via social media, and reviews-based data for sourcing talented incumbents are few effective techniques to build brand and help HEIs in getting potential incumbents.

3. Talent acquisition & hiring and competitive advantage

Application tracking system is another important and essential technique to understand the flow and bottlenecks in the process of hiring and guide for further improvements. Data gathered from each stage of hiring assist the hiring team to make well informed decisions. Data driven assessment of candidates improves the efficiency of overall hiring process (Boudreau, 2012). Analytics related to talent search can serve as a valuable element of assessment of applicants. Metrices such as 'Time to hire', 'Cost per hire', 'Quality of hire' and 'Attrition rate' are important ones to know the effectiveness of hiring policies in the HEIs. Predictive analytics in hiring can help both the employer and the incumbent by understanding the specific job roles. Metrices such as Time to hire, Cost per Hire, Performance of new Hire are important ones to measure the effectiveness of hiring process. Improved quality incumbents, reduced time to fill, cost efficient and reduced time to fill, enhanced candidate experience are a few advantages of applying data analytics in the hiring process. By keeping an eye on the effectiveness of the hiring process, HEIs can be benefitted and may have an edge over their competitors (Chaturvedi, 2016; Davenport et al., 2010). HEIs can significantly improve their hiring process by applying analytical tools and techniques.

4. Onboarding and Engagement and Competitive advantage

In HEIs, onboarding and engagement analytics plays a significant role as it analyses the experiences of new joinees and provide measures to engage them physically, mentally and spiritually. Analytics based onboarding and engagement process facilitate HEIs to make corrective actions for engaging newly hired employees in the organisation. Key metrices for onboarding and engagement are ' Time to value', 'Employee satisfaction' and 'Pulse surveys', these are crucial to unravel the effectiveness of onboarding and engagement practices. Apart from this, onboarding and engagement effectiveness can be understood via time to productivity, turnover of new hires, onboarding satisfaction and goal achievement. Engagement metrices focuses on employee satisfaction, employee feedback, turnover analysis and performance related feedback. Previou study posits that interactive and secure onboarding has impacts employee satisfaction positively (Tariq, 2024). It is imperative for the human resource department to be equipped with latest technologies. Normal, traditional performance appraisal methods prove to be inaccurate, when HR analytics is employed for the same it increases the trust employees have in the appraisal process (Jones, 2014).

These metrices are very useful for HEIs to make decisions which are based on robust data analysis. The benefits of onboarding and engagement analytics are many such as evidence based decision making, improved employees performance, reduced employee turnover and increased employee engagement. The key role of onboarding and engagement is to foster a positive and healthy environment by using a data driven approach and this can act as an advantage over others (Jones, 2023).

5. Performance management analytics and competitive advantage

In HEIs, there are many criteria to evaluate the performance of faculty and staff members however how often they make data driven decisions which are fair and equitable is a big question to be addressed. Inequality and unfair decisions lead to high labour turnover (Allport, 2015). Performance management analytics in HEIs involves tracking, evaluating and enhancing the performance of faculty and staff at different levels such as lower, middle and top and individual, group and organisational levels. Performance management analytics is beyond the conventional methods of appraising people's performance, it is a data driven approach where the performance of faculty, staff and students are measured on various dimensions. For example, for individual assessment, the outputs such as teaching contribution, contribution in institution building, research contribution and training and consultancy assignments can be used to evaluate faculty performance (Edger & Geare, 2013). The data generated from these dimensions can be further used to make informed decisions. Similarly for staff and students, HEIs can make use of data to examine the performance level and accordingly the feedback can be provided to them. For department level assessment also, the dimensions such as effectiveness of the programme, allocation of resources and benchmarking against the programmes may give input to better decisions. For organisational level performance in HEIs, data driven dimensions such as strategic planning at the institution level, the rankings and accreditations of HEIs and overall performance measures may be taken into consideration for further strategic moves at HEIs. There are many advantages of applying analytics in performance management such as improved performance at individual, department and organisational levels by tracking the data pertaining to several dimensions set by HEIs as performance criteria. Evidence based performance management system increases accountability and creates a transparent and open management system. It also helps in establishing an incremental but continuous improvement performance management system that may serve as a competitive advantage to HEIs (Shin, 2010; Hashim et al., 2024; Ter Bogt & Scapens, 2012). By leveraging data, HEIs can focus deeper on the strengths and areas of improvements and may have an edge over others.

6. Talent retention analytics and Competitive advantage

The role of talent management process in HEIs in the changing environments is discussed broadly in one of the studies by Cappelli & Keller, (2014). Zhang &Stewart, (2017) also addressed the concerns related to talent retention and mentioned how important retention data is to support the overall objectives of the organisation. Talent retention analytics in HEIs uses various tools and techniques to analyse the reasons for employees' turnover, absenteeism and leave patterns of employees. It is a data driven approach and helps HEIs to develop strategies to improve employee retention. Evidence based talent retention analytics is used to engage and create a more stable workforce. The main areas of employee retention are cost of employee turnover, turnover rate analysis, surveys of employees, exit interviews, performance data, compensation and demographic analysis. There are many advantages of talent retention analytics such as evidence-based decision making, improved employee morale, reduced attrition rate, increased productivity, improved reputation of HEIs and enhanced level of employees' motivation.

In the context of HEIs, practices such as reward & recognition and employee wellness were highlighted (Musakuro, 2022). The challenges and obstacles pertaining to managing talent in the organisation were highlighted in the studies conducted by Martin et al. (2022). Employee retention acts as a competitive advantage in the organisation as it creates an edge over the competitors.

7. Employee Wellness Analytics and Competitive Advantage in HEIs

Employee wellness analytics can act as a competitive advantage for HEIs. It involves using data analytics techniques to unravel and improve the welfare measures for the faculty, staff and other members of HEIs. It is an evidence-based approach to chalk out best practices for the well-being of the stakeholders of HEIs.

The prominent areas of employee wellness include health and wellness programs such as fitness classes, workshops related to stress management, meditation and recreational activities. Wellness analytics help us understand the effectiveness of these programs and uncover the areas of improvement. Regular employee surveys about physical and mental health, stress levels, work-life balance and other relevant issues provide great insights into the well-being of employees. The quality of work life is the key element of well-being. Vlachopoulos et al. (2011) explained the psychological needs in relation to regular exercise, which is relevant to employee wellness. Data related to absenteeism and presenteeism can give insights into potential problems and concerns. Disability claims data can also give relevant trends in employee health and inform preventive measures. Health insurance claims data also provides detailed information regarding employees' health and potential issues. The benefits of using employee wellness analytics are many, from improved health and wellness of employees to increased productivity to reduced healthcare costs to improved employee morale.

While the National Faculty and Staff Health Assessment, 2023 (NFSHA) ponders over health assessments, it highlights the relevance and importance of gathering data on employee health. Several previous studies discussed the role of analytics in higher education with special emphasis on the application of well-being analytics to create a healthier and inclusive environment, leading to more productive and engaged HEIs (Attaran et al., 2018).

CONCLUSION AND IMPLICATIONS

The chapter provides an in-depth description of the 7 key pillars of PA and provides a robust description for HEIs. By way of an in-depth examination of each pillar, this chapter aims to help academics and practitioners in applying PA in HEIs. It highlights that the role of PA is so pertinent as it involves a myriad of tasks such as planning effectively for the HEIs workforce, supplying the appropriate people and providing proper training. This provides the insights to apply metrics for all the seven pillars and helps HEIs remain globally competitive in the education field. The study has implications for all the stakeholders of HEIs, the management, the faculty members, the students, their parents and the society at large. The management team of any HEI can be benefitted by understanding the importance of applying data driven approach to manage people in their organisations specially for saving cost and improving the efficiency of their employees. Faculty members will also be benefitted by understanding the evidence-based approach used by the HEIs for analysing their performance. They will be treated more fairly in the organisation and this will eventually increase the retention rate. Evidence based hiring may also result in quality workforce for HEIs and would be beneficial for students as well. Quality faculty may help improve the quality of education and that would be a great relief to both the students and their parents.

By leveraging predictive analytics, HEIs can revolutionise practices like workforce and succession planning. With the help of data-driven insights, HR leaders can efficiently anticipate challenges, forecast talent needs and help the organisation productively grow. The integration of predictive analytics in HR strategy increases the competitiveness of an organisation(Bassi, 2011). People make up the most important asset of the HEIs, which is why heavy investments are made in them, the subsequent effect of this is witnessed in the rise of fields such as HR analytics (Pessach et al., 2020). The recruiting method of the HEIs must be foolproof to produce a talent pool of qualified candidates. Inefficient recruitment practices can have detrimental effects on the HEIs and can have spillover effects in the remuneration and profit relationships (Thiyagarajan, 2021). The hiring of a suitable workforce is deemed to be a highly challenging and strategic process for the organisation. Nonetheless, organisations must ensure that organisational goals are met along with the hiring of top talent (Pessach et al., 2020). As new disruptive technologies are being increasingly adopted, the recruitment process is now being revolutionised. The inclusion of such analytics can improve the effectiveness and efficiency of the organisation (Palshikar et al.,2019).

The evidence-based human resource management practices in HEIs are changing the HR landscape and redefining the experience (Gaur, 2020). This new approach focuses on advanced technologies and data analytics to improve the efficiency of

HEIs. Technological innovations such as AI-enabled HR functions and cloud-based systems are changing the workforce dynamics. Strategically, HEIs are leveraging analytics and helping leaders of HEIs to improve their overall productivity by improving the HR functions in general and reducing employee turnover in particular (Katiyar et al., 2023). To keep abrest with the latest advancement and to have an edge over other competitors, HEIs need to continuously invest in data driven decision making.

REFERENCES

Aljawarneh, N. M. (2024). The Mediating Role of Organization Agility between Business Intelligence & Innovative Performance. *Journal of Statistics Applications & Probability*, *13*(3), 929–938. DOI: 10.18576/jsap/130307

Allui, A., & Sahni, J. (2016). Strategic human resource management in higher education institutions: Empirical evidence from Saudi. *Procedia: Social and Behavioral Sciences*, *235*, 361–371. DOI: 10.1016/j.sbspro.2016.11.044

Andersen, M. K. (2017). Human capital analytics: The winding road. *Journal of Organizational Effectiveness: People and Performance*, *4*(2), 133–136. DOI: 10.1108/JOEPP-03-2017-0024

Aral, S., Brynjolfsson, E., & Wu, L. (2012). Three-way com plementarities: Performance pay, human resource analytics, and information technology. *Management Science*, *58*(5), 913–931. DOI: 10.1287/mnsc.1110.1460

Armstrong, M. (2006). *A handbook of human resource management practice*. Kogan Page Publishers.

Armstrong, M. (2009). *Armstrong's handbook of performance management: An evidence-based guide to delivering high performance*. Kogan Page Publishers.

Attaran, M., Stark, J., & Stotler, D. (2018). Opportunities and challenges for big data analytics in US higher education: A conceptual model for implementation. *Industry and Higher Education*, *32*(3), 169–182. DOI: 10.1177/0950422218770937

Baicker, K., Cutler, D., & Song, Z. (2010). Workplace wellness programs can generate savings. *Health Affairs*, *29*(2), 304–311. DOI: 10.1377/hlthaff.2009.0626

Balyasin, & Gebremerkel. (2020). Interaction between general management, human resource department and other academic departments (pp. 17–19).

Barney, J. B., & Arikan, A. M. (2005). The resource-based view: origins and implications. *The Blackwell handbook of strategic management*, 123-182, https://doi.org/DOI: 10.1111/b.9780631218616.2006.00006.x

Bassi, L. (2011). Raging debates in HR analytics. *People and Strategy*, *34*(2), 14–18.

Bendickson, J. S., Chandler, T. D., James, B. E., & Taylor, E. C. (2023). Sourcing human capital for organizational effectiveness: Sourcing strategy, determinants, and alignment. *International Journal of Human Resource Management*, *34*(5), 987–1014. zDOI: 10.1080/09585192.2021.2016888

Boles, M., Pelletier, B., & Lynch, W. (2004). The relationship between health risks and work productivity. *Journal of Occupational and Environmental Medicine, 46*(7), 737–745. DOI: 10.1097/01.jom.0000131830.45744.97

Boudreau, J. (2017), 'Hr must make people analytics more user-friendly', Harvard Business Review June, 1–5. https:// hbr.org/2017/06/hr-must-make-people-analytics -more- user-friendly

Boudreau, J. W. (2012). Decision Logic in Evidence-Based Management: Can Logical Models From Other Disciplines Improve Evidence-Based Human-Resource Decisions?.

Bryson, J. M., Ackermann, F., & Eden, C. (2007). Putting the resource-based view of strategy and distinctive competencies to work in public organizations. *Public Administration Review, 67*(4), 702–717. DOI: 10.1111/j.1540-6210.2007.00754.x

Bussin, Mark. *Remuneration and talent management.* eBook Partnership, 2014.

Cameron, K. (1978). Measuring organizational effectiveness in institutions of higher education. *Administrative science quarterly*, 604-632.2

Cameron, K. S. (1986). Effectiveness as paradox: Consensus and conflict in conceptions of organizational effectiveness. *Management Science, 32*(5), 539–553. DOI: 10.1287/mnsc.32.5.539

Cappelli, P., & Keller, J. R. (2014). Talent management: Conceptual approaches and practical challenges. *Annual Review of Organizational Psychology and Organizational Behavior, 1*(1), 305–331. DOI: 10.1146/annurev-orgpsych-031413-091314

Catteeuw, F., Flynn, E., & Vonderhorst, J. (2007). Employee engagement: Boosting productivity in turbulent times. *Organization Development Journal, 25*(2).

Chahar, B., Jain, S. R., & Hatwal, V. (2021). Mediating role of employee motivation for training, commitment, retention, and performance in higher education institutions. *Problems and Perspectives in Management, 19*(3), 95. DOI: 10.21511/ppm.19(3).2021.09

Chaturvedi, V. (2016). Talent analytics as an indispensable tool and an emerging facet of HR for organization building. *FIIB Business Review, 5*(3), 13–20. DOI: 10.1177/2455265820160302

Chen, S. H., Wang, H. H., & Yang, K. J. (2009). Establishment and application of performance measure indicators for universities. *The TQM Journal, 21*(3), 220–235. DOI: 10.1108/17542730910953004

Cotten, A. (2007). *Seven steps of effective workforce planning*. IBM Centre for the Business of Government.

Cross, R., Opie, T., Pryor, G., & Rollag, K. (2018). Connect and adapt: How network development and transformation improve retention and engagement in employees' first five years. *Organizational Dynamics*, *47*(2), 115–123. DOI: 10.1016/j.orgdyn.2017.08.003

Davenport, T. H., Harris, J. G., & Morison, R. (2010). *Analytics at work: Smarter decisions, better results*. Harvard Business Press.

De Bruecker, P., Van den Bergh, J., Beliën, J., & Demeulemeester, E. (2015). Workforce planning incorporating skills: State of the art. *European Journal of Operational Research, 243*(1), 1-16 https://doi.org/ rights and contentDOI: 10.1016/j.ejor.2014.10.038Get

Den Hartog, D. N., Boselie, P., & Paauwe, J. (2004). Performance management: A model and research agenda. *Applied Psychology*, *53*(4), 556–569. DOI: 10.1111/j.1464-0597.2004.00188.x

Dessler, G. (2004). *A framework for human resource management*. Pearson Education India.

Dilger, A. (2009). The principle of hiring the best available academics. *International Journal of Educational Management*, *23*(6), 523–532. DOI: 10.1108/09513540910981041

DiPiro, J. T. (2011). A culture of hiring for excellence. *American Journal of Pharmaceutical Education*, *75*(5). Advance online publication. DOI: 10.5688/ajpe75597

Ewing, M. T., Pitt, L. F., De Bussy, N. M., & Berthon, P. (2002). Employment branding in the knowledge economy. *International Journal of Advertising*, *21*(1), 3–22. DOI: 10.1080/02650487.2002.11104914

Fitz-Enz, J., & John Mattox, I. I. (2014). *Predictive analytics for human resources*. John Wiley & Sons.

Ford, J. K. (Ed.). (2014). *Improving training effectiveness in work organizations*. Psychology Press.

Fuming, X., & Jiliang, S. (2007). Research on job satisfaction of elementary and high school teachers and strategies to increase job satisfaction. *Chinese Education & Society*, *40*(5), 86–96. DOI: 10.2753/CED1061-1932400509

Gallo, A. (2015, October). Setting the record straight on switching jobs. *Harvard Business Review*, 34.

Gaur, B. (2020, July). HR4. 0: an analytics framework to redefine employee engagement in the fourth industrial revolution. In *2020 11th International Conference on Computing, Communication and Networking Technologies (ICCCNT)* (pp. 1-6). IEEE.

Gibbs, G. (2013). Reflections on the changing nature of educational development. *The International Journal for Academic Development*, *18*(1), 4–14. DOI: 10.1080/1360144X.2013.751691

Green, D. A., & Little, D. (2016). Family portrait: A profile of educational developers around the world. *The International Journal for Academic Development*, *21*(2), 135–150.

Guest, D., & Clinton, M. (2007). *Human resource management and university performance*. Research and Development Series. Leadership Foundation for Higher Education.

Hashim, M. A., Che Ibrahim, C. K. I., Jaafar, N. A. L., Kordi, N. E., Haron, A. T., & Umeokafor, N. (2024). Building data driven culture for digital competitiveness in construction industry: A theoretical exploration. *International Journal of Construction Management*, •••, 1–13.

Huisman, J., & Van der Wende, M. (2005). *On cooperation and competition II. Institutional responses to internationalisation, Europeanisation and globalisation*. Lemmens.

Hurst, K., & Kelley Patterson, D. (2014). Health and social care workforce planning and development–an overview. *International Journal of Health Care Quality Assurance*, *27*(7), 562–572. DOI: 10.1108/IJHCQA-05-2014-0062

Huselid, M. A. (1995). The impact of human resource management practices on turnover, productivity, and corporate financial performance. *Academy of Management Journal*, *38*(3), 635–672. DOI: 10.5465/256741

Irshad, M., & Afridi, F. (2007). Factors affecting employees retention: Evidence from literature. *Abasyn Journal of Social Sciences*, *4*(2), 307–339.

Jacobson, W. S. (2010). Preparing for tomorrow: A case study of workforce planning in North Carolina municipal governments. *Public Personnel Management*, *39*(4), 353–377. DOI: 10.1177/009102601003900404

Jones, C. M. (2023). *Comparing Approaches to Virtual Team Onboarding: the Influence of Synchrony and Cues on Impressions of Leaders During Encounter Phase Organizational Socialization* (Master's thesis, The University of Wisconsin-Milwaukee).

Jones, K. (2014). Conquering HR analytics: Do you need a rocket scientist or a crystal ball?. *Workforce Solutions Review, 5*(3).

Julius, D. J. (2000). Human Resources. *New Directions for Higher Education, 2000*(111).

Katiyar, A., Khan, C., & Sachan, V. S. (2023). Role of HR Analytics on Employees Performance. *International Journal for Modern Trends in Science and Technology, 9*, 925–933. DOI: 10.46501/IJMTST0905157

Katz, D., & Kahn, R. L. (1978). Organizations and the system concept. *Classics of organization theory, 80*(480), 27.

Kaur, R. (2017). Employee retention models and factors affecting employees retention in IT companies. *International Journal of Business Administration and Management, 7*(1), 161–174.

Kenny, N., Popovic, C., McSweeney, J., Knorr, K., Hoessler, C., Hall, S., & El Khoury, E. (2017). Drawing on the principles of SoTL to illuminate a path forward for the scholarship of educational development. *The Canadian Journal for the Scholarship of Teaching and Learning, 8*(2), n2.

Klein, H. J., & Polin, B. (2012). 14 Are Organizations On Board with Best Practices Onboarding?The Oxford handbook of organizational socialization, 267

Klein, H. J., Polin, B., & Leigh Sutton, K. (2015). Specific onboarding practices for the socialization of new employees. *International Journal of Selection and Assessment, 23*(3), 263–283. DOI: 10.1111/ijsa.12113

Levenson, A., Lawler, E. E., III, & Boudreau, J. W. (2005). Survey on HR Analytics and HR transformation: Feedback report. *Center for Effective Organizations, University of Southern California*, 131-42.

Lew, T. (2009). The relationships between perceived organizational support, felt obligation, affective organizational commitment and turnover intention of academics working with private higher educational institutions in Malaysia. *European Journal of Social Sciences, 9*(1), 72–87.

Mallillin, L. L. D. (2017). Human resource management in selected higher education institutions (HEI): Towards enhancing employees' work. *International Journal of Advanced Research in Management and Social Sciences, 6*(1), 58–74.

Mansour, H. F., Heath, G., & Brannan, M. J. (2015). Exploring the role of HR practitioners in pursuit of organizational effectiveness in higher education institutions. *Journal of Change Management, 15*(3), 210–230. DOI: 10.1080/14697017.2015.1045539

Marginson, S. (2007). The public/private divide in higher education: A global revision. *Higher Education, 53*, 307–333.

Marler, J. H., & Boudreau, J. W. (2017). An evidence-based review of HR Analytics. *International Journal of Human Resource Management, 28*(1), 3–26. DOI: 10.1080/09585192.2016.1244699

Marler, J. H., & Boudreau, J. W. (2017). An evidence-based review of HR Analytics. *International Journal of Human Resource Management, 28*(1), 3–26. DOI: 10.1080/09585192.2016.1244699

Marler, J. H., & Fisher, S. L. (2013). An evidence-based review of e-HRM and strategic human resource management. *Human Resource Management Review, 23*(1), 18–36. DOI: 10.1016/j.hrmr.2012.06.002

Martin, F., Sun, T., Westine, C. D., & Ritzhaupt, A. D. (2022). Examining research on the impact of distance and online learning: A second-order meta-analysis study. *Educational Research Review, 36*, 100438. DOI: 10.1016/j.edurev.2022.100438

Musakuro, R. N. (2022). A framework development for talent management in the higher education sector. *SA Journal of Human Resource Management, 20*, 1671. https://hdl.handle.net/10520/ejc-sajhrm_v20_i1_a1671

Nyambegera, S., Daniels, K., & Sparrow, P. (2001). Why fit doesn't always matter: The impact of HRM and cultural fit on job involvement of Kenyan employees. *Applied Psychology, 50*(1), 109–140. DOI: 10.1111/1464-0597.00050

Othman, M., Bhuiyan, N., & Gouw, G. J. (2011). A new approach to workforce planning. *International Journal of Computer and Systems Engineering, 5*(4), 858–864.

Owen, T. R. (2002). Student and Employee Wellness in Higher Education: A Literature Review.

Palshikar, G. K., Srivastava, R., Pawar, S., Hingmire, S., Jain, A., Chourasia, S., & Shah, M. (2019). Analytics-led talent acquisition for improving efficiency and effectiveness. *Advances in analytics and applications*, 141-160.

Pape, T. (2016). Prioritising data items for business analytics: Framework and application to human resources. *European Journal of Operational Research, 252*(2), 687–698. DOI: 10.1016/j.ejor.2016.01.052

Paul, M., & Jena, L. K. (2022). Workplace spirituality, teachers' professional well-being and mediating role of positive psychological capital: An empirical validation in the Indian context. *International Journal of Ethics and Systems, 38*(4), 633–660. DOI: 10.1108/IJOES-08-2021-0163

Pellert, A. (2007). Human resource management at universities. *Higher education management and development in central, southern and eastern. Europe*, •••, 104–109.

Pessach, D., Singer, G., Avrahami, D., Ben-Gal, H. C., Shmueli, E., & Ben-Gal, I. (2020). Employees recruitment: A prescriptive analytics approach via machine learning and mathematical programming. *Decision Support Systems*, *134*, 113290. DOI: 10.1016/j.dss.2020.113290

Ployhart, R. E. (2006). Staffing in the 21st century: New challenges and strategic opportunities. *Journal of Management*, *32*(6), 868–897. DOI: 10.1177/0149206306293625

Porter, M. E. (1980). *Competitive Strategy*. Free Press.

Powell, S., & Wood, D. (1999). Is recruitment the millennium time bomb for the industry worldwide? *International Journal of Contemporary Hospitality Management*, *11*(4), 138–141. DOI: 10.1108/09596119910263513

Powell, T. C. (2001). Competitive advantage: Logical and philosophical considerations. *Strategic Management Journal*, *22*(9), 875–888. DOI: 10.1002/smj.173

Raguseo, E. (2018). Big data technologies: An empirical investigation on their adoption, benefits and risks for companies. *International Journal of Information Management*, *38*(1), 187–195. DOI: 10.1016/j.ijinfomgt.2017.07.008

Roslender, R., Stevenson, J., & Kahn, H. (2006). Employee wellness as intellectual capital: An accounting perspective. *Journal of Human Resource Costing & Accounting*, *10*(1), 48–64. DOI: 10.1108/14013380610672675

Rosser, V. J., Johnsrud, L. K., & Heck, R. H. (2003). Academic deans and directors: • Assessing their effectiveness from individual and institutional perspectives. *The Journal of Higher Education*, *74*(1), 1–25. DOI: 10.1080/00221546.2003.11777185

Rumelt, R. P. (1991). How much does industry matter? *Strategic Management Journal*, *12*(3), 167–185. DOI: 10.1002/smj.4250120302

Sharif, S., Malik, S. A., Arooj, N., & Albadry, O. M. (2024). Human resource management (HRM) practices and organizational commitment in higher educational institution (HEI): A mediating role for work engagement. *Global Knowledge, Memory and Communication*. Advance online publication. DOI: 10.1108/GKMC-11-2023-0456

Shin, J. C. (2010). Impacts of performance-based accountability on institutional performance in the US. *Higher Education*, *60*, 47–68.

Spreitzer, G., & Porath, C. (2012). Creating sustainable performance. *Harvard Business Review*, *90*(1), 92–99.

Stein, M., & Christiansen, L. (2010). *Successful onboarding*. McGraw-Hill Professional Publishing.

Tariq, M. Z. (2024). Enhancing onboarding with AI: designing a modern conversational agent for onboarding. https://urn.fi/URN:NBN:fi-fe2024052737703

Tasmin, R., Huey, T. L., Nda, R. M., & Jaafar, I. (2022). What does it take to adopt big data management approach at Malaysian higher education institutions. *The Journal of Learning in Higher Education*, •••, 1–15. DOI: 10.5171/2022.924024

Taylor, F. W. (2004). *Scientific management*. Routledge.

Ter Bogt, H. J., & Scapens, R. W. (2012). Performance management in universities: Effects of the transition to more quantitative measurement systems. *European Accounting Review*, *21*(3), 451–497. DOI: 10.1080/09638180.2012.668323

Tursunbayeva, A., Di Lauro, S., & Pagliari, C. (2018). People analytics—A scoping review of conceptual boundaries and value propositions. *International Journal of Information Management*, *43*, 224–247. DOI: 10.1016/j.ijinfomgt.2018.08.002

Tursunbayeva, A., Pagliari, C., Di Lauro, S., & Antonelli, G. (2022). The ethics of people analytics: Risks, opportunities and recommendations. *Personnel Review*, *51*(3), 900–921. DOI: 10.1108/PR-12-2019-0680

Ulrich, D. (2013). Redefining our roles. *The Higher Education Workplace*, *5*(2), 26.

Ulrich, D., & Dulebohn, J. H. (2015). Are we there yet? What's next for HR? *Human Resource Management Review*, *25*(2), 188–204. DOI: 10.1016/j.hrmr.2015.01.004

van der Togt, J., & Rasmussen, T. H. (2017). Toward evidence-based HR. *Journal of Organizational Effectiveness: People and Performance*, *4*(2), 127–132. DOI: 10.1108/JOEPP-02-2017-0013

Vigoda, E. (2000). Organizational politics, job attitudes, and work outcomes: Exploration and implications for the public sector. *Journal of vocational Behavior, 57*(3), 326-347. https://doi.org/ rights and contentDOI: 10.1006/jvbe.1999.1742Get

Vlachopoulos, S. P., Kaperoni, M., & Moustaka, F. C. (2011). The relationship of self-determination theory variables to exercise identity. *Psychology of sport and exercise, 12*(3), 265-272. https://doi.org/ rights and contentDOI: 10.1016/j.psychsport.2010.11.006Get

Wang, T., Lund, B. D., Marengo, A., Pagano, A., Mannuru, N. R., Teel, Z. A., & Pange, J. (2023). Exploring the potential impact of artificial intelligence (AI) on international students in higher education: Generative AI, chatbots, analytics, and international student success. *Applied Sciences (Basel, Switzerland)*, *13*(11), 6716. DOI: 10.3390/app13116716

Wernerfelt, B. (1984). A resource-based view of the firm. *Strategic Management Journal*, *5*(2), 171–180. DOI: 10.1002/smj.4250050207

Zhang, C., & Stewart, J. (2017). Talent management and retention. *The Wiley Blackwell handbook of the psychology of recruitment, selection and employee retention*, 473-493.https://doi.org/DOI: 10.1002/9781118972472.ch22

Chapter 9
Advancing Organizational Resilience Through Learning and Development Analytics:
A Data-Driven Approach to Strategic Growth

A. Devikomathy
https://orcid.org/0009-0000-7350-3387
Rajalakshmi Engineering College, India

A. Devikomathy
SRM Institute of Science and Technology, India

S. K. Manivannan
https://orcid.org/0000-0002-4923-7864
SRM Institute of Science and Technology, India

ABSTRACT

This chapter explores data-driven strategies that can enhance decision-making, resource allocation, instruction effectiveness, and promote institutional openness to change. The study integrates new learning analytics trends, artificial intelligence in educational evaluation, data visualization techniques, and forecasting modeling to develop a multi-faceted approach to organizational resilience. The authors present a new Resilience Analytics Framework (RAF) that integrates diverse data sources and analytic techniques for strategic growth initiatives in higher education. The chapter also discusses the ethical implications and pragmatic challenges of

DOI: 10.4018/979-8-3373-7057-6.ch009

analytics use and provides actionable recommendations for institutions at different analytics maturity levels. The chapter concludes with potential research directions, citing future technologies like machine learning, natural language processing, and multimodal analytics to further improve organizational resilience and responsiveness in higher education.

INTRODUCTION

The landscape of higher education is going through an extraordinary era of change, with the demographics of students changing, changing workforce needs, technological disruption, and rising economic pressures. With institutions facing this challenging landscape, the ability to absorb organizational resilience—meaning being able to sense, prepare for, respond to, and adapt to incremental change and unexpected disruption—has come to be the key determinant of institutional sustainability and success (Heifetz et al., 2009). Conventional methods of institutional administration, based usually on precedent and intuitive choice, are increasingly unable to cope with the complex challenges confronting contemporary institutions of higher education (Macfadyen & Dawson, 2012).

Learning and development analytics, therefore, offer an influential tool for promoting organizational robustness through careful data gathering, examination, and deployment. Learning analytics, generally speaking, "the measurement, collection, analysis, and reporting of data about learners and their contexts, for purposes of understanding and optimizing learning and the environments in which it occurs" (Siemens, 2013, p. 1382), has mainly been geared towards enhancing students' outcomes. Nevertheless, its use can reach beyond the learning environment to provide insights for decision-making at an institutional level as well as strategic initiatives, hence organizational flexibility and resilience (Ifenthaler & Yau, 2022).

Institutional adoption of learning and development analytics is a paradigm shift away from intuition-based and toward evidence-based decision-making, consistent with the larger movement towards data-driven governance in higher education (Daniel, 2015). By leveraging diverse data sources—from student information systems and learning management platforms to faculty development records and institutional research—analytics can illuminate patterns, identify opportunities for intervention, and guide strategic planning efforts that strengthen institutional capacity to weather challenges and seize emerging opportunities (Dietz-Uhler & Hurn, 2013).

This chapter investigates the crossroads of learning and development analytics and organizational resilience in higher education, outlining a broad framework for utilizing data-informed methods to increase institutional adaptability and strategic expansion. Leveraging theoretical constructs from organizational science, educational data mining, and institutional effectiveness, the authors consider how analytics may guide decision-making across a variety of institutional spheres of activity, such as student success efforts, curriculum planning, faculty assistance, resource planning, and strategic planning (Ferguson et al., 2016).

At the center of this inquiry is the presentation of the Resilience Analytics Framework (RAF), a new conceptual framework that combines data collection, analysis, interpretation, and application processes in order to assist resilience-building initiatives within higher education institutions. The RAF offers a systematic method for capitalizing on various data sources and analytic approaches, providing a roadmap for institutions with different analytics maturity levels to increase their ability to adapt and innovate (Baker & Inventado, 2014).

By way of case studies derived from varied institutional settings, the chapter demonstrates real-life applications of the RAF, emphasizing successful approaches to adopting analytics-based resilience programs and overcoming typical setbacks encountered along the way. The case studies demonstrate how institutions have been able to effectively utilize analytics to solve vital challenges like student retention, curriculum design based on industry needs, faculty improvement, and strategic resource allocation, evincing the concrete advantages of data-driven strategies towards organizational resilience (Slade & Prinsloo, 2013).

Furthermore, the chapter explores ethical issues regarding the collection and utilization of learning data, including the need to protect privacy, be transparent, and ensure fairness in analytics implementation. Through its socio-technical approach, authors recognize that successful analytics projects will need to navigate technological potential along with organizational culture, stakeholder participation, and ethical guidelines if they are to have lasting effect (Gašević et al., 2015).

As higher education organizations continue to contend with unprecedented adversity—from the ongoing impacts of global disruptions to changing student expectations and new technologies—the ability for organizational resilience grows more critical. It is this chapter's contention that learning and development analytics, when carefully deployed as part of an integrated framework congruent with institutional mission and values, can act as a powerful driver for establishing the adaptive capacity required for sustainability and success in an uncertain future (Siemens et al., 2013).

To guide readers through this intersectional landscape, the chapter is structured as follows: Section 1 presents foundational theories of organizational resilience and the evolution of learning analytics. Section 2 introduces the Resilience Analytics Framework (RAF), detailing its components and data strategies. Section 3 discusses implementation strategies, success factors, and challenges. Section 4 explores emerging trends, ethical considerations, and cross-sector learnings. The chapter concludes with future research directions and a synthesized summary of implications for institutional leaders, technologists, and policy makers.

BACKGROUND

Theoretical Foundations of Organizational Resilience

Organizational resilience has become an essential field of research in organizational and management studies, especially when institutions are moving into more dynamic and turbulent contexts. The notion began in ecological systems theory where resilience is understood as the ability of a system to absorb perturbation while upholding fundamental structure and function (Holling, 1973). When applied to organizations, resilience encompasses the ability to anticipate potential threats, cope effectively with unexpected events, and adapt to changing circumstances while maintaining core operations (Lengnick-Hall et al., 2011).

Weick and Sutcliffe (2015) found five essential principles that define highly reliable organizations with robust resilience capabilities: (1) preoccupation with failure, (2) reluctance to oversimplify interpretations, (3) sensitivity to operations, (4) commitment to resilience, and (5) deference to expertise. These principles highlight the value of organizational mindfulness—a condition of active awareness about potential threats and opportunities—as a basis for resilience (Weick & Sutcliffe, 2015).

In higher education in particular, organizational resilience assumes special significance in light of the sector's distinctive features, such as multiple stakeholder groups, complex governance arrangements, and the interplay between tradition and innovation (Kezar, 2014). Institutions have to balance competing pressures while ensuring academic quality, financial viability, and responsiveness to social needs—a challenge that calls for flexible frameworks and evidence-based decision-making processes (Christensen & Eyring, 2011).

Scholarship more recently has broadened the definition of organizational resilience beyond survival or recuperation from hardship to include transformative capacity—the capability to use difficulties as chances for innovation and growth (Lengnick-Hall & Beck, 2016). This line of thinking concurs with requests for the transformation of higher education in light of shifting student demographics, technology, and changing workforce demands (Davidson, 2017). Whereas, as Heifetz et al. (2009) contend, these adaptive challenges call for new learning, innovation, and modifications in organizational behavior and values—very much the kind of abilities resilience frameworks aim to cultivate.

Evolution of Learning Analytics in Higher Education

Learning analytics has evolved from a niche concern to a cornerstone of strategic educational planning. Early iterations focused on descriptive insights—tracking performance and engagement (Clow, 2013). Subsequent advances introduced predictive analytics, enabling early identification of at-risk learners and forecasting institutional performance (Calvet Liñán & Juan Pérez, 2015). Current frontiers include prescriptive and diagnostic capabilities, supported by artificial intelligence (AI), to tailor interventions and understand causality (West et al., 2016; Baker & Inventado, 2014).

Recent literature emphasizes the role of **explainable AI (XAI)** in making analytics outcomes interpretable and trustworthy for stakeholders—particularly vital in educational settings where transparency and fairness are paramount (Arrieta et al., 2020). Furthermore, emerging technologies such as **federated learning** enable institutions to collaborate on predictive models while preserving data privacy across jurisdictions—an increasingly relevant consideration under global privacy regulations like GDPR and CCPA.

In tandem, **edge computing** and **real-time analytics** are reshaping the data infrastructure in learning environments, allowing for near-instant feedback and intervention in both physical and virtual classrooms (Blikstein & Worsley, 2016). These advancements extend the scope of learning analytics from static dashboards to dynamic, adaptive learning systems that enhance institutional responsiveness.

Despite this progress, integration between learning analytics and broader organizational resilience theory remains underdeveloped. While many frameworks address resilience and analytics separately, few explore their intersection systematically. This chapter seeks to fill that gap by demonstrating how integrated data strategies can inform not only learning success but also institutional agility, cultural adaptability, and strategic planning.

Bridging Learning Analytics and Organizational Development

The intersection of learning analytics and organizational development is a promising area for developing institutional resilience. While learning analytics has historically aimed at enhancing student outcomes, and organizational development has aimed at improving institutional structures and processes, the convergence of these fields holds the potential for data-driven strategies to develop adaptive capacity (Macfadyen et al., 2014).

This integration requires bridging multiple levels of analysis—from individual learning and teaching activities to program-level outcomes to institution-wide performance indicators (Greller & Drachsler, 2012). It also necessitates engaging diverse stakeholders, including faculty, administrators, instructional designers, and information technology professionals, in collaborative approaches to data collection, analysis, and application (West et al., 2016).

Several scholars have proposed frameworks for connecting analytics to organizational learning and development. For instance, Machi et al. (2018) presented the Continuous Improvement and Planning Framework, which connects learning analytics with strategic planning activities via repeated cycles of data collection, analysis, action, and assessment. Likewise, Carbonell et al. (2013) created the Analytics for Organizational Learning model, which focuses on the application of data to facilitate double-loop learning—the process by which organizations not only address current problems but also challenge and modify underlying assumptions and strategies.

Such integrative efforts are in line with broader trends in evidence-based management in higher education, evidencing increasing recognition that institutional decision-making should be data-driven and grounded in systematic analysis more than in tradition or intuition (Hora et al., 2017). By linking learning analytics with organizational development models, institutions can use data not just to resolve pressing problems but also to develop long-term adaptive capacity and resilience (Macfadyen & Dawson, 2012).

Data-Driven Decision Making in Educational Settings

Data-driven decision making (DDDM) in schools involves systematic data collection, analysis, and interpretation for the purpose of informing practice and policy decisions (Mandinach, 2012). Although DDDM has its origins in business intelligence and performance management, its use in educational settings poses distinctive challenges and opportunities concerning learning environments' complexity and stakeholder diversity (Marsh et al., 2006).

Studies of DDDM at the university level have found numerous factors that affect its effectiveness, which include the availability of data, analytical capability, organizational culture, top-management support, and stakeholder involvement (Hora et al., 2017). Institutions with robust data systems, effective analytical capacity, and organizational cultures that embrace evidence-based practices tend to apply DDDM more effectively than institutions without these features (Bichsel, 2012).

DDD use crosses institutional domains of operation such as student enrollment management, student success programming, curriculum planning, faculty assessment, and resource allocation (Daniel, 2015). In all domains, successful DDD needs not just strong technical infrastructure but also stakeholders' data literacy and unambiguous linkages between data analysis and actionable results (Macfadyen & Dawson, 2012).

In spite of its potential advantages, DDDM in education is also subject to some challenges, such as the possibility of over-reliance on quantifiable and easily measured data, the difficulty of quantifying complex educational outcomes, and conflict between standardization and contextualization (Mandinach & Schildkamp, 2021). Further, issues regarding data privacy, algorithmic bias, and analytics potentially exacerbating existing inequities need careful attention and ethical guidelines (Slade & Prinsloo, 2013).

To meet these challenges, researchers have called for balanced approaches to DDDM that combine quantitative and qualitative data, involve multiple stakeholders in the interpretation process, and keep educational values and mission in focus (Hora et al., 2017). By taking such balanced approaches, institutions can harness the strength of data without succumbing to reductionist approaches that can compromise educational quality and equity (Selwyn, 2019).

Technology Integration and Institutional Adaptation

Technology integration in higher education institutions is a crucial change driver and adaptation mechanism, as digital technologies have transformed teaching, learning, administrative processes, and communication patterns (Henderson et al., 2017). Successful implementation depends on factors such as technology infrastructure, support systems, faculty development, institutional policies, and organizational culture. Institutions that embrace technology integration as a socio-technical process, considering both technical competence and social dynamics, achieve more sustainable and transformative results (Trowler & Cooper, 2002). Technology integration and organizational resilience are intertwined, with technological expertise enhancing an institution's ability to identify potential problems, track performance, and adjust to new conditions (Macfadyen et al., 2014). Learning analytics platforms are particularly significant for institutional adoption, allowing institutions to gather, integrate, and analyze data from various sources, providing insights that inform decision-making (Siemens & Long, 2011). However, actualizing the potential of these technologies requires considerations such as data governance, stakeholder involvement, and alignment with institutional mission and values (Daniel, 2015). The embedding of learning analytics technologies promises to enrich adaptability and resilience through enhanced information flow, evidence-informed decision-making, and systematic methods for ongoing improvement. However, effective embedding requires careful consideration of organizational dynamics, stakeholder requirements, and ethical considerations of data-oriented strategies for educational practice and policy (Slade & Prinsloo, 2013). Theoretical insights and historical developments set the stage for operationalizing resilience through analytics. In the next section, we present the Resilience Analytics Framework (RAF)—a structured approach for integrating data systems and decision-making tools into organizational resilience initiatives.

Elements of the Resilience Analytics Framework

The Resilience Analytics Framework is a comprehensive framework designed to support data-driven resilience development in higher education institutions. It comprises five interlinked elements:

1. Data Ecosystem and Integration: This component involves creating the technical and organizational infrastructure to support good analytics, such as identifying and integrating relevant data sources institution-wide. It also includes formulating data governance policies, establishing interoperability standards, and developing data literacy and analysis capacity in stakeholders (Siemens et al., 2013).
2. Multi-level Analysis: This element involves systemic examination of data at various organizational levels to determine patterns, trends, and relationships applicable to resilience. This includes micro-level analysis of student learning interactions and behaviors, meso-level analysis of program performance, macro-level analysis of institutional performance indicators, and cross-level analysis of micro, meso, and macro factor relationships. By looking at data at multiple levels, institutions can gain a holistic view of their operations and find leverage points for building resilience throughout the organization (Slade & Prinsloo, 2013).
3. Resilience Indicators and Early Warning Systems: This element involves building metrics and monitoring systems specifically tailored to measure organizational resilience and detect potential issues before they become crises. It includes determining major indicators of resilience in various areas, setting initial measures and standards for indicators of resilience, having early warning systems that notify stakeholders about alarming trends or patterns, and designing dashboards and visualization tools that convey resilience indicators clearly to various stakeholder groups (Siemens & Long, 2011).
4. Evidence-Based Intervention Design: This element entails converting analytical insights into tangible interventions aimed at strengthening resilience. It includes building a set of evidence-based interventions to deal with typical obstacles to resilience in higher education, establishing protocols for connecting specific patterns of data to suitable interventions, developing interventions that tackle both short-term problems and deeper systemic causes, and involving stakeholders in the intervention development process (Machi et al., 2018).
5. Adaptive Implementation and Learning Cycles: This element emphasizes putting interventions into practice, measuring their impact, and applying the findings to drive future cycles of analysis and action. This includes setting up implementation procedures with explicit timelines, roles, resource allocation,

and success measures, creating evaluation systems that measure both the direct outcomes of interventions and their influence on overall organizational resilience, developing mechanisms for capturing lessons learned during implementation, and enabling organizational learning and reflection that probe assumptions, shakes up established practices, and fosters creative ways of building resilience (Kezar & Eckel, 2002) (Carbonell et al., 2013).

Data Sources and Analytical Methods

The Resilience Analytics Framework utilizes various data sources and methods of analysis to enable thorough understanding of organizational performance and responsiveness. Table 1 outlines major data sources applicable to resilience analytics in higher education, their possible uses, and limitations.

Table 1. Key Data Sources for Resilience Analytics

Data Source Category	Examples	Potential Applications	Limitations
Student Information Systems	Demographic data, enrolment patterns, academic performance records	Identifying at-risk populations, analysing retention patterns, tracking completion rates	Limited insight into student experiences and non-academic factors
Learning Management Systems	Course access patterns, assignment completion, discussion participation	Monitoring engagement, identifying course design issues, detecting early warning signs	Varies in depth based on instructor usage; may not capture offline activities
Course Evaluations and Surveys	Student satisfaction ratings, perceptions of teaching effectiveness, self-reported experiences	Assessing instructional quality, identifying program strengths and weaknesses	Self-report biases, response rate issues, potential for oversimplification
Faculty Development Records	Workshop participation, mentoring activities, innovation projects	Tracking professional growth, assessing development program impact	Often fragmented across departments; variable quality and consistency
Financial Systems	Budget allocations, expenditure patterns, revenue streams	Analysing resource utilization, identifying financial vulnerabilities	Limited connection to educational outcomes; focus on monetary factors
External Benchmarks	Peer institution data, employment outcomes, industry trends	Contextualizing institutional performance, identifying competitive positions	Comparability issues; may not account for institutional uniqueness
Qualitative Feedback	Focus group data, open-ended survey responses, exit interviews	Understanding stakeholder experiences, identifying emerging concerns	Resource-intensive to collect and analyze; challenges in systematization

Complementing these data sources, the RAF employs a range of analytical methods, each offering distinct capabilities for understanding organizational resilience. Table 2 outlines key analytical approaches incorporated in the framework.

Table 2. Analytical Methods in the Resilience Analytics Framework

Analytical Approach	Description	Applications in Resilience Analytics
Descriptive Analytics	Summarization of historical data to identify patterns and trends	Establishing baselines, monitoring key performance indicators, tracking changes over time
Diagnostic Analytics	Examination of causal relationships to understand why certain patterns occur	Identifying root causes of performance issues, understanding factors influencing student success
Predictive Analytics	Use of historical data to forecast future outcomes and trends	Early warning systems for student risk, enrollment projections, resource planning
Prescriptive Analytics	Recommendation of actions based on analytical insights	Intervention selection, resource allocation optimization, strategic initiative prioritization
Network Analysis	Examination of relationships and connections between entities	Identifying collaboration patterns, understanding information flow, mapping influence networks
Sentiment Analysis	Analysis of textual data to determine emotional tone and attitude	Monitoring organizational climate, tracking student and faculty sentiment, identifying emerging concerns
Process Mining	Discovery and analysis of actual processes from event logs	Identifying bottlenecks in student journeys, optimizing administrative workflows, improving service delivery
Multivariate Statistical Analysis	Examination of relationships between multiple variables simultaneously	Understanding complex relationships between factors affecting resilience, identifying key predictors of success

Institutions can improve their resilience by combining data sources and analysis techniques. However, effective implementation requires factors such as data quality and integration, analytical expertise, stakeholder engagement, ethical considerations, and organizational culture. Data quality ensures accurate, comprehensive data that can be combined meaningfully for analysis (Siemens et al., 2013). Analytical expertise builds capacity for advanced analysis through recruitment, training, and collaboration with outside experts (Macfadyen & Dawson, 2012). Stakeholder engagement helps in framing questions of analysis, interpreting findings, and creating response designs (Hora et al., 2017). Ethical considerations address privacy concerns, gaining consent, recognizing potential biases, and mitigating unintended outcomes of data-centric practices (Slade & Prinsloo, 2013). Organizational culture fosters an evidence-based, inquiry-friendly, and open-to-learning culture (Macfadyen et al.,

2014). By considering these variables, institutions can maximize the capabilities of multiple sources of data and analytical techniques.

Resilience Domains and Key Performance Indicators

The Resilience Analytics Framework highlights four main organizational domains of resilience in higher education, each reflecting an essential sphere of institutional performance and flexibility. For each of these domains, the framework provides specific key performance indicators (KPIs) that can be quantified and tracked to evaluate resilience status and monitor changes in resilience over time. These domains and indicators are detailed in Table 3.

Table 3. Resilience Domains and Key Performance Indicators

Resilience Domain	Definition	Key Performance Indicators
Learning Resilience	Capacity to maintain and enhance educational effectiveness amid disruptions and changing conditions	- Course completion rates - Learning outcome achievement - Student satisfaction and engagement - Instructional continuity during disruptions - Adaptability of pedagogical approaches
Operational Resilience	Ability to maintain core functions, allocate resources effectively, and adapt processes to changing circumstances	- Resource utilization efficiency- Process completion timeliness-Service quality metrics- Business continuity effectiveness- Administrative adaptability measures
Financial Resilience	Capacity to maintain financial stability, manage risks, and allocate resources strategically in response to changing conditions	- Revenue diversification index- Reserve adequacy measures- Budget flexibility indicators- Financial sustainability ratios- Investment in innovation and adaptation
Cultural Resilience	Organizational values, practices, and relationships that support adaptation, innovation, and collective response to challenges	- Collaboration network density- Innovation adoption rates- Psychological safety measures- Professional development engagement- Leadership succession planning indicators

Organizational resilience is influenced by four key areas: baseline measures, threshold values, benchmarks, and trend analyses. Deficits in any area can hinder an institution's ability to adapt. The RAF emphasizes the need for monitoring and improving these areas through specific analytics and interventions (Lengnick-Hall & Beck, 2016). Institutions can use baseline measures to observe changes over time, threshold values to identify areas that require intervention, benchmarks to place performance in context, and trend analyses to identify patterns relevant to resilience planning (Macfadyen et al., 2014) (West et al., 2016) (Daniel, 2015) (Few, 2006). These measures should be embedded within institutional dashboards and reporting tools, with visualizations and contextual explanatory information available for stakeholders (Few, 2006). However, qualitative indicators alone cannot fully represent organizational resilience, so qualitative measurements like stakeholder interviews and focus groups should be used (Hora et al., 2017). Monitoring these domains and indicators using systematic data collection and analysis helps institutions build a comprehensive picture of their resilience status, detect vulnerabilities, and monitor the effects of interventions to improve adaptive capacity. This method supports strategic decision-making, enhancing institutional capacity to anticipate challenges and capitalize on opportunities in a dynamic higher education environment (Macfadyen & Dawson, 2012).

EMERGING TRENDS AND POST-PANDEMIC CHALLENGES IN HIGHER EDUCATION ANALYTICS

Hybrid Learning and Institutional Agility

The COVID-19 pandemic permanently shifted the educational paradigm toward hybrid and blended learning models. Institutions must now monitor not only physical classroom engagement but also virtual presence, asynchronous participation, and device-level data to assess learning efficacy. Learning analytics systems should evolve to accommodate multimodal inputs and offer real-time dashboards that support agility in curriculum delivery and instructional resource allocation.

Mental Health Monitoring and Wellbeing Analytics

Mental health concerns among students have surged post-pandemic, prompting institutions to explore the use of learning data for early identification of stress, disengagement, or burnout. Behavioral analytics from learning management systems—such as irregular logins, missed assignments, and low discussion participation—can act as soft indicators of psychological distress. These must be triangulated with wellbeing surveys and counselor inputs to develop responsible support mechanisms. Ethical frameworks must explicitly address the boundaries of predictive mental health analytics.

Micro-learning and Granular Analytics

With the increasing prevalence of short-format, just-in-time learning interventions, analytics tools must shift from evaluating course-level outcomes to capturing engagement and effectiveness at the micro-learning object level. This demands finer-grained data collection and visualizations that reflect learner progress in modular formats. Micro-learning analytics also support personalization strategies, allowing institutions to recommend specific content paths based on granular behavioral data.

Federated Learning and Data Privacy Advances

Institutions are increasingly exploring federated learning models, which enable decentralized data processing. These models enhance privacy by keeping raw data on local servers while sharing learned model parameters across institutions. Federated analytics preserves data sovereignty and reduces the risks of data leakage in sensitive environments. Its potential is particularly strong for cross-institutional resilience studies and benchmarking without compromising participant privacy. Having defined the RAF and its analytical ecosystem, the next step is to understand how institutions can implement these strategies in real-world contexts. This section outlines institutional readiness models, common challenges, and evidence-based practices that enable sustainable deployment of resilience analytics.

IMPLEMENTATION STRATEGIES

Institutional Readiness and Maturity Models

The Resilience Analytics Framework (RAF) requires institutional readiness and strategy planning that aligns with an organization's analytics maturity level (Bichsel, 2012; Siemens et al., 2013).. The Analytics Maturity Model, proposed by Siemens et al. (2013), identifies five stages of institutional development in analytics capabilities: Awareness, Experimentation, Established, Strategic, and Transformative. Bichsel (2012) identified principal dimensions of analytics maturity: data management capacity, analytical skill, leadership support, and cultural preparedness.

The RAF implementation methodology focuses on essential readiness factors such as technical infrastructure, human capacity, governance structures, cultural factors, and leadership support. Institutions can evaluate these factors using self-assessment tools, peer benchmarking, and expert advice to establish their current maturity level and relevant areas for development (EDUCAUSE, 2023).

After evaluation, institutions can create strategies for implementation consistent with their maturity level, such as Building Foundations for early maturity institutions, Integration and Growth for mature institutions, and Transformation and Innovation for advanced institutions. This phased approach acknowledges that successful implementation requires alignment between analytics aspirations and institutional ability, avoiding the problem of starting projects beyond existing capacities. This approach ensures that the RAF effectively impacts institutional transformation and resilience-building projects (Macfadyen et al., 2014).

Implementation Challenges and Success Factors

Throughout the case studies described, a number of common challenges and success factors for implementation have emerged, offering useful insights for institutions looking to undertake analytics initiatives in order to increase organizational resilience. Table 4 outlines these essential factors.

Table 4. Analytics Implementation Challenges and Success Factors

Challenge Category	Common Challenges	Success Factors
Technical Challenges	Data quality and integration issues; Legacy system limitations; Analytical tool selection and implementation; Interoperability between systems	Establishing data governance frameworks; Incremental approach to integration; Building on existing infrastructure where possible; Prioritizing high-value data sources
Organizational Challenges	Siloed organizational structures; Competing priorities and initiatives; Resource constraints; Resistance to data-informed approaches	Executive sponsorship and clear governance; Alignment with strategic priorities; Demonstration of early wins and value; Integration with existing processes
Cultural Challenges	Data skepticism; Fear of evaluation or punishment; Limited data literacy; "Gut feeling" decision traditions	Emphasis on improvement rather than evaluation; Professional development for data literacy; Stakeholder involvement in design; Respecting domain expertise
Ethical Challenges	Privacy concerns; Potential algorithmic bias; Reductionist approaches to complex issues; Data security and access control	Transparent policies and practices; Ethical frameworks for data use; Combined quantitative and qualitative approaches; Attention to equity implications
Implementation Challenges	Project scope management; Stakeholder engagement; Change management; Sustainability beyond initial implementation	Phased implementation approaches; Clear communication strategies; Building internal capacity; Embedding in institutional processes

Analytics implementation is a complex process that requires a multifaceted approach that considers technical, organizational, cultural, and ethical aspects (Trowler & Cooper, 2002). Successful implementation requires strategic alignment with institutional priorities and challenges, involving key stakeholders throughout the design and implementation process (Macfadyen et al., 2014) (Hora et al., 2017). Capacity building is crucial for sustainable analytics implementation, as it involves developing human capacity through professional development and support resources (Mandinach & Gummer, 2013). Establishing clear ethical guidelines regarding data collection, analysis, and use helps address privacy concerns and prevent misuse (Slade

& Prinsloo, 2013). Continuous improvement is essential for enhancing effectiveness and adaptability to changing needs (Clow, 2012). By following these principles, institutions can navigate common implementation challenges and develop analytics approaches that enhance organizational resilience and adaptive capacity (Macfadyen & Dawson, 2012). By addressing these principles, institutions can develop analytics approaches that enhance organizational resilience and adaptive capacity.

ENHANCING ORGANIZATIONAL RESILIENCE:

Change Management Theory and Analytics Implementation

To ensure sustainable implementation of analytics initiatives, institutions must integrate change management theory into their approach. Kotter's 8-Step Change Model and Lewin's Change Management Theory offer structured processes for transitioning to data-driven cultures. Change management helps address resistance, foster stakeholder buy-in, and guide institutions through the emotional and operational shifts involved in analytics adoption. Incorporating change models enables smoother alignment between analytics deployment and institutional readiness for transformation.

Stakeholder Resistance and Mitigation Strategies

One of the most significant barriers to analytics adoption is stakeholder resistance, often rooted in fear of surveillance, job displacement, or lack of trust in data interpretations. Institutions should deploy proactive mitigation strategies, such as co-creation of analytics tools with end-users, transparent communication about data purposes, and capacity-building workshops. Participatory design and stakeholder-centered implementation increase perceived value and reduce defensive responses.

Technical Infrastructure: Cloud and Blockchain Implications

Cloud computing has revolutionized scalability and cost-effectiveness in analytics infrastructure. However, cloud dependency also raises concerns about vendor lock-in, latency, and regulatory compliance. Institutions must consider hybrid cloud strategies and local data caching to ensure resilience. Meanwhile, blockchain is emerging as a secure, tamper-resistant technology for educational data verification and decentralized learning records. Its potential to support cross-institutional data interoperability while ensuring integrity is especially relevant for credential verification and transcript portability.

Cross-Cultural and International Perspectives

The global adoption of learning analytics reveals substantial variation in implementation success based on cultural norms, data governance frameworks, and regulatory environments. In collectivist cultures, data-sharing may face fewer ethical objections, whereas in privacy-sensitive regions, stringent compliance may inhibit analytics depth. Comparative research across North America, Europe, Asia, and the Global South can illuminate effective localization strategies. Institutions should consider cultural agility and international benchmarks when designing analytics systems.

Cost-Benefit Analysis of Analytics Investments

Analytics initiatives are resource-intensive and require robust cost-benefit frameworks to evaluate feasibility and impact. Institutions should employ Total Cost of Ownership (TCO) models that account for software, infrastructure, personnel training, and maintenance. Simultaneously, Return on Learning Analytics Investment (ROLAI) models can assess outcomes in terms of student success, retention gains, process efficiency, and strategic alignment. Scenario planning and sensitivity analysis strengthen decision-making under uncertainty and help justify continued investment.

UNDER-EMPHASIZED CHALLENGES IN ANALYTICS IMPLEMENTATION

Data Privacy and Evolving Ethical Imperatives

While privacy is acknowledged in most learning analytics frameworks, its treatment is often cursory. In the wake of evolving data protection laws such as GDPR, FERPA, and CCPA, institutions must elevate privacy governance to a strategic level. Beyond anonymization, there is a growing need for **data sovereignty protocols**, granular consent mechanisms, and dynamic access controls. Institutional policies should account for the lifecycle of learning data—from collection and processing to archival and deletion—with stakeholder visibility and recourse options.

Algorithmic Bias and Equity Risks

Bias in analytics systems—stemming from skewed training data or opaque algorithmic logic—can reproduce or even amplify existing inequities. This is particularly problematic in predictive models used for retention alerts, admissions, or performance forecasting. Institutions should adopt **bias auditing protocols**, perform

equity impact assessments, and include **counterfactual reasoning** techniques in model validation. Fairness-aware machine learning should be positioned as a design requirement, not a post-hoc adjustment.

Resource Intensity and Capacity Constraints

Learning analytics systems demand considerable investments in infrastructure, software, skilled personnel, and ongoing training. For smaller institutions or those in low-resource settings, these requirements can be a significant barrier. A more honest acknowledgment of these constraints—coupled with strategies like shared services models, consortium analytics, and open-source platforms—would help democratize adoption. The chapter now outlines a **tiered implementation model** (Basic–Intermediate–Advanced) to guide institutions in scaling their initiatives incrementally.

Learning from Implementation Failures

The literature often emphasizes successful analytics case studies, but failures and missteps offer equally critical lessons. Common pitfalls include over-promising outcomes, poor stakeholder alignment, lack of technical readiness, and insufficient cultural support. Institutions must embed **failure documentation processes**, post-mortem reviews, and "fail-fast" experimentation loops into their analytics governance. Sharing anonymized lessons from failed pilots—via conferences or community repositories—can normalize setbacks and build collective intelligence across the sector.

ETHICAL CONSIDERATIONS IN RESILIENCE ANALYTICS

The ethical implementation of learning and development analytics for organizational resilience necessitates careful attention to privacy, equity, autonomy, and unintended consequences (Slade & Prinsloo, 2013). Institutions must establish robust privacy frameworks to safeguard individual rights while leveraging data effectively. Equity-oriented practices—such as informed consent, data minimization, and transparency—are essential to avoid reinforcing existing disparities. Ensuring stakeholder autonomy involves maintaining human judgment, offering algorithmic transparency, and enabling opt-out options (West et al., 2016).

Moreover, analytics initiatives may lead to unintended effects, including measurement bias, gaming behaviors, misallocated resources, and psychological stress (Selwyn, 2019). To mitigate these risks, institutions should deploy continuous monitoring systems that evaluate both intended and emergent impacts (Prinsloo & Slade, 2017). A proactive and inclusive ethical stance ensures analytics-driven resilience initiatives are both effective and equitable.

Ethical Framework for Resilience Analytics

To address these multifaceted ethical considerations, institutions implementing resilience analytics should develop comprehensive ethical frameworks that guide the design, implementation, and evaluation of initiatives. Table 5 summarizes the key roles and responsibilities of various stakeholder groups involved in analytics adoption.

Table 5. Ethical Framework Components for Resilience Analytics

Framework Component	Key Elements	Implementation Strategies
Ethical Principles	Articulation of core values guiding analytics use; Balance between individual and institutional interests; Commitment to beneficence, non-maleficence, justice, and respect for persons	Developing institutional ethics statements for analytics; Aligning analytics policies with broader institutional values; Establishing ethics review processes for new initiatives
Governance Structures	Clear roles and responsibilities for data stewardship; Oversight mechanisms for analytics initiatives; Processes for addressing ethical concerns and conflicts	Creating cross-functional data governance committees; Establishing ethics advisory boards with diverse membership; Developing escalation pathways for ethical issues
Transparency Practices	Clear communication about data collection and use; Explanations of analytical methodologies; Disclosure of limitations and uncertainty	Publishing data dictionaries and use policies; Providing plain-language explanations of algorithms; Disclosing confidence levels and error rates
Equity Safeguards	Processes for identifying and addressing bias; Inclusive design approaches; Regular equity impact assessments	Conducting algorithmic audits for bias; Engaging diverse stakeholders in design; Disaggregating outcomes data by relevant demographic factors
Continuous Reflection	Regular review of ethical implications; Adaptation to emerging ethical considerations; Learning from experience and stakeholder feedback	Establishing periodic ethical reviews of analytics initiatives; Creating feedback channels for ethical concerns; Supporting research on ethical aspects of analytics

This framework should be developed collaboratively with diverse stakeholders, regularly reviewed and updated based on emerging issues and experiences, and integrated into broader institutional governance structures rather than treated as a separate domain (Prinsloo & Slade, 2017). By approaching ethics as a fundamental aspect of analytics design and implementation rather than an afterthought, institutions can develop resilience-enhancing initiatives that align with educational values and build rather than undermine trust among stakeholders (Pardo & Siemens, 2014).

FUTURE RESEARCH DIRECTIONS

The convergence of learning and development analytics with organizational resilience presents emerging opportunities for empirical and applied inquiry. Future research should focus on five strategic areas:

1. Enhancing Resilience Measurement through Advanced Analytics

Improving resilience measurement will benefit from complexity science (e.g., agent-based modeling), longitudinal tracking of leading indicators, integration of mixed methods, and causal inference models (Meadows, 2008; Pearl & Mackenzie, 2018; Tashakkori & Teddlie, 2010). These methodologies can better capture the dynamic and systemic nature of resilience in complex educational institutions (Lengnick-Hall & Beck, 2016).

2. Leveraging Emerging Technologies

Emerging technologies such as AI, natural language processing, multimodal analytics, and blockchain offer new frontiers for educational resilience analytics (Baker & Inventado, 2014; Dawson et al., 2017; Chen et al., 2018). Research should also explore edge computing and IoT for timely and localized data insights (Siemens, 2013), while critically examining their organizational and ethical implications (Selwyn, 2019).

3. Advancing Human-Centered Analytics Design

Future work should investigate how decision-makers engage with analytics outputs, promote stakeholder participation in system design, and foster data literacy (Few, 2006; Mandinach & Gummer, 2013; Jarrahi, 2018). Emphasis should be placed on human-computer collaboration to ensure analytics are actionable and contextually relevant (Hora et al., 2017).

4. Ecosystem and Cross-Institutional Collaboration

Research should expand beyond institutional silos to examine shared resilience frameworks, ecosystem-wide analytics, and collective response mechanisms across education systems and sectors (Siemens et al., 2013; Kezar, 2014; Daniel, 2015). Such collaborations can enhance systemic adaptability and knowledge exchange (Macfadyen & Dawson, 2012).

5. Sustainability and Long-term Impact

As analytics systems mature, research should assess their long-term effectiveness, adaptive evolution, and ROI, considering both technical sustainability and institutional integration (Ferguson et al., 2016; Carbonell et al., 2013; Bichsel, 2012). Understanding how these systems endure and scale is vital to realizing lasting impact (Macfadyen et al., 2014).

ETHICAL AND SOCIAL IMPLICATIONS

The adoption of learning and development (L&D) analytics in organizational settings necessitates careful ethical scrutiny. As data increasingly informs human capital decisions, concerns around privacy, fairness, autonomy, and culture become central to responsible implementation.

Privacy and Data Protection

L&D analytics often involve extensive data collection—including behavioral, psychometric, and performance indicators—raising significant privacy concerns (Romero & Ventura, 2020). Organizations must ensure transparent data governance, inform employees about data use, and comply with regulations like GDPR and CCPA. Balancing data utility with privacy protection requires safeguards such as data minimization and anonymization (Greller & Drachsler, 2012).

Bias and Fairness

Analytics systems can embed algorithmic bias—via flawed sampling, assessment, or interpretation—leading to inequitable outcomes in promotions or training access (Holstein et al., 2019). To mitigate this, diverse teams, regular audits, and fairness-aware modeling are essential (Mehrabi et al., 2021). Institutions must also address disparities in digital literacy to avoid unintentionally disadvantaging certain employee groups.

Autonomy and Agency

Over-reliance on automated learning paths may restrict employee autonomy. Systems should empower user choice while providing recommendations, and offer appeals processes for algorithm-influenced decisions (Williamson, 2019). Human oversight remains essential to preserve agency in professional growth.

Transparency and Explainability

Advanced analytics can create opaque "black box" decision-making processes. Organizations should adopt explainable AI models and clearly communicate how analytics drive developmental outcomes (Arrieta et al., 2020). Transparency fosters trust and accountability among users and administrators.

Cultural and Social Dynamics

Data-driven L&D may shift focus away from qualitative development practices like mentorship or informal learning. Cultural alignment or guided transformation is vital to integrate analytics without eroding interpersonal values (Cameron & Quinn, 2011). Power dynamics must also be addressed by democratizing access to insights and ensuring data augments—rather than overrides—human judgment.

Ethical Framework for L&D Analytics

To address these multifaceted ethical concerns, organizations require a comprehensive ethical framework for L&D analytics implementation. Drawing on the work of Slade and Prinsloo (2013), we propose a six-dimensional framework encompassing:

1. **Informed Consent and Transparency**: Organizations must ensure that employees understand what data is being collected, how it will be used, and provide meaningful opportunities for consent or opt-out where appropriate.
2. **Privacy Protection and Data Security**: Robust technical and organizational measures must be implemented to protect sensitive learning and development data from unauthorized access or misuse.
3. **Fairness and Non-discrimination**: Analytics systems should be regularly audited for bias and designed with fairness constraints to prevent discriminatory outcomes across different demographic groups.

4. **Human Oversight and Accountability**: While algorithms may inform decisions, ultimate accountability should reside with human stakeholders who can explain, justify, and if necessary, override algorithmic recommendations.
5. **Proportionality and Purpose Limitation**: Data collection and analysis should be proportional to legitimate organizational needs and limited to specified purposes communicated to employees.
6. **Benefit Sharing and Inclusive Design**: The benefits of L&D analytics should be equitably distributed across the organization, with particular attention to ensuring that technologically disadvantaged groups are not excluded.

This ethical framework provides a foundation for responsible implementation of L&D analytics that balances organizational objectives with employee rights and wellbeing. Organizations that proactively address these ethical dimensions will likely achieve more sustainable and effective analytics implementation while building trust with their workforce.

FOSTERING A DATA-DRIVEN LEARNING CULTURE

The successful implementation of learning and development analytics requires more than sophisticated technological infrastructure or methodological expertise—it necessitates the cultivation of a data-driven learning culture that permeates all levels of the organization. This cultural dimension represents a critical yet often overlooked aspect of analytics implementation that significantly influences adoption, utilization, and ultimate impact on organizational resilience.

Characteristics of a Data-Driven Learning Culture

A data-driven learning culture in the context of L&D analytics exhibits several distinctive characteristics that differentiate it from traditional organizational learning approaches. First, it demonstrates a commitment to evidence-based decision-making, wherein learning interventions and development strategies are informed by empirical data rather than intuition or tradition (Bersin, 2015). This commitment manifests in systematic data collection, rigorous analysis, and the integration of insights into the developmental decision-making process.

Second, a data-driven learning culture embraces continuous improvement through iterative feedback loops. Organizations with mature data cultures regularly evaluate the effectiveness of learning initiatives, identify areas for enhancement, and implement refined approaches based on empirical findings. This cyclical process of implementation, evaluation, and refinement enables organizations to progressively optimize their learning ecosystem to better support organizational resilience and strategic objectives (Macfadyen et al., 2014).

Third, data-driven learning cultures are characterized by democratized access to relevant insights. Rather than confining analytical capabilities to specialized units or senior leadership, these organizations make appropriate data and insights accessible to stakeholders at various organizational levels, empowering informed decision-making across the learning ecosystem (Guenole et al., 2018). This democratization is facilitated through intuitive dashboards, visualization tools, and targeted reports that translate complex data into actionable insights for diverse user groups.

Barriers to Cultural Transformation

Despite the compelling benefits of a data-driven learning culture, organizations frequently encounter significant barriers to cultural transformation that impede the effective implementation of L&D analytics. One primary obstacle involves entrenched resistance to change among stakeholders accustomed to traditional, intuition-based approaches to learning and development. This resistance often stems from skepticism regarding the value of data-driven methodologies, concerns about the quantification of inherently qualitative aspects of learning, or apprehension about the implications of analytics for existing roles and responsibilities (Bichsel, 2012).

Technical literacy limitations represent another substantial barrier to cultural transformation. Many L&D professionals and organizational leaders lack the data literacy required to effectively interpret and utilize analytical insights, creating a significant skill gap that hinders the integration of data-driven approaches into organizational practices (Rienties et al., 2017). This skill deficit can manifest as misinterpretation of analytical findings, reluctance to engage with data resources, or over-reliance on simplified metrics that fail to capture the complexity of learning processes.

Organizational silos further complicate the cultivation of data-driven learning cultures by impeding the free flow of information across functional boundaries. When learning data remains isolated within specific departments or systems, organizations cannot develop the comprehensive understanding necessary for effective analytics implementation (Macfadyen & Dawson, 2012). These silos not only fragment the data landscape but also reinforce compartmentalized approaches to learning and development that undermine collaborative, data-informed strategies.

Strategies for Cultural Transformation

Organizations must adopt strategies for cultural transformation to foster a data-driven learning culture. Leadership commitment is crucial, involving resource allocation, policy development, and personal engagement with analytical initiatives. Capacity building initiatives are essential, addressing technical literacy limitations and equipping stakeholders with the necessary skills (Guenole et al., 2018). Cross-functional collaboration mechanisms, such as learning analytics committees and collaborative governance structures, help dismantle organizational silos and integrate diverse perspectives. Narrative development helps stakeholders understand the practical value of data-driven approaches, translating abstract concepts into concrete examples. Incentive alignment ensures that organizational reward systems and performance evaluation mechanisms reinforce data-driven behaviours and decision-making processes. Recognition and rewards for data utilization can encourage adoption and sustainability of these approaches.

Cultural Maturity Model for L&D Analytics

To assess and guide cultural transformation efforts, organizations can utilize a cultural maturity model that delineates progressive stages of development in data-driven learning cultures. Building on the work of Cosic et al. (2012), we propose a five-stage maturity model encompassing:

1. **Initial Stage**: Organization exhibits ad hoc, isolated uses of data in learning and development, with limited awareness of analytics potential and significant resistance to data-driven approaches.
2. **Developing Stage**: Organization begins systematic data collection and basic analysis, with pockets of engagement among early adopters but continued skepticism among many stakeholders.
3. **Defined Stage**: Organization implements standardized analytical methodologies and governance structures, with growing acceptance of data-driven approaches and emerging evidence of improved outcomes.
4. **Managed Stage**: Organization integrates analytics throughout the learning ecosystem, with widespread data literacy, collaborative analytical practices, and demonstrated impact on organizational performance.
5. **Optimizing Stage**: Organization exhibits a pervasive data culture where analytics is seamlessly embedded in learning and development processes, continuous innovation in analytical approaches, and clear linkage between L&D analytics and organizational resilience.

This maturity model provides organizations with a roadmap for cultural transformation, enabling them to assess their current state, identify specific development needs, and implement targeted strategies for advancing along the maturity continuum. By systematically addressing cultural dimensions of analytics implementation, organizations can create an environment conducive to effective utilization of L&D analytics for enhanced organizational resilience.

INTEGRATING L&D ANALYTICS INTO ORGANIZATIONAL SYSTEMS

The efficacy of learning and development analytics in fostering organizational resilience is substantially influenced by the degree to which analytical capabilities are integrated into broader organizational systems. This integration enables a holistic approach to data-driven decision-making that transcends functional boundaries and aligns learning initiatives with strategic objectives across the organization.

Systems Integration Approach

Effective integration of L&D analytics necessitates a comprehensive systems approach that acknowledges the interconnected nature of organizational processes and technologies. Rather than implementing analytics as an isolated capability within the learning function, organizations should conceptualize it as a component of an integrated ecosystem that spans multiple domains including human resources, operations, finance, and strategic planning (Bersin, 2015). This systemic perspective facilitates the bidirectional flow of data and insights between L&D and other organizational functions, enabling more comprehensive analysis and more impactful interventions.

The systems integration approach encompasses several key dimensions. Technical integration involves establishing interoperability between learning management systems, talent management platforms, human resource information systems, and business intelligence tools to create a unified data architecture that supports comprehensive analytics (Gašević et al., 2015). Process integration focuses on aligning analytical workflows with existing business processes to ensure seamless incorporation of data-driven insights into decision-making routines across the organization. Governance integration establishes consistent policies, standards, and procedures for data management, quality assurance, and ethical utilization across functional boundaries (Gagné, 2018).

Integration with Human Resource Management Systems

The integration of L&D analytics with human resource management systems (HRMS) creates particularly valuable synergies for organizational resilience development. This integration enables organizations to correlate learning activities with broader talent management processes including recruitment, performance management, succession planning, and compensation (Isson & Harriott, 2016). By linking these previously siloed data domains, organizations can develop more sophisticated understanding of how learning interventions influence talent outcomes and ultimately contribute to organizational resilience.

Several specific integration points between L&D analytics and HRMS warrant examination. The connection with recruitment analytics allows organizations to identify effective learning pathways for different entry profiles, optimize onboarding programs based on pre-hire characteristics, and align recruitment strategies with identified skill gaps (Guenole et al., 2018). Integration with performance management systems enables the correlation of learning activities with performance outcomes, assessment of learning transfer effectiveness, and personalization of development plans based on performance data (Van den Broeck et al., 2018). Succession planning integration facilitates the identification of critical skill development needs for key positions, evaluation of readiness trajectories based on learning progress, and implementation of targeted interventions to accelerate leadership development (Dai et al., 2013).

Integration with Business Intelligence and Strategic Planning

The alignment of L&D analytics with business intelligence and strategic planning functions represents another critical dimension of systems integration. This connection enables organizations to directly link learning investments with business outcomes, assess the contribution of capability development to strategic objectives, and calibrate learning initiatives to address emerging organizational challenges (Minbaeva, 2018). By integrating these domains, organizations can elevate L&D analytics from an operational tool focused on learning efficiency to a strategic resource that informs resilience-building initiatives.

The integration with business intelligence functions typically involves correlating learning metrics with key performance indicators from operations, finance, customer service, and other business domains (Fitz-enz & Mattox, 2014). This correlation enables organizations to quantify the business impact of learning interventions, identify capability gaps that undermine performance, and prioritize development investments based on potential return. Integration with strategic planning processes ensures that learning analytics insights inform scenario planning, capability forecasting, and strategic workforce development initiatives that enhance organizational preparedness for future disruptions (Minbaeva, 2018).

Technical Infrastructure for Systems Integration

Comprehensive systems integration requires a robust technical infrastructure that facilitates data exchange, analytical processing, and insight delivery across organizational boundaries. This includes a unified Enterprise Data Architecture, Integration Middleware, Analytics Platform, Visualization and Reporting Layer, and Security Framework. The Enterprise Data Architecture standardizes data structures, establishes consistent taxonomies, and implements data governance mechanisms. Integration Middleware facilitates seamless data exchange between systems, supports various analytical methodologies, and provides user-friendly interfaces for comprehension and action. The Security Framework ensures compliance with regulatory requirements and organizational policies.

Implementation Challenges and Mitigation Strategies

The implementation of integrated L&D analytics systems presents numerous challenges that organizations must proactively address to ensure successful outcomes. Data quality and consistency issues frequently arise when integrating information from disparate systems with varying standards, collection methodologies, and update frequencies (Siemens et al., 2013). These challenges can be mitigated through the implementation of master data management practices, data quality assessment protocols, and remediation workflows that systematically address inconsistencies across integrated data sources.

Technical compatibility constraints emerge when attempting to connect systems built on different technological foundations, particularly when legacy systems with limited interoperability capabilities must be incorporated into the integrated ecosystem (Nunn et al., 2016). Organizations can address these constraints through the implementation of middleware solutions, development of custom integration interfaces, or adoption of standards-based approaches that facilitate communication between heterogeneous systems.

Cross-functional governance complexities represent another significant challenge, as the integration of systems across organizational boundaries necessitates collaborative decision-making processes that balance the interests and requirements of multiple stakeholders (Gagné, 2018). These complexities can be managed through the establishment of cross-functional governance committees, development of clear decision rights frameworks, and implementation of escalation procedures for resolving conflicts or competing priorities.

Change management challenges inevitably accompany systems integration initiatives, as stakeholders must adapt to new processes, technologies, and decision-making approaches that span traditional functional boundaries (Hornstein, 2015).

Organizations can mitigate these challenges through comprehensive stakeholder analysis, targeted communication strategies, phased implementation approaches, and dedicated support resources that assist users in navigating the transition to integrated analytics systems.

MEASURING THE IMPACT OF L&D ANALYTICS ON ORGANIZATIONAL RESILIENCE

The implementation of learning and development analytics represents a significant investment for organizations, necessitating rigorous evaluation of its impact on organizational resilience and strategic outcomes. While traditional learning evaluation models assess training effectiveness at individual or program levels, measuring the contribution of L&D analytics to organizational resilience requires more sophisticated approaches that capture systemic effects across multiple dimensions and timeframes.

Conceptual Framework for Impact Measurement

A comprehensive framework for measuring the impact of L&D analytics on organizational resilience must encompass multiple levels of analysis, diverse outcome domains, and various temporal horizons. Building on the work of Phillips and Phillips (2016) and extending it to the specific context of L&D analytics and resilience, we propose a multi-dimensional framework organized around four primary evaluation dimensions:

1. **Analytical Capability Maturity**: Assessing the organization's progression in developing and deploying analytical capabilities within the learning and development function. This dimension examines technical infrastructure, methodological sophistication, data governance practices, and analytical competencies that collectively determine the organization's capacity to generate actionable insights from learning data.
2. **Learning System Effectiveness**: Evaluating improvements in the efficiency, effectiveness, and responsiveness of learning and development systems resulting from analytics implementation. This dimension focuses on operational enhancements within the learning function, including optimization of resource allocation, personalization of learning experiences, acceleration of capability development processes, and alignment of learning initiatives with organizational priorities.

3. **Workforce Capability Enhancement**: Measuring changes in individual and collective capabilities that contribute to organizational resilience, including technical skills, adaptive competencies, collaboration patterns, and knowledge distribution. This dimension examines how analytics-improves workforce environment.

CONCLUSION AND SYNTHESIS

The convergence of learning and development analytics with organizational resilience represents a paradigm shift in higher education. By leveraging multi-level data systems, predictive intelligence, and inclusive governance, institutions can not only survive disruption but proactively adapt and thrive. The Resilience Analytics Framework offers a roadmap for this transformation—aligning technical innovation with strategic foresight and ethical accountability.

To move from aspiration to action, institutions must invest in foundational infrastructure, foster a culture of data-driven inquiry, and adopt flexible implementation models that match their readiness levels. Integrating lessons from both success and failure, this chapter underscores that resilience is not a static trait but an evolving institutional capacity—cultivated through continuous learning, stakeholder engagement, and technology-enabled insight.

As higher education grapples with the post-pandemic reality, talent shortages, and global competition, analytics will increasingly shape decisions about pedagogy, policy, and performance. Ensuring that this transformation is responsible, equitable, and sustainable remains a shared challenge—and opportunity—for educational leaders, researchers, and practitioners worldwide.

REFERENCES

Arrieta, A. B., Díaz-Rodríguez, N., Ser, J. D., Bennetot, A., Tabik, S., Barbado, A., & Herrera, F. (2020). Explainable artificial intelligence (XAI): Concepts, taxonomies, opportunities, and challenges toward responsible AI. *Information Fusion, 58*, 82–115. DOI: 10.1016/j.inffus.2019.12.012

Baker, R. S., & Inventado, P. S. (2014). Educational data mining and learning analytics. In Larusson, J. A., & White, B. (Eds.), *Learning analytics: From research to practice* (pp. 61–75). Springer., DOI: 10.1007/978-1-4614-3305-7_3

Bichsel, J. (2012). *Analytics in higher education: Benefits, barriers, progress, and recommendations.* EDUCAUSE Center for Applied Research. https://www.educause.edu/ecar/research-publications/analytics-higher-education-benefits-barriers-progress-and-recommendations

Blikstein, P., & Worsley, M. (2016). Multimodal learning analytics and education data mining: Using computational technologies to measure complex learning tasks. *Journal of Learning Analytics, 3*(2), 220–238. DOI: 10.18608/jla.2016.32.11

Calvet Liñán, L., & Juan Pérez, A. (2015). Educational data mining and learning analytics: Differences, similarities, and their relationship to open education. *International Journal of Educational Technology in Higher Education, 12*(3), 98–112. DOI: 10.7238/rusc.v12i3.2515

Cameron, K. S., & Quinn, R. E. (2011). *Diagnosing and changing organizational culture: Based on the competing values framework* (3rd ed.). John Wiley & Sons.

Carbonell, K. B., Dailey-Hebert, A., & Gijselaers, W. H. (2013). Unleashing the creative potential of faculty to create hybrid courses: A framework for business analytics in higher education. *Research in Learning Technology, 21*(1), 1–17. DOI: 10.3402/rlt.v21.21399

Chen, G., Xu, B., Lu, M., & Chen, N. S. (2018). Exploring blockchain technology and its potential applications for education. *Smart Learning Environments, 5*(1), 1–10. DOI: 10.1186/s40561-018-0070-8

Christensen, C. M., & Eyring, H. J. (2011). *The innovative university: Changing the DNA of higher education from the inside out*. John Wiley & Sons.

Clow, D. (2012). The learning analytics cycle: Closing the loop effectively. *Proceedings of the 2nd International Conference on Learning Analytics & Knowledge (LAK'12)*, 134-138. https://doi.org/DOI: 10.1145/2330601.2330636

Clow, D. (2013). An overview of learning analytics. *Teaching in Higher Education, 18*(6), 683–695. DOI: 10.1080/13562517.2013.827653

Daniel, B. (2015). Big data and analytics in higher education: Opportunities and challenges. *British Journal of Educational Technology, 46*(5), 904–920. DOI: 10.1111/bjet.12230

Davidson, C. N. (2017). *The new education: How to revolutionize the university to prepare students for a world in flux*. Basic Books.

Dawson, S., Mirriahi, N., & Gašević, D. (2017). Improving student outcomes and analytics: A framework for university-wide implementation. *Proceedings of the Seventh International Learning Analytics & Knowledge Conference (LAK'17)*, 153-162.

Dietz-Uhler, B., & Hurn, J. E. (2013). Using learning analytics to predict (and improve) student success: A faculty perspective. *Journal of Interactive Online Learning, 12*(1), 17–26.

EDUCAUSE. (2023). Analytics maturity in higher education: Progress, gaps, and recommendations. https://library.educause.edu/resources/2023/2/analytics-maturity-2023

Ferguson, R., Brasher, A., Clow, D., Cooper, A., Hillaire, G., & Rienties, B. (2016). Learning analytics: Visions of the future. *Proceedings of the Sixth International Learning Analytics & Knowledge Conference (LAK'16)*, 520-525.

Few, S. (2006). *Information dashboard design: The effective visual communication of data*. O'Reilly Media.

Gašević, D., Dawson, S., & Siemens, G. (2015). Let's not forget: Learning analytics are about learning. *TechTrends, 59*(1), 64–71. DOI: 10.1007/s11528-014-0822-x

Greller, W., & Drachsler, H. (2012). Translating learning into numbers: A generic framework for learning analytics. *Journal of Educational Technology & Society, 15*(3), 42–57.

Heifetz, R., Grashow, A., & Linsky, M. (2009). *The practice of adaptive leadership: Tools and tactics for changing your organization and the world*. Harvard Business Press.

Holling, C. S. (1973). Resilience and stability of ecological systems. *Annual Review of Ecology and Systematics, 4*, 1–23.

Ifenthaler, D., & Yau, J. Y. K. (2022). Utilising learning analytics to support student engagement in higher education during COVID-19. *Educational Technology Research and Development, 70*, 393–406. DOI: 10.1007/s11423-021-10006-9

Kezar, A. (2014). *How colleges change: Understanding, leading, and enacting change*. Routledge.

Macfadyen, L. P., & Dawson, S. (2012). Numbers are not enough: Why e-learning analytics failed to inform an institutional strategic plan. *Journal of Educational Technology & Society*, *15*(3), 149–163.

Meadows, D. H. (2008). *Thinking in systems: A primer*. Chelsea Green Publishing.

Pardo, A., & Siemens, G. (2014). Ethical and privacy principles for learning analytics. *British Journal of Educational Technology*, *45*(3), 438–450. DOI: 10.1111/bjet.12152

Selwyn, N. (2019). Should robots replace teachers? AI and the future of education. *Learning, Media and Technology*, *44*(1), 1–17. DOI: 10.1080/17439884.2019.1590622

Siemens, G. (2013). Learning analytics: The emergence of a discipline. *The American Behavioral Scientist*, *57*(10), 1380–1400.

Slade, S., & Prinsloo, P. (2013). Learning analytics: Ethical issues and dilemmas. *The American Behavioral Scientist*, *57*(10), 1510–1529.

Weick, K. E., & Sutcliffe, K. M. (2015). *Managing the unexpected: Resilient performance in an age of uncertainty*. John Wiley & Sons.

Chapter 10
Artificial Intelligence (AI) and Critical Thinking Endorsement:
Investigating Higher Education Institutional Tools and Strategies

Hany Zaky
https://orcid.org/0000-0003-0342-8814
Eastern International College, USA

ABSTRACT

In the aftermath of COVID-19, colleges and universities have faced many challenges that negatively impacted students' Critical Thinking (CR). Integrating Artificial Intelligence (AI) into learning and teaching processes positively affects learners' self-efficacy, motivation, and regulated learning abilities. Artificial Intelligence (AI) has increasingly become a transformative educational power, offering unprecedented opportunities to enhance learning experiences and outcomes. This literature review examines the effects of AI-assisted learning applications on Critical Thinking skills in higher education. It provides valuable presentations of AI tools, Critical Thinking elements, and research-based strategies to integrate AI technologies properly into higher education classrooms. The review also addresses the negative impact of excessive use of AI on developing learners' independent problem-solving abilities. Therefore, balanced integration is crucial to ensure the use of AI as a complement in the teaching process. The report, therefore, suggests a more robust framework promoting CR skills in synthesizing AI-generated information. The implications of the findings were discussed, and pedagogical strategies were recommended to

DOI: 10.4018/979-8-3373-7057-6.ch010

prepare students for the challenges of AI-driven knowledge. Additionally, educators' guided grids were shared to stimulate self-reflection, increase awareness of learning progress, and make performance levels visible.

INTRODUCTION

Technology has hit its boiling point, yet students are yearning for more—empathy, understanding, and connections that make them feel seen, heard, and understood. For competitiveness in the midst of rapid changes in societies, students require core academic knowledge and an understanding of twenty-first-century skills such as critical thinking, problem-solving, creativity, innovation, communication, and collaboration. Critical thinking is at the heart of the educational curriculum and is understood to mean reasonable reflective thinking focused on deciding what to believe or do. Norris and Ennis classified CR into six elements: 1) determining the credibility of sources and observations, 2) inferring and judging deductive conclusions, 3) definitions and identification of assumptions, 4) planning induction experiments and predicting probable consequences, 5) inferring and judging inductive conclusions and 6) semantics (Wannapiroon, 2008). Developing CR skills in higher education classes is an indicator of the program's effectiveness and success toward quality education.

Researchers investigate a variety of pedagogical teaching tools to deepen CR teaching. Research has revealed that students' critical thinking abilities are significantly higher when taught through inquiry-based learning than traditional teaching methods (Wongkam et al., 2014). Additionally, the institutional instructional model shapes the effectiveness of CR in teaching and learning. For example, the model provides educators with the tools to foster the whole student body. It includes five stages: First, engagement: Teachers assess their students' prior knowledge and engage them in new conceptual discussions to promote curiosity and elicit new knowledge. Second, Exploration: The teachers provide students with several cooperative exploration activities designed to help them use their prior knowledge in different contexts to generate new related ideas, explore new questions, and conduct new investigations. Third, Explanation: During this stage, students focus on new explorations and opportunities to demonstrate conceptual understanding and processing skills with the teachers' guidance and scaffolding. Fourth, elaboration: Teachers challenge their students with a new conceptual understanding of Thoreau's new related experiences, such as using case studies reflecting the context of the content in practicality. Fifth, evaluation, teachers encourage their students to ass their understanding and abilities and provide opportunities for assessing the progress of their students' achievement toward educational objectives (Bybee et al., 2014).

Technology. In this context provides educators with the opportunity to assure the smooth transition among the CR training journey.

Artificial Intelligence (AI) has emerged as a transformative force across various sectors, and its impact on higher education (HE) is widely noticed in academic literature (Crompton & Burke, 2023; Yusuf et al., 2024). Integrating AI into HE offers many innovative solutions to enhance teaching and learning (Bhutoria, 2022). AI in higher education presents a paradigm shift to revolutionize the traditional pedagogical approaches and open many new possibilities for students and educators to deepen their knowledge and skills by content generation, improving thinking competencies, and fostering academic writing skills (Tlili et al., 2023; Yusuf et al., 2024; Yilmaz & Yilmaz, 2023; Parycek et al., 2023). The integration of AI in higher education, though, captured the attention of many researchers and educators due to its potential to transform traditional pedagogical practices and promote critical skills such as collaboration and critical thinking

Educators use Artificial intelligence (AI) to ease the implementation of CR training. Generative AI is a subarea of information automation that involves the development of the intelligence of humans and platforms to analyze, raise, and act intelligently (Valentin, 2021). Artificial intelligence is the power of a computer to execute cognitive work that typically connects with human minds. It is the theory and the creation of programs that can carry tasks that usually call for intelligence from humans (Soeffiner, 2023; Rahman, 2021). Rust (2018) stated that AI can make decisions by itself; therefore, it might replace human intelligence, offer knowledge, and boost productivity. Therefore, the AI-related research trends were expanded to personalized learning, precision education, and assessment (Hui Luan, 2020).

The use of AI applications in higher education has become a hotly debated topic among educators due to the variety of learning and teaching opportunities these applications offer. For example, ChatGPT capacities increase students' involvement in their learning. Students can ask questions and get a prompt answer. This quick feedback encourages active learning and fosters students' involvement (Cotton et al., 2023; Rawas, 2023). ChatGPT provides students with individualized learning support by examining those students' questions and learning trends. This individualized learning support accommodates learners' preferences and fosters a more welcoming learning atmosphere (Adiguzel et al., 2023; Fuchs, 2023). Nevertheless, educators need to investigate the reliability of the generative -AI tools constantly.

The flow of ideas and the credibility of the accumulated data using AI- tools negatively impact students' learning and stiffen their academic growth. ChatGPT, for example, may unintentionally produce and disseminate false information due to the hallucination experience, which could lead students astray in learning environments. If ChatGPT's users are unaware of this false information, they will reach incorrect conclusions in their research (De Angelis et al., 2023). Research reveals that the heavy use of ChatGPT negatively impacts students' critical thinking abilities. To this end, Genuine learning and intellectual growth can be hampered by relying on AI for solutions to comprehend embodied concepts (Fuchs, 2023; Iskender, 2023). To this end, training students to properly use AI tools is of paramount importance. At this point, researchers might ask, "What do thinking skills refer to? The components of thinking skills are the focus of many taxonomies, such as Bloom's Cognitive taxonomy. Bloom addressed three core thinking stages: synthesis, analysis, and evaluation (Swartz & McGuinness, 2004). These skills are searching for meaning (analytical thinking), creative thinking, critical thinking, problem-solving, and metacognition. Reflective thinking is also a component of higher-order thinking skills (Costa, 1985; Schön, 1992; Swartz & Parks, 2004). Therefore, considering the proper taxonomy and the available AI tools, educators secure a lot of teaching opportunities to build their student's CR skills.

The AI text generators play an influential role in the endorsement of critical thinking skills. Critical Thinking (CR) is reflective thinking aimed at decision-making and conceptualization, application, analysis, synthesis, and information evaluation based on observation, experience, reflection, reasoning, and communication (Ennis, 1989; Bukoye & Oyelere, 2019; Calma & Davies, 2021). Bloom's taxonomy is a relevant framework for addressing how AI text generators enhance critical thinking by evaluating educational learning objectives (Schoepp, 2019; Calma & Davies, 2021). Bloom classified the cognitive skills into distinctive levels: Remembering, understanding, applying, analyzing, evaluating, and creating, reflecting the progressive complexity of critical thinking (Bloom et al., 1956; Krathwohl, 2002). Gen-AI can play a role in education by creating scenarios for students to analyze and evaluate, aligning with Bloom's taxonomy (JISC 2023). Moreover, interacting with AI text generators can encourage students to generate innovative solutions, stimulating the highest cognitive skill level in Bllom taxonomy (Rudolph et al., 2023).

The HE experiences a high volume of using AI-generated texts in scholarly research and academic assignments. Therefore, Institutions were engaged in a debate regarding cheating and plagiarism issues. Scholars argue that integrating Gen-AI into educational teaching and research might increase productivity, augment learning outcomes, and foster creativity. Critics raise many concerns about the negative effect of such integration on students' critical thinking skills and the overall integrity of academic work due to the authenticity, credibility, and validity of AI-generated texts (Yusuf et al., 2024; Al Naqbi et al., 2024; Habib et al., 2024; Chan & Hu, 2023; Ipek et al., 2023). To this point, ethical considerations such as attributions, ownership, and potential misuse should be considered to ensure the responsible use of AI technologies.

Ethical concerns applications require the application of Critical thinking skills to evaluate and synthesize AI-generated texts. Critical Thinking encompasses a range of cognitive abilities, including analysis, interpretation, inference, evaluation, explanation, and self-regulation (Dwyer et al., 2014; Fahim & Eslamdoost, 2014; Shanto et al., 2024). Critical Thinking embodies the skillful examination and evaluation of information, emphasizing the importance of skepticism, objectivity, and analytical reasoning. Thinking, therefore, encompasses the cognitive processes involved in mental activity, such as perception, reasoning, and problem-solving (Murawski, 2014; Ruggiero, 2012). Informed judgments and sound decisions are the outcomes of systematic information analysis, considering the multiple perspectives and the application of logical reasoning to make informed judgments and sound decisions. Critical Thinking skills enable individuals to critically assess the quality, credibility, and reliability of information (Shanto et al., 2024; Bates et al., 2020; Çela et al., 2024). Therefore, a well-researched framework ensures the quality instruction.

The paucity of frameworks guiding students to evaluate and build upon AI-generated information critically causes inconsistency in the in-class teaching processes. One of the published frameworks is "AI-CRITIQUE," This framework includes areas for improvements regarding the process and the time duration (Shanto et al., 2024). Training students in critical thinking, though, is deemed an essential stage in the process of properly using the information generated by AI technologies. To this point, the integration of AI into educational settings has revolutionized numerous aspects of teaching and learning. AI has introduced novel methods for enhancing personalized learning, improving assessments, and reducing administrative burdens for educators. AI is an effective teaching tool in analyzing student data, enabling the customization of learning experiences to individual requirements (Ayala-Pazmiño, 2023). However, educators and students should consider the unintentional risks and inaccurate information.

Educators highlight the potential risks of using AI in their classes. Data security and privacy are the two prominent concerns about using AI in educational settings. Educators deem the lack of appropriate context and accuracy of the generated content by AI tools (Cardona et al., 2023). Therefore, AI tools are considered critical instruments for redefining classroom dynamics and enhancing students' engagement in teaching-learning processes. Educators and administrators raise their concerns regarding the excessive use of AI technologies to undermine students' problem-solving skills and reduce their capacities to independently address complex issues (Pavlenko & Syzenko, 2024). This integrative literature review investigates the impact of AI technological tools on students' critical thinking skills. Through this comprehensive analysis, the benefits and drawbacks of the tools are presented with a focus on the implications and pedagogical practices of some of these commonly used tools.

This review addresses the following questions:

R Q1: How can Artificial Intelligence technological tools transform the higher education landscape?

R Q 2: To what extent do Gen-AI applications provide learning opportunities to develop Critical Thinking skills in higher education?

METHODOLOGY

An integrative literature review was conducted, which focused on describing the topic from theoretical and conceptual viewpoints to answer the research questions. The data collection passed three stages: First, an initial search for appropriate sources was conducted using Google Scholar and electronic databases from several academic fields, such as education and psychology, to identify articles related to critical thinking and artificial intelligence (AI). A variety of research terms were used, including different variations and combinations of the following terms: Critical Thinking Skills, Teaching Critical Thinking, Innovative way to teach Critical Thinking, Artificial intelligence (AI) in teaching, Higher Education Classroom and AI, Gen-AI, and teaching and learning and using AI effectively in classrooms. Second, the abstracts were read to screen the initial list of articles for the five main topics (Critical Thinking and Teaching, Assessing and Teaching Critical Thinking, Critical Thinking Taxonomy, Critical Thinking and Technology, Artificial Intelligence (AI), and Critical Thinking in Higher Education). These five research areas were used to form the report's conceptual framework. Third, the conceptual framework was designed to summarize the key findings from the report and answer the research questions. This integrative literature review focused on the peer-reviewed theoretical and empirical studies on teaching Critical Thinking and utilizing AI applications in higher education classrooms.

Gen-AI and Digital Transformation of Higher Education Landscape (Q1)

Artificial intelligence (AI) has emerged as a disruptive force reshaping societies worldwide in recent years. It supports organizations in various ways, identifying more effective economic strategies to improve decision-making. The noticeable digital transformation in higher education has been driven by technological advancement (De Nito et al., 2023; Peres et al., 2023). The integration of AI in reshaping traditional teaching methods represents a major shift in educational practices, merging technology, teaching, and learning (O'Dea & O'Dea, 2023). These various evolutions in technology brought novel challenges and related opportunities for developing critical thinking skills. With Gen-AI, educators could create various learning content guided by the differentiation principles in the learning environments, such as audio, text, images, and videos (Davenport & Mittal, 2022; McKinsey, 2023). The text generator ChatGpt demonstrated the potential of Gen-AI to transform education and provide educators with the tools to discover new realms in educational settings (Cano et al., 2014; Rudolph et al., 2023). The new Chatbots and other AI tools offer a variety of skills and developmental instruments for more innovative learning experiences (Hwang & Chang, 2023). To this point, AI provides diverse perspectives to foster creativity and rigorous analysis among students, deepening their overall critical thinking skills (Bearman at. al., 2023; Hooda, et., al., 202).

AI and Learning Transformation

The growing integration of Generative AI in education brought many opportunities to personalize the learning experiences (Moscardini et al., 2022). By bringing educational digitalization to the learning and teaching environment, educators gained many opportunities to differentiate their instructions and address the needs of all their students (Lodge et al., 2023; Olga et al., 2023). Research reveals a strong connection between students' perceived value of Gen-AI and their intention to use it. This relation highlights a widespread acceptance and readiness for a transformative role in education and underscores the promising capacities of these technological applications to improve educational processes, outcomes, and experiences.

The adoption of AI text generators such as ChatGPT in the educational landscape can bring significant time efficiency. ChaptGPT can foster critical thinking skills by allowing learners to access information from various analytical angles (Lacka et al., 2021; Lim et al., 2023; Kremantzis, 2023). This incentivizes institutions to integrate AI-driven tools into their learning systems to facilitate student learning engagement. However, the integration process should not aim to adopt new technological applications but to prepare students for a future where AI will likely be a ubiquitous part of those students' daily lives. Therefore, a policy framework that ensures equitable access to these technologies for all students regardless of their socio-economic background should be created.

The growing integration of Generative AI in education brought many opportunities to personalize the learning experiences (Moscardini et al., 2022). By bringing educational digitalization to the learning and teaching environment, educators gained many opportunities to differentiate their instructions and address the needs of all their students (Lodge et al., 2023; Olga et al., 2023). Research reveals a strong connection between students' perceived value of Gen-AI and their intention to use it. This relation highlights a widespread acceptance and readiness for a transformative role in education and underscores the promising capacities of these technological applications to improve educational processes, outcomes, and experiences.

For example, adopting AI text generators such as ChatGPT in the educational landscape can bring significant time efficiency. ChaptGPT can foster critical thinking skills by allowing learners to access information from various analytical angles (Lacka et al., 2021; Lim et al., 2023; Kremantzis, 2023). This incentivizes institutions to integrate AI-driven tools into their learning systems to facilitate student learning engagement. However, the integration process should not aim to adopt new technological applications but to prepare students for a future where AI will likely be a ubiquitous part of those students' daily lives. Therefore, creating a policy framework ensures equitable access to these technologies for all students regardless of their background.

AI has two major dimensions: Human-like thinking and rational action. AI is a machine that imitates human cognitive functions such as learning and problem-solving, as well as managing the complexity and the experience that might drive the situation. Stephen Hawking once warned that AI might end humanity due to the very fundamental operations these technologies might complete (Cellan-Jones, 2014). Researchers categorize AI into three levels: Artificial narrow intelligence, artificial general intelligence, and artificial super intelligence (Siau & Yang, 2017; Zhang & Xie, 2018). Narrow AI is labeled weak AI, which refers to the computer system that focuses on narrow tasks such as self-driving cars. Gen-AI is labeled a strong AI as it imitates human-like intelligence to perform more complicated and complex cognitive tasks. Super AI is a system smarter than the best human brains in science-related fields (Russell & Norvig, 2009).

Human intelligence is a form of developing expertise from the novice to the more experienced (Sternberg, 1999). Therefore, learners should experience multiple learning (Implicit and Explicit) and thinking (Critical and Creative) processes. The 21st-century skills provide a way to shape any educational system's goals for more balanced competencies learners should obtain. Communication, Collaboration, Critical Thinking, and Creativity (4Cs) are the fundamental skills for creating knowledge-seekers and equipping learners with the practical tools to develop themselves and their communities. The 4 Cs are interrelated with logic and epistemology in the form of the 3 Rs: Re-examining, reasoning, and reflecting. Re-examining is related to the observation processes as an inception for inquiry. Reasoning is the method of evaluating thoughts by practicing elimination and engaging in solving challenging problems. Reflecting on the individual performance in the life-long enterprise of solving challenging problems is a higher kind of meta-cognitive activity (Ericsson et al., 1993). Therefore, the intricacy of the 3Rs leads to many Critical Thinking frameworks.

A Framework of Critical Thinking

For a deeper understanding of Critical thinking, it is essential to consider the many definitions and related frameworks addressing the concept and its implementations. critical thinking is a multidimensional and multifaceted human capability. Critical Thinking has been interpreted from Education, Psychology, and Epistemology (Figure 1). This framework provides a visual presentation of the four dimensions: Abilities (Educational perspectives), dispositions (Psychological perspectives), levels (Epistemological perspectives), and time to emphasize the critical thinking nature in terms of a specific context. In the developmental approach, Critical Thinking involves accumulative skills, dispositions, and other psych-socio-related variables such as motivation, context, criteria, and knowledge. This developmental approach proceeds from experience to various forms of inquiry, investigation, examination of evidence, exploration of alternatives, argumentation, testing conclusions, rethinking assumptions, and reflecting on the entire process (Spector, 2019). Experience and engagement are progressive throughout the process, proceeding from a relatively simple experience to a more complex interaction, such as manipulating the observing effects and the related artifacts. This approach also involves a variety of non-cognitive states, assisting students to become more purposeful and goal-directed individuals.

Metacognition and self-regulation are two crucial cognitive capabilities necessary for critical thinking. Research reveals that metacognition has two essential components: the awareness of one's thoughts and the ability to regulate one's cognitive processes. Metacognition has received considerable emphasis in the last decades as the capacity to monitor the quality of one's thinking process and accordingly make proper changes (Davies, 2015; APA, 2020). Metacognition, though, involves awareness and self-regulation and stresses the individual proper control. Considering metacognition and self-regulation enables individuals to create a self-regulatory mechanism, which regulates corresponding skills such as observation, interpretation, explanation, reasoning, analysis, evaluation, synthesis, and judgment. Therefore, students can regulate their learning using a variety of variables, such as technological tools.

Figure 1. Critical Thinking Visual Presentation (Adapted from Spector, 2019)

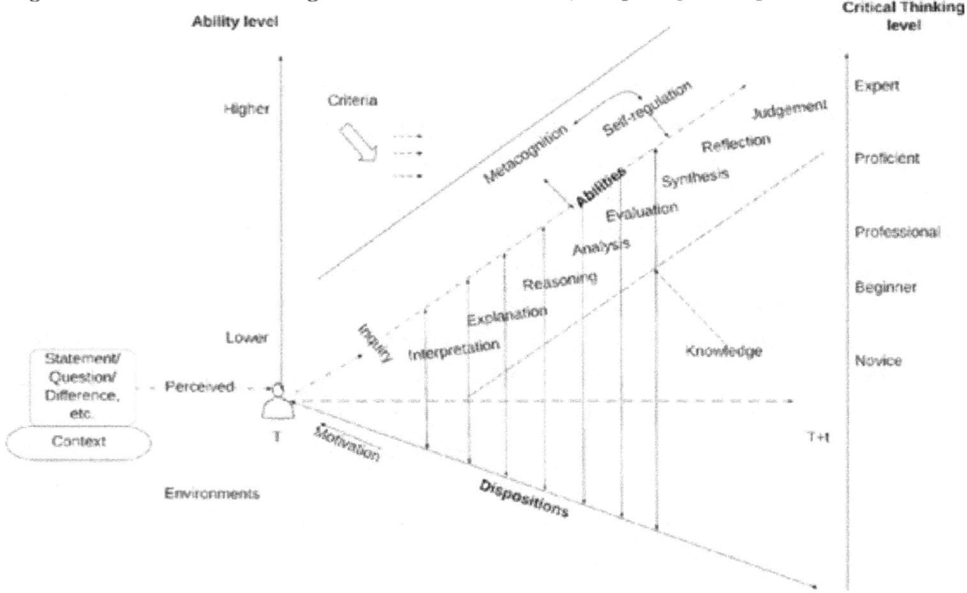

Educators, therefore, should consider the various stages of embedded critical thinking. Critical thinking starts with a simple experience, such as observation of differences, encountering questions or a challenge, or questioning someone's statement, and leads to an inquiry that proceeds to a complex experience, such as interaction and application (logical reasoning, questioning assumptions, considering and evaluating alternative explanations). Therefore, Critical thinking and disposition involve interrelated cognitive constructs such as interpretation, explanation, reasoning, evaluation, synthesis, reflection, judgment, metacognition, and self-regulation (Dwyer et al., 2014; Davies, 2015; Ennis, 2018; Hitchcock, 2018).

Critical Thinking and Cognitive Processes

Critical thinking is a cognitive process that includes analyzing, inferring, and solving problems (Rodzalan, 2015; Chen, 2017; Jatmiko et al., 2018). Systematic thinking is paramount to formulating findings and obtaining justifiable assumptions (Sari et al., 2019). critical thinking skills encourage students to be competent in dealing with natural and social environments more practically and effectively (Mahanal, 2019). Learning innovation depends on deepening the critical thinking processes and understanding of curricula (Anggraini, 2016; Bahous et al., 2011; Hong & Yu, 2017). Research reveals the positive impact of various frameworks such as inquiry and Mind-mapping models, addressing the construction of CR in the higher education realm.

The inquiry model provides educators and learners with ample tools to improve their high-level thinking skills (Prince et al., 2006; Arsal, 2017; Zubaidah et al., 2017). The model emphasizes constructing science by building experience and knowledge through investigation to activate thinking skills. It emphasizes the process of problem-solving and active learning processes to increase students' learning motivation (Ruzaman & Rosli, 2020; Bayram et. al., 2013). Additionally, mind mapping is an effective tool for fostering critical thinking skills and learning motivations. It is recommended that the inquiry model be complemented, as it provides students with step-by-step operations to build their knowledge about the selected topic. Mind mapping helps students construct knowledge and activate the brain's work steps. Mind mapping can help students adapt to the required developmental needs (Barra et al., 2019; Buzan, 2002 a/ b). Therefore, Mind-mapping strategies encourage students to participate actively in the learning process.

Developing the Inquiry mind-map

The inquiry activity is one of the learning steps of the inquiry learning models. The inquiry model is a model developed by Richard Sucman. The model uses the constructivist learning theory. It unfolds student-centered learning by prioritizing the Socratic approach through questions and answers as the teacher facilitates the learning activities. High-level thinking forms the core practice at the heart of the inquiry syntax (Zubaidah et al., 2017; Joyce. et.. al., 2000). The mind map is a tool to organize ideas, concepts, and information and make thinking effective and systematic. It activates the brain's work through color, shapes, and writing variations. It also allows students to independently search for knowledge and experiences (Buzan, 2006; Wette, 2017). Consequently, it is an effective model for constructing knowledge and developing competencies according to learning goals and objectives. The updated technological mind map software is a learning media that presents a more structured learning journey. The software could be used on computers and tablets for easy accessibility for students and educators. It provides educators and students with many opportunities to track the achievement of their objectives (Sagita et al.,2018). To this end, the inquiry mind map gives students many ways to assess their thinking and discover various ways to expand their knowledge.

Figure 2. Figure of Inquiry Mind Map (Adapted from Wette, 2017; Zubaidah et al., 2017; Joyce. et.. al., 2000)

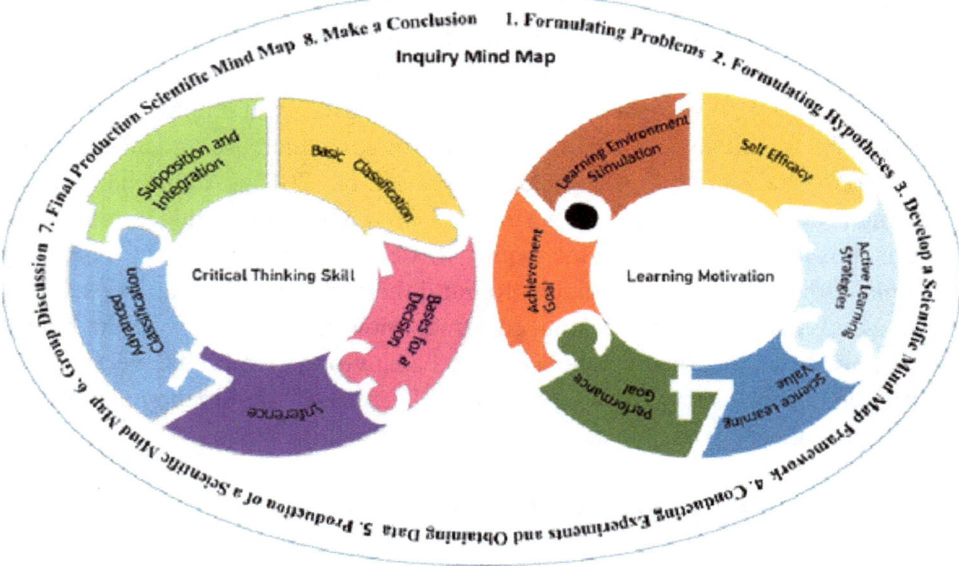

Additionally, the generative AI created the following table to present the inquiry mind map model developed by Richard Sucman. The table addresses the model's key elements with a short description illustrating its function.

Table 1. Inquiry Mind Map Model by Richard Sucman (Developed by Gen-AI, 2024)

Category	Element	Description
Central Question	Description	The main question that drives the inquiry process.
	Example	"How does integrating generative AI impact student learning outcomes in higher education?"
Key Concepts	Generative AI	AI technologies capable of generating content, such as text, images, or code, used in educational settings.
	Higher Education	The context of universities, colleges, and other post-secondary institutions where AI is integrated.
	Learning Outcomes	The measurable skills, knowledge, and attitudes that students are expected to gain through education.
Assumptions	Personalization	AI can personalize learning experiences.
	Educator Training	Educators are trained to use AI tools effectively.

continued on following page

Table 1. Continued

Category	Element	Description
Evidence	Research Studies	Studies on AI in education that provide data and insights.
	Student Performance Metrics	Data related to student grades, engagement, and other performance indicators.
Implications	Teaching Methodologies	Potential shifts in how educators teach, incorporating more technology-driven approaches.
	Policy Adjustments	Changes to institutional policies to accommodate and regulate AI use in classrooms.
Alternative Perspectives	Ethical Considerations	Moral and ethical issues surrounding AI deployment in education, such as privacy and bias.
	Equity in Access	Ensuring all students have equal access to AI tools, preventing disparities based on socioeconomic status.

Critical thinking skills are essential in the learning process. John Dewey perceived CR as a process that begins with a problem, pursues it through a self-directed search and interrogation of knowledge, and ends with a solution and self-interpretation. The process starts with a question that evokes students' natural curiosity and simulates learning and critical thinking using the various cognitive skills that increase the probability of a desirable outcome. To this point, Critical thinking is purposeful, reasoned, and goal-directed. It involves solving problems, formulating inferences, calculating possibilities, and making decisions. Learners, therefore, are aware of the process as they have a conscious intent, evaluate the outcomes of their thought processes, calculate how good a decision is, and how effectively a problem has been solved (Bean, 2011; Harplen, 1997).

ChatGPT and Critical Thinking Support

Critical thinking is a tool of inquiry and a powerful resource in personal and civic lives. Research reveals that Critical Thinking encompasses various elements such as reasoning, inferences, critical judgments, and critical creativity (Paul, 1984; Facione, 2011). Artificial Intelligence has revolutionized various aspects of daily life, from mimicking human-like behaviors to advancing applications like machine learning (Wnag, 2019; Shukla, 2013). AI utilizes large language models and a generative pretraining transformer (GPT). ChaptGPT is trained using machine learning algorithms on vast text data sets, making it adept at interactive applications. It can accomplish various tasks, such as summarizing, answering, and chatting (Kasneci et al., 2013; Bitzenbauer, 2013). Conversely, CHatGPT as an educational tool brings many limitations: First, the reliability and accuracy of the created data by ChatGPT; Second, citation and referencing as many articles are nonexistent; third, lack of creativity as ChatGPT promptly shares the required knowledge; therefore, students do not spend time thinking about creative presentation of the data. Additionally, students notice that the quality of response varies dramatically by the clarity and specificity of the prompt (Association of College & Research Libraries, 2023; American et al., 2023; Halaweh, 2023).

The Integration of AI in Higher Education Classrooms- Social Cognitive Lense

Research reveals that social cognitive theories introduced a much more accessible tool for understanding the complex interactions between the various elements of the environment, behaviors, and cognitive processes. The Social Cognitive Theories prove their practicality and effectiveness in education and healthcare as they imply individual skills, qualifications, and understanding (Main, 2023; Rahman, 2018). The awareness level of users shapes the effectiveness of using AI to acquire knowledge of the process. However, Gen-AI integration in higher education classrooms is shaped by an institutional understanding of human learning within a dynamic interaction of personal, behavioral, and environmental factors. Below are key insights and variables framed within this perspective (See Figure 2)

Table 2. Integration of Generative AI into Higher Education Classrooms from a Social Cognitive Lens (Generated by Gen-AI, 2024)

Category	Variable/Factor	Description
Personal Factors	Self-Efficacy	Students' belief in their ability to effectively use AI tools for learning.
	Motivation	The drive to engage with AI technologies to enhance academic performance.
Behavioral Factors	Usage Patterns	How often and in what ways do students and educators interact with AI tools?
	Skill Development	The acquisition of skills is necessary to utilize AI effectively in educational tasks.
Environmental Factors	Social Support	Support from peers, instructors, and the institution in adopting AI technologies.
	Cultural Attitudes	Prevailing attitudes towards AI in the educational environment.
Outcome Expectations	Academic Performance	Anticipated improvements in grades and understanding due to AI integration.
	Engagement Levels	Expected increase in student engagement and participation through AI tools.
Reciprocal Determinism	Interaction Effects	The dynamic relationship between personal beliefs, behaviors, and environmental influences in the context of AI use.
	Feedback Loops	How experiences with AI influence future use and perceptions of the technology.

Personalized Learning

Using personalized learning experiences through AI applications fosters learning. Personalized learning is the experience that is customized for each learner's individuality to encourage this student's academic achievement by recognizing their unique learning requirements, interests, and goals. Personalization is the learning experience through which the mentor directs his/ her mentees to evaluate, design, work collaboratively, keep its outline, and demonstrate their study using various media. Therefore, building personalized learning experiences with a virtual operating medium is one example of how artificial intelligence (AI) can be utilized in education. This approach provides massive access by removing geographical barriers to learning. Learners can manage the learning process by manipulating their learning pace from anywhere and fostering their learning ownership. They can track their progress by establishing their learning objectives and choosing activities to deepen their interest in the topic. This type of practice simulates a high level of participation and a greater sense of independence and responsibility (Rahman, 2023).

Gen-AI applications and Functionality

Technological applications are increasingly developed to fulfill human needs while becoming more intelligent (Monika Hooda, 2022; Lin, 2023). In higher education, evaluation dramatically impacts students' learning by offering various learning opportunities. For example, analyzing the available data, finding structures, and deciding the common patterns using Artificial intelligence (AI) can assist nurses in diagnosing and treating their patients more accurately. These tools enable students to interact with their course content and foster their engagement with the materials. For example, ChatGPT can facilitate interactive learning by generating real-time responses to students' queries. By incorporating tools like Google Docs, Canva, and Zoom into the instructional time, educators can create dynamic and interactive learning experiences that cater to various learning preferences and accordingly provide students with a variety of ways to examine the content from different perspectives (Lin, 2023; Bansal, et al., 2024). Using some technological applications such as Claude.ai, ChatGPT, Gemini, Latimer, Copilot, WolframAlpha, and Meta AI brings a natural human-related interaction to the learning process. These tools facilitate the creation and distribution of educational content and promote critical skills such as critical thinking skills and collaboration among students (Moustaq et al., 2023; Bozkurt, 2021; Wang, 2019; Hasan, 2020). However, the methodological use of the application is at the heart of its effectiveness in the educational realm (See Table 3).

The following are some of the most widely used Gen-AI applications in higher education and their impact on teaching and learning processes.

Table 3. AI Application and Working Mechanism in Class Settings (Adapted from Orduno et al., 2023; Pavlik, 2023; Yu et al., 2023; Branig, 2022)

The Application	The Tool Description
Claude.ai Claude.ai	Sonnet 3.5 is GREAT and currently FREE. There is also a smaller Haiku and a larger Opus. Claude (in workbench mode) also now allows you to control the "temperature" from most random to most predictable.
ChatGPT ChatGPT	ChatGPT, developed by Open AI, San Francisco, CA, USA is a tool that can generate coherent and contextual responses to user queries. From its inception the ChatGPT is progressively presents adult educators to a countless opportunities to foster their teaching. ChatGPT Plus, and ChaptGPT 4.0 and ChatGPT 40 (Omni) are faster tools. ChatGPT host virtual discussions on different approaches in education. Students can ask questions and receives answers generated by the tool to explore diverse perspectives and prompt critical thinking skills.
Gemini Gemini	It is formerly Google Bard. Gemini Advanced is commonly used by adults.
Latimer Latimer	It is a tool that represents a diverse community of knowledge by adding deeper training from books, oral histories, and sources from communities of color.
CoPilot Copilot	CoPilot is another version of ChatGPT. It is interacted with Microsoft projects. Mircosoft ensures its compliance with FERPA and HIPPA. The creative button of CoPIlot includes GPT 4 and Turbo functions.
PI Pi	The tool focuses on conversational communication between AI and the human. Dialogue and role-playing has a good voice interface.
Huggingface Huggingface	This tool is a chatbot running on Llama. The user does not need a lohin to start the interaction with the AI.
Perplexity Perplexity.ai	The tool is an a chatbot. The user can conduct the interaction and the tool uses the online citation mechanism to formulate the responses. Therefore, the user gets the responses of the shared questions with the sources cited using multiple frontier models.
Consensus Consensus. app	This tools is an academic research tool taking its data from 200M published papers and uses ChatGPT to filter the research by claims, methodology, sample size, and more. It is a very helpful tool for researchers while conducting a thorough literature review.
Storm Storm	This is a Stanford created AI tool. It is a new research tool that creates a WIkipedia-like report on the topic of choice. It looks at the related content, summarize the related content from different perspectives according to the focus of the research such as the Sociologist's perspectives, Psychologist's perspectives …etc. Additionally it tell the user what sources are used to address the topic of discussion and comparing the results.
NotebookLM NotebookLM	It is a Google version of a research assistant, It operate on the document (Microsoft Word, PDF) you upload. The used could upload up to 50 documents (up to 500,000 words). The user provide, therefore, the tool with specific instructions such as to summarize the book, provide a report regarding some specific criteria…..etc. It also creates a podcast based on the provided content. Teachers could use it to foster their students critical thinking skills by asking them to create podcasts addressing various higher-order thinking. Teachers could use it to provide their students with instant analytical and constructive feedback on their work by uploading students work and the used rubric.

continued on following page

Table 3. Continued

The Application	The Tool Description
YOU.COM You.com	It is a tool to summarize long documents and texts. It helps students understand academic articles by highlighting the ket ponts and essential relationships. It is a crucial functionality to develop critical thinking by allowing students to identify and evaluate the relevance of the information in the selected discipline. The tools is used to summarize academic articles on educational intervention strategies. The summary; therefore, could be used to conduct an online discussion using other tools such as Google Docencouraging critical thinking as they reflect on the ideas presented.
Chat-PDF	It is a tool, allowing students to interact with PDF documents through natural conversations. The tool facilitates the exploration and analysis of complex documents, allowing students to ask questions and obtain contextual answers. PDF chat is useful for critically analyzing case studies and other detailed materials. This tool provides students with a PDF document containing a case study about an academic related issue to the course content. Then students can use the PDF chat to interact with the document by asking questions, analyzing data, and discussing possible intervention approaches in a virtual forum on Zoom. This practice promotes critical thinking by allowing students to explore the case study interactively.
Tome AI	It is a tool to generate summaries and analyses of relevant documents. Students can use Tom AI to break down complex texts into manageable and meaningful parts. It supports students' comprehension of the material and foster their analytical skills, enabling them to synthesize information effectively. Educators could start dividing students into groups and assign different educational interventions or related scientific concepts to generate summaries or analyses. Then each group uses Google Doc to collaborate to design an intervention proposal based on the collected information. At the end, all groups can present their proposals in class or Zoom/ Google Mee/ Microsoft Team.
Canva	It is an online platform enabling collaboration and the creation of visual resources such as mind maps, presentations, and graphics. It is used for group projects in higher education settings as students can work together to visualize concepts and related discipline projects. It encourages teamwork and creativity, which are essential for developing collaborative and critical thinking skills. . Educators could ask students to use Canva to create a mind map to visualize the discussed issue. Then, in an online form discussion using Google Docs or the Learning Management System Discussion Boards, students can share their mind maps and discuss the similarities and differences between the proposals. This activity encourages collaborative work by facilitating the joint creation and review of ideas while promoting critical thinking and topic analyses.
Google Doc	Google Docs is an online productivity suite that allows students to collaborate in real-time to create and edit documents. It is a tool for collaborative projects in which students work together to investigate and analyze a specific problem in their field of study. They can use the comments features to discuss and debate different perspectives, promoting critical thinking. At the end of the task, students could use educational video tools such as Zoom, Google Meet, or Microsoft Teams to present their findings.
Zoom	Zoom is a video conferencing platform that revolutionized communication in education during and after COVID-19. It allows students and educators to interact in real time, share resources, and collaborate on projects.

CHALLENGES AND SOLUTIONS FOR STUDENTS' ENHANCEMENT

1- Plagiarism & Academic Integration

Integrity is one of the crucial pillars of higher education. Various higher education policies highlight the commitment to six core values as an accepted definition of academic integrity: truthfulness, justice, equity, morality, transparency, and fearlessness (Mohammad, 2023; Mehta, 2023). Using AI tools to create content without crediting the sources is unacceptable. However, the importance of text phrasing may vary according to the topic (King, 2023).

2- Security and data privacy

The global shift to a post-industrial culture impacts educational systems; however, online learning resources secure many opportunities for more progress (Kamenskih, 2022). For example, the online course's adaptable structure makes it possible to update the course without affecting the other sections within the system. Therefore, it is beneficial that policymakers think about AI's support of privacy, even though it might challenge conceptions of privacy. As AI expands, the confidentiality of personal information has surfaced. AI requires vast amounts of personal data to acquire knowledge and make predictions, which raises questions about how these data are collected, handled, and kept. Research, therefore, is in progress regarding the security and privacy of the collected data (AL-Khassawneh, 2023; Kumar, 2023; David Elliott, 2024).

To this end, Integrating technology in higher education is paramount to enhancing learning experiences and motivating students to engage and self-regulate their learning experiences. Recent studies have revealed the significant impact of technology on student engagement, skills development, and learning outcomes. Technology integration equips students with the tools to strive in the digital world. However, these rapid changes in technological application demand continuous adaptation and innovation from educators to integrate these technological tools into their instruction and assessments properly. Nevertheless, ethical considerations, such as fairness and transparency in AI algorithms. are paramount to their responsible use in education. To this point, educators can leverage AI to create more inclusive learning experiences by considering ethical factors (Weng, 2023; Muca et al., 2022).

Gen-AI Applications and Critical Thinking Teaching Endorsement (Q2)

Higher education fosters collaborative and critical thinking to prepare students for the workforce. Technology is essential to achieve this goal by providing tools for communication, problem-solving and collaboration. It enables students to work together seamlessly regardless of the physical location. Technological applications foster students' critical thinking by providing them with opportunities to access diverse perspectives, analyze information critically, and engage in more meaningful conversations about their content (Iba et al., 2023; Peramunugamage et al., 2023; Hemachandran et al., 2022). Therefore, incorporating technology into educational practices is vital for building these skills in students.

Critical thinking involves analyzing, evaluating, and synthesizing information reflectively and deliberately, questioning assumptions, examining evidence, identifying biases and forming informed conclusions. AI tools improve students' abilities to analyze, evaluate, synthesize, and draw conclusions by providing sufficient resources (Halaweh, 2023; Michel-Villarreal et al., 2023). Using AI tools develops a greater depth of thinking by challenging students to explore and question different approaches and solutions. In a critical thinking context, analysis refers to breaking down information into smaller components and understanding the available relationships. Evaluation refers to the ability to judge the quality, relevance, and credibility of information. Creativity involves the ability to create new ideas and address a variety of perspectives to understand complex problems. To this point, educators need to consider the AI tool to create a more structural framework to realize how generative AI can be integrated into teaching activities, encourage critical thinking and collaborative work, and precisely identify the tool's function in the fabric of the instructional process. The following table presents AI tools to endorse critical thinking and promote more profound collaborative learning (See Table 4).

Table 4. Gen-AI Applications and Critical Thinking Endorsement (Adapted from Halaweh, 2023; Michel-Villarreal et al., 2023)

Tools to Generate Critical Thinking	Tools for collaborative work
ChatGPT allows users to chat with each other in real-time. It can raise questions and frame discussions by providing feedback on students' critical thinking.	Google Docs allows students to collaborate on creating, editing, and presenting their production in real-time.
YOU.COM and NootebookLM automatically summarize research documents and long texts. They help students understand and recognize the text's key concepts and the various relationships among these textual pillars.	Zoom, Google Meet, and Microsoft Teams are video conferencing platforms that allow students to meet virtually and collaborate in real-time. These platforms also allow users to share their content and presentations.
Claudi and Chat PDF allow students to interact with the document through natural conversation. They help analyze complex documents, encourage students to raise questions, and generate various discussions related to the text's focus.	Canva allows students to collaborate on creating graphic designs, presentations, and other visual resources. It facilitates collaboration on creative projects.
Tome AI, Consensus, and Perplexity help facilitate understanding the concepts and analyze long texts, promoting critical thinking by identifying and synthesizing relevant information.	

Toward a Conceptualized Use of AI in Teaching

Big data and artificial intelligence (AI) have profoundly transformed education and pedagogical practices in higher education. Gen-AI can deliver personalized learning experiences and pinpoint learning difficulties to foster academic progress. AI can accomplish many teaching operations, such as personalized instruction, autonomous learning, and an intelligent campus environment. AI, therefore, profoundly reshapes management approaches and pedagogies in higher education classrooms as it impacts students' cognitive learning capacities and motivation (Chen et al., 2020; Singh & Haran, 2022). Higher education institutions use Gen-AI applications to foster their organizational skills based on these tools' functionality (See Table 5).

Table 5. Gen-AI Applications and Educational Organizations

Scenarios of AI Education	AI-Related Technology
Assessment of students and schools	Adaptive learning methodologies and personalized learning approach, academic analytics such as Claudi.Ai, perpexity, Consensus, and Storm.
Grading and evaluation of papers and exams	Image recognition, computer vision, and prediction systems like NootbookLM, ChatGPT, and CoPilot.
Personalized intelligent teaching	Data mining or Bayesian knowledge interference, intelligent teaching systems, learning analytics such as Pi, Claudi, and ChatGPT
Smart facilities	Facial recognition, speech recognition, virtual labs, A/R, V/R, hearing and sensing technologies such as ChatGPT, Perplexity, Storm and Tom.You.

Research outlines Gen-AI in terms of application area, discipline, capacities, and functionality. Using ChatGpt 0.4, the author created the following table to address the various applications of Gen-AI in educational settings, along with a short description, benefits, and examples.

Table 6. Applications of Generative AI in Education (created by Gen-AI, 2024)

Application Area	Description	Benefits	Examples
Personalized Learning	Tailoring educational content and experiences to individual student needs, preferences, and learning styles using AI-driven insights.	- Enhanced student engagement - Improved learning outcomes - Increased motivation	- Adaptive learning platforms like DreamBox - Personalized lesson plans generated by AI
Content Creation	Automatically generating educational materials, such as textbooks, quizzes, and multimedia resources, using AI models.	- Saves time for educators - Ensures up-to-date content - Facilitates diverse materials	- AI-generated practice questions - Interactive AI-driven textbooks
Tutoring and Support	Providing AI-powered virtual tutors and assistants to help students with homework, explanations, and study strategies.	- 24/7 availability - Immediate feedback - Supports diverse learning paces	- Chatbots like ChatGPT for homework help - AI-driven study assistants
Assessment and Evaluation	Automating grading, providing instant feedback, and analyzing student performance data to identify areas for improvement.	- Reduces grading time - Provides consistent evaluations - Identifies learning gaps	- Automated essay grading systems - AI analytics for performance tracking

continued on following page

Table 6. Continued

Application Area	Description	Benefits	Examples
Administrative Tasks	Streamlining administrative processes such as scheduling, enrollment, and communication using AI tools.	- Increases operational efficiency - Reduces administrative burden - Enhances accuracy	- AI-driven enrollment systems - Automated scheduling assistants
Language Learning	Assisting in language acquisition through AI-powered translation, pronunciation guides, and interactive language practice tools.	- Facilitates immersive learning - Provides personalized language practice - Enhances accessibility	- Duolingo's AI-driven lessons - AI translation tools for multilingual support
Accessibility Enhancements	Creating inclusive learning environments by providing AI tools that support students with disabilities, such as text-to-speech, speech-to-text, and personalized learning aids.	- Promotes inclusivity - Enhances learning for all students - Removes barriers to education	- AI-powered captioning for lectures - Customized learning tools for students with disabilities
Research and Development	Assisting educators and researchers in developing curricula, conducting research, and analyzing educational trends using AI-driven data analysis.	- Accelerates research processes - Provides deep insights - Supports evidence-based decision-making	- AI tools for curriculum development - Data analytics platforms for educational research
Virtual and Augmented Reality	Enhancing immersive learning experiences through AI-integrated VR and AR applications, enabling simulations and interactive learning environments.	- Enhances engagement - Facilitates experiential learning - Provides safe simulation environments	- AI-driven VR science labs - AR applications for interactive history lessons
Career Guidance and Counseling	Utilizing AI to provide personalized career advice and counseling based on student interests, skills, and market trends.	- Offers tailored career paths - Enhances student decision-making - Aligns education with job market needs	- AI career assessment tools - Personalized counseling chatbots

AI technology has brought many advantages to the higher education setting, yet its impact on students' cognitive capacities, specifically Critical Thinking, remains unclear (25,27). The factors affecting Critical Thinking are diverse, including self-efficacy, learning motivation, cognition, emotional intelligence, and the learning environment. Digital learning applications such as Google Classrooms, Canvas, and Blackboard can influence critical thinking through self-regulated learning and motivation. General self-efficacy may alter learning goals and self-assessments using AI tools. Therefore, it is essential to investigate how AI capabilities impact critical thinking through the available mediating variable (Liu et al., 2023; Bayram et al., 2019; Abbas et al., 2023). Therefore, this report provides the framework for educators to recognize how AI shapes critical thinking and enhances pedagogical practices.

Increasing educators' critical awareness in teaching content is supported by considering artificial intelligence capabilities and general self-efficacy. Institutional access to resources and the methods of using these resources efficiently have a significant impact on institutional effectiveness. Resource-based theory (RBT), which was proposed by Penrose (1959) and Barny (1991), underscores the significance of internal resources and organizational capabilities such as AI data, application platforms, and strategic assets. (See Figure 3)

Figure 3. RBT Theory- The core competencies and organizational capabilities of institutions

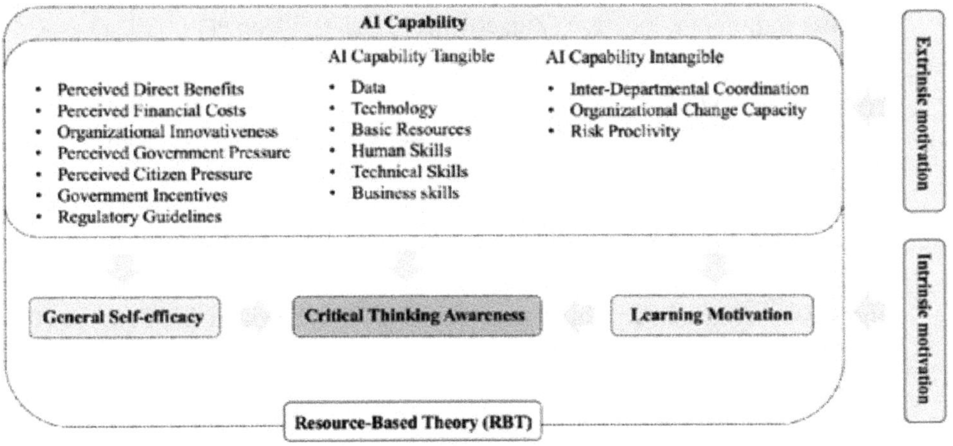

AI capability refers to the ability of artificial intelligence to pertain the capability of executing tasks typically required by humans. AI's multifaceted functions have the potential to significantly shape the educational landscape with applications including personalized learning and adaptive assessment to hone students' learning outcomes achievements (SLOs) (Chen et al.., 2020). AI technologies can foster personalized engagement and offer tailored educational experiences for students. Research reveals the impact of AI on improvement in educational settings, such as the pedagogical practices and the learning environments for quality education (Peng et al., 2023). The RBT introduces three important factors shaping higher education effectiveness:

1-Critical Thinking awareness is recognized as a fundamental competency for university students. It encompasses students' abilities to analyze, evaluate, synthesize, and resolve various challenges (Utami et al., 2017). It shapes students' learning, cognition, analysis, and decision-making. It shapes students' academic success in higher education. Therefore, it is essential to adequately embody CR in curricula to ensure students' academic and professional growth (Alwehaibi, 2012; Benítez & Canales,2013).

2-General self-efficacy as an individual belief to accomplish formulated tasks and attained objectives has been examined extensively in higher education. Studies demonstrate that self-efficacy beliefs play a crucial role in psychological adaptation, physical well-being, and creating strategies for behavioral change (Spector & Ma, 2019). Within the sociocultural contexts, Bandura (1995) underscored the importance of self-efficacy in shaping the trajectory of individual academic growth. Self-efficacy, therefore, alleviates the stress levels among college students and fosters their academic performance. Academic self-efficacy is linked to students' persistence and predicts the students' success in higher education (Zajacova et al.., 2005; Ren et al., 2021).

3-Leaning motivation refers to the intrinsic and extrinsic factors that drive individuals to engage in learning activities. It plays a crucial role in shaping students' attitudes, behaviors, and academic performance. Research reveals that learning motivation gives students the mental focus and attention required for effective learning. Motivation, therefore, influences the level of students' engagement and their interest in the learning processes. Research also reveals that there is a strong correlation between teaching styles, learning motivation, and students' academic achievement (Emda, 2018; Silviana, 2023; Atma et al., 2021). To this end, learning motivation profoundly affects students' attitudes and academic achievements.

Critical Thinking Awareness and AI capability

Research reveals that AI capability is an essential resource fostering thinking skills as it is a tool to enhance individual cognitive abilities. Research suggests that educational institutions should effectively leverage AI to enhance critical thinking skills and students' satisfaction. Integrating emotional intelligence into AI significantly influences students' motivation and abilities, which fosters teaching effectiveness (Kawakami et al., 2021; Ling et al.,2022; Farhan et al., 2021). For example, the integration of AI in teaching increases classroom engagement in project-based learning. AI technological applications foster autonomous learning, curiosity, and intrinsic motivation, which are elements of social learning and peer interactions (Lopez-Gazpio, 2022; Sun, 2021; Oudeyer, 2017). Additionally, research reveals the impact of students' motivation to use AI on students' engagement. Institutions, in this context, could regularly organize learning-sharing sessions, allowing students to showcase their successful experiences while using AI applications to achieve their learning goals. Institutions could periodically administer surveys to gather students' needs and understand the difficulties and obstacles they might experience while using AI tools in their learning discourses. Consequently, addressing these challenges and needs through guided sessions could bolster their academic growth and sharpen their use of technology in their study.

Critical Thinking and Related Pedagogical Implications

Institutions could follow a variety of pedagogical implications to bolster students' critical thinking awareness by using the AI application in their learning experiences:

1-Self-efficacy enhancement: The institutions could regularly host AI project exhibitions for students to present and exchange their experiences, increasing their confidence and sharpening their use of AI applications. The process of sharing and seeking feedback deepens knowledge use.

2-Personlized Learning Experiences: Institutions could encourage students to use AI applications to create personalized learning experiences with the academic content. Students could start activating their prior knowledge by engaging with AI in timely-manner conversations to assess their knowledge level. Applications such as Claudi, PI, and NootbookLM help students activate their prior knowledge before starting their learning journey.

3-Learning patterns: Educators could use AI to analyze learning patterns, creating tailored plans for each student. For example, educators could assign students specific topics based on their interests to stimulate enthusiasm. Additionally, educators could use AI to create interactive course materials, use AI for real-time Q&A, and assess reports.

4-Fostering Critical Thinking Awareness: Educators could use AI to develop content that integrates AI to analyze learning performance and provide immediate feedback to help students understand their progress and identify areas for improvement.

Overall, AI applications for monitoring educational achievements, identifying areas for improvement, and implementing tailored corrective measures provide educators with actionable insights to gain a comprehensive understanding of students' skill mastery.

Pedagogical Opportunities and Challenges

AI tools are commonly used educational and teaching instruments in higher education. They are used for research, instruction, and assessment. AI tools make information available online and condense it to provide an overview of the topic. Therefore, it is impactful in the learning process if it is used as a tool to spark information. Therefore, educators need to guide their students to use AI tools to deepen their critical thinking skills properly. Students could be engaged with the AI applications in a progressive conversation regarding the content to either activate their prior knowledge or identify various ways to implement the content. These questions approach while using the Gen-AI applications to empower students to move beyond the knowledge surface level and achieve a meaningful, transformative learning experience (Messeri & Crockett, 2024; Jarrahi et al., 2023). The mechanism of integrating AI technology into learning and teaching is of paramount importance to building learners' skills. Students need to be aware of the following outcomes due to their excessive use of AI tools:

1-Shallow learning: They use AI tools to generate facts and data without any further use of these data to sharpen their critical and analytical skills.
2-Overconfidence: Students might feel they have mastered the content due to the available data.

These analyses, evaluations, and applications of knowledge are stagnant. Conversely, Gen-AI addresses some of the challenges and tools to address them properly, as illustrated in Table 7.

Table 7. Challenges and Solutions with Gen-AI Integration in Higher Education Settings (Created by Gen-AI, 2024)

Challenge	Description	Potential Solutions
Data Privacy Concerns	Risk of student data being misused or inadequately protected.	Implement strict data governance policies and use secure AI platforms.
Bias in AI Algorithms	systems may perpetuate or amplify existing biases in educational materials and assessments.	Use diverse training datasets and regularly audit AI systems for bias.
h Implementation Costs	Financial barriers to adopting advanced AI technologies.	Seek grants, partnerships, and scalable AI solutions that fit budget constraints.
Resistance to Change	Educators and administrators may be hesitant to adopt new AI tools and methodologies.	Provide comprehensive training and demonstrate the benefits of AI integration through pilot programs.
Technical Issues and Maintenance	Ensuring AI tools are reliable, up-to-date, and properly maintained.	Establish dedicated IT support teams and choose reputable AI vendors with strong support services.
Ethical and Responsible Use	Ensuring AI is used in ways that respect student autonomy and promote positive educational outcomes.	Develop ethical guidelines and policies for AI use in education.

Teaching Critical Thinking Skills- Strategies and Procedures

Students who excessively use the Gen-AI application might bring shallow learning and overconfidence due to access to a huge source of related knowledge. Therefore, educators' responsibility is to guide their students in properly integrating Gen-AI into their learning to develop their CR skills. Research reveals that class discussions, problem-based learning, collaborative learning, discussion methods, questioning techniques, and evidence-based projects are practical teaching tools to foster critical thinking (Kuhn, 1999). Additionally, Lawrence (2008) reported that critiquing journal articles, engaging students in debates, evaluating case studies, and discussing questions foster critical thinking in higher education. Research reveals the effectiveness of a variety of strategies in higher education settings, such as:

1-Questioning techniques: Research reveals the effectiveness of the Socratic questioning tactic as a powerful teaching approach that guides students to generate thoughtful questions and foster CR skills. Educators could provide students with the main areas of questioning. Therefore, students reframe their questions and converse with AI-generated response tools such as ChatGPT and PI. Students write a report summarizing the outcome of the conversation conducted with the AI. The report could be uploaded on the LMS discussion board.

2-Discussion Techniques: Using the discussions as a teaching approach develops high-order cognitive skills. During these discussion activities, students produce their interpretation of the content. The discussions foster the flow of ideas and the development of thinking. However, the effectiveness of the discussions is shaped by the following manipulated steps: Defining the goals of the discussion, selecting the content, which is students' reports on the conversations with AI, preparing a set of related questions to guide the discussions, planning the mechanics of the discussions and the evaluation of the discussions. This discussion organization motivates students to deepen their self-discovery and develop reasoning skills. To this end, these procedures encourage planned, meaningful, and prepared discussions (Yang et al., 2005; Hansen & Salemi, 2012; Salleh et al., 2012; Bozkurt, 2021).

Assessing the effectiveness of AI activities

The assessment of AI-powered activities' effectiveness in educational settings encompasses multiple dimensions. Educators, therefore, need to consider the following areas during the creation and evaluation processes:

1-Students' Learning Outcomes Achievement: Educators need to align the AI-generative activities used with the SLOs and Learning objectives. For example, educators need to evaluate their students' understanding of new concepts and their ability to apply their knowledge.
2-Data Collection: Educators need to collect qualitative and quantitative data regarding students' feedback on Gen-AI activities. They also need to observe their students' engagement and collaboration during the implementation stage of these activities.
3-Evaluating the resources Quality: Educators could use AI tools to evaluate the quality of the course contents and their students' work performance, such as the originality and coherence of the tasks' productions.
4-Students' performance: Educators need to evaluate their students' performance progressively during the study using formative and summative methods that measure students' skills development, considering cognitive and socio-emotional aspects. Tailoring assessment strategies to Gen-AI applications and specific objectives is crucial to addressing teaching challenges. Therefore, understanding the content and teaching modality enables educators to identify the proper Gen-AI tools.

CONCLUSION

Gen-AI applications' use in teaching and academics is becoming increasingly prevalent due to their significance in enlightening learning outcomes, enhancing security, and maintaining data privacy. The integration of AI can be a game-changer as AI can help students learn faster and provide educators with valuable insights into their students' academic performance (Al-Hattami, 2023). This report explores the integration of Gen-AI in teaching and assessment, the functionality of some of the available AI tools, critical thinking awareness, and the practical procedures of integration of AI-generative activities in higher education. The report addresses some of the challenges of integrating AI-generative activities in teaching, such as privacy and academic integrity-related issues, such as using AI-powered essay grading systems. The report provides institutional administrators with valuable content to formulate effective internal policies regarding the proper integration of AI tools in the curriculum. This analysis provides academicians with useful insights to improve their teaching and content delivery.

From a practical perspective, increased awareness of Gen-AI applications has spurred academic discourse on teaching practices related to technology integration. The report framework the research-based integration of AI applications into teaching in higher education classrooms to provide practical guidance to the progressive development of inquiry and critical thinking skills in adult education. In this context, educators are not merely users of technology but facilitators of knowledge creation, critical thinkers, and change agents. To this end, integrating Gen-AI into higher education classroom pedagogy presents a transformative opportunity to enhance accessibility, inclusivity, engagement, and critical thinking and reasoning skills. However, achieving these goals requires institutional support and a commitment to quality education.

To this end, Gen-AI has immense potential to transform higher education institutions by enhancing personalized learning, streamlining administrative tasks and training, creating teaching-engaged content, and supporting educators and students in self-regulating their assignments. Integrating Gen-AI into institutional instructions and administrative tasks fosters efficiency, inclusivity, and educational outcomes. However, addressing the challenges related to data privacy, biases, integrity, and ethical use is crucial to ensure the reliable use of AI applications to benefit the educational community.

Funding

The author(s) received no financial support for this article's research, authorship, and/or publication.

Authors and Affiliations

Hany Zaky, Eastern International College, NJ, USA

Contributions

Hany Zaky, the primary author, completed the project.

Ethics declarations/ Ethics approval

The study follows the relevant guidelines and regulations of the American Psychological Association (APA).

Availability of data and material

Not Applicable

Competing interests

The author declares no competing interests.

REFERENCES

Abbas, S. Umangap, & W. Amin, A (2023). Collaborative group investigation and self-efficacy on pre-service science teachers' critical thinking skills. J. Pendidik. Sains Indonesia. 2023, pp. 11, 1–11.

Adiguzel, T., Kaya, M., & Cansu, F. (2023). Revolutionizing education with AI: Exploring the transformative potential of ChatGPT. *Contemporary Educational Technology*, *15*(3), 1–13. DOI: 10.30935/cedtech/13152

Alwehaibi, H. (2012). Novel program to promote critical thinking among higher education students: Empirical study from Saudi Arabia. *Asian Social Science*, *2012*(8), 193–204.

Al-Hattami, H. (2023). Understanding perceptions of academics toward technology acceptance in accounting education. *Heliyon*, *9*(1). Advance online publication. DOI: 10.1016/j.heliyon.2023.e13141

Arsal, Z. (2017). The Impact of Inquiry-Based Learning on The Critical Thinking Dispositions of Pre-Service Science Teachers. *International Journal of Science Education*, *39*(10), 1326–1338. DOI: 10.1080/09500693.2017.1329564

Association of College & Research Libraries. (2023). Framework for information literacy for higher education. http://www.ala.org/acrl/ standards/framework (accessed October 2023).

Anggraini, I. (2016). Motivasi Belajar dan Faktor-Faktor yang Berpengaruh: Sebuah Kajian pada Interaksi Pembelajaran Mahasiswa. *Premiere Educandum: Jurnal Pendidikan Dasar Dan Pembelajaran*, *1*(02). Advance online publication. DOI: 10.25273/pe.v1i02.39

Atma, B. A., Azahra, F. F., Mustadi, A., & Adina, C. A. (2021). Teaching style, learning motivation, and learning achievement: Do they have significant and positive relationships? *J. Prima Edukasia*, *2021*(9), 23–31.

Bahous, R., Bacha, N., & Nabhani, M. (2011). Motivating Students in the EFL Classroom: A Case Study of Perspectives. *English Language Teaching*, *4*(3), 33. DOI: 10.5539/elt.v4n3p33

Bansal, G., Mitchell, A., & Li, D. A. (2024). Panel Report on Higher Education in the Age of AI from the Perspective of Academic Leaders in the Midwest U.S. *Communications of the Association for Information Systems*, *2024*(54), 360–375.

Bayram, Z., Oskay, Ö. Ö., Erdem, E., Özgür, S. D., & Şen, Ş. (2013). Effect of Inquiry-based Learning Method on Students' Motivation. *Procedia: Social and Behavioral Sciences, 106*, 988–996. DOI: 10.1016/J.SBSPRO.2013.12.112

Barra, W. N., Wilujeng, I., & Kuswanto, H. (2019). The Effect of Inductive Learning Model Assisted Mindmap Mindjet MindManager towards Critical Thinking Skills of Students. *Journal of Physics: Conference Series, 1233*(1). Advance online publication. DOI: 10.1088/1742- 6596/1233/1/012046

Bayram, D., Kurt, G., & Atay, D. (2019). The implementation of webquest-supported critical thinking instruction in pre-service English teacher education: The Turkish context. *Particip. Educ. Res., 6*, 144–157.

Benítez, C., & Canales, E. (2013). Critical thinking as a resilience factor in an engineering program. *Creative Education, 2013*(04), 611–613.

Branig, M.; Engel, C.; Schmalfus-Schwarz, J.; Muller, E.F.;Weber, G. (2022). Where Are We with Inclusive Digital Further Education? Accessibility Through Digitalization. Lect. Notes Netw. Syst. 2022, 389 LNNS, 21–33. [CrossRef]

Buzan, T. (2006). The Buzan Study Skills Handbook. BBC Active. https://books.google. co. id/books/about/The_Buzan_Study_Skills_Handbook.html?id=719lVhWXTvAC&redir_ esc=y

Bloom, B. S., Englehart, M. D., Furst, E. J., Hill, W. H., & Krathwohl, D. R. (1956). Taxonomy of Educational Objectives, Handbook I: The Cognitive Domain. New York.

Bozkurt, A. A.-R. (2021, January 15). "Artificial Intelligence and Reflections from Educational Landscape: A Review of AI Studies in Half a Century.

Bukoye, T., & Oyelere, M. (2019). "Assessing the Value of Capstone Unit in Developing Critical Thinking Skills in MSc Students." In BAM 2019 Conference, Aston University, Birmingham, UK. British Academy of Management.

Bybee, R. (February 2014). [Online]. The BSCS 5E Instructional Model: Origins, Effectiveness, and Applications. Available: http://bscs.org/sites/default/files/_legacy/BSCS_5E_Instructional_Model Executive_Summary_0.pdf

Buzan, T. (2002a). *How to Mind Map: The Ultimate Thinking Tool That Will Change Your Life*. Thorson.

Buzan, T. (2002b). *Mind Maps*. Thorson.

Calma, A., & Davies, M. (2021). Critical Thinking in Business Education: Current Outlook and Future Prospects. *Studies in Higher Education, 46*(11), 2279–2295. DOI: 10.1080/03075079.2020.1716324

Cano, Y. M., Venuti, F., & Cellan-Jones, R. H. (2014). Stephen Hawking warns that artificial intelligence could end humanity. BBC. News. 2, 2014 (2014) M.T.H. Chi, R. Glaser, E. Rees, in Advances in the Psychology of Human Intelligence, ed. by R. S. Sternberg. Expertise in problem-solving (Erlbaum)

Chen, L. (2017). Understanding Critical Thinking in Chinese Sociocultural Contexts: A Case Study in A Chinese College. Thinking Skills and Creativity, pp. 24, 140–151. https://doi. org/DOI: 10.1016/J.TSC.2017.02.015

Chen, L.; Chen, P.; Lin, Z.(2020). Artificial intelligence in education: A review. IEEE Access 2020, 8, 75264–75278.

Dwyer, C. P., Hogan, M. J., & Stewart, I. (2014). An integrated critical thinking framework for the 21st century. *Thinking Skills and Creativity*, *12*, 43–52.

Cotton, D. R., Cotton, P. A., & Shipway, J. R. (2023). Chatting and cheating: Ensuring academic integrity in the era of ChatGPT. *Innovations in Education and Teaching International*, •••, 1–12. DOI: 10.1080/14703297.2023.2190148

Davies, . (2015). *Higher education: Handbook of theory and research. A Model of Critical Thinking in Higher Education* (pp. 41–92). Springer.

Emda, A. (2018). Kedudukan motivasi belajar siswa dalam pembelajaran. *Lantanida J.*, *2018*(5), 172.

Ennis, R. H. (1989). Critical thinking and subject specificity: Clarification and needed research. *Educational Researcher*, *18*, 4–10.

Ennis, R. H. (2018). Critical thinking across the curriculum: A vision. *Topoi*, *37*(1), 165–184.

Ericsson, R. T., & Krampe, C. (1993). Tesch-Römer, The role of deliberate practice in the acquisition of expert performance. *Psychological Review*, *100*(3), 363–406.

Facione, P. (2011). Critical thinking: What it is and why it counts. *Insight Assessment*, *1*(1), 1–23.

Fuchs, K. (2023). Exploring the opportunities and challenges of NLP models in higher education: Is Chat GPT a blessing or a curse? *Frontiers in Education*, *8*(May), 1166682.

Farhan, F., & Rofi'ulmuiz, M. (2021). Religiosity and emotional intelligence on Muslim student learning achievement. *Int. J. Eval. Res. Educ. IJERE*, *2021*(10), 404.

Halaweh, M. (2023). ChatGPT in education: Strategies for responsible implementation. Contemp. Educ. Technol. 2023, pp. 15, 421.

Hansen, W., & Salemi, M. (2012). Improving classroom discussion in economics courses. In Hoyt, G., & McGoldrick, K. (Eds.), *International handbook on teaching and learning economics* (pp. 68–78). Edward Elgar.

Hemachandran, K., Verma, P., Pareek, P., Arora, N., Rajesh Kumar, K. V., Ahanger, T. A., Pise, A. A., & Ratna, R. (2022). Artificial Intelligence: A Universal Virtual Tool to Augment Tutoring in Higher Education. *Computational Intelligence and Neuroscience*, *2022*(2022), 1–8.

Hong, S., & Yu, P. (2017). Comparison of The Effectiveness of Two Styles of Case-Based Learning Implemented in Lectures for Developing Nursing Students' Critical Thinking Ability: A Randomized Controlled Trial. *International Journal of Nursing Studies*, *68*, 16–24. DOI: 10.1016/J.IJNURSTU.2016.12.008

Hitchcock, D. (2018). Critical thinking. Retrieved from https://plato.stanford.edu/entries/critical-thinking/

Iskender, A. (2023). Holy or Unholy? Interview with Open AI's ChatGPT. European Journal of Tourism Research, pp. 34, 1–11. https://doi.org/DOI: 10.54055/ejtr.v34i.3169

Jarrahi, M. H., Askay, D., Eshraghi, A., & Smith, P. (2023). Artificial intelligence and knowledge management: A partnership between human and AI. *Business Horizons*, *66*(1), 87–99.

Jatmiko, B., & Prahani, B. K., Munasir, Supardi, Z. A. I., Wicaksono, I., Erlina, N., Pandiangan, P., Althaf, R. & Zainuddin. (2018). The Comparison of Oripa Teaching Model and Problem-Based Learning Model Effectiveness to Improve Critical Thinking Skills of PreService Physics Teachers. *Journal of Baltic Science Education*, *17*(2), 300–319. DOI: 10.33225/jbse/18.17.812

Joyce, B. R., Weil, M., & Calhoun, E. (2000). *Models of Teaching*. Allyn and Bacon.

Kawakami, N., Imamura, K., Watanabe, K., Sekiya, Y., Sasaki, N., & Sato, N. (2021). Effectiveness of an internet-based machine-guided stress management program based on cognitive behavioral therapy for improving depression among workers: Protocol for a randomized controlled trial. *JMIR Research Protocols*, *2021*(10), e30305.

Krathwohl, D. R. (2002). A Revision of Bloom's Taxonomy: An Overview. *Theory into Practice*, *41*(4), 212–218. DOI: 10.1207/s15430421tip4104_2

Kremantzis, M. D. (2023). Employability and Student Engagement from a Business Analytics Perspective.

Kuhn, D. (1999). A developmental model of critical thinking. *Educational Researcher, 28*(2), 16–46.

Lacka, E., T. C. Wong, & M. Y. Haddoud. (2021). "Can Digital Technologies Improve Students' Efficiency? Exploring the Role of Virtual Learning Environment and Social Media Use in Higher Education." Computers & Education 163:104099. https://doi.org/. 104099.DOI: 10.1016/ j.compedu.2020

Lawrence, N., Serdikoff, S., Zinn, T., & Baker, S. (2008). Have we demystified critical thinking. In Dunn, D., Halonen, J., & Smith, R. (Eds.), *Teaching Critical Thinking in Psychology* (1st ed.). Wiley-Blackwell.

Lim, W. M., Gunasekara, A., Pallant, J. L., Pallant, J. I., & Pechenkina, E. (2023). Generative AI and the Future of Education: Ragnarök or Reformation? A Paradoxical Perspective from Management Educators. *International Journal of Management Education, 21*(2), 100790. DOI: 10.1016/j.ijme.2023.100790

Lin, Z. (2023). Why and how to embrace AI such as ChatGPT in your academic life. R. Soc. Open Sci. 2023, pp. 10, 1–11.

Liu, C., Tang, M., Wang, M., Chen, L., & Sun, X. (2023). Critical thinking disposition and academic achievement among Chinese high school students: A moderated mediation model. *Psychology in the Schools, 2023*(60), 3103–3113.

Ling, Y., Zhou, J., Li, Y., & Huang, J. (2022). Learner satisfaction-based research on the application of artificial intelligence science popularization kits. *Frontiers in Psychology, 2022*(13), 901191.

Lopez-Gazpio, I. (2022). Gaining student engagement through project-based learning: A competitive 2d game construction case study. IEEE Access 2022, 10, 1881–1892.

Lodge, J. M., Thompson, K., & Corrin, L. (2023). Mapping Out a Research Agenda for Generative Artificial Intelligence in Tertiary Education. *Australasian Journal of Educational Technology, 39*, 1–8. DOI: 10.14742/ajet.8695

Mahanal, S., Zubaidah, S., Sumiati, I. D., Sari, T. M., & Ismirawati, N. (2019). RICOSRE: A Learning Model to Develop Critical Thinking Skills for Students with Different Academic Abilities. *International Journal of Instruction, 12*(2), 417–434. DOI: 10.29 333/iji.2019.12227a

Michel-Villarreal, R., Vilalta-Perdomo, E., & Salinas-Navarro, D. (2023). Thierry-Aguilera, R., and Gerardou, F. S. (2023). Challenges and opportunities of generative AI for higher education as explained by ChatGPT. *Education in Science, 2023*(13), 856.

Messeri, L., & Crockett, M. J. (2024). Artificial intelligence and illusions of understanding in scientific research. *Nature*, *627*(8002), 49–58.

Moscardini, A. O., Strachan, R., & Vlasova, T. (2022). The Role of Universities in Modern Society. *Studies in Higher Education*, *47*(4), 812–830. DOI: 10.1080/03075079.2020.1807493

Muca, E., Cavallini, D., Odore, R., Baratta, M., Bergero, D., & Valle, E. (2022). Are Veterinary Students Using Technologies and Online Learning Resources for Didactic Training? A Mini-Meta Analysis. *Education in Science*, *2022*(12), 573.

Oudeyer, P. (2017). Autonomous development and learning in artificial intelligence and robotics: Scaling up deep learning to human-like learning. Behav. Brain Sci. 2017, p. 40, e275.

Olga, A., A. Saini, G. Zapata, D. Searsmith, B. Cope, M. Kalantzis, V. Castro, T. Kourkoulou, J. Jones & R. A. da Silva. (2023). Generative AI: Implications and Applications for Education. arXiv Prepr. arXiv2305.07605.

Orduno-Osuna, J., Cota-Rivera, E., Raygoza, L., Jimenez-Sanchez, R., Limón-Molina, G., Bravo-Zanoguera, M., Mercado-Herrera, A., & Rico, F. (2023). Exploring the challenges and applications of generative AI on engineering education in Mexico. In *Facilitating Global Collaboration and Knowledge Sharing in Higher Education with Generative AI* (pp. 259–286). IGI Global.

Peng, M., Xie, J., Mao-hua, X., & Liu, Y. (2023). Artificial intelligence education in primary and secondary schools from the perspective of thinking quality. *J. Contemp. Educ. Res.*, *2023*(7), 41–46.

Pavlik, J. (2023). Collaborating with ChatGPT: Considering the Implications of Generative Artificial Intelligence for Journalism and Media Education. J. (2023). *Mass Commun. Educ.*, *2023*(78), 84–93.

Paul, R. W. (1984). Critical thinking: Fundamental to education for a free society. *Educational Leadership*, *42*(1), 4–14.

Prince, M. J., & Felder, R. M. (2006). Inductive Teaching and Learning Methods: Definitions, Comparisons, and Research Bases. *Journal of Engineering Education*, *95*(2), 123–138. DOI: 10.1002/j.2168-9830.2006.tb00884.x

Rahman, M. T. (2018). Cloud Computing: User's Perceptions About Security Issues. Information and knowledge management, 8(4). Retrieved from https://www.iiste.org/ Journals/index.php/IKM/article/view/41882/0

Peramunugamage, A., Ratnayake, U., & Karunanayaka, S. (2023). Systematic review on mobile collaborative learning for engineering education. *Journal of Computers in Education*, *2023*(10), 83–106.

Rahman, M. Tuhinur & Singh, Rahul. (2023). Impact of social influence on continuous use of mobile game applications" (2023). AMCIS 2023 Proceedings. https://aisel.aisnet.org/amcis2023/soc_inclusion/social_inclusion/5 Rahman, M. Tuhinur & Palvia, Prashant. (2023). How is my IT department leading to Digital Innovation Success?" (2023). AMCIS 2023 Proceedings. 7. https://aisel.aisnet.org/amcis2023/sig_dite/sig_dite/

Rust, Ming-Hui Huang, & Roland T. (2018). Artificial Intelligence in Service. https://journals.sagepub.com/doi/full/10.1177/1094670517752459

Rawas, S. (2023). ChatGPT: Empowering lifelong learning in the digital age of higher education. *Education and Information Technologies*, •••, 1–14. DOI: 10.1007/s10639-023-12114-8

Rudolph, J., Samson Tan, & Shannon Tan. (2023). ChatGPT: Bullshit Spewer or the End of Traditional Assessments in Higher Education? *Journal of Applied Learning and Teaching*, *6*(1), 342–363. DOI: 10.37074/jalt.2023.6.1.9

Schoepp, K. (2019). The state of course learning outcomes at leading universities. *Studies in Higher Education*, *44*(4), 615–627.

Ren, K., Liu, X., Feng, Y., Li, C., Sun, D., & Qiu, K. (2021). The relationship between physical activity and academic procrastination in Chinese college students: The mediating role of self-efficacy. *International Journal of Environmental Research and Public Health*, *2021*(18), 11468.

Rodzalan, S., & Saat, M. (2015). The Perception of Critical Thinking and ProblemSolving Skills among Malaysian Undergraduate Students. *Procedia: Social and Behavioral Sciences*, *172*, 725–732. DOI: 10.1016/J.SBSPRO.2015.01.425

Ruzaman, N., & Rosli, D. (2020). Inquiry-Based Education: Innovation in Participatory Inquiry Paradigm. *International Journal of Emerging Technologies in Learning*, *15*(10), 4. DOI: 10.3991/ijet.v15i10.11460

Salleh, S., Tasir, Z., & Shukor, N. (2012). Web-Based Simulation Learning Framework to Enhance Students' Critical Thinking Skills. International Educational Technology Conference, IETC2012, Procedia-Social and Behavioral Sciences, Elsevier Ltd., 64(2012), 372-381.Shukla

Sagita, A., Nurlaela, L., & Widodo, W. (2018). Mind Maple Lite Software. *Improve Student's Learning Outcomes and Stimulating Metacognition in Nutrition Science Subject.*, *112*, 1–5. DOI: 10.2991/iconhomecs-17.2018.1

Sari, R. Sumarmi, Komang Astina, I. Utomo, D. & Ridhwan. (2019). Measuring Students Scientific Learning Perception and Critical Thinking Skill Using Paper-Based Testing: School and Gender Differences. *International Journal of Emerging Technologies in Learning*, *14*(19). Advance online publication. DOI: 10.3991/ijet.v14i19.10968

Siau, K., & Yang, Y. (2017). In Twelve Annual Midwest Association for Information Systems Conference (MWAIS 2017). Impact of Artificial Intelligence, robotics, and Machine Learning on Sales and Marketing (2017), pp. 18–19

Singh, S., & Hiran, K. (2022). The Impact of AI on Teaching and Learning in Higher Education Technology. *Journal of Higher Education Theory and Practice*, *2022*(22), 135.

Spector, J. M. (2019). Smart Learning Environments: Concepts and Issues. In G. Chamblee & L. Langub (Eds.), Proceedings of Society for Information Technology & Teacher Education International Conference (pp. 2728–2737). (Association for the Advancement of Computing in Education (AACE), Savannah, GA, United States, 2016). Retrieved June 4, 2019 from https://www.learntechlib.org/primary/p/172078/

Spector, J. M. (2019). Complexity, Inquiry Critical Thinking, and Technology: A Holistic and Developmental Approach. In Mind, Brain and Technology (pp. 17–25). (Springer, Cham, 2019). Jisc [WWW Document]. Accessed March 28, 2023. URL https://www.jisc.ac.uk/news/does-chatgpt-mean-the-end-of-the-essay-as-an-assessment-tool-10-jan2023

Spector, J., & Ma, S. (2019). Inquiry and critical thinking skills for the next generation: From artificial intelligence back to human intelligence. *Smart Learn. Environ.*, *2019*(6), 8.

Silviana, D., Musafik, M., & Sulistyanto, I. (2023). The effect of internet media usage toward learning interest through learning motivation as a moderator variable. *J. Pendidik. Bhs. Ingg. Profic.*, *2023*(5), 37.

Sun, X. (2021). 5G. (2021). Joint artificial intelligence technology in the innovation and reform of university English education. *Wireless Communications and Mobile Computing*, *2021*, 4892064.

Swartz, R., & Parks, S. (2004). infusing the teaching of critical and creative thinking into content instruction. California: The Critical Thinking Co.

Swartz, S., & McGuinness, C. (2004). *Developing and Assessing Thinking Skills Project Part 1*. National Center for Teaching Thinking.

Utami, B., Saputro, S., Ashadi, A., Masykuri, M., & Widoretno, S. (2017). Critical Thinking Skills Profile of High School Students in Learning Chemistry. *Int. J. Sci. Appl. Sci. Conf. Ser., 2017*(1), 124.

Wannapiroon, P. (2008). Development of a Problem-Based Learning Model to Develop Undergraduate Student's Critical Thinking Skills, Ph.D. dissertation, Dept. Curriculum, Instruction, and Educational Technology, Chulalongkorn Univ., Bangkok, Thailand.

Wang, P. (2019). On defining artificial intelligence. *Journal of Artificial General Intelligence, 10*(2), 1–37.

Wette, R. (2017). Using Mind Maps to Reveal and Develop Genre Knowledge in A Graduate Writing Course. *Journal of Second Language Writing, 38*, 58–71. https://www.mdpi.com/2071-1050/13/18/10424. DOI: 10.10 16/J.JSLW.2017.09.005Doi

Weng, J. C. (2023). *Putting Intellectual Robots to Work: Implementing Generative AI Tools in Project Management*. NYU SPS Applied Analytics Laboratory.

Wongkam, N. Pinsuwan, D. & Chaowakeeratipong, N. (February 2014). The Effects of Using the 7Es Learning Management Approach Emphasizing Critical Thinking Activities in the Topic of Homeostasis on Learning Achievement and Critical Thinking Ability of Mathayom Suksa IV Students at Piriyalai Changwat Phara School in Phare Province. Available: http://www.stou.ac.th/thai/grad_stdy/Masters/%E0%B8%9D%E0%B8%AA%E0%B8%AA/research/2nd/FullPaper/SS/Oral/OSS%

Yang, Y., Newby, T., & Bill, R. (2005). Using Socratic questioning to promote critical thinking skills through asynchronous discussion forums in distance learning environments. *American Journal of Distance Education, 19*(3), 163–181.

Yu, P. Mulli, J. Syed, Z.A.S. Umme, L. (2023). Facilitating Global Collaboration and Knowledge Sharing in Higher Education with Generative AI; IGI Global: Hershey, PA, USA, 2023; pp. 1–356.

Zajacova, A., Lynch, S. M., & Espenshade, T. (2005). Self-efficacy, stress, and academic success in college. *Research in Higher Education, 2005*(46), 677–706.

Zhang, M. Xie (2018). Artificial Intelligence's Digestion and Reconstruction for Humanistic Feelings. In 2018 International Seminar on Education Research and Social Science (ISERSS 2018) (Atlantis Press, Paris, 2018).

Zubaidah, S., Fuad, N., Mahanal, S., & Suarsini, E. (2017). Improving Creative Thinking Skills of Students Through Differentiated Science Inquiry Integrated with Mind Map. *Journal of Turkish Science Education*, *14*(4), 77–91. DOI: 10.12973/tused.10214a

Compilation of References

Abbas, S. Umangap, & W. Amin, A (2023). Collaborative group investigation and self-efficacy on pre-service science teachers' critical thinking skills. J. Pendidik. Sains Indonesia. 2023, pp. 11, 1–11.

Abdulrahaman, M. D., Faruk, N., Oloyede, A. A., Surajudeen-Bakinde, N. T., Olawoyin, L. A., Mejabi, O. V., Imam-Fulani, Y. O., Fahm, A. O., & Azeez, A. L. (2020). Multimedia tools in the teaching and learning processes: A systematic review [Review of Multimedia tools in the teaching and learning processes: A systematic review]. Heliyon, 6(11). Elsevier BV. https://doi.org/DOI: 10.1016/j.heliyon.2020.e05312

Adel, A. (2024). The convergence of intelligent tutoring, robotics, and IoT in smart education for the transition from industry 4.0 to 5.0. *Smart Cities*, *7*(1), 325–369.

Adeshina, A. E. (2024). From Theory to Practice: A Framework for Inclusive Technology Integration in Education. *International Journal of Instructional Technology and Educational Studies*, *5*(1), 1–6.

Adeshola, I., & Adepoju, A. P. (2023). The opportunities and challenges of ChatGPT in education. *Interactive Learning Environments*. Advance online publication. DOI: 10.1080/10494820.2023.2253858;WEBSITE:WEBSITE:TFOPB;PAGE-GROUP:STRING:PUBLICATION

Adiguzel, T., Kaya, M., & Cansu, F. (2023). Revolutionizing education with AI: Exploring the transformative potential of ChatGPT. *Contemporary Educational Technology*, *15*(3), 1–13. DOI: 10.30935/cedtech/13152

Aheleroff, S., Huang, H., Xu, X., & Zhong, R. Y. (2022). Toward sustainability and resilience with Industry 4.0 and Industry 5.0. *Frontiers in Manufacturing Technology*, *2*, 951643.

Ahmad, M., Ho, W. Y., Goyes Robalino, A. P., Maqsood, M., Ahmad, M., Ho, W. Y., Goyes Robalino, A. P., & Maqsood, M. (2025). Theoretical Implications of Generative AI for Content Generation in Geoinformatics Training. In A. Anna A. (Ed.), *Integration Strategies of Generative AI in Higher Education* (pp. 101–130). IGI Global Scientific Publishing. https://doi.org/DOI: 10.4018/979-8-3693-5518-3.CH005

Ajani, O. A., Gamede, B. T., & Bansal, R. (2024). Challenges and Opportunities of Integrating Industry 5.0 and Emerging Technologies in Higher Education for Enhancing Employability Skills. *Industry 5.0 and Emerging Technologies: Transformation Through. Technology and Innovation*, •••, 217–230.

Alam, A. (2022). Employing adaptive learning and intelligent tutoring robots for virtual classrooms and smart campuses: Reforming education in the age of artificial intelligence *Advanced computing and intelligent technologies* [Springer.]. *Proceedings of ICACIT, 2022*, 395–406.

Alamäki, A., Khan, U. A., Kauttonen, J., & Schlögl, S. (2024). An Experiment of AI-Based Assessment: Perspectives of Learning Preferences, Benefits, Intention, Technology Affinity, and Trust. *Education Sciences 2024, Vol. 14, Page 1386, 14*(12), 1386. https://doi.org/DOI: 10.3390/EDUCSCI14121386

Alamri, H. A., Watson, S., & Watson, W. (2021). Learning technology models that support personalization within blended learning environments in higher education. *TechTrends*, *65*(1), 62–78.

Alavi, S. M., & Bordbar, S. (2018). Differential item functioning analysis of high-stakes test in terms of gender: A Rasch model approach. *MOJES: Malaysian Online Journal of Educational Sciences*, *5*(1), 10–24.

Albadarin, Y., Saqr, · Mohammed, Pope, N., & Tukiainen, M. (2024). A systematic literature review of empirical research on ChatGPT in education. *Discover Education 2024 3:1, 3*(1), 1–26. https://doi.org/DOI: 10.1007/S44217-024-00138-2

Al-Haddad, S., Chick, N., & Safi, F. (2024). Teaching Statistics: A Technology-Enhanced Supportive Instruction (TSI) Model During the Covid-19 Pandemic and Beyond. *Journal of Statistics and Data Science Education: An Official Journal of the of the American Statistical Association*, *32*(2), 129. DOI: 10.1080/26939169.2024.2315939

Al-Hattami, H. (2023). Understanding perceptions of academics toward technology acceptance in accounting education. *Heliyon*, *9*(1). Advance online publication. DOI: 10.1016/j.heliyon.2023.e13141

Ali, A. (2006). Role and importance of the simulator instructor (Master's thesis). World Maritime University, Malmö, Sweden.

Ali, M. H., Kainat, M., Maqsood, M., Fernandez, S. F., Ali, S., & Ahmad, M. (2024). Chatbots in Academic Literacy Exploring AI in Education. In *Enhancing Higher Education and Research With OpenAI Models* (pp. 37–59). IGI Global.

Aljawarneh, N. M. (2024). The Mediating Role of Organization Agility between Business Intelligence & Innovative Performance. *Journal of Statistics Applications & Probability*, *13*(3), 929–938. DOI: 10.18576/jsap/130307

Allen, K., Donoghue, G. M., Pahlevansharif, S., Jimerson, S. R., & Hattie, J. (2020). Assessment practices in Philippine higher STEAM education. *Journal of University Teaching & Learning Practice*, *17*(5). Advance online publication. DOI: 10.53761/1.17.5.18

Allui, A., & Sahni, J. (2016). Strategic human resource management in higher education institutions: Empirical evidence from Saudi. *Procedia: Social and Behavioral Sciences*, *235*, 361–371. DOI: 10.1016/j.sbspro.2016.11.044

Almumen, H. A. (2020). Universal Design for Learning (UDL) Across Cultures: The Application of UDL in Kuwaiti Inclusive Classrooms. *SAGE Open*, *10*(4). Advance online publication. DOI: 10.1177/2158244020969674

Alsadoon, E., Alkhawajah, A., & Suhaim, A. B. (2022). Effects of a gamified learning environment on students' achievement, motivations, and satisfaction. *Heliyon*, *8*(8). Advance online publication. DOI: 10.1016/j.heliyon.2022.e10249 PMID: 36042749

Alvarez, A. I., & Conati, C. (2020). Towards using artificial intelligence for adaptive learning in online learning environments. *Journal of Educational Technology & Society*, *23*(4), 33–45.

Alwehaibi, H. (2012). Novel program to promote critical thinking among higher education students: Empirical study from Saudi Arabia. *Asian Social Science*, *2012*(8), 193–204.

Andersen, E. B. (1977). Sufficient statistics and latent trait models. *Psychometrika*, *42*, 69–81.

Andersen, M. K. (2017). Human capital analytics: The winding road. *Journal of Organizational Effectiveness: People and Performance*, *4*(2), 133–136. DOI: 10.1108/JOEPP-03-2017-0024

Andrich, D., & Hagquist, C. (2015). Real and Artificial Differential Item Functioning in Polytomous Items. *SAGE Journals, 75*(2), 185–205. https://doi.org.uplib.idm.oclc.org/10.1177/0013164414534258

Andrich, A. (2004). Controversy and the Rasch Model: A Characteristic of Incompatible Paradigms? *Medical Care*, *42*(1), 1–7. PMID: 14707751

Andrich, D. (2011). *Rasch models for measurement*. Sage.

Angeioplastis, A., Papaioannou, N., Tsimpiris, A., Kamilali, A., & Varsamis, D. (2024). Predicting student specializations: a Machine Learning Approach based on Academic Performance.

Anggraini, I. (2016). Motivasi Belajar dan Faktor-Faktor yang Berpengaruh: Sebuah Kajian pada Interaksi Pembelajaran Mahasiswa. *Premiere Educandum: Jurnal Pendidikan Dasar Dan Pembelajaran*, *1*(02). Advance online publication. DOI: 10.25273/pe.v1i02.39

Ansar, M., & George, G. (2022). Gamification in education and its impact on student motivation—a critical review. *Emerging IT/ICT and AI Technologies Affecting Society*, 161-170.

Anselmi, P., Colledani, D., & Robusto, E. (2019). A Comparison of Classical and Modern Measures of Internal Consistency. *Frontiers in Psychology*, *10*(2714), 1–10. DOI: 10.3389/fpsyg.2019.02714 PMID: 31866905

Anumanthan, S., & Hashim, H. (2022). Improving the Learning of Regular Verbs through TikTok among Primary School ESL Pupils. *Creative Education*, *13*(3), 896. DOI: 10.4236/ce.2022.133059

Aral, S., Brynjolfsson, E., & Wu, L. (2012). Three-way com plementarities: Performance pay, human resource analytics, and information technology. *Management Science*, *58*(5), 913–931. DOI: 10.1287/mnsc.1110.1460

Armstrong, M. (2006). *A handbook of human resource management practice*. Kogan Page Publishers.

Armstrong, M. (2009). *Armstrong's handbook of performance management: An evidence-based guide to delivering high performance*. Kogan Page Publishers.

Arrieta, A. B., Díaz-Rodríguez, N., Ser, J. D., Bennetot, A., Tabik, S., Barbado, A., & Herrera, F. (2020). Explainable artificial intelligence (XAI): Concepts, taxonomies, opportunities, and challenges toward responsible AI. *Information Fusion*, *58*, 82–115. DOI: 10.1016/j.inffus.2019.12.012

Arsal, Z. (2017). The Impact of Inquiry-Based Learning on The Critical Thinking Dispositions of Pre-Service Science Teachers. *International Journal of Science Education*, *39*(10), 1326–1338. DOI: 10.1080/09500693.2017.1329564

Aryadoust, V., Ng, L. Y., & Sayama, H. (2021). A comprehensive review of Rasch measurement in language assessment: Recommendations and guidelines for research. *Language Testing*, *38*(1), 6–40.

Asoodar, M., Janesarvatan, F., Yu, H., & de Jong, N. (2024). Theoretical foundations and implications of augmented reality, virtual reality, and mixed reality for immersive learning in health professions education. *Advances in Simulation (London, England)*, *9*(1), 36. PMID: 39252139

Assefa, E. A., & ZENEBE, C. K. (2024). Fostering inclusive excellence: Strategies for effective diversity management in schools. *International Journal of Research in Education Humanities and Commerce*, *5*(2), 189. DOI: 10.37602/ijrehc.2024.5216

Association of College & Research Libraries. (2023). Framework for information literacy for higher education. http://www.ala.org/acrl/ standards/framework (accessed October 2023).

Atma, B. A., Azahra, F. F., Mustadi, A., & Adina, C. A. (2021). Teaching style, learning motivation, and learning achievement: Do they have significant and positive relationships? *J. Prima Edukasia*, *2021*(9), 23–31.

Attaran, M., Stark, J., & Stotler, D. (2018). Opportunities and challenges for big data analytics in US higher education: A conceptual model for implementation. *Industry and Higher Education*, *32*(3), 169–182. DOI: 10.1177/0950422218770937

Autsadee, Y., Jeevan, J., Othman, M. R. B., & Salleh, N. H. B. M. (2025). Maritime Society 5.0: A global transition on human economy and civilisation for maritime sustainability. *Australian Journal of Maritime and Ocean Affairs*, *17*(1), 1–26. DOI: 10.1080/18366503.2023.2287872

AYDIN YILDIZ, T. (2023). The Impact of ChatGPT on Language Learners' Motivation. *Journal of Teacher Education and Lifelong Learning*, *5*(2). Advance online publication. DOI: 10.51535/tell.1314355

Babcock, B., & Hodge, K. J. (2020). Rasch Versus Classical Equating in the Context of Small Sample Sizes. *Educational and Psychological Measurement*, *80*(3), 499–521. DOI: 10.1177/0013164419878483 PMID: 32425217

Bahous, R., Bacha, N., & Nabhani, M. (2011). Motivating Students in the EFL Classroom: A Case Study of Perspectives. *English Language Teaching*, *4*(3), 33. DOI: 10.5539/elt.v4n3p33

Baicker, K., Cutler, D., & Song, Z. (2010). Workplace wellness programs can generate savings. *Health Affairs*, *29*(2), 304–311. DOI: 10.1377/hlthaff.2009.0626

Baker, L., Phelan, S., Woods, N. N., Boyd, V., Rowland, P., & Ng, S. (2021). Re-envisioning paradigms of education: Towards awareness, alignment, and pluralism. *Advances in Health Sciences Education : Theory and Practice*, *26*(3), 1045. DOI: 10.1007/s10459-021-10036-z

Baker, R. S. (2016). Staying in control: Automated education with learning management systems and artificial intelligence. *Journal of Educational Data Mining*, *8*(1), 12–25.

Baker, R. S., & Inventado, P. S. (2014). Educational data mining and learning analytics. In Larusson, J. A., & White, B. (Eds.), *Learning analytics: From research to practice* (pp. 61–75). Springer., DOI: 10.1007/978-1-4614-3305-7_3

Balalle, H., & Pannilage, S. (2025). Reassessing academic integrity in the age of AI: A systematic literature review on AI and academic integrity. *Social Sciences & Humanities Open*, *11*, 101299. DOI: 10.1016/j.ssaho.2025.101299

Baldauf, M., & Procee, S. (2014). Augmented reality in ships bridge operation. *Isis*, *2014*, 170–178.

Balyasin, & Gebremerkel. (2020). Interaction between general management, human resource department and other academic departments (pp. 17–19).

Bansal, G., Mitchell, A., & Li, D. A. (2024). Panel Report on Higher Education in the Age of AI from the Perspective of Academic Leaders in the Midwest U.S. *Communications of the Association for Information Systems*, *2024*(54), 360–375.

Barney, J. B., & Arikan, A. M. (2005). The resource-based view: origins and implications. *The Blackwell handbook of strategic management*, 123-182, https://doi.org/DOI: 10.1111/b.9780631218616.2006.00006.x

Barocas, S., Guo, A., Kamar, E., Krones, J., Morris, M. R., Vaughan, J. W., Wadsworth, W. D., & Wallach, H. (2021). Designing Disaggregated Evaluations of AI Systems: Choices, Considerations, and Tradeoffs. *AIES 2021 - Proceedings of the 2021 AAAI/ACM Conference on AI, Ethics, and Society*, 368–378. https://doi.org/DOI: 10.1145/3461702.3462610;CTYPE:STRING:BOOK

Barra, W. N., Wilujeng, I., & Kuswanto, H. (2019). The Effect of Inductive Learning Model Assisted Mindmap Mindjet MindManager towards Critical Thinking Skills of Students. *Journal of Physics: Conference Series*, *1233*(1). Advance online publication. DOI: 10.1088/1742- 6596/1233/1/012046

Barteit, S., Lanfermann, L., Bärnighausen, T., Neuhann, F., & Beiersmann, C. (2021). Augmented, mixed, and virtual reality-based head-mounted devices for medical education: Systematic review. *JMIR Serious Games*, *9*(3), e29080. PMID: 34255668

Barty, G., Boyer, N., Chrysikos, A., Griffith, M. L., House, K., Laughlin, T., Ossiannilsson, E., Ward, R., & Zanville, H. A. (2024). *Developing a More Granular and Equitable Approach to the Learner-Earner Journey. The Role of Badging*. Micro-Credentials and Twenty-first Century Skills Within Higher Education to Enable Future Workforce Development. In Zukunft der Hochschulbildung., DOI: 10.1007/978-3-658-42948-5_23

Basak, S. K. (2017). A framework on the factors affecting to implement maritime education and training system in educational institutions: A review of the literature. *Procedia Engineering*, *194*, 345–350.

Bassi, L. (2011). Raging debates in HR analytics. *People and Strategy*, *34*(2), 14–18.

Bayram, D., Kurt, G., & Atay, D. (2019). The implementation of webquest-supported critical thinking instruction in pre-service English teacher education: The Turkish context. *Particip. Educ. Res.*, *6*, 144–157.

Bayram, Z., Oskay, Ö. Ö., Erdem, E., Özgür, S. D., & Şen, Ş. (2013). Effect of Inquiry-based Learning Method on Students' Motivation. *Procedia: Social and Behavioral Sciences*, *106*, 988–996. DOI: 10.1016/J.SBSPRO.2013.12.112

Belbase, S., Mainali, B. R., Kasemsukpipat, W., Tairab, H., Gochoo, M., & Jarrah, A. (2022). At the dawn of science, technology, engineering, arts, and mathematics (STEAM) education: Prospects, priorities, processes, and problems. *International Journal of Mathematical Education in Science and Technology*, *53*(11), 2919–2955.

Bendickson, J. S., Chandler, T. D., James, B. E., & Taylor, E. C. (2023). Sourcing human capital for organizational effectiveness: Sourcing strategy, determinants, and alignment. *International Journal of Human Resource Management*, *34*(5), 987–1014. zDOI: 10.1080/09585192.2021.2016888

Benítez, C., & Canales, E. (2013). Critical thinking as a resilience factor in an engineering program. *Creative Education*, *2013*(04), 611–613.

Bennett, R. E. (2023). Toward a Theory of Socioculturally Responsive Assessment. *Educational Assessment*, *28*(2), 83. DOI: 10.1080/10627197.2023.2202312

Bichsel, J. (2012). *Analytics in higher education: Benefits, barriers, progress, and recommendations*. EDUCAUSE Center for Applied Research. https://www.educause.edu/ecar/research-publications/analytics-higher-education-benefits-barriers-progress-and-recommendations

Biggs, J. (1996). Enhancing teaching through constructive alignment. *Higher Education*, *32*(3), 347–364. DOI: 10.1007/BF00138871/METRICS

Binhammad, M. H. Y., Othman, A., Abuljadayel, L., Mheiri, H. A., Alkaabi, M., & Almarri, M. (2024). Investigating How Generative AI Can Create Personalized Learning Materials Tailored to Individual Student Needs. *Creative Education*, *15*(7), 1499. DOI: 10.4236/ce.2024.157091

Blikstein, P., & Worsley, M. (2016). Multimodal learning analytics and education data mining: Using computational technologies to measure complex learning tasks. *Journal of Learning Analytics*, *3*(2), 220–238. DOI: 10.18608/jla.2016.32.11

Bloom, B. S., Englehart, M. D., Furst, E. J., Hill, W. H., & Krathwohl, D. R. (1956). Taxonomy of Educational Objectives, Handbook I: The Cognitive Domain. New York.

Blundell, C. (2021). Teacher use of digital technologies for school-based assessment: a scoping review [Review of Teacher use of digital technologies for school-based assessment: a scoping review]. Assessment in Education Principles Policy and Practice, 28(3), 279. Routledge. https://doi.org/DOI: 10.1080/0969594x.2021.1929828

Bogusławski, K., Gil, M., Nasur, J., & Wróbel, K. (2022). Implications of autonomous shipping for maritime education and training: The cadet's perspective. *Maritime Economics & Logistics*, *24*(2), 327–343. DOI: 10.1057/s41278-022-00217-x

Boles, M., Pelletier, B., & Lynch, W. (2004). The relationship between health risks and work productivity. *Journal of Occupational and Environmental Medicine*, *46*(7), 737–745. DOI: 10.1097/01.jom.0000131830.45744.97

Bond, T. G., & Fox, C. M. (2015). *Applying the Rasch Model: Fundamental measurement in the human sciences* (3rd ed.). Routledge.

Bonefont, V., Carbino, B., & Zakerzadeh, R. (2022). Addressing Test Anxiety Using Game-Based Assessment. *Biomedical Engineering Education*, *2*(2), 319. DOI: 10.1007/s43683-022-00082-3 PMID: 35856077

Boone, J. W. (2016). Rasch Analysis for Instrument Development: Why, When, and How? *CBE Life Sciences Education*, *15*(4), 1–7. DOI: 10.1187/cbe.1604-0148 PMID: 27856555

Boone, J. W., & Rogan, J. (2005). Rigour in quantitative analysis: The promise of Rasch analysis techniques, *African Journal of Research in Mathematics. Science and Technology Education*, *9*(1), 25–38. DOI: 10.1080/10288457.2005.10740574

Boone, J. W., Staver, J. R., & Yale, M. S. (2014). *Rasch analysis in the human Sciences*. Springer.

Boudreau, J. (2017), 'Hr must make people analytics more user-friendly', Harvard Business Review June, 1–5. https:// hbr.org/2017/06/hr-must-make-people-analytics -more- user-friendly

Boudreau, J. W. (2012). Decision Logic in Evidence-Based Management: Can Logical Models From Other Disciplines Improve Evidence-Based Human-Resource Decisions?.

Bourke, R. (2020). Assessment to Incite and Reconceptualize Learning. In Oxford Research Encyclopedia of Education. https://doi.org/DOI: 10.1093/acrefore/9780190264093.013.1213

Boutros, M.-B. F., Jawad, D., & Ghanimeh, S. (2023). The Implementation of Enterprise Resource Planning Systems for Roads and Infrastructure Construction Companies in Developing Countries. International Conference on Civil Infrastructure and Construction/Proceedings of the ... International Conference on Civil Infrastructure and Construction, 269. https://doi.org/DOI: 10.29117/cic.2023.0038

Bozkurt, A. A.-R. (2021, January 15). "Artificial Intelligence and Reflections from Educational Landscape: A Review of AI Studies in Half a Century.

Branig, M.; Engel, C.; Schmalfus-Schwarz, J.; Muller, E.F.;Weber, G. (2022). Where Are We with Inclusive Digital Further Education? Accessibility Through Digitalization. Lect. Notes Netw. Syst. 2022, 389 LNNS, 21–33. [CrossRef]

Brennan, R. L. (2010). Generalizability Theory and Classical Test Theory. *Applied Measurement in Education*, *24*(1), 1–21. DOI: 10.1080/08957347.2011.532417

Bryant, L., & Hemsley, B. (2024). Augmented reality: A view to future visual supports for people with disability. *Disability and Rehabilitation. Assistive Technology*, *19*(3), 800–813. PMID: 36149835

Bryson, J. M., Ackermann, F., & Eden, C. (2007). Putting the resource-based view of strategy and distinctive competencies to work in public organizations. *Public Administration Review*, *67*(4), 702–717. DOI: 10.1111/j.1540-6210.2007.00754.x

Bukoye, T., & Oyelere, M. (2019). "Assessing the Value of Capstone Unit in Developing Critical Thinking Skills in MSc Students." In BAM 2019 Conference, Aston University, Birmingham, UK. British Academy of Management.

Buledi, M. H., & Badariah, T. A. T. (2024). Exploring Digital Technology Usage among English Language Instructors at a Saudi Higher Education Institution and Validating a Hierarchical Structure of Usage Based on the SAMR Model. *IIUM Journal of Educational Studies*, *12*(1), 90–111.

Bunmi, E. E., Esegbona-Isikeh, O. M., Oriakhi, V. N., Akiotu, C. A., Emakporuena, D., & Matthew, U. O. (2024). STEM application in education: Implication of STEM computational paradigm on employment prospects. *HAFED POLY Journal of Science. Management and Technology*, *6*(1), 131–148.

Bussin, Mark. *Remuneration and talent management*. eBook Partnership, 2014.

Buzan, T. (2006). The Buzan Study Skills Handbook. BBC Active. https://books.google. co. id/books/about/The_Buzan_Study_Skills_Handbook.html?id=719lVhWXTvAC&redir_ esc=y

Buzan, T. (2002a). *How to Mind Map: The Ultimate Thinking Tool That Will Change Your Life*. Thorson.

Buzan, T. (2002b). *Mind Maps*. Thorson.

Bybee, R. (February 2014). [Online]. The BSCS 5E Instructional Model: Origins, Effectiveness, and Applications. Available: http://bscs.org/sites/default/files/_legacy/BSCS_5E_Instructional_Model Executive_Summary_0.pdf

Cai, H., Lin, Z., Zhan, Y., Li, Y., Gong, R., Zhou, Y., Zhang, J., & Wang, B. (2024). SciAssess: Benchmarking LLM proficiency in scientific literature analysis. arXiv. https://arxiv.org/abs/2403.01976

Calma, A., & Davies, M. (2021). Critical Thinking in Business Education: Current Outlook and Future Prospects. *Studies in Higher Education*, *46*(11), 2279–2295. DOI: 10.1080/03075079.2020.1716324

Calvet Liñán, L., & Juan Pérez, A. (2015). Educational data mining and learning analytics: Differences, similarities, and their relationship to open education. *International Journal of Educational Technology in Higher Education*, *12*(3), 98–112. DOI: 10.7238/rusc.v12i3.2515

Cameron, K. (1978). Measuring organizational effectiveness in institutions of higher education. *Administrative science quarterly*, 604-632.2

Cameron, K. S. (1986). Effectiveness as paradox: Consensus and conflict in conceptions of organizational effectiveness. *Management Science*, *32*(5), 539–553. DOI: 10.1287/mnsc.32.5.539

Cameron, K. S., & Quinn, R. E. (2011). *Diagnosing and changing organizational culture: Based on the competing values framework* (3rd ed.). John Wiley & Sons.

Cano, Y. M., Venuti, F., & Cellan-Jones, R. H. (2014). Stephen Hawking warns that artificial intelligence could end humanity. BBC. News. 2, 2014 (2014) M.T.H. Chi, R. Glaser, E. Rees, in Advances in the Psychology of Human Intelligence, ed. by R. S. Sternberg. Expertise in problem-solving (Erlbaum)

Cappelli, P., & Keller, J. R. (2014). Talent management: Conceptual approaches and practical challenges. *Annual Review of Organizational Psychology and Organizational Behavior, 1*(1), 305–331. DOI: 10.1146/annurev-orgpsych-031413-091314

Carayannis, E. G., Kostis, P. C., Kafka, K. I., & Valvi, T. (2024). *Toward Industry 6.0 and Techno-Centric vs Human-Centric Smart Balancing: The Journey from Industry and Society 4.0 toward Industry and Society 5.0 and Beyond Sustainable Economic Development*. Routledge.

Carayannis, E. G., & Morawska, J. (2023). *University and education 5.0 for emerging trends, policies and practices in the concept of industry 5.0 and society 5.0 Industry 5.0: Creative and Innovative Organizations*. Springer.

Carayannis, E. G., & Morawska-Jancelewicz, J. (2022). The futures of Europe: Society 5.0 and Industry 5.0 as driving forces of future universities. *Journal of the Knowledge Economy, 13*(4), 3445–3471. DOI: 10.1007/s13132-021-00854-2 PMID: 40477679

Carbonell, K. B., Dailey-Hebert, A., & Gijselaers, W. H. (2013). Unleashing the creative potential of faculty to create hybrid courses: A framework for business analytics in higher education. *Research in Learning Technology, 21*(1), 1–17. DOI: 10.3402/rlt.v21.21399

Caronni, A., Ramella, M., Arcuri, P., Salatino, C., Pigini, L., Saruggia, M., Folini, C., Scarano, S., & Converti, R. M. (2023). The Rasch Analysis Shows Poor Construct Validity and Low Reliability of the Quebec User Evaluation of Satisfaction with Assistive Technology 2.0 (QUEST 2.0) Questionnaire. *International Journal of Environmental Research and Public Health, 20*(1036), 1–16. DOI: 10.3390/ijerph20021036 PMID: 36673791

Carpenter, C. D., Ray, M. S., & Bloom, L. A. (1995). Portfolio assessment: Opportunities and challenges. *Intervention in School and Clinic, 31*(1), 34–41.

Castañeda, L., Marín, V. I., & Villar-Onrubia, D. (2024). Relational topologies in the learning activity spaces: Operationalising a sociomaterial approach. *Educational Technology Research and Development, 72*(5), 2793–2815.

Catteeuw, F., Flynn, E., & Vonderhorst, J. (2007). Employee engagement: Boosting productivity in turbulent times. *Organization Development Journal, 25*(2).

CEALLAIGH, T. Ó., & Connolly, C. (2024). Navigating transformative assessment and feedback in teacher education: Unveiling challenges and innovative practices. *European Journal of Teacher Education*, *47*(2), 197. DOI: 10.1080/02619768.2024.2352816

Chahar, B., Jain, S. R., & Hatwal, V. (2021). Mediating role of employee motivation for training, commitment, retention, and performance in higher education institutions. *Problems and Perspectives in Management*, *19*(3), 95. DOI: 10.21511/ppm.19(3).2021.09

Chang, C. Y., Yang, C. L., Jen, H. J., Ogata, H., & Hwang, G. H. (2024). Facilitating nursing and health education by incorporating ChatGPT into learning designs. *Journal of Educational Technology & Society*, *27*(1). Advance online publication. DOI: 10.30191/ETS.202401_27(1).TP02

Chang, S. L., & Kabilan, M. K. (2022). Using social media as e-Portfolios to support learning in higher education: A literature analysis. *Journal of Computing in Higher Education*, *36*(1), 1. DOI: 10.1007/s12528-022-09344-z

Chaturvedi, V. (2016). Talent analytics as an indispensable tool and an emerging facet of HR for organization building. *FIIB Business Review*, *5*(3), 13–20. DOI: 10.1177/2455265820160302

Chen, L. (2017). Understanding Critical Thinking in Chinese Sociocultural Contexts: A Case Study in A Chinese College. Thinking Skills and Creativity, pp. 24, 140–151. https://doi. org/DOI: 10.1016/J.TSC.2017.02.015

Chen, L.; Chen, P.; Lin, Z.(2020). Artificial intelligence in education: A review. IEEE Access 2020, 8, 75264–75278.

Chen, G., Xu, B., Lu, M., & Chen, N. S. (2018). Exploring blockchain technology and its potential applications for education. *Smart Learning Environments*, *5*(1), 1–10. DOI: 10.1186/s40561-018-0070-8

Chen, S. H., Wang, H. H., & Yang, K. J. (2009). Establishment and application of performance measure indicators for universities. *The TQM Journal*, *21*(3), 220–235. DOI: 10.1108/17542730910953004

Chen, Z., & Singh, C. (2025). Opportunities and Challenges in Harnessing Digital Technology for Effective Teaching and Learning. *Trends in Higher Education*, *4*(1), 6. DOI: 10.3390/higheredu4010006

Chimero, F. (2015). *The shape of design*.

Chinta, S. V., Wang, Z., Yin, Z., Hoang, N. N. M., Gonzalez, M., Quy, T. L., & Zhang, W. (2024). FairAIED: Navigating Fairness, Bias, and Ethics in Educational AI Applications. arXiv (Cornell University). https://doi.org//arxiv.2407.18745DOI: 10.48550

Chiu, T. K. F., Xia, Q., Zhou, X., Chai, C. S., & Cheng, M. (2023). Systematic literature review on opportunities, challenges, and future research recommendations of artificial intelligence in education. In *Computers and Education* (Vol. 4). Artificial Intelligence., DOI: 10.1016/j.caeai.2022.100118

Chiziwa, W., & Kunkwenzu, E. D. (2021). Investigating Teacher Assessment Practices in the Teaching of Social Studies in Malawian Primary Schools. *Open Journal of Social Sciences*, *9*(7), 480. DOI: 10.4236/jss.2021.97035

Choudhary, K. (2024). An Approach to Enhancing Continuous Evaluation through Self-Reflection among Students of the Foundation Program in Design Course. *Creative Education, 15*(6), 1003. DOI: 10.4236/ce.2024.156061

Christensen, C. M., & Eyring, H. J. (2011). *The innovative university: Changing the DNA of higher education from the inside out.* John Wiley & Sons.

Clow, D. (2012). The learning analytics cycle: Closing the loop effectively. *Proceedings of the 2nd International Conference on Learning Analytics & Knowledge (LAK'12)*, 134-138. https://doi.org/DOI: 10.1145/2330601.2330636

Clow, D. (2013). An overview of learning analytics. *Teaching in Higher Education*, *18*(6), 683–695. DOI: 10.1080/13562517.2013.827653

Combrinck, C. (2018). *The use of Rasch Measurement Theory to address measurements and analysis challenges in social science research.* [Doctoral Thesis]. University of Pretoria.

Combrinck, C. (2020). Is this a useful instrument? An Introduction to Rasch Measurement Models. In S. Kramer, S. Laher, A. Fynn, & H. H. Janse van Vuuren (Eds.), (pp. 1–48), *Online Readings in Research Methods.* Psychological Society of South Africa: Johannesburg. https://doi.org/DOI: 10.17605/OSF.I0/BNPFS

Combrinck, C. (2019). *Rasch unidimensional measurements models: Analysis data in RUMM2030 handout.* University of Pretoria, Centre for Evaluation and Assessment.

Combrinck, C. (2024). Not liking the Likert? A Rasch analysis of forced-choice format and usefulness in survey design. *SAGE Open*, *14*(4), 1–18. DOI: 10.1177/21582440241295501

Cossette-Lefebvre, H., & Maclure, J. (2022). AI's fairness problem: Understanding wrongful discrimination in the context of automated decision-making. *AI and Ethics*, *3*(4), 1255. DOI: 10.1007/s43681-022-00233-w

Costa, E. (2024). Industry 5.0 and SDG 9: A symbiotic dance towards sustainable transformation. *Sustainable Earth Reviews*, *7*(1), 4.

Cotten, A. (2007). *Seven steps of effective workforce planning*. IBM Centre for the Business of Government.

Cotton, D. R., Cotton, P. A., & Shipway, J. R. (2023). Chatting and cheating: Ensuring academic integrity in the era of ChatGPT. *Innovations in Education and Teaching International*, •••, 1–12. DOI: 10.1080/14703297.2023.2190148

Creed, C., Al-Kalbani, M., Theil, A., Sarcar, S., & Williams, I. (2023). Inclusive AR/VR: Accessibility barriers for immersive technologies. *Universal Access in the Information Society*, *23*(1), 59. DOI: 10.1007/s10209-023-00969-0

Cross, R., Opie, T., Pryor, G., & Rollag, K. (2018). Connect and adapt: How network development and transformation improve retention and engagement in employees' first five years. *Organizational Dynamics*, *47*(2), 115–123. DOI: 10.1016/j.orgdyn.2017.08.003

Cutumisu, M., Chin, D. B., & Schwartz, D. L. (2019). A digital game-based assessment of feedback-seeking behavior and its relation to academic achievement. *British Journal of Educational Technology*, *50*(6), 2977–3003. DOI: 10.1111/bjet.12832

Cwilewicz, R., & Tomczak, L. (2008). Improvement of ship operational safety as a result of the application of virtual reality engine room simulators. *WIT Transactions on Information and Communication Technologies*, *39*, 535–544.

Dahal, N., Luitel, B. C., Pant, B. P., & Rajbanshi, R. (2022). Enhancing Student-Teachers Assessment Skills: A Self-and Peer-Assessment Tool in Higher Education. *International Journal of Education and Practice*, *10*(4), 313. DOI: 10.18488/61.v10i4.3173

Dakakni, D., & Safa, N. (2023). Artificial intelligence in the L2 classroom: Implications and challenges on ethics and equity in higher education: A 21st century Pandora's box. *Computers and Education Artificial Intelligence*, *5*, 100179. DOI: 10.1016/j.caeai.2023.100179

Dakkaki, J., Drouri, S., Dhoum, S., Mayou, R., & Jabri, M. (2021). Evaluation Grids for Endodontics Preclinical Practical Activities. *Education Research International*, *1*. Advance online publication. DOI: 10.1155/2021/8829119

Damaševičius, R., & Sidekerskienė, T. (2024). Virtual worlds for learning in metaverse: A narrative review. *Sustainability, 16*(5), 2032.

Daniel, B. (2015). Big data and analytics in higher education: Opportunities and challenges. *British Journal of Educational Technology, 46*(5), 904–920. DOI: 10.1111/bjet.12230

Davenport, T. H., Harris, J. G., & Morison, R. (2010). *Analytics at work: Smarter decisions, better results*. Harvard Business Press.

David, L. T., & Hein, M. (2012). Student portfolio–A tool to achieve quality in training. *Bulletin of the Transilvania University of Braşov. Series VII: Social Sciences• Law*, 169-174.

Davidson, C. N. (2017). *The new education: How to revolutionize the university to prepare students for a world in flux*. Basic Books.

Davies, . (2015). *Higher education: Handbook of theory and research. A Model of Critical Thinking in Higher Education* (pp. 41–92). Springer.

Davis, M. H., & Ponnamperuma, G. G. (2005). Portfolio assessment. *Journal of Veterinary Medical Education, 32*(3), 279–284. PMID: 16261482

Dawson, S., Mirriahi, N., & Gašević, D. (2017). Improving student outcomes and analytics: A framework for university-wide implementation. *Proceedings of the Seventh International Learning Analytics & Knowledge Conference (LAK'17)*, 153-162.

De Bruecker, P., Van den Bergh, J., Beliën, J., & Demeulemeester, E. (2015). Workforce planning incorporating skills: State of the art. *European Journal of Operational Research, 243*(1), 1-16 https://doi.org/ rights and contentDOI: 10.1016/j.ejor.2014.10.038Get

De Villiers, C. (2024). The Impact of Society 5.0 on Curriculum Development in Higher Education. *Journal of Ethics in Higher Education*, (4), 1–25.

Den Hartog, D. N., Boselie, P., & Paauwe, J. (2004). Performance management: A model and research agenda. *Applied Psychology, 53*(4), 556–569. DOI: 10.1111/j.1464-0597.2004.00188.x

Dessler, G. (2004). *A framework for human resource management*. Pearson Education India.

Diaz, E., Brooks, G., & Johanson, G. (2021). Detecting Differential Item Functioning: Item Response Theory Methods Versus the Mantel-Haenszel Procedure. *International Journal of Assessment Tools in Education, 8*(2), 376–378.

Dieterle, E., Dede, C., & Walker, M. E. (2022). The cyclical ethical effects of using artificial intelligence in education. *AI & Society*, *39*(2), 633. DOI: 10.1007/s00146-022-01497-w

Dietz-Uhler, B., & Hurn, J. E. (2013). Using learning analytics to predict (and improve) student success: A faculty perspective. *Journal of Interactive Online Learning*, *12*(1), 17–26.

Dilger, A. (2009). The principle of hiring the best available academics. *International Journal of Educational Management*, *23*(6), 523–532. DOI: 10.1108/09513540910981041

Dillenbourg, P., Schneider, D., & Synteta, P. (2022). Virtual learning environments: Integrating AI tools for effective collaboration and learning. *AI and Education Journal*, *39*(3), 56–78.

DiPiro, J. T. (2011). A culture of hiring for excellence. *American Journal of Pharmaceutical Education*, *75*(5). Advance online publication. DOI: 10.5688/ajpe75597

Dogucu, M., Johnson, A. A., & Ott, M. Q. (2023). Framework for Accessible and Inclusive Teaching Materials for Statistics and Data Science Courses. *Journal of Statistics and Data Science Education: An Official Journal of the of the American Statistical Association*, *31*(2), 144. DOI: 10.1080/26939169.2023.2165988

Do, H., Bich, N., & Nguyen, M. H. (2023). 3How do constructivism learning environments generate better motivation and learning strategies? The Design Science Approach. *Heliyon*, *9*(12). Advance online publication. DOI: 10.1016/j.heliyon.2023.e22862

Dong, C. (2024). How to build an AI tutor using LLM and RAG. arXiv. https://arxiv.org/abs/2311.17696

Driessen, E. (2017). Do portfolios have a future? *Advances in Health Sciences Education: Theory and Practice*, *22*, 221–228. PMID: 27025510

Dwork, C., Hardt, M., Pitassi, T., Reingold, O., & Zemel, R. (2012). Fairness through awareness. *ITCS 2012 - Innovations in Theoretical Computer Science Conference*, 214–226. https://doi.org/DOI: 10.1145/2090236.2090255;JOURNAL:JOURNAL:ACMCONFERENCES;PAGEGROUP:STRING:PUBLICATION

Dwyer, C. P., Hogan, M. J., & Stewart, I. (2014). An integrated critical thinking framework for the 21st century. *Thinking Skills and Creativity*, *12*, 43–52.

Ebenbeck, N., & Gebhardt, M. (2022). Simulating computerized adaptive testing in special education based on inclusive progress monitoring data. *Frontiers in Education*, *7*(945733), 1–4. DOI: 10.3389/feduc.2022.945733

EDUCAUSE. (2023). Analytics maturity in higher education: Progress, gaps, and recommendations. https://library.educause.edu/resources/2023/2/analytics-maturity-2023

EDUCAUSE. (2024). *The future of AI in higher education*. EDUCAUSE AI Landscape Study. Retrieved from https://www.educause.edu/ecar/research-publications/2024/2024-educause-ai-landscape-study/the-future-of-ai-in-higher-education

El Mekkaoui, S., Benabbou, L., Caron, S., & Berrado, A. (2023). Deep learning-based ship speed prediction for intelligent maritime traffic management. *Journal of Marine Science and Engineering*, *11*(1), 1–18. DOI: 10.3390/jmse11010191

Elangovan, N., & Sundaravel, E. (2021). Method of preparing a document for survey instrument validation by experts. *MethodsX*, *8*, 101326. DOI: 10.1016/j.mex.2021.101326

Elbanna, S., & Armstrong, L. (2024). Exploring the integration of ChatGPT in education: Adapting for the future. *Management and Sustainability*, *3*(1). Advance online publication. DOI: 10.1108/MSAR-03-2023-0016

Elfman, L. (2023). Crafting Equitable Access and Engagement. *Women in Higher Education*, *32*(12), 6. DOI: 10.1002/whe.21345

Elhan, A., Kutlay, Ş., Küçükdeveci, A. A., Cotuk, C., Ozturk, G., Tesio, L., & Tennant, A. (2005). Psychometric properties of the Mini-Mental State Examination in patients with acquired brain injury in Turkey. *Journal of Rehabilitation Medicine*, *37*(5), 306–310. DOI: 10.1080/16501970510037573 PMID: 16203619

Ellinger, E., Mini, T., Gregory, R., & Widjaja, T. (2021). Facilitating Collective Action in Agentic IS Platforms: The Case of Decentralized Autonomous Organizations. *University of Miami Business School Research Paper*(3938489).

Elnegahy, S., Jin, H., & Kim, H. (2021). Fairness, Justice, and Language Assessment. *Language Assessment Quarterly*, *19*(1), 102. DOI: 10.1080/15434303.2021.1922412

Emad, G., & Roth, W. M. (2008). Contradictions in the practices of training for and assessment of competency: A case study from the maritime domain. *Education + Training*, *50*(3), 260–272. DOI: 10.1108/00400910810874026

Emda, A. (2018). Kedudukan motivasi belajar siswa dalam pembelajaran. *Lantanida J.*, *2018*(5), 172.

Ennis, R. H. (1989). Critical thinking and subject specificity: Clarification and needed research. *Educational Researcher, 18*, 4–10.

Ennis, R. H. (2018). Critical thinking across the curriculum: A vision. *Topoi, 37*(1), 165–184.

Ericsson, R. T., & Krampe, C. (1993). Tesch-Römer, The role of deliberate practice in the acquisition of expert performance. *Psychological Review, 100*(3), 363–406.

Esseme, A. C. B., Oladipupo, M. A., Ogechukwu, O. N., Andrew-Vitalis, N., Akpan, E. E., Oseni, V. E., & Matthew, U. O. (2025). Healthcare Applications of Augmented Reality (AR) and Virtual Reality (VR): Immersive Simulation in Medical-Clinical Education. In Mazhar Hussain, S., & Nawaz Hakro, A. (Eds.), *Creating Immersive Learning Experiences Through Virtual Reality (VR)* (pp. 201–238). IGI Global.

Estefan, M., Selbin, J. C., & MacDonald, S. (2023). From Inclusive to Equitable Pedagogy: How to Design Course Assignments and Learning Activities That Address Structural Inequalities. *Teaching Sociology, 51*(3), 262. DOI: 10.1177/0092055x231174515

Evans, T., & Jeong, I. (2023). Concept maps as assessment for learning in university mathematics. *Educational Studies in Mathematics, 113*(3), 475. DOI: 10.1007/s10649-023-10209-0

Ewing, M. T., Pitt, L. F., De Bussy, N. M., & Berthon, P. (2002). Employment branding in the knowledge economy. *International Journal of Advertising, 21*(1), 3–22. DOI: 10.1080/02650487.2002.11104914

Facione, P. (2011). Critical thinking: What it is and why it counts. *Insight Assessment, 1*(1), 1–23.

Fang, L. (2024). Exploring the impact of artificial intelligence-based assistants in modern education: The case of ChatGPT. *Applied and Computational Engineering, 35*(1). Advance online publication. DOI: 10.54254/2755-2721/35/20230379

Farhan, F., & Rofi'ulmuiz, M. (2021). Religiosity and emotional intelligence on Muslim student learning achievement. *Int. J. Eval. Res. Educ. IJERE, 2021*(10), 404.

Farrokhnia, M., Banihashem, S. K., Noroozi, O., & Wals, A. (2024). A SWOT analysis of ChatGPT: Implications for educational practice and research. *Innovations in Education and Teaching International, 61*(3). Advance online publication. DOI: 10.1080/14703297.2023.2195846

Ferguson, R., Brasher, A., Clow, D., Cooper, A., Hillaire, G., & Rienties, B. (2016). Learning analytics: Visions of the future. *Proceedings of the Sixth International Learning Analytics & Knowledge Conference (LAK'16)*, 520-525.

Feuerriegel, S., Hartmann, J., Janiesch, C., & Zschech, P. (2023). Generative AI. *Business & Information Systems Engineering, 66*(1), 111. DOI: 10.1007/s12599-023-00834-7

Few, S. (2006). *Information dashboard design: The effective visual communication of data*. O'Reilly Media.

Filho, R. L. C. S., Brito, K., & Adeodato, P. J. L. (2023). Leveraging Causal Reasoning in Educational Data Mining: An Analysis of Brazilian Secondary Education. *Applied Sciences (Basel, Switzerland), 13*(8), 5198. DOI: 10.3390/app13085198

Fink, A. (2019). *Conducting research literature reviews: From the internet to paper*. Sage publications.

Fischer, L., Rohm, T., Carstensen, C. H., & Gnambs, T. (2021). Linking of Rasch-Scaled Tests: Consequences of Limited Item Pools and Model Misfit. *Frontiers in Psychology, 12*(633896), 1–9. DOI: 10.3389/fpsyg.2021.633896 PMID: 34295279

Fisher, W. (1992). Reliability Statistics. *Rasch Measurement Transactions, 3*(6), 238.

Fitria, T. N. (2023). Artificial intelligence (AI) technology in OpenAI ChatGPT application: A review of ChatGPT in writing English essay. *ELT Forum: Journal of English Language Teaching, 12*(1). https://doi.org/DOI: 10.15294/elt.v12i1.64069

Fitria, T. N. (2024). Choosing Objective and Non-objective Test as Instrument for Assessment of EFL Student Learning Outcomes. *Globish: An English-Indonesian Journal for English. Education and Culture, 13*(1). Advance online publication. DOI: 10.31000/globish.v13i1.9601

Fitz-Enz, J., & John Mattox, I. I. (2014). *Predictive analytics for human resources*. John Wiley & Sons.

Flanagan, L. (n.d.). Understanding Warm Colors and Cool Colors: Color Examples and How to Use Color Palettes at Home. Retrieved from: https://www.thespruce.com/understanding-warm-and-cool-colors-1976480

Flanagan, S., & Morgan, J. J. (2021). Ensuring Access to Online Learning for All Students Through Universal Design for Learning. *Teaching Exceptional Children, 53*(6), 459. DOI: 10.1177/00400599211010174

Ford, J. K. (Ed.). (2014). *Improving training effectiveness in work organizations*. Psychology Press.

Foster, T. C., Moroney, W. F., Phillips, H. L., & Lilienthal, M. G. (2024). Human Factors in Simulation and Training: An Overview. *Human Factors in Simulation and Training*, 1-64.

Fuchs, K. (2023). Exploring the opportunities and challenges of NLP models in higher education: Is Chat GPT a blessing or a curse? *Frontiers in Education*, *8*(May), 1166682.

Fuming, X., & Jiliang, S. (2007). Research on job satisfaction of elementary and high school teachers and strategies to increase job satisfaction. *Chinese Education & Society*, *40*(5), 86–96. DOI: 10.2753/CED1061-1932400509

Gallo, A. (2015, October). Setting the record straight on switching jobs. *Harvard Business Review*, 34.

Gašević, D., Dawson, S., & Siemens, G. (2015). Let's not forget: Learning analytics are about learning. *TechTrends*, *59*(1), 64–71. DOI: 10.1007/s11528-014-0822-x

Gaur, B. (2020, July). HR4. 0: an analytics framework to redefine employee engagement in the fourth industrial revolution. In *2020 11th International Conference on Computing, Communication and Networking Technologies (ICCCNT)* (pp. 1-6). IEEE.

Gibbs, G. (2013). Reflections on the changing nature of educational development. *The International Journal for Academic Development*, *18*(1), 4–14. DOI: 10.1080/1360144X.2013.751691

Gill, S. S., Xu, M., Patros, P., Wu, H., Kaur, R., Kaur, K., Fuller, S., Singh, M., Arora, P., Parlikad, A. K., Stankovski, V., Abraham, A., Ghosh, S. K., Lutfiyya, H., Kanhere, S. S., Bahsoon, R., Rana, O., Dustdar, S., Sakellariou, R., & Buyya, R. (2024). Transformative effects of ChatGPT on modern education: Emerging Era of AI Chatbots. *Internet of Things and Cyber-Physical Systems*, *4*. Advance online publication. DOI: 10.1016/j.iotcps.2023.06.002

Giray, L., Silos, P. Y. D., Adornado, A., Buelo, R. J. V., Galas, E. M., Reyes-Chua, E., Santiago, C. S., & Ulanday, Ma. L. (2024). Use and Impact of Artificial Intelligence in Philippine Higher Education: Reflections from Instructors and Administrators. *Internet Reference Services Quarterly*, *28*(3), 315. DOI: 10.1080/10875301.2024.2352746

Gligorea, I., Cioca, M., Oancea, R., Gorski, A.-T., Gorski, H., & Tudorache, P. (2023). Adaptive Learning Using Artificial Intelligence in e-Learning: A Literature Review. *Education Sciences*, *13*(12), 1216.

Goel, A., Masurkar, S., & Pathade, G. R. (2024). An Overview of Digital Transformation and Environmental Sustainability: Threats, Opportunities, and Solutions. *Sustainability*, *16*(24), 11079.

Gombert, S., Fink, A., Giorgashvili, T., Jivet, I., Di Mitri, D., Yau, J., Frey, A., & Drachsler, H. (2024). From the Automated Assessment of Student Essay Content to Highly Informative Feedback: A Case Study. *International Journal of Artificial Intelligence in Education*. Advance online publication. DOI: 10.1007/s40593-023-00387-6

Gonzalez, M. A., & de Vicente, M. J. (2021). Generative AI in learning management systems: Opportunities and challenges. *AI and Learning Sciences Review*, *7*(1), 41–58.

Gouseti, A., James, F., Fallin, L., & Burden, K. (2024). The ethics of using AI in K-12 education: A systematic literature review. *Technology, Pedagogy and Education*, *1*. Advance online publication. DOI: 10.1080/1475939x.2024.2428601

Green, D. A., & Little, D. (2016). Family portrait: A profile of educational developers around the world. *The International Journal for Academic Development*, *21*(2), 135–150.

Greller, W., & Drachsler, H. (2012). Translating learning into numbers: A generic framework for learning analytics. *Journal of Educational Technology & Society*, *15*(3), 42–57.

Groenendijk, T., Kárpáti, A., & Haanstra, F. (2020). Self-assessment in art education through a visual rubric. *International Journal of Art & Design Education*, *39*(1), 153–175.

Gronseth, S. (2023). Strategically Inclusive E-Learning Design. *Journal of Technology-Integrated Lessons and Teaching*, *2*(1), 68. DOI: 10.13001/jtilt.v2i1.7673

Guest, D., & Clinton, M. (2007). *Human resource management and university performance*. Research and Development Series. Leadership Foundation for Higher Education.

Gumel, A. A., & Abdullahi, A. B., & O, U. M. (2019). *The Need for a Multimodal Means of Effective Digital Learning through Data Mining and Institutional Knowledge Repository: A Proposed System for Polytechnics in Northern Nigeria*. Paper presented at the Proceedings of the 2019 5th International Conference on Computer and Technology Applications.

Gunning, D., Stefik, M., Choi, J., Miller, T., Stumpf, S., & Yang, G. Z. (2019). XAI—Explainable artificial intelligence. *Science Robotics*, *4*(37). Advance online publication. DOI: 10.1126/SCIROBOTICS.AAY7120

Gupta, S., Ranjan, R., & Singh, S. N. (2024). *A Comprehensive Survey of Retrieval-Augmented Generation (RAG)*. Evolution, Current Landscape and Future Directions.

Gupta, S., Wilcocks, K., Matava, C., Wiegelmann, J., Kaustov, L., & Alam, F. (2023). Creating a Successful Virtual Reality–Based Medical Simulation Environment: Tutorial. *JMIR Medical Education*, *9*, e41090. PMID: 36787169

Gu u, B. M., & Popescu, N. (2024). Exploring Data Analysis Methods in Generative Models: From Fine-Tuning to RAG Implementation. In *Computers* (Vol. 13, Issue 12). Multidisciplinary Digital Publishing Institute (MDPI). https://doi.org/DOI: 10.3390/computers13120327

Hagel, P. (2014). Testing Rating scale Unidimensionality Using the Principal Component Analysis (PCA)/t-test Protocol with the Rasch Model: The Primacy of Theory over Statistics. *Open Journal of Statistics*, *4*, 456–459. DOI: 10.4236/ojs.2014.46044

Hagquist, C., & Andrich, D. (2017). Recent advances in analysis of differential item functioning in health research using the Rasch model. *Health and Quality of Life Outcomes*, *15*(181), 1–8. DOI: 10.1186/s12955-017-0755-0 PMID: 28927468

Halaweh, M. (2023). ChatGPT in education: Strategies for responsible implementation. Contemp. Educ. Technol. 2023, pp. 15, 421.

Halaweh, M. (2023). ChatGPT in education: Strategies for responsible implementation. *Contemporary Educational Technology*, *15*(2). Advance online publication. DOI: 10.30935/cedtech/13036

Haleem, A., Javaid, M., Vaishya, R., & Deshmukh, S. G. (2021). Areas of applications of Artificial Intelligence (AI) in maritime industry: A review. *Ocean Engineering*, *234*, 109276. DOI: 10.1016/j.oceaneng.2021.109276

Han, S., Wang, M., Zhang, J., Li, D., & Duan, J. (2024). A Review of Large Language Models: Fundamental Architectures, Key Technological Evolutions, Interdisciplinary Technologies Integration, Optimization and Compression Techniques, Applications, and Challenges. In *Electronics (Switzerland)* (Vol. 13, Issue 24). Multidisciplinary Digital Publishing Institute (MDPI). https://doi.org/DOI: 10.3390/electronics13245040

Hansen, W., & Salemi, M. (2012). Improving classroom discussion in economics courses. In Hoyt, G., & McGoldrick, K. (Eds.), *International handbook on teaching and learning economics* (pp. 68–78). Edward Elgar.

Hanzu-Pazara, R., Lupu-Dima, L., & Vasilache, S. (2008). The impact of the new learning models on the development of e-learning systems. *Informações Econômicas*, *12*(2), 34–39.

Harris, H. S., & Greer, M. (2020). Using Multimedia for Instructor Presence in Purposeful Pedagogy-Driven Online Technical Writing Courses. *Journal of Technical Writing and Communication*, *52*(1), 110. DOI: 10.1177/0047281620978360

Hashim, M. A., Che Ibrahim, C. K. I., Jaafar, N. A. L., Kordi, N. E., Haron, A. T., & Umeokafor, N. (2024). Building data driven culture for digital competitiveness in construction industry: A theoretical exploration. *International Journal of Construction Management*, •••, 1–13.

Heifetz, R., Grashow, A., & Linsky, M. (2009). *The practice of adaptive leadership: Tools and tactics for changing your organization and the world*. Harvard Business Press.

Heim, A. B., Duke, J., & Holt, E. A. (2022). Design, Discover, and Decipher: Student-Developed Escape Rooms in the Virtual Ecology Classroom. *Journal of Microbiology & Biology Education*, *23*(1). Advance online publication. DOI: 10.1128/jmbe.00015-22 PMID: 35784618

Hemachandran, K., Verma, P., Pareek, P., Arora, N., Rajesh Kumar, K. V., Ahanger, T. A., Pise, A. A., & Ratna, R. (2022). Artificial Intelligence: A Universal Virtual Tool to Augment Tutoring in Higher Education. *Computational Intelligence and Neuroscience*, *2022*(2022), 1–8.

Hernandez-de-Menendez, M., Escobar Díaz, C., & Morales-Menendez, R. (2020). Technologies for the future of learning: State of the art. [IJIDeM]. *International Journal on Interactive Design and Manufacturing*, *14*(2), 683–695.

Herur-Raman, A., Almeida, N. D., Greenleaf, W., Williams, D., Karshenas, A., & Sherman, J. H. (2021). Next-generation simulation—Integrating extended reality technology into medical education. *Frontiers in Virtual Reality*, *2*, 693399.

Herzog-Punzenberger, B., Altrichter, H., Brown, M., Burns, D., Nortvedt, G. A., Skedsmo, G., Wiese, E., Nayır, F., Fellner, M., McNamara, G., & O'Hara, J. (2020). Teachers responding to cultural diversity: Case studies on assessment practices, challenges and experiences in secondary schools in Austria, Ireland, Norway and Turkey. *Educational Assessment, Evaluation and Accountability*, *32*(3), 395. DOI: 10.1007/s11092-020-09330-y

Hetland, L., Winner, E., Veenema, S., & Sheridan, K. (2014). *Studio thinking 2*. Teachers College Press.

Hickey, D. T., & Harris, T. (2021). Reimagining online grading, assessment, and testing using situated cognition. *Distance Education*, *42*(2), 290. DOI: 10.1080/01587919.2021.1911627

Hitchcock, D. (2018). Critical thinking. Retrieved from https://plato.stanford.edu/entries/critical-thinking/

Hjelmervik, K., Nazir, S., & Myhrvold, A. (2018). Simulator training for maritime complex tasks: An experimental study. *WMU Journal of Maritime Affairs*, *17*(1), 17–30. DOI: 10.1007/s13437-017-0136-7

Hoare, A., Hondzel, C. D., Wagner, S. L., & Church, S. (2024). A course-based approach to conducting program review. *Discover Education*, *3*(1). Advance online publication. DOI: 10.1007/s44217-023-00085-4

Hobson, E. G. (2015). *Using the Rasch model in a computer adaptive testing application to enhance the measurement quality of emotional intelligence*. University of Johannesburg.

Hohensinn, C., & Kubinger, K. D. (2011). On the impact of missing values on item fit and the model validness of the Rasch model. *Psychological Test and Assessment Modeling*, *53*(3), 380–393. https://www.proquest.com/scholarly-journals/on-impact-missing-values-item-fit-model-validness/docview/1399684427/se-2

Holling, C. S. (1973). Resilience and stability of ecological systems. *Annual Review of Ecology and Systematics*, *4*, 1–23.

Holmes, W., Bialik, M., & Fadel, C. (2019). *Artificial intelligence in education: Promises and implications for teaching and learning*. Center for Curriculum Redesign.

Hong, S., & Yu, P. (2017). Comparison of The Effectiveness of Two Styles of Case-Based Learning Implemented in Lectures for Developing Nursing Students' Critical Thinking Ability: A Randomized Controlled Trial. *International Journal of Nursing Studies*, *68*, 16–24. DOI: 10.1016/J.IJNURSTU.2016.12.008

Hontvedt, M., & Arnseth, H. C. (2013). On the bridge to learn: Analysing the social organization of nautical instruction in a ship simulator. *International Journal of Computer-Supported Collaborative Learning*, *8*, 89–112. DOI: 10.1007/s11412-013-9167-6

Hopfenbeck, T. N., Zhang, Z., Sun, S. Z., Robertson, P., & McGrane, J. A. (2023). Challenges and opportunities for classroom-based formative assessment and AI: A perspective article. *Frontiers in Education*, *8*. Advance online publication. DOI: 10.3389/feduc.2023.1270700

Hosseini, M., & Nimehchisalem, V. (2021). Self-Assessment in English Language Teaching and Learning in the Current Decade (2010-2020): A Systematic Review [Review of Self-Assessment in English Language Teaching and Learning in the Current Decade (2010-2020): A Systematic Review]. Open Journal of Modern Linguistics, 11(6), 854. Scientific Research Publishing. https://doi.org/DOI: 10.4236/ojml.2021.116066

HOUNGUE, P., HOUNTONDJI, M., & DAGBA, T. (2022). An Effective Decision-Making Support for Student Academic Path Selection using Machine Learning. *International Journal of Advanced Computer Science and Applications*, *13*(11). Advance online publication. DOI: 10.14569/ijacsa.2022.0131184

Huang, L., Yu, W., Ma, W., Zhong, W., Feng, Z., Wang, H., Chen, Q., Peng, W., Feng, X., Qin, B., & Liu, T. (2023). *A Survey on Hallucination in Large Language Models: Principles*. Taxonomy, Challenges, and Open Questions., DOI: 10.1145/3703155

Huisman, J., & Van der Wende, M. (2005). *On cooperation and competition II. Institutional responses to internationalisation, Europeanisation and globalisation*. Lemmens.

Hurst, K., & Kelley Patterson, D. (2014). Health and social care workforce planning and development–an overview. *International Journal of Health Care Quality Assurance*, *27*(7), 562–572. DOI: 10.1108/IJHCQA-05-2014-0062

Huselid, M. A. (1995). The impact of human resource management practices on turnover, productivity, and corporate financial performance. *Academy of Management Journal*, *38*(3), 635–672. DOI: 10.5465/256741

Huxham, M., Campbell, F., & Westwood, J. (2012). Oral versus written assessments: A test of student performance and attitudes. *Assessment & Evaluation in Higher Education*, *37*(1). Advance online publication. DOI: 10.1080/02602938.2010.515012

Ifenthaler, D., & Yau, J. Y. K. (2022). Utilising learning analytics to support student engagement in higher education during COVID-19. *Educational Technology Research and Development*, *70*, 393–406. DOI: 10.1007/s11423-021-10006-9

Inside Higher Ed. (2024). *How will AI influence higher ed in 2025?* Retrieved from https://www.insidehighered.com/news/tech-innovation/artificial-intelligence/2024/12/19/how-will-ai-influence-higher-ed-2025

International Maritime Organization (IMO). (2024). *Report of the Working Group on the Comprehensive Review of the 1978 STCW Convention and Code* (HTW 10/WP.3).

Irshad, M., & Afridi, F. (2007). Factors affecting employees retention: Evidence from literature. *Abasyn Journal of Social Sciences*, *4*(2), 307–339.

Iskender, A. (2023). Holy or Unholy? Interview with Open AI's ChatGPT. European Journal of Tourism Research, pp. 34, 1–11. https://doi.org/DOI: 10.54055/ejtr.v34i.3169

Ismail, R., Noh, M. Z. M., Ismail, N. H., & Tamil, A. M. (2015). A tale of two construct validation analysis: Rasch model and exploratory factor analysis approach for three-factor eating questionnaire (TFEQ-R21) among Malaysian male workers. *The Medical Journal of Malaysia*, *70*(3), 169–175. PMID: 26248780

Jacobson, W. S. (2010). Preparing for tomorrow: A case study of workforce planning in North Carolina municipal governments. *Public Personnel Management*, *39*(4), 353–377. DOI: 10.1177/009102601003900404

Jagannathan, S., Ra, S., & Maclean, R. (2019). *Education and skills for inclusive growth, green jobs and the greening of economies in Asia: Case study summaries*. Springer.

Jagatheesaperumal, S. K., Ahmad, K., Al-Fuqaha, A., & Qadir, J. (2024). Advancing education through extended reality and internet of everything enabled metaverses: Applications, challenges, and open issues. *IEEE Transactions on Learning Technologies*.

Jain, A., Maleki, A., & Saade, N. (2024, August 7). *Methods for adapting large language models*. ai.meta.com. https://ai.meta.com/blog/adapting-large-language-models-llms/

James, W., Oates, G., & Schönfeldt, N. (2024). Improving retention while enhancing student engagement and learning outcomes using gamified mobile technology. *Accounting Education*, *1*. Advance online publication. DOI: 10.1080/09639284.2024.2326009

Jankowski, N. (2022). Reframing Assessment to Center Equity: A Resource to Inform Practice. *Assessment Update*, *34*(2), 6. DOI: 10.1002/au.30294

Jarrahi, M. H., Askay, D., Eshraghi, A., & Smith, P. (2023). Artificial intelligence and knowledge management: A partnership between human and AI. *Business Horizons*, *66*(1), 87–99.

Jatmiko, B., & Prahani, B. K., Munasir, Supardi, Z. A. I., Wicaksono, I., Erlina, N., Pandiangan, P., Althaf, R. & Zainuddin. (2018). The Comparison of Oripa Teaching Model and Problem-Based Learning Model Effectiveness to Improve Critical Thinking Skills of PreService Physics Teachers. *Journal of Baltic Science Education*, *17*(2), 300–319. DOI: 10.33225/jbse/18.17.812

Jatto, E. O., & Aladesusi, G. A. (2025). *Empowering Pre-Service Teachers for Inclusive Education Through Technology: Strategies, Tools, and Innovations Empowering Pre-Service Teachers to Enhance Inclusive Education Through Technology*. IGI Global Scientific Publishing.

Jeganathan, S., Raj, L. A., Parthasarathy, S., Khan, A. A. A., & Sathick, K. J. (2024). OptCatB: Optuna Hyperparameter Optimization Model to Forecast the Educational Proficiency of Immigrant Students based on CatBoost Regression. *Journal of Internet Services and Information Security*, *14*(3), 111. DOI: 10.58346/jisis.2024.i2.008

Jiang, H., Vimalesvaran, S., Wang, J. K., Lim, K. B., Mogali, S. R., & Car, L. T. (2022). Virtual reality in medical students' education: Scoping review. *JMIR Medical Education*, *8*(1), e34860. PMID: 35107421

Jiang, Z., Zhang, H., & Ni, J. (2023). Active Retrieval Augmented Generation for knowledge-intensive tasks. arXiv. https://arxiv.org/abs/2305.06983

Jibril, A. U., Abdullahi, N. M., Ali, A. S., Abdulkadir, H., Matthew, U. O., & Haruna, K. (2022). Motivational aspects of digital games in learning process. *Science in Information Technology Letters*, *3*(1), 1–9.

Joh, J. (2021). Implementing Peer Assessment for Optimal Effects : Learners' Voice. *The Journal of AsiaTEFL*, *18*(1), 1. DOI: 10.18823/asiatefl.2021.18.1.1.1

Johnson, A., Smith, B., & Thomas, L. (2019). Challenges in Maritime Education: Bridging Theory and Practice. *Journal of Marketing Education*, *42*(3), 115–128.

Johnson, S. L., Allen, J., Fernandez, L., Garikiparthy, V., Renovato, L., Land, M., Favela, L., Becerra, K., Belmares, R., Holland, N., & Chacon, J. (2023). Closing the digital divide: Developing a platform to conduct training, outreach, and education for employment skills. *Digital Health*, *9*. Advance online publication. DOI: 10.1177/20552076231154383 PMID: 36756645

Jones, C. M. (2023). *Comparing Approaches to Virtual Team Onboarding: the Influence of Synchrony and Cues on Impressions of Leaders During Encounter Phase Organizational Socialization* (Master's thesis, The University of Wisconsin-Milwaukee).

Jones, K. (2014). Conquering HR analytics: Do you need a rocket scientist or a crystal ball?. *Workforce Solutions Review*, *5*(3).

Joyce, B. R., Weil, M., & Calhoun, E. (2000). *Models of Teaching*. Allyn and Bacon.

Julius, D. J. (2000). Human Resources. *New Directions for Higher Education*, *2000*(111).

Junker, W. B. (2015). *Factor Analysis and Latent Structure: IRT and Rasch Models* (2nd ed.). International Encyclopedia of the Social & Behavioral Sciences., https://doi.org/https://doi.org/10.1016/B978-0-08-097086-8.24126-4

Kamalov, F., Santandreu Calonge, D., & Gurrib, I. (2023). New Era of Artificial Intelligence in Education: Towards a Sustainable Multifaceted Revolution. *Sustainability (Switzerland)*, *15*(16). Advance online publication. DOI: 10.3390/su151612451

Kaplan, A. D., Cruit, J., Endsley, M., Beers, S. M., Sawyer, B. D., & Hancock, P. A. (2021). The effects of virtual reality, augmented reality, and mixed reality as training enhancement methods: A meta-analysis. *Human Factors*, *63*(4), 706–726. PMID: 32091937

Kapsali, M., Bayer, S., Brailsford, S., & Bolt, T. (2022). The agency role of simulation models in model-building groups. *The Journal of the Operational Research Society*, *73*(7), 1423–1443.

Karim, M. S. (2022). Maritime cybersecurity and the IMO legal instruments: Sluggish response to an escalating threat? *Marine Policy*, *143*, 105138. DOI: 10.1016/j.marpol.2022.105138

Kartal, G. (2024). The influence of ChatGPT on thinking skills and creativity of EFL student teachers: A narrative inquiry. *Journal of Education for Teaching*, *50*(4). Advance online publication. DOI: 10.1080/02607476.2024.2326502

Karunanayaka, S. P., & Naidu, S. (2021). Impacts of authentic assessment on the development of graduate attributes. *Distance Education*, *42*(2), 231. DOI: 10.1080/01587919.2021.1920206

Katiyar, A., Khan, C., & Sachan, V. S. (2023). Role of HR Analytics on Employees Performance. *International Journal for Modern Trends in Science and Technology*, *9*, 925–933. DOI: 10.46501/IJMTST0905157

Katz, D., & Kahn, R. L. (1978). Organizations and the system concept. *Classics of organization theory, 80*(480), 27.

Kaur, R. (2017). Employee retention models and factors affecting employees retention in IT companies. *International Journal of Business Administration and Management*, *7*(1), 161–174.

Kawakami, N., Imamura, K., Watanabe, K., Sekiya, Y., Sasaki, N., & Sato, N. (2021). Effectiveness of an internet-based machine-guided stress management program based on cognitive behavioral therapy for improving depression among workers: Protocol for a randomized controlled trial. *JMIR Research Protocols*, *2021*(10), e30305.

Kenny, N., Popovic, C., McSweeney, J., Knorr, K., Hoessler, C., Hall, S., & El Khoury, E. (2017). Drawing on the principles of SoTL to illuminate a path forward for the scholarship of educational development. *The Canadian Journal for the Scholarship of Teaching and Learning*, *8*(2), n2.

Kezar, A. (2014). *How colleges change: Understanding, leading, and enacting change*. Routledge.

Killen, R. (2010). *Teaching Strategies Quality Teaching & Learning: Outcome-based assessment*. Juta Publishers.

Kim, D., & Mallam, S. (2020). Human factors considerations for the design and implementation of autonomous ships. *Journal of Marine Science and Engineering*, *8*(5), 308. DOI: 10.3390/jmse8050308

Kim, J., Lee, C., Jeong, M., Cho, E., & Lee, Y. (2023). Identifying optimal approaches for sustainable maritime education and training: Addressing technological, environmental, and epidemiological challenges. *Sustainability*, *15*(10), 8092. DOI: 10.3390/su15108092

Kim, W.-H., & Kim, J.-H. (2020). Individualized AI tutor based on developmental learning networks. *IEEE Access: Practical Innovations, Open Solutions*, *8*, 176594–176607. DOI: 10.1109/ACCESS.2020.3026359

Klein, H. J., & Polin, B. (2012). 14 Are Organizations On Board with Best Practices Onboarding?The Oxford handbook of organizational socialization, 267

Klein, H. J., Polin, B., & Leigh Sutton, K. (2015). Specific onboarding practices for the socialization of new employees. *International Journal of Selection and Assessment*, *23*(3), 263–283. DOI: 10.1111/ijsa.12113

Kooli, C. (2023). Chatbots in Education and Research: A Critical Examination of Ethical Implications and Solutions. *Sustainability (Switzerland)*, *15*(7). Advance online publication. DOI: 10.3390/su15075614

Koolivand, H., Shooreshi, M. M., Safari-Faramani, R., Borji, M., Mansoory, M. S., Moradpoor, H., Bahrami, M., & Azizi, S. M. (2024). Comparison of the effectiveness of virtual reality-based education and conventional teaching methods in dental education: A systematic review. *BMC Medical Education*, *24*(1). Advance online publication. DOI: 10.1186/s12909-023-04954-2

Koraishi, O. (2023). Teaching English in the Age of AI: Embracing ChatGPT to Optimize EFL Materials and Assessment. *Language Education & Technology Journal, 3*(1).

Korkmaz, N. (2025). *Büyük Dil Modelleri ve İstem Mühendisliği.* https://bilgem.tubitak.gov.tr/yte/

Kose, U., & Deperlioglu, O. (2020). Intelligent learning systems: Integration of AI into LMS for personalized education. *International Journal of Artificial Intelligence in Education, 30*(2), 183–203.

Krathwohl, D. R. (2002). A Revision of Bloom's Taxonomy: An Overview. *Theory into Practice, 41*(4), 212–218. DOI: 10.1207/s15430421tip4104_2

Kremantzis, M. D. (2023). Employability and Student Engagement from a Business Analytics Perspective.

Kubiszyn, T., & Borich, G. D. (2024). *Educational testing and measurement : classroom application and practice*. 14.

Kuhn, D. (1999). A developmental model of critical thinking. *Educational Researcher, 28*(2), 16–46.

Kulgemeyer, C., Riese, J., Vogelsang, C., Buschhüter, D., Borowski, A., Weißbach, A., Jordans, M., Reinhold, P., & Schecker, H. (2023). How authenticity impacts validity: Developing a model of teacher education assessment and exploring the effects of the digitisation of assessment methods. *Zeitschrift für Erziehungswissenschaft, 26*(3), 601. DOI: 10.1007/s11618-023-01154-y PMID: 37359180

Kumar, N., & Rajini, G. (2024). Reimaging maritime education and training using latest technologies. Salud, Ciencia y Tecnología – Serie de Conferencias, 3, 895. https://doi.org/.DOI: 10.56294/sctconf2024895

Kumar, P. S. (2023). Transformative Role of ICT in 21st Century Learning: Enhancing Educational Effectiveness and Equitability. *International Journal for Research in Applied Science and Engineering Technology, 11*(12), 91. DOI: 10.22214/ijraset.2023.57028

Kumar, V., & Vivek, S. (2021). AI in education: Application of natural language processing (NLP) in learning management systems. *International Journal of Learning Analytics and Artificial Intelligence for Education, 4*(1), 45–67.

Kuon, T., Philbrick, J., & Gill, D. (2024). Reflections on Implementing an ePortfolio as a Capstone Project for an LIS Master's Degree Program. *Journal of Education for Library and Information Science, 65*(4), 455–461.

Kurniawan, E. S., & Sofyan, H. (2020). Application of problem based learning model to improve problem solving ability of student of XI science grade in chemistry. *Journal of Physics: Conference Series, 1440*(1), 12014. DOI: 10.1088/1742-6596/1440/1/012014

Laamanen, M., Ladonlahti, T., Uotinen, S., Okada, A., Bañeres, D., & Koçdar, S. (2021). Acceptability of the e-authentication in higher education studies: Views of students with special educational needs and disabilities. *International Journal of Educational Technology in Higher Education, 18*(1). Advance online publication. DOI: 10.1186/s41239-020-00236-9 PMID: 34778518

Lacka, E., T. C. Wong, & M. Y. Haddoud. (2021). "Can Digital Technologies Improve Students' Efficiency? Exploring the Role of Virtual Learning Environment and Social Media Use in Higher Education." Computers & Education 163:104099. https://doi.org/. 104099.DOI: 10.1016/ j.compedu.2020

Lampropoulos, G., & Kinshuk. (2024). Virtual reality and gamification in education: A systematic review. *Educational Technology Research and Development, 72*(3), 1691–1785.

Lau, Y. Y., & Ng, A. K. (2015). The motivations and expectations of students pursuing maritime education. *WMU Journal of Maritime Affairs, 14*, 313–331. DOI: 10.1007/s13437-015-0080-5

Lavanya, K., Somu, L. K., & Mishra, S. K. (2024). Effectiveness of Scenario-based Roleplay as a Method of Teaching Soft Skills for Undergraduate Medical Students. *International Journal of Applied & Basic Medical Research, 14*(2), 78–84. PMID: 38912358

Lawrence, N., Serdikoff, S., Zinn, T., & Baker, S. (2008). Have we demystified critical thinking. In Dunn, D., Halonen, J., & Smith, R. (Eds.), *Teaching Critical Thinking in Psychology* (1st ed.). Wiley-Blackwell.

Lawrence, W. J., & Mathis, J. (2020). Multimodal assessments: Affording children labeled 'at-risk' expressive and receptive opportunities in the area of literacy. *Language and Education, 34*(2), 135. DOI: 10.1080/09500782.2020.1724140

Lee, H., Hsia, C.-C., Tsoy, A., Choi, S., Hou, H., & Ni, S. (2023). *VisionARy: Exploratory research on Contextual Language Learning using AR glasses with ChatGPT.* Paper presented at the Proceedings of the 15th Biannual Conference of the Italian SIGCHI Chapter.

Lee, D., Bathish, M. A., & Nelson, J. (2024). Transforming Nursing Education: Developing Augmented Reality Procedural Training. *Cyberpsychology, Behavior, and Social Networking*. PMID: 38407873

Lee, J., & Choi, H. (2017). What affects learner's higher-order thinking in technology-enhanced learning environments? The effects of learner factors. *Computers & Education, 115*, 143–152. DOI: 10.1016/j.compedu.2017.06.015

Lee, M., Horii, C. V., Austin, A. E., Avery, L., DeSanctis, M., Finkelstein, N. D., Miller, E., & Schaal, B. A. (2023). An Instructional-Workforce Framework for Co-ordinated Change in Undergraduate Education. *Change The Magazine of Higher Learning*, *55*(1), 54. DOI: 10.1080/00091383.2023.2151809

Levenson, A., Lawler, E. E., III, & Boudreau, J. W. (2005). Survey on HR Analytics and HR transformation: Feedback report. *Center for Effective Organizations, University of Southern California*, 131-42.

Lewis, P. R., & Sarkadi, Ş. (2024). Reflective Artificial Intelligence. *Minds and Machines*, *34*(2). Advance online publication. DOI: 10.1007/s11023-024-09664-2

Lew, T. (2009). The relationships between perceived organizational support, felt obligation, affective organizational commitment and turnover intention of academics working with private higher educational institutions in Malaysia. *European Journal of Social Sciences*, *9*(1), 72–87.

Li, B., Bonk, C. J., Wang, C., & Kou, X. (2024). Reconceptualizing Self-Directed Learning in the Era of Generative AI: An Exploratory Analysis of Language Learning. *IEEE Transactions on Learning Technologies*, *17*, 1515. DOI: 10.1109/tlt.2024.3386098

Li, L., & Duan, L. (2025). Human centric innovation at the heart of industry 5.0–exploring research challenges and opportunities. *International Journal of Production Research*, •••, 1–33.

Lim, W. M., Gunasekara, A., Pallant, J. L., Pallant, J. I., & Pechenkina, E. (2023). Generative AI and the Future of Education: Ragnarök or Reformation? A Paradoxical Perspective from Management Educators. *International Journal of Management Education*, *21*(2), 100790. DOI: 10.1016/j.ijme.2023.100790

Lin, Z. (2023). Why and how to embrace AI such as ChatGPT in your academic life. R. Soc. Open Sci. 2023, pp. 10, 1–11.

Linacre, J. M. (1994). *Many-Facet Rasch Measurement* (2nd ed.). Mesa Press.

Linacre, J. M. (2010). Predicting Responses from Rasch measures. *Journal of Applied Measurement, 11*(1), 1–9. PMID: 20351444

Ling, Y., Zhou, J., Li, Y., & Huang, J. (2022). Learner satisfaction-based research on the application of artificial intelligence science popularization kits. *Frontiers in Psychology, 2022*(13), 901191.

LinkedIn Advice. (n.d.). Student Engagement: How can portfolios align with curriculum standards and learning outcomes? Retried from: https://www.linkedin.com/advice/0/how-can-portfolios-align-curriculum-standards

Lippmann, M. (2021). Inquiry-Based Learning in Psychology. In *Springer international handbooks of education* (p. 1). Springer Nature., DOI: 10.1007/978-3-030-26248-8_59-2

Liu, C., Tang, M., Wang, M., Chen, L., & Sun, X. (2023). Critical thinking disposition and academic achievement among Chinese high school students: A moderated mediation model. *Psychology in the Schools, 2023*(60), 3103–3113.

Liu, J. Y. W., Mak, P. Y., Chan, K., Cheung, D. S. K., Cheung, K., Fong, K. N., & Maximo, T. (2024). The Effects of Immersive Virtual Reality–Assisted Experiential Learning on Enhancing Empathy in Undergraduate Health Care Students Toward Older Adults With Cognitive Impairment: Multiple-Methods Study. *JMIR Medical Education, 10*, e48566. PMID: 38358800

Li, Y. (2023). The Potential Application of ChatGPT in Higher Education Management. *Lecture Notes in Education Psychology and Public Media, 25*(1). Advance online publication. DOI: 10.54254/2753-7048/25/20230750

Lodge, J. M., Thompson, K., & Corrin, L. (2023). Mapping Out a Research Agenda for Generative Artificial Intelligence in Tertiary Education. *Australasian Journal of Educational Technology, 39*, 1–8. DOI: 10.14742/ajet.8695

Lodhia, S., Kaur, A., & Williams, B. (2020). Integrated reporting in the public sector. In *Routledge eBooks* (p. 227). Informa., DOI: 10.4324/9780429279621-15

Lokuketagoda, M. G., Miwa, T., Jayasinghe, S., & Dev Ranmuthugala, P. (2018). Training engineers for remotely operated ships of the future. In *Proceedings of the 19th Annual General Assembly (AGA), International Association of Maritime Universities (IAMU)* (pp. 17–19). Barcelona, Spain.

Lopez-Gazpio, I. (2022). Gaining student engagement through project-based learning: A competitive 2d game construction case study. IEEE Access 2022, 10, 1881–1892.

Lungu, A. J., Swinkels, W., Claesen, L., Tu, P., Egger, J., & Chen, X. (2021). A review on the applications of virtual reality, augmented reality and mixed reality in surgical simulation: An extension to different kinds of surgery. *Expert Review of Medical Devices*, *18*(1), 47–62. PMID: 33283563

Luo, H. (2024). *Instructional Design with Emerging Technologies: Theory, Practice, and Research*. Taylor & Francis.

Lu, P. C. (2007). The integration of blog platform and e-portfolio in art assessment. *The International Journal of Arts Education*, *5*(2), 154–185.

MacDonald, C., Backhaus, I., Vanezi, E., Yeratziotis, A., Clendinneng, D., Seriola, L., Häkkinen, S., Cassar, M., Mettouris, C., & Papadopoulos, G. A. (2021). European Union Digital Education quality standard framework and companion evaluation toolkit. *Open Learning*, *39*(1), 85. DOI: 10.1080/02680513.2021.1936476

Macfadyen, L. P., & Dawson, S. (2012). Numbers are not enough: Why e-learning analytics failed to inform an institutional strategic plan. *Journal of Educational Technology & Society*, *15*(3), 149–163.

Mahanal, S., Zubaidah, S., Sumiati, I. D., Sari, T. M., & Ismirawati, N. (2019). RICOSRE: A Learning Model to Develop Critical Thinking Skills for Students with Different Academic Abilities. *International Journal of Instruction*, *12*(2), 417–434. DOI: 10.29 333/iji.2019.12227a

Makhubele, M. (2019). Using the Trauma Symptom Checklist for Children-Short form (TSCC-SF) on abused children in South Africa: Confirmatory factor analysis and Rasch models. *Child Abuse & Neglect*, *98*(104241), 1–9. DOI: 10.1016/j.chiabu.2019.104241 PMID: 31704542

Mallam, S. C., Nazir, S., Renganayagalu, S. K., Ernstsen, J., Veie, S., & Edwinson, A. E. (2019). Design of experiment comparing users of virtual reality head-mounted displays and desktop computers. In *Proceedings of the 20th Congress of the International Ergonomics Association (IEA 2018)* (pp. 240–249). Springer. https://doi.org/DOI: 10.1007/978-3-319-96071-5_28

Mallillin, L. L. D. (2017). Human resource management in selected higher education institutions (HEI): Towards enhancing employees' work. *International Journal of Advanced Research in Management and Social Sciences*, *6*(1), 58–74.

Manley, E. D., Urness, T., Migunov, A., & Reza, M. A. (2024). Examining student use of AI in CS1 and CS2. *Journal of Computing Sciences in Colleges*, *39*(6), 41–51.

Mansour, H. F., Heath, G., & Brannan, M. J. (2015). Exploring the role of HR practitioners in pursuit of organizational effectiveness in higher education institutions. *Journal of Change Management*, *15*(3), 210–230. DOI: 10.1080/14697017.2015.1045539

Manuel, M. E. (2017). Vocational and academic approaches to maritime education and training (MET): Trends, challenges and opportunities. *WMU Journal of Maritime Affairs*, *16*(3), 473–483. DOI: 10.1007/s13437-017-0135-8

Marginson, S. (2007). The public/private divide in higher education: A global revision. *Higher Education*, *53*, 307–333.

Marler, J. H., & Boudreau, J. W. (2017). An evidence-based review of HR Analytics. *International Journal of Human Resource Management*, *28*(1), 3–26. DOI: 10.1080/09585192.2016.1244699

Marler, J. H., & Fisher, S. L. (2013). An evidence-based review of e-HRM and strategic human resource management. *Human Resource Management Review*, *23*(1), 18–36. DOI: 10.1016/j.hrmr.2012.06.002

Martin, F., Sun, T., Westine, C. D., & Ritzhaupt, A. D. (2022). Examining research on the impact of distance and online learning: A second-order meta-analysis study. *Educational Research Review*, *36*, 100438. DOI: 10.1016/j.edurev.2022.100438

Martin, F., Zhuang, M., & Schaefer, D. (2024). A systematic review of the use of artificial intelligence in K–12 education (2017–2022). Computers & Education. *Artificial Intelligence*, *6*, 100195. DOI: 10.1016/j.caeai.2023.100195

Martín-Sómer, M., Casado, C., & Gómez-Pozuelo, G. (2023). Utilising interactive applications as educational tools in higher education: Perspectives from teachers and students, and an analysis of academic outcomes. *Education for Chemical Engineers*, *46*, 1. DOI: 10.1016/j.ece.2023.10.001

Masuwai, A., Zulkifli, H., & Hamzah, M. I. (2024). Evaluation of content validity and face validity of secondary school Islamic education teacher self-assessment instrument. *Cogent Education*, *11*(1). Advance online publication. DOI: 10.1080/2331186x.2024.2308410

Ma, T. (2023). The Influence of ChatGPT on Autonomous Learning for College Students. *Lecture Notes in Education Psychology and Public Media*, *25*(1). Advance online publication. DOI: 10.54254/2753-7048/25/20230708

Mathew, U. O., Rodriguez, D. Z., Rosa, R. L., Ayub, M. S., & Adasme, P. (2024). *Advancing healthcare 5.0 through federated learning: Opportunity for security enforcement using blockchain.* Paper presented at the 2024 International Conference on Software, Telecommunications and Computer Networks (SoftCOM).

Matthew, U. O., Bakare, K. M., Ebong, G. N., Ndukwu, C. C., & Nwanakwaugwu, A. C. (2023). Generative Artificial Intelligence (AI) Educational Pedagogy Development: Conversational AI with User-Centric ChatGPT4. *Journal of Trends in Computer Science and Smart Technology*, *5*(4), 401–418.

Matthew, U. O., Kazaure, A. S., Kazaure, J. S., Hassan, I. M., Nwanakwaugwu, A. C., & Okafor, N. U. (2022). Educational Technology Adaptation & Implication for Media Technology Adoption in the Period of COVID-19. *Journal of Trends in Computer Science and Smart Technology*, *4*(4), 226–245.

Matthew, U. O., & Kazaure, J. S. (2020). Multimedia e-learning education in nigeria and developing countries of Africa for achieving SDG4. [IJICTHD]. *International Journal of Information Communication Technologies and Human Development*, *12*(1), 40–62.

Matthew, U. O., Kazaure, J. S., Kazaure, A. S., Nwamouh, U. C., & Chinonso, A. (2022). ICT Policy Implementation as Correlate for Achieving Educational Sustainability: Approaching Development in Multi ICT Dimensions. *Journal of Information Technology*, *4*(4), 250–269.

Matthew, U. O., Kazaure, J. S., Ndukwu, C. C., Ebong, G. N., Nwanakwaugwu, A. C., & Nwamouh, U. C. (2024). *Artificial Intelligence Educational Pedagogy Development: ICT Pedagogy Development for Education 5.0 Educational Perspectives on Digital Technologies in Modeling and Management*. IGI Global.

Matthew, U. O., Oyekunle, D. O., Akpan, E. E., Oladipupo, M. A., Chukwuebuka, E. S., Adekunle, T. S., & Onumaku, V. C. (2024). *Generative Artificial Intelligence (AI) on Sustainable Development Goal 4 for Tertiary Education: Conversational AI With User-Centric ChatGPT-4 Impacts of Generative AI on Creativity in Higher Education*. IGI Global.

McDaniel, M. A., Wildman, K. M., & Anderson, J. L. (2012). Using quizzes to enhance summative-assessment performance in a web-based class: An experimental study. *Journal of Applied Research in Memory and Cognition*, *1*(1). Advance online publication. DOI: 10.1016/j.jarmac.2011.10.001

McMillan, J. H. (2023). *Classroom assessment: Principles and practice for effective standards-based instruction* (8th ed.). Pearson.

McNally, D., & Speak, K. D. (2010). *Be your own brand: Achieve more of what you want by being more of who you are*. Berrett-Koehler Publishers.

Meadows, D. H. (2008). *Thinking in systems: A primer*. Chelsea Green Publishing.

Medvedev, O. N., & Krägeloh, C. U. (2022). Rasch Measurement Model. In Medvedev, O. N., Krägeloh, C. U., Siegert, R. J., & Singh, N. N. (Eds.), *Handbook of Assessment in Mindfulness Research*. Springer., DOI: 10.1007/978-3-030-77644-2_4-1

Meier, D. (2003). *In schools we trust: Creating communities of learning in an era of testing and standardization*. Beacon Press.

Messeri, L., & Crockett, M. J. (2024). Artificial intelligence and illusions of understanding in scientific research. *Nature*, *627*(8002), 49–58.

Meylani, R. (2024). A Comparative Analysis of Traditional and Modern Approaches to Assessment and Evaluation in Education. [WAJES]. *The Western Anatolia Journal of Educational Sciences*, *15*(1), 520–555. DOI: 10.51460/BAEBD.1386737

Mhlongo, S., Mbatha, K., Ramatsetse, B., & Dlamini, R. (2023). Challenges, opportunities, and prospects of adopting and using smart digital technologies in learning environments: An iterative review. *Heliyon*, *9*(6). Advance online publication. DOI: 10.1016/j.heliyon.2023.e16348 PMID: 37274691

Michel-Villarreal, R., Vilalta-Perdomo, E., & Salinas-Navarro, D. (2023). Thierry-Aguilera, R., and Gerardou, F. S. (2023). Challenges and opportunities of generative AI for higher education as explained by ChatGPT. *Education in Science*, *2023*(13), 856.

Michel-Villarreal, R., Vilalta-Perdomo, E., Salinas-Navarro, D. E., Thierry-Aguilera, R., & Gerardou, F. S. (2023). Challenges and Opportunities of Generative AI for Higher Education as Explained by ChatGPT. *Education Sciences*, *13*(9). Advance online publication. DOI: 10.3390/educsci13090856

Millikin, C. C. (2023). Future-Proof your Instructional Design with Universal Design for Learning and Translanguaging. *Literacy Information and Computer Education Journal*, *14*(1), 3709. DOI: 10.20533/licej.2040.2589.2023.0488

Mislevy, R. J., Almond, R. G., & Lukas, J. F. (2003). A BRIEF INTRODUCTION TO EVIDENCE-CENTERED DESIGN. *ETS Research Report Series*, *2003*(1), i–29. DOI: 10.1002/J.2333-8504.2003.TB01908.X;PAGE:STRING:ARTICLE/CHAPTER

Mittal, S., Agarwal, R., Bansal, S., & Sharma, A. (2025). ChatGPT in Financial Education: Assessing its Role in Improving Financial Literacy and Investor Knowledge. *International Journal of Electronic Finance*, *1*(1). Advance online publication. DOI: 10.1504/ijef.2025.10062488

Mizrahi, M., Mazor, Y., Goldberg, Y., & Berant, J. (2024). State of what art? A call for multi-prompt LLM evaluation. arXiv. https://arxiv.org/abs/2401.00595

Mobo, F. D. (2024). *Education 5.0: Navigating the Future of Learning Preconceptions of Policies, Strategies, and Challenges in Education 5.0*. IGI Global.

Molinari, A., & Sandri, S. (2024). Evolution of LMS design and implementation in the age of AI and large language models. In *Proceedings of the 2nd International Workshop on Artificial Intelligence Systems in Education (AIxEDU 2024)*. CEUR Workshop Proceedings.

Monib, W. K., Qazi, A., & Mahmud, M. M. (2024). Exploring learners' experiences and perceptions of ChatGPT as a learning tool in higher education. *Education and Information Technologies*, *30*(1), 917–939. DOI: 10.1007/S10639-024-13065-4/METRICS

Moradi, M., Yan, K., Colwell, D., Samwald, M., & Asgari, R. (2025). A Critical Review of Methods and Challenges in Large Language Models. In *Computers, Materials and Continua* (Vol. 82, Issue 2, pp. 1681–1698). Tech Science Press. https://doi.org/DOI: 10.32604/cmc.2025.061263

Morjaria, L., Burns, L., Bracken, K., Levinson, A. J., Ngo, Q. N., Lee, M., & Sibbald, M. (2024). Examining the Efficacy of ChatGPT in Marking Short-Answer Assessments in an Undergraduate Medical Program. *International Medical Education*, *3*(1). Advance online publication. DOI: 10.3390/ime3010004

Moscardini, A. O., Strachan, R., & Vlasova, T. (2022). The Role of Universities in Modern Society. *Studies in Higher Education*, *47*(4), 812–830. DOI: 10.1080/03075079.2020.1807493

Mourtzis, D., Angelopoulos, J., & Panopoulos, N. (2023). Smart manufacturing and Industry 5.0: Human-centered approaches and skill development strategies. *Journal of Manufacturing Systems*, *68*, 162–174. DOI: 10.1016/j.jmsy.2023.02.003

Mowling, C. M., & Sims, S. (2021). The Metacognition Journey: Strategies for Teacher Candidate Exploration of Self and Student Metacognition. *Strategies (La Jolla, Calif.)*, *34*(2), 13. DOI: 10.1080/08924562.2020.1867268

Mthimkhulu, S. (2023). *Examining PIRLS 2021: Differential item functioning across English and isiZulu language groups*. [Master's Dissertation]. University of Pretoria.

Muca, E., Cavallini, D., Odore, R., Baratta, M., Bergero, D., & Valle, E. (2022). Are Veterinary Students Using Technologies and Online Learning Resources for Didactic Training? A Mini-Meta Analysis. *Education in Science*, *2022*(12), 573.

Mudhol, A. C. (2024). Innovative Assessment Methods for Measuring Practical Skills in Higher Education. In Advances in economics, business and management research/Advances in Economics, Business and Management Research (p. 78). Atlantis Press. https://doi.org/DOI: 10.2991/978-94-6463-374-0_8

Muirhead, P. M. (2004). New technology and maritime training in the 21st century: Implications and solutions for MET institutions. *WMU Journal of Maritime Affairs*, *3*, 139–158.

Muller, M. (2020). Item fit statistics for Rasch analysis: Can we trust them? *Journal of Statistical Distributions and Applications*, *7*(5), 1–11. DOI: 10.1186/s40488-020-00108-7

Musakuro, R. N. (2022). A framework development for talent management in the higher education sector. *SA Journal of Human Resource Management*, *20*, 1671. https://hdl.handle.net/10520/ejc-sajhrm_v20_i1_a1671

Mustafa, F., Nguyen, H. T. M., & Gao, X. (2024). The challenges and solutions of technology integration in rural schools: A systematic literature review. *International Journal of Educational Research*, *126*, 102380. DOI: 10.1016/j.ijer.2024.102380

Naaj, M. A., Mehdi, R., Mohamed, E. A., & Nachouki, M. (2023). Analysis of the Factors Affecting Student Performance Using a Neuro-Fuzzy Approach. *Education Sciences*, *13*(3), 313. DOI: 10.3390/educsci13030313

Nandini, N., Indora, P., & Singh, R. (2024). Artificial Intelligence in Journalism: An Overview of its Applications and Uses. *Journal of Communication Management (London)*, *3*(3), 237. DOI: 10.58966/jcm2024337

Navarro-Parra, S. L., & Chiappe, A. (2024). Simulated Learning Environments as an Interdisciplinary Option for Vocational Training: A Systematic Review. *Simulation & Gaming*, *55*(2), 135–158.

Naveed, H., Khan, A. U., Qiu, S., Saqib, M., Anwar, S., Usman, M., Akhtar, N., Barnes, N., & Mian, A. (2023). *A Comprehensive Overview of Large Language Models*. https://arxiv.org/abs/2307.06435

Ndawo, G. (2022). The development of self skills in an authentic learning environment: A qualitative study. *Curationis*, *45*(1). Advance online publication. DOI: 10.4102/curationis.v45i1.2198

Neerupa, C., Naveen Kumar, R., Pavithra, R., & John William, A. (2024). Game on for learning: A holistic exploration of Gamification's impact on student engagement and academic performance in educational environments. *Management Matters*, *21*(1), 38–53.

Nguyen, L. (2018). 9 experts discuss the skills seafarers need in the future. *Informa Connect*. Retrieved September 21, 2024, from https://knect365.com/shipping/article/c17e1ac8-6e3a-4e33-855c-5adbb3bad9aa/

Nguyen, P., Cao, L., & Trương, H. (2023). Integrating ChatGPT with Virtual Reality and Augmented Reality Technology in Teaching Biology at High Schools in Vietnam.

Nguyen, H. M., & Goto, D. (2024). Unmasking academic cheating behavior in the artificial intelligence era: Evidence from Vietnamese undergraduates. *Education and Information Technologies*. Advance online publication. DOI: 10.1007/s10639-024-12495-4

Nicholas, M., Veresov, N., & Clark, J. C. (2021). Guided reading – Working within a child's zone of proximal development. *Learning, Culture and Social Interaction*, *30*, 100530. DOI: 10.1016/j.lcsi.2021.100530

Nkhoma, C., Nkhoma, M., Thomas, S., & Le, N. Q. (2020). The Role of Rubrics in Learning and Implementation of Authentic Assessment: A Literature Review [Review of The Role of Rubrics in Learning and Implementation of Authentic Assessment: A Literature Review]. Informing Science and IT Education Conference, 237. Informing Science Institute. https://doi.org/DOI: 10.28945/4606

Novak, K. (2023). How UDL Creates an Equitable Environment for Students. https://www.edutopia.org/article/universal-design-learning-promotes-equity

Ntorukiri, T. B., Kirugua, J. M., & Kirimi, F. (2022). Policy and infrastructure challenges influencing ICT implementation in universities: a literature review [Review of Policy and infrastructure challenges influencing ICT implementation in universities: a literature review]. Discover Education, 1(1). Springer Science+Business Media. https://doi.org/DOI: 10.1007/s44217-022-00019-6

Nyambegera, S., Daniels, K., & Sparrow, P. (2001). Why fit doesn't always matter: The impact of HRM and cultural fit on job involvement of Kenyan employees. *Applied Psychology*, *50*(1), 109–140. DOI: 10.1111/1464-0597.00050

Oberer, B., & Erkollar, A. (2022). *Education 5.0: the effectiveness of game based learning strategies on post-pandemic educational competences.* Paper presented at the The International Symposium for Production Research.

Olanipekun, S. O. (2025). Ethical frameworks for AI in journalism: Balancing technological innovation and journalistic integrity. *World Journal of Advanced Research and Reviews*, *25*(1), 1342. DOI: 10.30574/wjarr.2025.25.1.0187

Olga, A., A. Saini, G. Zapata, D. Searsmith, B. Cope, M. Kalantzis, V. Castro, T. Kourkoulou, J. Jones & R. A. da Silva. (2023). Generative AI: Implications and Applications for Education. arXiv Prepr. arXiv2305.07605.

Omorogiuwa, K. O. (2012). *Benefits and challenges of feedback in formative assessment of distance learners*. https://uir.unisa.ac.za/handle/10500/8558

Onesi-Ozigagun, O., Ololade, Y. J., Eyo-Udo, N. L., & Ogundipe, D. O. (2024). Revolutionizing education through ai: a comprehensive review of enhancing learning experiences [review of revolutionizing education through ai: a comprehensive review of enhancing learning experiences]. International Journal of Applied Research in Social Sciences, 6(4), 589. Fair East Publishers. https://doi.org/DOI: 10.51594/ijarss.v6i4.1011

Ong, C. W., Tan, M. C. J., Lam, M., & Koh, V. T. C. (2021). Applications of extended reality in ophthalmology: Systematic review. *Journal of Medical Internet Research*, *23*(8), e24152. PMID: 34420929

Orduno-Osuna, J., Cota-Rivera, E., Raygoza, L., Jimenez-Sanchez, R., Limón-Molina, G., Bravo-Zanoguera, M., Mercado-Herrera, A., & Rico, F. (2023). Exploring the challenges and applications of generative AI on engineering education in Mexico. In *Facilitating Global Collaboration and Knowledge Sharing in Higher Education with Generative AI* (pp. 259–286). IGI Global.

Oriakhi, V. N., Esegbona-Isikeh, O. M., Esseme, B., Claude, A., Emakporuena, D., Nwanakwaugwu, A. C., & Matthew, U. O. (2024). Generative artificial intelligence in education: ChatGPT-4 experiences to anticipated ChatGPT-5. *HAFED POLY Journal of Science. Management and Technology*, *6*(1), 149–169.

Ortega-Sanchez, C. (2016). Written Exams: How Effectively are We Using Them? *Procedia: Social and Behavioral Sciences*, *228*. Advance online publication. DOI: 10.1016/j.sbspro.2016.07.021

Osterman, C., & Boström, M. (2021). Workplace bullying and harassment at sea: A structured literature review. *Marine Policy*, *136*, 104910. DOI: 10.1016/j.marpol.2021.104910

Oteng, B., Mensah, R. O., Babah, P. A., & Swanzy-Impraim, E. (2023). Social studies and history curriculum assessment in colleges of education in Ghana: Reflective practices of teacher educators. *Cogent Education*, *10*(1). Advance online publication. DOI: 10.1080/2331186x.2023.2175515

Othman, H., Asshaari, I., Bahaludin, H., Nopiah, Z. M., & Ismail, N. A. (2012). Application of Rasch measurement model in reliability and quality evaluation of examination paper for Engineering Mathematics courses. *Procedia: Social and Behavioral Sciences*, *60*, 163–171. DOI: 10.1016/j.sbspro.2012.09.363

Othman, M., Bhuiyan, N., & Gouw, G. J. (2011). A new approach to workforce planning. *International Journal of Computer and Systems Engineering*, *5*(4), 858–864.

Oudeyer, P. (2017). Autonomous development and learning in artificial intelligence and robotics: Scaling up deep learning to human-like learning. Behav. Brain Sci. 2017, p. 40, e275.

Owan, V. J., Abang, K. B., Idika, D. O., Etta, E. O., & Bassey, B. A. (2023). Exploring the potential of artificial intelligence tools in educational measurement and assessment. In *Eurasia Journal of Mathematics, Science and Technology Education* (Vol. 19, Issue 8). https://doi.org/DOI: 10.29333/ejmste/13428

Owen, T. R. (2002). Student and Employee Wellness in Higher Education: A Literature Review.

Oyekunle, D. O. T., Okwudili Matthew, U., Preston, D., & Boohene, D. (2024). Trust beyond technology algorithms: A theoretical exploration of consumer trust and behavior in technological consumption and AI projects. *Journal of Computer and Communications, 12*(06), 10.4236.

Oyekunle, D., Claude, B. E. A., Waliu, A. O., Adekunle, T. S., & Matthew, U. O. (2024). Cloud based adaptive learning system: virtual reality and augmented reality assisted educational pedagogy development on clinical simulation. *Journal of Digital Health*, 49-62.

Oyekunle, D., Ugochukwu, O. M., Rosa, R. L., Rodriguez, D. Z., & Fatai, L. O. (2024). Novel Approaches in Clinical Simulation: Immersive Educational Technology to Enhance Nursing Education. *INFOCOMP Journal of Computer Science, 23*(1).

Oyekunle, D. O., Nwaiku, M., Matthew, U. O., Ogechukwu, O. N., Nwanakwaugwu, A. C., Adebola, N. T., & Olawoyin, O. O. (2025). *Transition to Sustainable Human-Centric Education in Emerging Artificial Intelligence Industry 5.0: Conversational AI With User-Centric ChatGPT-5 Higher Education and Quality Assurance Practices*. IGI Global Scientific Publishing.

Oyekunle, D., Matthew, U. O., Waliu, A. O., & Fatai, L. O. (2024). Healthcare applications of Augmented Reality (AR) and Virtual Real-ity (VR) simulation in clinical ceducation. *Journal of Clinical Images and Medical Case Reports*, *5*(6), 3141.

Palada, B., Chandan, V. S., & Gowda, C. P., & Nikitha, Prof. (2024). The Role of Augmented Reality (AR) in Education. *International Journal for Research in Applied Science and Engineering Technology*, *12*(3), 1400. DOI: 10.22214/ijraset.2024.59079

Pallant, J. F., Miller, R. L., & Tennant, A. (2006). Evaluation of the Edinburgh Post Natal Depression Scale using Rasch analysis. *BMC Psychiatry*, *6*(28), 1–9. DOI: 10.1186/1471-244X-6-28 PMID: 16768803

Palshikar, G. K., Srivastava, R., Pawar, S., Hingmire, S., Jain, A., Chourasia, S., & Shah, M. (2019). Analytics-led talent acquisition for improving efficiency and effectiveness. *Advances in analytics and applications*, 141-160.

Papanastasiou, G., Drigas, A., Skianis, C., Lytras, M., & Papanastasiou, E. (2019). Virtual and augmented reality effects on K-12, higher and tertiary education students' twenty-first century skills. *Virtual Reality (Waltham Cross)*, *23*(4), 425–436.

Pape, T. (2016). Prioritising data items for business analytics: Framework and application to human resources. *European Journal of Operational Research*, *252*(2), 687–698. DOI: 10.1016/j.ejor.2016.01.052

Pardo, A., & Siemens, G. (2014). Ethical and privacy principles for learning analytics. *British Journal of Educational Technology*, *45*(3), 438–450. DOI: 10.1111/bjet.12152

Parwoto, P., Ilyas, S. N., Bachtiar, M. Y., & Marzuki, K. (2024). Fostering creativity in kindergarten: The impact of collaborative project-based learning. *South African Journal of Childhood Education*, *14*(1). Advance online publication. DOI: 10.4102/sajce.v14i1.1462

Pascanu, R., Mikolov, T., & Bengio, Y. (2013). *On the difficulty of training recurrent neural networks*.

Paul, M., & Jena, L. K. (2022). Workplace spirituality, teachers' professional well-being and mediating role of positive psychological capital: An empirical validation in the Indian context. *International Journal of Ethics and Systems*, *38*(4), 633–660. DOI: 10.1108/IJOES-08-2021-0163

Paul, R. W. (1984). Critical thinking: Fundamental to education for a free society. *Educational Leadership*, *42*(1), 4–14.

Pavlik, J. (2023). Collaborating with ChatGPT: Considering the Implications of Generative Artificial Intelligence for Journalism and Media Education. J. (2023). *Mass Commun. Educ.*, *2023*(78), 84–93.

Pellert, A. (2007). Human resource management at universities. *Higher education management and development in central, southern and eastern. Europe*, •••, 104–109.

Pelton, T. (2002, April). Where are the limits to the Rasch advantage? In *The International Objective Measurement Workshop*, New Orleans.

Peng, M., Xie, J., Mao-hua, X., & Liu, Y. (2023). Artificial intelligence education in primary and secondary schools from the perspective of thinking quality. *J. Contemp. Educ. Res., 2023*(7), 41–46.

Peramunugamage, A., Ratnayake, U., & Karunanayaka, S. (2023). Systematic review on mobile collaborative learning for engineering education. *Journal of Computers in Education, 2023*(10), 83–106.

Perišić, A., Perisic, I., Lazić, M., & Perišić, B. (2023). The foundation for future education, teaching, training, learning, and performing infrastructure - The open interoperability conceptual framework approach. *Heliyon, 9*(6). Advance online publication. DOI: 10.1016/j.heliyon.2023.e16836 PMID: 37484382

Pessach, D., Singer, G., Avrahami, D., Ben-Gal, H. C., Shmueli, E., & Ben-Gal, I. (2020). Employees recruitment: A prescriptive analytics approach via machine learning and mathematical programming. *Decision Support Systems, 134*, 113290. DOI: 10.1016/j.dss.2020.113290

Philippe, S., Souchet, A. D., Lameras, P., Petridis, P., Caporal, J., Coldeboeuf, G., & Duzan, H. (2020). Multimodal teaching, learning and training in virtual reality: a review and case study. In Virtual Reality & Intelligent Hardware (Vol. 2, Issue 5, p. 421). Elsevier BV. https://doi.org/DOI: 10.1016/j.vrih.2020.07.008

Pitura, J., Kaplan-Rakowski, R., & Asotska-Wierzba, Y. (2025). The VR-AI–Assisted Simulation for Content Knowledge Application in Pre-Service EFL Teacher Training. *TechTrends, 69*(1), 100–110.

Plooy, E. du, Casteleijn, D., & Franzsen, D. (2024). Personalized adaptive learning in higher education: a scoping review of key characteristics and impact on academic performance and engagement [Review of Personalized adaptive learning in higher education: a scoping review of key characteristics and impact on academic performance and engagement]. Heliyon, 10(21). Elsevier BV. https://doi.org/DOI: 10.1016/j.heliyon.2024.e39630

Ployhart, R. E. (2006). Staffing in the 21st century: New challenges and strategic opportunities. *Journal of Management, 32*(6), 868–897. DOI: 10.1177/0149206306293625

Plummer, R., Blythe, J., Gurney, G. G., Witkowski, S., & Armitage, D. (2022). Transdisciplinary partnerships for sustainability: An evaluation guide. *Sustainability Science, 17*(3), 955. DOI: 10.1007/s11625-021-01074-y

Popenici, S., & Kerr, S. (2017). Exploring the impact of artificial intelligence on teaching and learning in higher education. *Research and Practice in Technology Enhanced Learning, 12*(1), 1–14. PMID: 30595727

Porter, M. E. (1980). *Competitive Strategy*. Free Press.

Powell, S., & Wood, D. (1999). Is recruitment the millennium time bomb for the industry worldwide? *International Journal of Contemporary Hospitality Management, 11*(4), 138–141. DOI: 10.1108/09596119910263513

Powell, T. C. (2001). Competitive advantage: Logical and philosophical considerations. *Strategic Management Journal, 22*(9), 875–888. DOI: 10.1002/smj.173

Prince, M. J., & Felder, R. M. (2006). Inductive Teaching and Learning Methods: Definitions, Comparisons, and Research Bases. *Journal of Engineering Education, 95*(2), 123–138. DOI: 10.1002/j.2168-9830.2006.tb00884.x

Qin, C. (2024). Discussion on the Curriculum Design and Implementation of Competency-Based Vocational Education. *Journal of Modern Educational Theory and Practice, 1*(2).

Qu, X., & Cross, B. (2023). UDL for inclusive higher education—What makes group work effective for diverse international students in UK? *International Journal of Educational Research, 123*, 102277. DOI: 10.1016/j.ijer.2023.102277

Raguseo, E. (2018). Big data technologies: An empirical investigation on their adoption, benefits and risks for companies. *International Journal of Information Management, 38*(1), 187–195. DOI: 10.1016/j.ijinfomgt.2017.07.008

Rahman, M. T. (2018). Cloud Computing: User's Perceptions About Security Issues. Information and knowledge management, 8(4). Retrieved from https://www.iiste.org/ Journals/index.php/IKM/article/view/41882/0

Rahman, M. Tuhinur & Singh, Rahul. (2023). Impact of social influence on continuous use of mobile game applications" (2023). AMCIS 2023 Proceedings. https://aisel.aisnet.org/amcis2023/soc_inclusion/social_inclusion/5 Rahman, M. Tuhinur & Palvia, Prashant. (2023). How is my IT department leading to Digital Innovation Success?" (2023). AMCIS 2023 Proceedings. 7. https://aisel.aisnet.org/amcis2023/sig_dite/sig_dite/

Raiaan, M. A. K., Mukta, M. S. H., Fatema, K., Fahad, N. M., Sakib, S., Mim, M. M. J., Ahmad, J., Ali, M. E., & Azam, S. (2024). A Review on Large Language Models: Architectures, Applications, Taxonomies, Open Issues and Challenges. *IEEE Access: Practical Innovations, Open Solutions*, *12*, 26839–26874. DOI: 10.1109/ACCESS.2024.3365742

Ramkissoon, L. (2024). AI: Powering Sustainable Innovation in Higher Ed *The Evolution of Artificial Intelligence in Higher Education* (pp. 203-229): Emerald Publishing Limited.

Rane, N., Choudhary, S., & Rane, J. (2023a). Education 4.0 and 5.0: Integrating artificial intelligence (AI) for personalized and adaptive learning: Nov.

Rane, N., Choudhary, S., & Rane, J. (2023c). Enhanced product design and development using Artificial Intelligence (AI), Virtual Reality (VR), Augmented Reality (AR), 4D/5D/6D Printing, Internet of Things (IoT), and blockchain: A review. *Virtual Reality (VR), Augmented Reality (AR) D, 4.*

Rane, N., Choudhary, S., & Rane, J. (2023b). Education 4.0 and 5.0: Integrating Artificial Intelligence (AI) for personalized and adaptive learning. *Available at SSRN* 4638365.

Ravi, L. (2020). Maritime education in India—The "theory–practice" conundrum. *IIRE Journal of Maritime Research and Development*, *4*(2), 15–22.

Rawas, S. (2023). ChatGPT: Empowering lifelong learning in the digital age of higher education. *Education and Information Technologies*, •••, 1–14. DOI: 10.1007/s10639-023-12114-8

Redecker, C., Leis, M., Leendertse, M., Punie, Y., Gijsbers, G., Kirschner, P., & Hoogveld, B. (2010). *The future of learning: New ways to learn new skills for future jobs. Results from an online expert consultation. Technical Note JRC60869*. JRC-IPTS.

Reed, S. (2015). Collecting evidence for your portfolio. In Collecting evidence for your portfolio (Second Edition ed., pp. 39-56). SAGE Publications, Inc., https://doi.org/DOI: 10.4135/9781473922419

Renganayagalu, S. K., Mallam, S. C., & Hernes, M. (2022). Maritime education and training in the COVID-19 era and beyond. TransNav. *International Journal on Marine Navigation and Safety of Sea Transportation*, *16*(1), 59–69. DOI: 10.12716/1001.16.01.06

Ren, K., Liu, X., Feng, Y., Li, C., Sun, D., & Qiu, K. (2021). The relationship between physical activity and academic procrastination in Chinese college students: The mediating role of self-efficacy. *International Journal of Environmental Research and Public Health*, *2021*(18), 11468.

Rincón-Flores, E. G., Castano, L., Solis, S. L. G., Lopez, O. O., Rodríguez-Hernández, C. F., Lara, L. A. C., & Aldape, P. (2024). Improving the learning-teaching process through adaptive learning strategy. *Smart Learning Environments*, *11*(1). Advance online publication. DOI: 10.1186/s40561-024-00314-9

Rodriguez, R., Martinez-Ulloa, L., & Flores-Bustos, C. (2022). E-portfolio as an evaluative tool for emergency virtual education: Analysis of the case of the University Andres Bello (Chile) during the COVID-19 pandemic. *Frontiers in Psychology*, *13*, 1–10. DOI: 10.3389/fpsyg.2022.892278 PMID: 35783798

Rodzalan, S., & Saat, M. (2015). The Perception of Critical Thinking and ProblemSolving Skills among Malaysian Undergraduate Students. *Procedia: Social and Behavioral Sciences*, *172*, 725–732. DOI: 10.1016/J.SBSPRO.2015.01.425

Romanowski, M. H. (2022). Controlling higher education from a distance: Using foucault's governmentality to better understand accreditation. *Cogent Education*, *9*(1). Advance online publication. DOI: 10.1080/2331186x.2022.2073631

Roschelle, J., & Teasley, S. D. (2023). Collaborative learning with AI: Integrating GPT in learning management systems for enhanced educational outcomes. *Journal of Learning Analytics*, *10*(2), 75–92.

Roshanaei, M., Olivares, H., & Lopez, R. R. (2023). Harnessing AI to Foster Equity in Education: Opportunities, Challenges, and Emerging Strategies. *Journal of Intelligent Learning Systems and Applications*, *15*(4), 123. DOI: 10.4236/jilsa.2023.154009

Roslender, R., Stevenson, J., & Kahn, H. (2006). Employee wellness as intellectual capital: An accounting perspective. *Journal of Human Resource Costing & Accounting*, *10*(1), 48–64. DOI: 10.1108/14013380610672675

Rosli, R., Abdullah, M., Siregar, N. C., Hamid, N. S. A., Abdullah, S., Beng, G. K., Halim, L., Daud, N. M., Bahari, S. A., Majid, R. A., & Bais, B. (2020). Student Awareness of Space Science: Rasch Model Analysis for Validity and Reliability. *World Journal of Education*, *10*(3), 170–177.

Rosser, V. J., Johnsrud, L. K., & Heck, R. H. (2003). Academic deans and directors: • Assessing their effectiveness from individual and institutional perspectives. *The Journal of Higher Education*, *74*(1), 1–25. DOI: 10.1080/00221546.2003.11777185

Rothe, L., & Snyder, C. K. (2024). Using Bloom's taxonomy to visualise antiracist teaching strategies. *Whiteness and Education*, •••, 1–19.

Roux, K. (2020). Examining the Equivalence of the PIRLS 2016 Released Texts in South Africa Across Three Languages. [Doctoral Thesis]. University of Pretoria.

Rudolph, J., Samson Tan, & Shannon Tan. (2023). ChatGPT: Bullshit Spewer or the End of Traditional Assessments in Higher Education? *Journal of Applied Learning and Teaching*, *6*(1), 342–363. DOI: 10.37074/jalt.2023.6.1.9

Rumelt, R. P. (1991). How much does industry matter? *Strategic Management Journal*, *12*(3), 167–185. DOI: 10.1002/smj.4250120302

Rust, Ming-Hui Huang, & Roland T. (2018). Artificial Intelligence in Service. https://journals.sagepub.com/doi/full/10.1177/1094670517752459

Ruzaman, N., & Rosli, D. (2020). Inquiry-Based Education: Innovation in Participatory Inquiry Paradigm. *International Journal of Emerging Technologies in Learning*, *15*(10), 4. DOI: 10.3991/ijet.v15i10.11460

Sagita, A., Nurlaela, L., & Widodo, W. (2018). Mind Maple Lite Software. *Improve Student's Learning Outcomes and Stimulating Metacognition in Nutrition Science Subject.*, *112*, 1–5. DOI: 10.2991/iconhomecs-17.2018.1

Sahin, A., Thompson, N., & Ercikan, K. (2024). Opportunities and Challenges of AI in Educational Assessment. *Journal of Measurement and Evaluation in Education and Psychology*, *15*, 260–262. DOI: 10.21031/EPOD.1607441

Salleh, S., Tasir, Z., & Shukor, N. (2012). Web-Based Simulation Learning Framework to Enhance Students' Critical Thinking Skills. International Educational Technology Conference, IETC2012, Procedia-Social and Behavioral Sciences, Elsevier Ltd., 64(2012), 372-381.Shukla

Samaras, S., Adkins, C. L., & White, C. D. (2021). Developing critical thinking skills: Simulations vs. cases. *Journal of Education for Business*, *97*(4), 270. DOI: 10.1080/08832323.2021.1932703

Samuel, O., Joseph, E., Sylvia, M., & Charles, O. (2025). Artificial intelligence in higher education institutions: Review of innovations, opportunities, and challenges. *Frontiers in Education*, *10*, 1530247.

Sari, R. Sumarmi, Komang Astina, I. Utomo, D. & Ridhwan. (2019). Measuring Students Scientific Learning Perception and Critical Thinking Skill Using Paper-Based Testing: School and Gender Differences. *International Journal of Emerging Technologies in Learning*, *14*(19). Advance online publication. DOI: 10.3991/ijet.v14i19.10968

Saul, C., & Wuttke, H. D. (2013). E-assessment meets personalization. *IEEE Global Engineering Education Conference, EDUCON*. https://doi.org/DOI: 10.1109/EduCon.2013.6530106

Savaglio, C., Ganzha, M., Paprzycki, M., Bădică, C., Ivanović, M., & Fortino, G. (2020). Agent-based Internet of Things: State-of-the-art and research challenges. *Future Generation Computer Systems*, *102*, 1038–1053.

Schoepp, K. (2019). The state of course learning outcomes at leading universities. *Studies in Higher Education*, *44*(4), 615–627.

Scouller, K. (1998). The influence of assessment method on students' learning approaches: Multiple choice question examination versus assignment essay. *Higher Education*, *35*(4), 453–472. DOI: 10.1023/A:1003196224280/METRICS

Selwyn, N. (2019). Should robots replace teachers? AI and the future of education. *Learning, Media and Technology*, *44*(1), 1–17. DOI: 10.1080/17439884.2019.1590622

Seyyed, K., Banihashem, Dragon, G. & Omid, N. (2025). A critical review of using learning analytics for formative assessment: Progress, pitfalls, and the way forward. *Journal of Computer Assisted Learning*.

Sharif, H., & Atif, A. (2024). The Evolving Classroom: How Learning Analytics Is Shaping the Future of Education and Feedback Mechanisms. *Education Sciences*, *14*(2), 176. DOI: 10.3390/educsci14020176

Sharif, S., Malik, S. A., Arooj, N., & Albadry, O. M. (2024). Human resource management (HRM) practices and organizational commitment in higher educational institution (HEI): A mediating role for work engagement. *Global Knowledge, Memory and Communication*. Advance online publication. DOI: 10.1108/GKMC-11-2023-0456

Sharma, A., Channa, A., Malhotra, P., Jain, A., & Kumar, S. (2025). *Leveraging XR for Environmental Communication and Behavior Change: A Media Perspective Exploring the Impact of Extended Reality (XR) Technologies on Promoting Environmental Sustainability*. Springer.

Sharoff, L. (2022). Student's Perception of vSim for Nursing® using the Simulation Effectiveness Tool—Modified. *Clinical Simulation in Nursing*, *68*, 1. DOI: 10.1016/j.ecns.2022.04.006 PMID: 36718189

Shavelson, R. J., Webb, N. M., & Rowley, G. L. (1992). Generalizability theory. *Methodological Issues & Strategies in Clinical Research.*, 233–256. https://doi.org/DOI: 10.1037/10109-051

Shen, Y. (2024). Personalised Education: A study on the relationship between student assessment methods and student development. *SHS Web of Conferences, 199*, 01002. https://doi.org/DOI: 10.1051/SHSCONF/202419901002

Sheppard-Jones, K., Goldstein, P., Leslie, M., Singleton, P., Gooden, C., Rumrill, P. D., Mullis, L., & Bard, C. E. (2020). Reframing workplace inclusion through the lens of universal design: Considerations for vocational rehabilitation professionals in the wake of COVID-19. *Journal of Vocational Rehabilitation*, *54*(1), 71. DOI: 10.3233/jvr-201119

Shin, J. C. (2010). Impacts of performance-based accountability on institutional performance in the US. *Higher Education*, *60*, 47–68.

Siau, K., & Yang, Y. (2017). In Twelve Annual Midwest Association for Information Systems Conference (MWAIS 2017). Impact of Artificial Intelligence, robotics, and Machine Learning on Sales and Marketing (2017), pp. 18–19

Siemens, G. (2013). Learning analytics: The emergence of a discipline. *The American Behavioral Scientist*, *57*(10), 1380–1400.

Silviana, D., Musafik, M., & Sulistyanto, I. (2023). The effect of internet media usage toward learning interest through learning motivation as a moderator variable. *J. Pendidik. Bhs. Ingg. Profic.*, *2023*(5), 37.

Singh, K., Deshpande, S., & Patwardhan, S. (2025). Refining the Giants: A Comprehensive Review of Fine-Tuning Strategies for Large Language Models. *Lecture Notes in Networks and Systems*, *1144*, 65–82. DOI: 10.1007/978-981-97-7839-3_5

Singh, N., Misra, R., Quan, W., Radić, A., Lee, S.-M., & Han, H. (2024). An analysis of consumer's trusting beliefs towards the use of e-commerce platforms. *Humanities & Social Sciences Communications*, *11*(1). Advance online publication. DOI: 10.1057/s41599-024-03395-6

Singh, S., & Hiran, K. (2022). The Impact of AI on Teaching and Learning in Higher Education Technology. *Journal of Higher Education Theory and Practice*, *2022*(22), 135.

Slade, S., & Prinsloo, P. (2013). Learning analytics: Ethical issues and dilemmas. *The American Behavioral Scientist, 57*(10), 1510–1529.

Smith, A. B., Rush, R., Fallowfield, L. J., Velikova, G., & Sharpe, M. (2008). Rasch fit statistics and sample size considerations for polytomous data. *BMC Medical Research Methodology, 8*(33), 1–10. DOI: 10.1186/1471-2288-8-33 PMID: 18510722

Smith, B. A. C. (2018). *DP sea time validation: An in-depth review of the commonly utilized DP validation practices and suggestions for how the industry can improve*. Dynamic Positioning Committee.

Smith, B., & Wyness, L. (2024). What makes professional teacher development in universities effective? Lessons from an international systematised review. *Professional Development in Education, 1*. Advance online publication. DOI: 10.1080/19415257.2024.2386666

Smith, J., & Noble, H. (2014). Bias in research. *Evidence-Based Nursing, 17*(4), 100–101. PMID: 25097234

Smith, R. C. (1993). *Basic graphic design*. Prentice Hall.

Söken, A. (2023). Universal Design for Learning: Increasing Inclusive Teaching for Graduate Students. *Journal of Technology-Integrated Lessons and Teaching, 2*(1), 60. DOI: 10.13001/jtilt.v2i1.7675

Son, T. (2024). Intelligent Tutoring Systems in Mathematics Education: A Systematic Literature Review Using the Substitution, Augmentation, Modification, Redefinition Model. *Computers, 13*(10), 270.

Souza, M. A. P., Coster, W. J., Mancini, M. C., Dutra, F. C. M. S., Kramer, J., & Sampaaio, R. F. (2017). Rasch Analysis of the participation scale (P-scale): Usefulness of the P-scale to a rehabilitation service network. *Bio Med Central. Public Health, 17*(934), 1–3. DOI: 10.1186/s12889-017-4945-9 PMID: 29216914

Soysal, S., Arikan, Ç. A., & Inal, H. (2016). Impact of Missing Data on Rasch Model Estimations. *The Turkish Online Journal of Educational Technology*, (Special issue), 1166–1175.

Spector, J. M. (2019). Complexity, Inquiry Critical Thinking, and Technology: A Holistic and Developmental Approach. In Mind, Brain and Technology (pp. 17–25). (Springer, Cham, 2019). Jisc [WWW Document]. Accessed March 28, 2023. URL https://www.jisc.ac.uk/news/does-chatgpt-mean-the-end-of-the-essay-as-an-assessment-tool-10-jan2023

Spector, J. M. (2019). Smart Learning Environments: Concepts and Issues. In G. Chamblee & L. Langub (Eds.), Proceedings of Society for Information Technology & Teacher Education International Conference (pp. 2728–2737). (Association for the Advancement of Computing in Education (AACE), Savannah, GA, United States, 2016). Retrieved June 4, 2019 from https://www.learntechlib.org/primary/p/172078/

Spector, J., & Ma, S. (2019). Inquiry and critical thinking skills for the next generation: From artificial intelligence back to human intelligence. *Smart Learn. Environ., 2019*(6), 8.

Spowart, L., & Turner, R. (2021). Institutional Accreditation and the Professionalisation of Teaching in the HE Sector. In *IntechOpen eBooks*. IntechOpen., DOI: 10.5772/intechopen.99805

Spreitzer, G., & Porath, C. (2012). Creating sustainable performance. *Harvard Business Review, 90*(1), 92–99.

Srivastava, S., Varshney, A., Katyal, S., Kaur, R., & Gaur, V. (2021). A smart learning assistance tool for inclusive education. *Journal of Intelligent & Fuzzy Systems, 40*(6), 11981. DOI: 10.3233/jifs-210075

Stein, M., & Christiansen, L. (2010). *Successful onboarding*. McGraw-Hill Professional Publishing.

Stemler, S. E., & Naples, A. (2021). Rasch Measurement vs. Item Response Theory: Knowing when to cross the line. *Practical Assessment, Research & Evaluation, 26*(11), 1–12. DOI: 10.7275/v2gd-4441

Stoll, L. (2020). Creating capacity for learning: Are we there yet? *Journal of Educational Change, 21*(3), 421. DOI: 10.1007/s10833-020-09394-z

Stolt, M., Kottorp, A., & Suhonen, R. (2022). The use and quality of reporting of Rasch analysis in nursing research: A methodological scoping review. *International Journal of Nursing Studies, 132*, 104244. PMID: 35635906

Strobl, C., Kopf, J., & Zeileis, A. (2015). Rasch Trees: A new method for detecting differential item functioning in the Rasch model. *Psychometrika, 80*(2), 289–295. DOI: 10.1007/S11336-013-9388-3 PMID: 24352514

Sun, X. (2021). 5G. (2021). Joint artificial intelligence technology in the innovation and reform of university English education. *Wireless Communications and Mobile Computing, 2021*, 4892064.

Supriya, Y., Bhulakshmi, D., Bhattacharya, S., Gadekallu, T. R., Vyas, P., Kaluri, R., & Mahmud, M. (2024). Industry 5.0 in smart education: Concepts, applications, challenges, opportunities, and future directions. *IEEE Access: Practical Innovations, Open Solutions.*

Swartz, R., & Parks, S. (2004). infusing the teaching of critical and creative thinking into content instruction. California: The Critical Thinking Co.

Swartz, S., & McGuinness, C. (2004). *Developing and Assessing Thinking Skills Project Part 1.* National Center for Teaching Thinking.

Swidan, A., Lee, S. Y., & Romdhane, S. B. (2025). College Students' Use and Perceptions of AI Tools in the UAE: Motivations, Ethical Concerns and Institutional Guidelines. *Education Sciences, 15*(4), 461. DOI: 10.3390/educsci15040461

Swiecki, Z., Khosravi, H., Chen, G., Martínez-Maldonado, R., Lodge, J. M., Milligan, S., Selwyn, N., & G sević, D. (2022). Assessment in the age of artificial intelligence. *Computers and Education Artificial Intelligence, 3*, 100075. DOI: 10.1016/j.caeai.2022.100075

Swist, T., Shum, S. B., & Gulson, K. N. (2024). Co-producing AIED Ethics Under Lockdown: An Empirical Study of Deliberative Democracy in Action. *International Journal of Artificial Intelligence in Education, 34*(3), 670. DOI: 10.1007/s40593-023-00380-z

Syzdykova, Z., Koblandin, K., Mikhaylova, N., & Akinina, O. (2021). Assessment of E-portfolio in higher education. *International Journal of Emerging Technologies in Learning (Online), 16*(2), 120.

Tai, J., Ajjawi, R., Bearman, M., Boud, D., Dawson, P., & Jorre, T. J. de S. (2022). Assessment for inclusion: Rethinking contemporary strategies in assessment design. *Higher Education Research & Development, 42*(2), 483. DOI: 10.1080/07294360.2022.2057451

Tai, J., Dollinger, M., Ajjawi, R., Jorre, T. J. de S., Krattli, S., McCarthy, D., & Prezioso, D. (2022). Designing assessment for inclusion: An exploration of diverse students' assessment experiences. *Assessment & Evaluation in Higher Education, 48*(3), 403. DOI: 10.1080/02602938.2022.2082373

Talagala, N. (2022). Data as The New Oil Is Not Enough: Four Principles For Avoiding Data Fires. Retrieved from: https://www.forbes.com/sites/nishatalagala/2022/03/02/data-as-the-new-oil-is-not-enough-four-principles-for-avoiding-data-fires/#:~:text=Generally%20credited%20to%20mathematician%20Clive,entity%20that%20drives%20profitable%20activity

Tang, Y. M., Chau, K. Y., Kwok, A. P. K., Zhu, T., & Ma, X. (2022). A systematic review of immersive technology applications for medical practice and education-trends, application areas, recipients, teaching contents, evaluation methods, and performance. *Educational Research Review*, *35*, 100429.

Tariq, M. Z. (2024). Enhancing onboarding with AI: designing a modern conversational agent for onboarding. https://urn.fi/URN:NBN:fi-fe2024052737703

Tasmin, R., Huey, T. L., Nda, R. M., & Jaafar, I. (2022). What does it take to adopt big data management approach at Malaysian higher education institutions. *The Journal of Learning in Higher Education*, •••, 1–15. DOI: 10.5171/2022.924024

Taylor, F. W. (2004). *Scientific management*. Routledge.

Ter Bogt, H. J., & Scapens, R. W. (2012). Performance management in universities: Effects of the transition to more quantitative measurement systems. *European Accounting Review*, *21*(3), 451–497. DOI: 10.1080/09638180.2012.668323

Thomas, D. S. M. (1998). The use of portfolio learning in medical education. *Medical Teacher*, *20*(3), 192–199.

Timotheou, S., Miliou, O., Dimitriadis, Y., Villagrá-Sobrino, S., Giannoutsou, N., Cachia, R., Martínez-Monés, A., & Ioannou, A. (2022). Impacts of digital technologies on education and factors influencing schools' digital capacity and transformation: A literature review [Review of Impacts of digital technologies on education and factors influencing schools' digital capacity and transformation: A literature review]. Education and Information Technologies, 28(6), 6695. Springer Science+Business Media. https://doi.org/DOI: 10.1007/s10639-022-11431-8

Topsakal, O., & Topsakal, E. (2022). Framework for a foreign language teaching software for children utilizing AR, voicebots and ChatGPT (large language models). *The Journal of Cognitive Systems*, *7*(2), 33–38.

Tossell, C. C., Tenhundfeld, N. L., Momen, A., Cooley, K., & De Visser, E. J. (2024). Student Perceptions of ChatGPT Use in a College Essay Assignment: Implications for Learning, Grading, and Trust in Artificial Intelligence. *IEEE Transactions on Learning Technologies*, *17*. Advance online publication. DOI: 10.1109/TLT.2024.3355015

Tursunbayeva, A., Di Lauro, S., & Pagliari, C. (2018). People analytics—A scoping review of conceptual boundaries and value propositions. *International Journal of Information Management*, *43*, 224–247. DOI: 10.1016/j.ijinfomgt.2018.08.002

Tursunbayeva, A., Pagliari, C., Di Lauro, S., & Antonelli, G. (2022). The ethics of people analytics: Risks, opportunities and recommendations. *Personnel Review*, *51*(3), 900–921. DOI: 10.1108/PR-12-2019-0680

Ulrich, D. (2013). Redefining our roles. *The Higher Education Workplace, 5*(2), 26.

Ulrich, D., & Dulebohn, J. H. (2015). Are we there yet? What's next for HR? *Human Resource Management Review, 25*(2), 188–204. DOI: 10.1016/j.hrmr.2015.01.004

Ünal, N. Ü., Karal, M. A., & Tan, S. (2020). Developing Accessible Lesson Plans with Universal Design for Learning (UDL). *International Journal of Disability Development and Education, 69*(4), 1442. DOI: 10.1080/1034912x.2020.1812539

UNESCO. (2025). *Artificial intelligence in education.* Retrieved from https://www.unesco.org/en/digital-education/artificial-intelligence

Utami, B., Saputro, S., Ashadi, A., Masykuri, M., & Widoretno, S. (2017). Critical Thinking Skills Profile of High School Students in Learning Chemistry. *Int. J. Sci. Appl. Sci. Conf. Ser., 2017*(1), 124.

van As, J., & Cooke, R. (2024). *Immersive Virtual Community Engagement: Unleashing the Potential of AI Avatars and Virtual Reality in Education to Enhance Learning Excellence Integrating Cutting-Edge Technology Into the Classroom.* IGI Global.

van der Togt, J., & Rasmussen, T. H. (2017). Toward evidence-based HR. *Journal of Organizational Effectiveness: People and Performance, 4*(2), 127–132. DOI: 10.1108/JOEPP-02-2017-0013

Varoquaux, G., & Colliot, O. (2023). Evaluating Machine Learning Models and Their Diagnostic Value. In Neuromethods (p. 601). Humana Press. https://doi.org/ DOI: 10.1007/978-1-0716-3195-9_20

Vaswani, A., Shazeer, N., Parmar, N., Uszkoreit, J., Jones, L., Gomez, A. N., Kaiser, L., & Polosukhin, I. (2017). *Attention Is All You Need.* https://arxiv.org/abs/1706.03762

Vaughan, N., Gabrys, B., & Dubey, V. N. (2016). An overview of self-adaptive technologies within virtual reality training. *Computer Science Review, 22*, 65–87. DOI: 10.1016/j.cosrev.2016.10.001

Veldkamp, E. L., Bygvraa, D. A., Dawicki, H. E., Dawicki, M. G., & Center for Ocean Policy & Economics (COPE) Working Group. (2022). Psychological safety, bullying, sexual assault and harassment in the maritime sector. *Medical Sciences Forum, 13*(1), 25. https://doi.org/DOI: 10.3390/msf2022013025

Verhagen, J., Levy, R., Millsap, R. E., & Fox, J. P. (2016). Evaluating evidence for invariant items: A Bayes factor applied to testing measurement invariance in IRT models. *Journal of Mathematical Psychology, 72*, 171–182.

Vieriu, A. M., & Petrea, G. (2025). The Impact of Artificial Intelligence (AI) on Students' Academic Development. *Education Sciences 2025, Vol. 15, Page 343, 15*(3), 343. https://doi.org/DOI: 10.3390/EDUCSCI15030343

Vigoda, E. (2000). Organizational politics, job attitudes, and work outcomes: Exploration and implications for the public sector. *Journal of vocational Behavior, 57*(3), 326-347. https://doi.org/ rights and contentDOI: 10.1006/jvbe.1999.1742Get

Villegas-Ch, W., García-Ortiz, J., & Sánchez-Viteri, S. (2024). Educational advances in the metaverse: Boosting learning through virtual and augmented reality and artificial intelligence. *IEEE Access: Practical Innovations, Open Solutions.*

Vlachopoulos, S. P., Kaperoni, M., & Moustaka, F. C. (2011). The relationship of self-determination theory variables to exercise identity. *Psychology of sport and exercise, 12*(3), 265-272. https://doi.org/ rights and contentDOI: 10.1016/j.psychsport.2010.11.006Get

Voulgarides, C. K., Etscheidt, S., & Hernández-Saca, D. I. (2023). Educational inequality and the paradox of dis/Ability rights in a schooled society: Moving towards an intersectional discursive, material, and emotive approach*. *Educational Review, 76*(1), 181. DOI: 10.1080/00131911.2023.2181313

Wahyuni, L. G. E., Dewi, N. L. P. E. S., & Paramartha, A. A. G. Y. (2021). Authentic Assessment Practice. Advances in Social Science, Education and Humanities Research. *Advances in Social Science, Education and Humanities Research.* Advance online publication. DOI: 10.2991/assehr.k.210407.258

Waliu, A. O., Matthew, U. O., Oseni, V. E., Oyekunle, D. O., Oladipupo, M. A., Adekunle, T. S., & Esseme, A. C. B. (2025). *Immersive Educational Pedagogy Development: Cloud-Based Adaptive System for Higher Education Generative AI Approaches to Sustainable Development in Higher Education.* IGI Global Scientific Publishing.

Waliu, A. O., Muojekwu, E. E., Matthew, U. O., Kazaure, J. S., Oseni, V. E., Ononiwu, C. C., & Haruna, K. (2025). *Clinical Simulation in nursing education: Immersive Educational Tech for nurses and midwives Creating Immersive Learning Experiences Through Virtual Reality (VR).* IGI Global.

Wang, X. (2023). How can technology leverage university teaching & learning innovation? A longitudinal case study of diffusion of technology innovation from the knowledge creation perspective. https://link.springer.com/article/10.1007/s10639-023-11780-y

Wang, L. (2020). Evaluating Competency-Based Maritime Training Programs. *International Maritime Journal*, *36*(2), 77–90.

Wang, P. (2019). On defining artificial intelligence. *Journal of Artificial General Intelligence*, *10*(2), 1–37.

Wang, T., Lund, B. D., Marengo, A., Pagano, A., Mannuru, N. R., Teel, Z. A., & Pange, J. (2023). Exploring the potential impact of artificial intelligence (AI) on international students in higher education: Generative AI, chatbots, analytics, and international student success. *Applied Sciences (Basel, Switzerland)*, *13*(11), 6716. DOI: 10.3390/app13116716

Wang, X., & Feng, Y. (2023). An Experimental Study of ChatGPT-Assisted Improvement of Chinese College Students' English Reading Skills: A Case Study of Dear Life. *ACM International Conference Proceeding Series*. https://doi.org/DOI: 10.1145/3629296.3629300

Wannapiroon, P. (2008). Development of a Problem-Based Learning Model to Develop Undergraduate Student's Critical Thinking Skills, Ph.D. dissertation, Dept. Curriculum, Instruction, and Educational Technology, Chulalongkorn Univ., Bangkok, Thailand.

Wattoo, M. U., Du, J., Shahzad, F., & Kousar, S. (2025). Shaping E-commerce Experiences: Unraveling the Impact of Service Quality on Youth Customer Behavior in a Developing Nation. *SAGE Open*, *15*(1). Advance online publication. DOI: 10.1177/21582440241311786

Webb, J. J. (2023). Proof of Concept: Using ChatGPT to Teach Emergency Physicians How to Break Bad News. *Cureus*. Advance online publication. DOI: 10.7759/cureus.38755

Weick, K. E., & Sutcliffe, K. M. (2015). *Managing the unexpected: Resilient performance in an age of uncertainty*. John Wiley & Sons.

Weng, J. C. (2023). *Putting Intellectual Robots to Work: Implementing Generative AI Tools in Project Management*. NYU SPS Applied Analytics Laboratory.

Wernerfelt, B. (1984). A resource-based view of the firm. *Strategic Management Journal*, *5*(2), 171–180. DOI: 10.1002/smj.4250050207

Wette, R. (2017). Using Mind Maps to Reveal and Develop Genre Knowledge in A Graduate Writing Course. *Journal of Second Language Writing*, *38*, 58–71. https://www.mdpi.com/2071-1050/13/18/10424. DOI: 10.10 16/J.JSLW.2017.09.005Doi

Wibowo, H. A. (2025). An explication of how website design actually shapes online customer loyalty: Incorporating sem and person-items map analysis. *International Journal of Social Service and Research*, *5*(1), 123. DOI: 10.46799/ijssr.v5i1.1190

Winget, M., & Persky, A. M. (2022). A Practical Review of Mastery Learning [Review of A Practical Review of Mastery Learning]. American Journal of Pharmaceutical Education, 86(10). Elsevier BV. https://doi.org/DOI: 10.5688/ajpe8906

Wongkam, N. Pinsuwan, D. & Chaowakeeratipong, N. (February 2014). The Effects of Using the 7Es Learning Management Approach Emphasizing Critical Thinking Activities in the Topic of Homeostasis on Learning Achievement and Critical Thinking Ability of Mathayom Suksa IV Students at Piriyalai Changwat Phara School in Phare Province. Available: http://www.stou.ac.th/thai/grad_stdy/Masters/%E0%B8%9D%E0%B8%AA%E0%B8%AA/research/2nd/FullPaper/SS/Oral/OSS%

Wright, D. B., & Stone, M. H. (1999). Measurement essentials (2nd ed.). Wide range.

Wright, B. D. (1995). 3PL IRT or Rasch? *Rasch Measurement Transactions*, *9*, 408.

Wright, D. B. (1997). Solving measurement problems with the Rasch model. *Journal of Educational Measurement*, *14*, 97–116.

Xia, Q., Weng, X., Ouyang, F., Lin, T., & Chiu, T. K. F. (2024). A scoping review on how generative artificial intelligence transforms assessment in higher education [Review of A scoping review on how generative artificial intelligence transforms assessment in higher education]. International Journal of Educational Technology in Higher Education, 21(1). Springer Nature. https://doi.org/DOI: 10.1186/s41239-024-00468-z

Xu, J. J., Sun, X. F., Liu, Y. N., Zhang, S. Y., & Zhou, Q. (2025). Effects of Game-Based Learning on Students' Motivation in Chemistry: A Meta-analysis. *Journal of Chemical Education*.

Xu, W., Yang, Z., Ng, D. W. K., Levorato, M., Eldar, Y. C., & Debbah, M. (2023). Edge learning for B5G networks with distributed signal processing: Semantic communication, edge computing, and wireless sensing. *IEEE Journal of Selected Topics in Signal Processing*, *17*(1), 9–39.

Yadav, S. (2025). *Leveraging AI to Enhance Teaching and Learning in Education: The Role of Artificial Intelligence in Modernizing Classroom Practices Optimizing Research Techniques and Learning Strategies With Digital Technologies*. IGI Global Scientific Publishing.

Yang, J. (2023). *Technology-Enhanced Preclinical Medical Education (Anatomy, Histology and Occasionally, Biochemistry): A Practical Guide Biomedical Visualisation: Volume 17–Advancements in Technologies and Methodologies for Anatomical and Medical Education*. Springer.

Yang, Y., Newby, T., & Bill, R. (2005). Using Socratic questioning to promote critical thinking skills through asynchronous discussion forums in distance learning environments. *American Journal of Distance Education, 19*(3), 163–181.

Yao, K., Huang, W., Hsu, L.-C., Yang, C.-K., & Lai, J.-Y. (2020). Evaluation of the Established IoT Smart Home Robot Teaching Module Based on Embedded Thematic-Approach Strategy. *Mathematical Problems in Engineering, 1*. Advance online publication. DOI: 10.1155/2020/6696155

Yao, Y., Zhang, Y., Ma, Y., & Zhao, Y. (2024). A survey on large language model security and privacy. *High-Confidence Computing, 4*(2), 100211. DOI: 10.1016/j.hcc.2024.100211

Yaseen, H., Mohammad, A. S., Ashal, N., Abusaimeh, H., Ali, A. A. A., & Sharabati, A. A. (2025). The Impact of Adaptive Learning Technologies, Personalized Feedback, and Interactive AI Tools on Student Engagement: The Moderating Role of Digital Literacy. *Sustainability, 17*(3), 1133. DOI: 10.3390/su17031133

Yeganeh, L. N., Fenty, N. S., Chen, Y., Simpson, A., & Hatami, M. (2025). The Future of Education: A Multi-Layered Metaverse Classroom Model for Immersive and Inclusive Learning. *Future Internet, 17*(2), 63.

Yi, S.-Y., Jung, M., & Lee, S.-I. (2025). *Adapting to change: International maritime education and training for future seafarers – focusing on the comprehensive review of the STCW convention and code. Journal of International Maritime Safety*. Environmental Affairs, and Shipping., DOI: 10.1080/25725084.2025.2464486

Yu, P. Mulli, J. Syed, Z.A.S. Umme, L. (2023). Facilitating Global Collaboration and Knowledge Sharing in Higher Education with Generative AI; IGI Global: Hershey, PA, USA, 2023; pp. 1–356.

Yu, C. H. (2020). Objective Measurement: How Rasch Modeling Can Simplify and Enhance Your Assessment. In Khine, M. (Ed.), *Rasch Measurement*. Springer., DOI: 10.1007/978-981-15-1800-3_4

Yu, H. (2024). Enhancing creative cognition through project-based learning: An in-depth scholarly exploration. *Heliyon, 10*(6). Advance online publication. DOI: 10.1016/j.heliyon.2024.e27706 PMID: 38533042

Zaabalawi, R. S., & Zaabalawi, J. (2024). Portfolios versus exams: A study to gauge the better student assessment tool. *Language Testing in Asia*, *14*(1), 28.

Zafar, M. H., Langås, E. F., & Sanfilippo, F. (2024). Exploring the synergies between collaborative robotics, digital twins, augmentation, and industry 5.0 for smart manufacturing: A state-of-the-art review. *Robotics and Computer-integrated Manufacturing*, *89*, 102769.

Zajacova, A., Lynch, S. M., & Espenshade, T. (2005). Self-efficacy, stress, and academic success in college. *Research in Higher Education*, *2005*(46), 677–706.

Zanon, C., Hutz, S. C., Yoo, H. H., & Hambleton, K. R. (2016). An Application of Item Response Theory to psychological test development. *Psicologia: Reflexão e Crítica: Revista Semestral do Departamento de Psicologia da UFRGS*, *29*(18), 1–10. https://doi.org/https://10.1186?s41155-016-0040-x

Zawacki-Richter, O., Marín, V. I., Bond, M., & Gouverneur, F. (2019). Systematic review of research on artificial intelligence applications in higher education: Where are the educators? *International Journal of Educational Technology in Higher Education*, *16*(1), 1–27. DOI: 10.1186/s41239-019-0171-0

Zhai, X., Nyaaba, M., & Ma, W. (2024). Can Generative AI and ChatGPT Outperform Humans on Cognitive-Demanding Problem-Solving Tasks in Science? *Science and Education*. Advance online publication. DOI: 10.1007/s11191-024-00496-1

Zhang, C., & Stewart, J. (2017). Talent management and retention. *The Wiley Blackwell handbook of the psychology of recruitment, selection and employee retention*, 473-493.https://doi.org/DOI: 10.1002/9781118972472.ch22

Zhang, M. Xie (2018). Artificial Intelligence's Digestion and Reconstruction for Humanistic Feelings. In 2018 International Seminar on Education Research and Social Science (ISERSS 2018) (Atlantis Press, Paris, 2018).

Zhang, X. (2023). How can technology leverage university teaching & learning innovation? A longitudinal case study of diffusion of technology innovation from the perspective of knowledge creation. https://link.springer.com/content/pdf/10.1007/s10639-023-11780-y.pdf

Zheng, X., Luo, L., & Liu, C. (2022). Facilitating Undergraduates' Online Self-Regulated Learning: The Role of Teacher Feedback. *The Asia-Pacific Education Researcher*, *32*(6), 805. DOI: 10.1007/s40299-022-00697-8

Zubaidah, S., Fuad, N., Mahanal, S., & Suarsini, E. (2017). Improving Creative Thinking Skills of Students Through Differentiated Science Inquiry Integrated with Mind Map. *Journal of Turkish Science Education*, *14*(4), 77–91. DOI: 10.12973/tused.10214a

Zumbo, B. (1999). *A handbook on the theory and methods of differential item functioning: Logistic regression modelling as a unitary framework for binary and Likert-type item scores.* Directorate of Human Resource Research and Evaluation.

Zuñiga-Aviles, L. A., & Cruz-Martinez, G. M. (2024). *Designing Exoskeletons.* CRC Press.

About the Contributors

Hany Zaky is an international scholar. Dr. Zaky's diverse teaching capacities have allowed him to work effectively with diverse linguistic learners. Throughout his career, Dr. Zaky has remained passionate about education, first as a middle and high school teacher and then as a university Professor. He has several publications in peer-reviewed journals and scholarly presentations at national and international conferences. He is an active member of several Adult Education TESOL and Composition studies organizations. His research interests include using technology to enhance Teacher Reflection, Action Research, Reflective Teaching, Educational Technology, Assessment and evaluation, Professional development for diversity, Culturally Responsive Pedagogy, and Language Teachers' Identity.

***

A. Devikomathy is a research scholar at the Faculty of Management, SRM Institute of Science and Technology (IST), Kattankulathur, Tamil Nadu. Her primary research interests lie in Learning and Development (L&D), HR Analytics, and L&D Analytics. With a deep passion for understanding how data-driven approaches can enhance human capital development, her work focuses on bridging academic theory with practical organizational needs. She is committed to contributing scholarly insights that support evidence-based decision-making in talent management, employee engagement, and strategic workforce planning.

Munir Ahmad is a seasoned professional in the realm of Spatial Data Infrastructure (SDI), Geo-Information Productions, Information Systems, and Information Governance, boasting over 25 years of dedicated experience in the field. With a PhD in Computer Science, Dr. Ahmad's expertise spans Spatial Data Production, Management, Processing, Analysis, Visualization, and Quality Control. Throughout his career, Dr. Ahmad has been deeply involved in the development and deployment of SDI systems specially in the context of Pakistan, leveraging his proficiency in Spatial Database Design, Web, Mobile & Desktop GIS, and Geo Web Services Architecture. His contributions to Volunteered Geographic Information (VGI) and Open Source Geoportal & Metadata Portal have significantly enriched the geospatial community. As a trainer and researcher, Dr. Ahmad has authored over 50 publications, advancing the industry's knowledge base and fostering innovation in Geo-Tech, Data Governance, and Information Infrastructure, and Emerging Technologies. His commitment to Research and Development (R&D) is evident in his role as a dedicated educator and mentor in the field.

Andi Asrifan is an accomplished educator and academic leader with a Doctorate in Education, specializing in English Language Education from Universitas Negeri Makassar. With a strong academic foundation, he holds a Master's degree in the same field and a Bachelor's degree in Secondary Education. His dissertation focused on developing bilingual educational materials, reflecting his commitment to enhancing language education. Dr. Asrifan has extensive experience in various educational roles, including serving as the Head of the International Affairs Office at Politeknik Negeri Nunukan and as the Head of the Institute for Student Development and Alumni at Universitas Muhammadiyah Sidenreng Rappang. He is also an active member of several professional organizations, including the Linguistics Society of Indonesia and TEFLIN. In addition to his administrative roles, Dr. Asrifan is a passionate advocate for educational innovation and has participated in numerous international conferences and webinars, sharing his insights on language teaching and curriculum development. His dedication to professional development is evident through his participation in various training programs.

Andi Asrifan is an accomplished educator and academic leader with a Doctorate in Education, specializing in English Language Education from Universitas Negeri Makassar. With a strong academic foundation, he holds a Master's degree in the same field and a Bachelor's degree in Secondary Education. His dissertation focused on developing bilingual educational materials, reflecting his commitment to enhancing language education. Dr. Asrifan has extensive experience in various educational roles, including serving as the Head of the International Affairs Office at Politeknik Negeri Nunukan and as the Head of the Institute for Student Development and Alumni at Universitas Muhammadiyah Sidenreng Rappang. He is also an active member of several professional organizations, including the Linguistics Society of Indonesia and TEFLIN. In addition to his administrative roles, Dr. Asrifan is a passionate advocate for educational innovation and has participated in numerous international conferences and webinars, sharing his insights on language teaching and curriculum development. His dedication to professional development is evident through his participation in various training programs.

Metin Celik is a Professor of Maritime Faculty at Istanbul Technical University and co-founder of Blueanalytica Maritime established in 2021. He published 5 book chapters, 70+ SCI/SSCI indexed journal papers (h-index 30; 2500+ citations in Wos/WoK) and 70+ international conference papers. He has conducting granted 18 different maritime research and technology projects. He has completed the supervision of 7 PhD dissertations and 12 MSc theses in the maritime era. Professor Celik has been featured among the World's Top 2% Scientists List, according to a Stanford University ranking study, published in 2020–2024. His main research topics include marine safety engineering, maritime skill transition, human reliability, compliance management, operation excellence.

Mgbike Francisca Chinenye is a renowned academic doctor in Counselling Psychology, dedicated to shaping the minds of future generations as a lecturer at Federal College of Education (Technical) Umunze. With a passion for research, psychology, and mentorship, she has established herself as a respected authority in her field. Through her work as a counsellor, researcher, and educator, Dr. Mgbike empowers students, colleagues, and individuals to reach their full potential, fostering a culture of growth, well-being, and academic excellence."

Kadir Cicek is an Associate Professor in the Marine Engineering Department at Istanbul Technical University (ITU) and a Co-Founder of Blueanalytica Maritime R&D and Information Technologies Inc. He obtained his BSc degree in Marine Engineering from ITU in 2003, followed by an MSc in Maritime Transportation Engineering in 2008 and a PhD in Industrial Engineering in 2013, both from ITU. During his doctoral studies, he conducted research at the Liverpool Logistics Offshore and Marine Research Institute (LOOM) of Liverpool John Moores University, focusing on risk-based decision making in operational fleet management for a period of six months. His research interests include predicting future skill sets required by digitalisation in the maritime industry and developing marine engineering program curricula accordingly.

Vedat Dogancan is a Research Assistant in the Maritime Transportation and Management Engineering Department at Istanbul Technical University (ITU). He received his BSc degree in Maritime Transportation and Management Engineering Department from Dokuz Eylul University in 2021. He served as Oceangoing Watchkeeping Officer onboard container ships between 2021 and 2023. He is currently pursuing an MSc degree in Maritime Transportation Engineering at ITU.

Godwin Nse Ebong is a scholarly AI enthusiast with a strong academic record and years of experience in machine learning research. I specialize in applying statistics and data mining techniques to develop decision-making systems that drive strategic improvements and predict future trends for businesses. With a deep understanding of Hadoop and text analytics, I excel in extracting valuable insights.

Arushi Handa is a business administration student, specialising in International Business and Analytics, from Amity University, Noida. She enjoys reading and is deeply interested in research work. She wants to pursue higher studies in research and development. Ms. Handa also enjoys public speaking and has a flair for writing. She looks forward to building a career in marketing research.

Isumarni, S.Pd., M.Pd., is a dedicated lecturer in the English Education Program at Universitas Muhammadiyah Sidenreng Rappang (UMS), South Sulawesi, Indonesia. She earned her Bachelor's degree in English Education from Universitas Negeri Makassar (UNM) in 2012 and continued her academic journey by completing a Master's degree in English Education at the UNM Graduate Program in 2016. Born in Sandakan, Malaysia, Isumarni brings a cross-cultural perspective to her work in language education. With a strong commitment to advancing English language teaching, she actively engages in teaching, academic writing, and educational research. Her interests span curriculum development, instructional strategies, and educational innovation in rural and multicultural contexts. In addition to her academic career, Isumarni is also an entrepreneur, balancing her professional responsibilities with business ventures. Her work reflects a passion for empowering students and educators through thoughtful pedagogy and research-driven practices. She continues to contribute to academic discourse by writing educational books and participating in scholarly collaborations. Isumarni's multidisciplinary engagement positions her as a proactive educator and a role model for aspiring teachers in the region.

A. Devikomathy is a seasoned academic and researcher serving as a Corresponding Author from the Department of Management Studies, Rajalakshmi Engineering College, Tamil Nadu, India. As a dedicated faculty member, she actively engages in teaching, research, and academic development. Her core research interests include Learning and Development (L&D), HR Analytics, and L&D Analytics, with a focus on leveraging data-driven insights to enhance organizational effectiveness and employee growth. She is widely recognized for her commitment to academic excellence, student mentorship, and meaningful contributions to the evolving landscape of human resource management and workplace learning.

Ma Joan M. Delda, a dedicated educator born on February 4, 1971, in Naval, Biliran Province, Philippines, has dedicated her career to inspiring young minds. She holds a Bachelor of Science in Medical Technology and a Master of Arts in Teaching - Science, and is currently pursuing a Doctor of Education at the University of Cebu Graduate School. Her passion for knowledge is evident in her role as an Assistant Professor 1 at Biliran Province State University, where she teaches Chemistry for Engineers and General Education subjects like Human Reproduction, Science, Technology, and Society, Understanding the Self, Ethics, and Readings in Philippine History.. Ma Joan's commitment to education shines through her pursuit of higher learning and her dedication to shaping the future of her students.

Rashmi Maini is a faculty member of HR/OB at Amity International Business School, Amity University, Noida. With a PhD in Human Resource Management from the Faculty of Management Studies, University of Delhi, she has been teaching management students for over fifteen years. She also holds a degree in labour management and a certified HR Analyst from from XLRI, Jamshedpur. During her Ph.D tenure, she earned scholarships (JRF and SRF) from the UGC and has presented several papers at National and International Conferences in India and abroad. Dr. Maini's research work has been acknowledged by Middlesex University, UK, IIT Delhi & XLRI Jamshedpur, India to name a few. She has published various research papers in reputed journals, including those listed in ABDC and SCOPUS indexed. She has been a guest editor of Global Business and organizational Excellence Journal (ABDC indexed). She has organized various research conferences in Indian and Abroad. Recently, a conference on Diversity Equity Inclusion and Belonging was organized at Amity University [in] London in collaboration with Global Business and Organisational Excellence Journal.

Ugochukwu O. Matthew, presently is an Academic scholar with Hussaini Adamu Federal Polytechnic, Nigeria, in the Department of Computer Science with specialty in AI, Big Data Science, Cloud Computing, Internet of Things, Data Mining, Multimedia and E-Learning Education. A Member of Nigeria Computer Society (NCS), Nigeria Institute of Management (NIM), International Association of Computer Science & Information Technology (IACSIT), European Alliance for Innovation(EAI) and also a member of Teaching & Education Research Association (TERA). Ugochukwu O. Matthew hold Masters in Computer Applications from Bayero University Kano, Nigeria. Ugochukwu O. Matthew had reviewed several Journals and a member of Review Board Committee of Journals Indexed by Scopus and Web of Science including IEEE Access, SN Computer Science (Springer), International Journal of Information Communication Technologies & Human Development(IJICTHD), International Journal of Business Data Communications and Networking (IJBDCN), International Journal of Cloud Applications and Computing (IJCAC). Ugochukwu O. Matthew is a cofounder of U&J Digital Consult Limited, an IT and Educational Consulting Firm in Nigeria.

Maemuna Muhayyang, M.Pd. is a distinguished academic and lecturer at Universitas Negeri Makassar, where she holds the position of Lektor Kepala (Associate Professor). She was born in Ma'rang on July 5, 1974, and has built a solid educational foundation with degrees in English education, educational theory, and communication culture from reputable institutions in Indonesia. Over the years, she has developed expertise in teaching courses such as Phonology, Bilingualism, Educational Psychology, and Research in English Language Teaching (ELT). Her research spans various aspects of language learning, including enhancing vocabulary skills in students through innovative methods and exploring the effectiveness of corrective feedback in English writing instruction. She has actively contributed to community development programs by providing training for teachers in interpersonal communication and academic writing. Dr. Muhayyang has published numerous articles in both national and international journals, focusing on blended learning, students' perceptions of weekly quizzes, and teachers' professional competencies in English language education. Her work also extends to presenting at several international conferences, where she has discussed issues like the role of English as a foreign language (EFL) teachers in classroom management and factors influencing student learning. In addition to her academic articles, Dr. Muhayyang has authored books, including a collection of hybrid learning poems and a guidebook on educational research fundamentals. Her dedication to advancing English education in Indonesia is reflected in her extensive research, publications, and community engagement efforts.

Syamsiarna Nappu, M.Pd., is a senior lecturer in the field of Technology in Teaching and Learning English at Universitas Muhammadiyah Makassar, Indonesia. She holds the academic position of Associate Professor (Lektor Kepala) and has extensive experience in integrating digital platforms into English language education. Her academic expertise focuses on improving teaching effectiveness through educational technology, with an emphasis on vocabulary development, online learning environments, and project-based instruction. Her research portfolio includes a wide range of studies on mother tongue interference in EFL writing, students' experiences in synchronous online learning, and the use of applications such as Toontastic, Edmodo, Schoology, and visual media in large classroom settings. These works reflect her commitment to making English language instruction more accessible, interactive, and contextually relevant. In addition to her scholarly contributions, Dr. Syamsiarna is actively engaged in community outreach and teacher training, promoting the use of technology to enhance both teaching practices and student learning outcomes. Her approach blends pedagogical theory with practical application, making her a leading advocate for digital transformation in language education. She continues to mentor pre-service and in-service teachers in adopting innovative, student-centered methods for English language teaching in the digital age.

Morgan Nwaiku is a dedicated cybersecurity professional with a strong foundation in software development and a background in computer engineering. With a focus on building and monitoring systems that utilize anomaly detection and artificial intelligence, Morgan ensures that software products are both secure and user-friendly, balancing the critical aspects of security and usability. His passion for technology extends beyond his professional work, as he actively mentors aspiring tech enthusiasts and contributes to the tech community through volunteering and knowledge sharing. Morgan's expertise spans across various tools and technologies, including Azure cloud services, SQL and NoSQL databases, Python programming, application testing, and API. By integrating AI into their anomaly detection systems, Morgan stays at the cutting edge of cybersecurity innovation. This diverse skill set, coupled with a commitment to staying at the forefront of technological advancements, positions Morgan as a valuable asset in the technology space.

Matthew Abiola Oladipupo is the Lead Data Analyst at Perch Group Ltd in Manchester, United Kingdom. He earned his Master of Science in Data Science from The University of Salford and holds a Bachelor of Technology in Electronics and Electrical Engineering, as well as a Postgraduate Diploma, from Ladoke Akintola University of Technology. As a passionate scholar in Artificial Intelligence, he brings years of experience in researching machine learning and boasts a distinguished academic profile. His expertise spans across applied statistics and data mining techniques, enabling him to develop decision-making systems for business organizations. This involves collecting extensive datasets and transforming them into actionable insights and reports, aiding organizations in strategic decision-making, business improvement, and future trend prediction.

Amaonwu Onyebuchi is a lecturer in the Department of Computer Science, Hussaini Adamu Federal Polytechnic Kazaure, Jigawa State, Nigeria. Onyebuchi is a seasoned IT professional, registered with Nigeria Computer Society (NCS) with speciality in Artificial Intelligence, Cloud Technology Management, Information System Security, Internet of Things and E-Learning Education. Onyebuchi hold Masters of Science Degree in Computer Science from Kampala University Uganda.

Ogechukwu Nkiruka Onyedibe (PhD) is a Registry staff in the Federal University of Technology Owerri, for over 13 years, and have served in the different units of the university, her quest for administrative excellence spinning from Digitalization of academic work environment has birthed many research work on ICT and Education. Dr. Mrs. Ogechukwu Onyedibe was born and raised in the vibrant city of Onitsha, Anambra State, Nigeria. From a young age, she displayed an unwavering thirst for knowledge and a strong desire to contribute to the betterment of society. Her passion for seasoned administrative process in university education with technology positioned her as a distinguished researcher and leader in her field. Throughout her career, Dr. Onyedibe has been a pivotal force in driving the adoption of digital solutions in educational administration. Her research outputs have provided valuable insights into the benefits and challenges of digitalization in academic environments, influencing policy and practice within and beyond her institution.

David Oyekunle is a highly esteemed expert with extensive education and experience in the fields of information technology research, project management, business analysis and artificial intelligence. He earned his Bachelor of Science degree in Statistics from the University of Ilorin in Nigeria. Furthering his education, he obtained a Postgraduate Diploma in International Business Administration and Management from the National Open University in Nigeria, and a (Summer online) Master of Business Administration in Leadership and Team Building from the University of New Haven in the United States of America. He excelled as a postgraduate research scholar at the University of Salford, graduating with a Master of Science degree in project management with distinctions. David significant organizational experience includes leading cross-functional teams, crafting strategic project policies, implementing logistics, ensuring adherence to risk standards and compliance, and analyzing vast datasets to uncover trends and patterns. Among his accomplishments are the successful implementation of intelligent lean management and Six Sigma with data analysis, the delivery of comprehensive business reports, and the utilization of technological innovation for more effective customer service improvements. Currently serving as an educational consultant at U& J Digital Consult Limited in Nigeria, David continues to contribute significantly to the fields of information technology and educational consulting. His research, published in global journals, spans various subjects, including strategic management, project management, international business, business informatics, and ethics in project management. Demonstrating his commitment to academic collaboration and human capital development, David actively participates in volunteer positions and committee memberships at conferences both locally and internationally. David aims to continue leveraging his expertise to drive innovation and excellence in the field of research, education, project management and information technology.

Rismawati Sudirman is a distinguished academic and consultant with a robust focus on sustainability reporting. She currently holds the position of lecturer and Head of the Quality Assurance Institute at Universitas Muhammadiyah Palopo, where she has been pivotal in ensuring the quality of university processes and outputs since February 2020. Additionally, she serves as an Assurer for Sustainability Reporting at the National Center for Sustainability Reporting in Jakarta, specializing in the evaluation of sustainability reports for mining companies across Indonesia. Her academic qualifications are extensive, comprising a Bachelor's degree in Economics and Accounting, a Master's degree in Accounting Science, and a Doctorate in Accounting from Universitas Brawijaya, Malang. Rismawati is also a certified specialist in sustainability reporting, risk management, and tax planning, holding several prestigious certifications including Certified Sustainability Reporting Specialist (CSRS) and Certified Risk Management Practitioner (CRMP). In her professional capacity, she has provided consultancy services in financial management and tax compliance for companies such as PT. Reski Barito Timur and PT. Helay Raya. Furthermore, she has authored multiple publications on taxation and management, contributing significantly to the academic community. Her interests in reading, writing, and travel reflect her commitment to lifelong learning and professional growth in her field.

Vinita Sharma is an Associate Professor at Amity University, Noida. Dr. Sharma has more than 24 years of academic experience. A seasoned academician, author and trainer with proficiency in new and upcoming areas such as Business analytics, Machine Learning, Deep Learning, Data visualisation, and emerging technologies. She has multiple Research Papers in Scopus-listed Journals and many book chapters to her credit. She is an avid researcher in analytical domains and has been a resource for EDPs, MDPs, and FDPs in various information technology and analytics areas. She has been guiding Ph.D and postgraduate dissertations in technology and Management.

Nurfaida Tasni is a lecturer at STKIP YPUP Makassar, where she has been teaching since 2012. She holds a Bachelor's and Master's degree in Mathematics Education from Universitas Negeri Makassar, and earned her Doctoral degree from Universitas Negeri Malang in 2019, specializing in Mathematics Education. Throughout her career, Dr. Tasni has been deeply involved in academic research, focusing on mathematical problem-solving and cognitive development in students. She has contributed extensively to scholarly publications, serving as both an author and a reviewer for various national and international journals. Among her roles, she is a member of the editorial board for Jurnal Lebesgue at Universitas Bina Bangsa, and a reviewer for multiple academic journals, including PEPATUDZU and

Jurnal Pendidikan Indonesia. Dr. Tasni is also an active participant in professional organizations, such as the Indonesian Mathematics Educators Society (I-MES) and the Indonesian Association of Educators and Educational Developers (APPI). Her research primarily explores mathematical thinking, problem-solving skills, and the application of cooperative learning models in mathematics education. She is highly committed to enhancing the quality of education in Indonesia, with a strong focus on integrating technology and innovative teaching methods in her field.

Wahira, M.Pd., is a senior academic specializing in Educational Management and Arts Education at the Faculty of Education, Universitas Negeri Makassar. With a functional position as Lektor Kepala (Associate Professor, IV/c), she has demonstrated an outstanding commitment to higher education, research, and community engagement over the span of more than 30 years. She earned her Bachelor's degree in Dance Education from Universitas Negeri Surabaya, followed by two Master's degrees—one in Educational Management from Universitas Negeri Makassar and another in Arts Education from Universitas Negeri Semarang. Her academic trajectory culminated in a doctoral degree in Educational Management from Universitas Negeri Semarang in 2012. Prof. Wahira has made significant scholarly contributions through research funded by national grants, focusing on school leadership, supervision models, curriculum development, and the integration of local cultural values in character education. She has published extensively in national and international journals and has authored nine academic books. Her innovative work has been recognized with multiple registered copyrights (HKI) in the area of educational models. Her expertise is further reflected in her supervision of over 240 undergraduate, master's, and doctoral students. Prof. Wahira remains actively engaged in scholarly dissemination through conference presentations and continues to advance the discourse in educational management and pedagogical innovation.

Index

A

C

D

E

F

G

H

I

L

M

O

P

R

S

V

www.ingramcontent.com/pod-product-compliance
Lightning Source LLC
LaVergne TN
LVHW060006031026
849161LV00025B/1508